TEXT

T E X T

Transactions of the Society
for Textual Scholarship

3

Edited by

D. C. GREETHAM

and

W. SPEED HILL

AMS PRESS
NEW YORK

T E X T

Transactions of the Society
for Textual Scholarship

INTERNATIONAL STANDARD BOOK NUMBER

Set: 0–404–62550–9
Volume 3: 0–404–62553–3

INTERNATIONAL STANDARD SERIALS NUMBER
0736–3974

Manufactured in the United States of America

Contents

v

Notes on Contributors

ELIZABETH AUBREY is Assistant Professor of Musicology and Director of the Collegium Musicum at the University of Iowa. In addition to on-going research into the manuscripts, melodies, and literature of the troubadours, she is preparing a book on singing the monophonic songs of medieval France.

JOHN BARNARD is Professor of English Literature, School of English, The University of Leeds. He has published work on the Restoration (Etherege, Dryden, and Congreve), on Pope, and on Keats.

FREDSON BOWERS is Linden Kent Memorial Professor of English Emeritus at the University of Virginia, and editor of the annual *Studies in Bibliography*. In addition to writing two books on editorial theory—*Textual and Literary Criticism* and *Bibliography and Textual Criticism* and a volume of collected essays, *Essays in Bibliography, Text, and Editing*—he has edited the texts of Thomas Dekker, Christopher Marlowe, Nathaniel Hawthorne, Stephen Crane, and selected texts of Shakespeare, Dryden, Fielding, Walt Whitman, and (as general editor) Beaumont and Fletcher. He is at present textual editor of the ongoing *The Works of William James* in the ACLS–Harvard University Press edition.

ROBERT H. ELIAS, Goldwin Smith Professor of English Literature and American Studies, Emeritus, Cornell University, is the editor of *Letters of Theodore Dreiser* and, with the late Eugene D. Finch, *Letters of Thomas Attwood Digges (1742-1821)*. He has written *Theodore Dreiser: Apostle of Nature* and *"Entangling Alliances with None": An Essay on the Individual in the American Twenties*, as well as numerous articles on American writers. At present he is a lecturer at the Nathan Mayhew Seminars of Martha's Vineyard in Massachusetts, where he teaches courses in American literature.

HANS WALTER GABLER pursued post-doctoral research in bibliography and textual criticism at the University of Virginia and subsequently taught there. Now professor in the Department of English, University of Munich, Germany, he is General Editor of the critical edition of James Joyce in progress and volume editor of the recently published *Ulysses*.

WILLIAM H. HARDESTY teaches Victorian and twentieth-century British literature at Miami University (Ohio). The author of articles on Conrad, Rossetti, and science fiction, he is currently President of the Science Fiction Research Association. With David D. Mann, he has written extensively on Stevenson's *Treasure Island*.

LOUIS HAY, Director of the Centre National de la Recherche Scientifique (France) has founded in Paris l'Institut des Textes et Manuscrits Modernes and has encouraged a series of researches that concentrate on the creative literary process through authors' manuscripts (''genetic criticism''). He directs the collection ''Textes et Manuscrits'' which includes such notable works as *Essais de critique genetique*; *Le genèse du texte*; *Les modèles linguistiques*; *Ecritures, création, communication*. In the field of critical editions, he has overseen the publication of *La Publication des manuscrits inédits* and *Edition et interpretation*. In 1985, he was honored with the volume *Leçons d'écriture / Homage à Louis Hay*.

T. H. HOWARD-HILL, Professor of English at the University of South Carolina, continues to work on the Revels Plays edition of Middleton's *A Game at Chess* and manuscripts associated with Middleton's scribe, Ralph Crane.

KLAUS HURLEBUSCH, University Library of Hamburg (West Germany), is Co-editor of the historical-critical edition of the works and letters of Friedrich Gottlieb Klopstock (Berlin and New York, 1974 *subseq.*).

GUNILLA IVERSEN, Reader in Latin at the University of Stockholm, is jointly responsible for the Corpus Troporum research project on medieval liturgical poetry. She has published critical editions and analytical studies on tropes and sequences and now is preparing a critical edition of tropes and sequences to the Sanctus in the *Corpus Troporum* series and an illustrated anthology of tropes, *Florilegium Troporum*.

GEORGE KILLOUGH, Associate Professor of Language and Literature at the College of St. Scholastica in Duluth, Minnesota, has published ''Punctuation and Caesura in Chaucer,'' *Studies in the Age of Chaucer*, 4 (1982), 87-107. He is presently preparing an edition of a diary of Sinclair Lewis.

PAUL OSKAR KRISTELLER is Woodbridge Professor of Philosophy Emeritus at Columbia University. He is the author of many books and articles dealing with the history of philosophy, especially with the intellectual history of the Renaissance. As an editor of Renaissance Latin and Italian texts, he has been concerned with the problems of textual criticism, and as an intellectual historian, with the growing disregard of contemporary literary critics and theorists for textual and documentary evidence.

JEAN-LOUIS LEBRAVE is a researcher at l'Institute des Textes et Manuscrits Moderne at the Centre National de la Recherche Scientifique. Among his publications is ''Programmation et sciences humaine,'' a special issue of *Le traitement automatique des brouillons* in which he discusses at length the development of a computerized system for tracking the manuscript variants in the poetry of Heinrich Heine.

GERALD MacLEAN is Assistant Professor of English at Wayne State University. In addition to several articles on seventeenth-century poetry and feminist critical theory, he has edited Poullain de La Barre's *The Woman as Good as the Man* and is the author of the forthcoming study *Time's Witness: Historical Representation in English Poetry, 1603-60*. In addition to editing the English poems commemorating the Stuart Restoration, he is writing a book "The Living Memory: Studies in English Popular culture, 1642–1984."

JOHN McCLELLAND is Professor of French and Comparative Literature at the University of Toronto and, in 1988, Visiting Professor at the University of California at Santa Barbara. He has published a critical edition of the *Erreurs amoureuses* of Pontus de Tyard and several articles and papers on physical bibliography and textual criticism in the context of the French Renaissance.

JO-ANN McEACHERN, Assistant Professor of French at the University of Western Ontario, has completed a bibliography of Rousseau's *Emile* which is scheduled to appear in 1987. Currently she is working on a bibliography of *La Nouvelle Héloïse*, and she is General Editor, with R. A. Leigh, of the *Bibliography of J.-J. Rousseau to 1800* (ten volumes projected).

JEROME J. McGANN is the Commonwealth Professor of English, University of Virginia. His most recent book is *Social Values and Poetic Acts*, published in 1987 by Harvard University Press.

DAVID D. MANN teaches bibliography and eighteenth-century British literature at Miami University (Ohio). He is the author of concordances to William Congreve (Cornell) and Sir George Etherege (Greenwood) and has edited the plays of Theophilus and Susannah Cibber (Garland) and well as compiling a reference guide to Etherege (G. K. Hall). With William H. Hardesty, he has written extensively on Stevenson's *Treasure Island*.

MARCIA SMITH MARZEC is Associate Professor of English at the College of St. Francis. She is a member of a team of scholars editing the early fifteenth-century *Regiment of Princes* by Thomas Hoccleve. Besides editing some 1000 lines of the 5500-line poem, she also has been responsible for the genealogy of the forty-three extant manuscripts of the work. She has published articles of the sources of the *Regiment* and on scribal practices in the manuscripts.

EDWARD MENDELSON is Professor of English and Comparative Literature at Columbia University and the Literary Executor of the Estate of W. H. Auden. His edition of Auden's complete works will begin to appear in 1988.

HERSHEL PARKER, H. Fletcher Brown Professor of American Literature at the University of Delaware, is Associate General Editor of the Northwestern–Newberry Edition of the Writings of Herman Melville and author of *Flawed Texts and Verbal Icons: Literary Authority and American Fiction* (Evanston, Ill.: Northwestern University Press, 1984).

ROBERT ROSENBERG is finishing his dissertation for the Ph.D. degree in the history of science from the Johns Hopkins University. Currently he is an Editorial Associate at the Thomas A. Edison Papers, Rutgers, The State University of New Jersey.

The late E. RUBINSTEIN was Coordinator of Cinema Studies at the College of Staten Island, City University of New York. He wrote on a variety of literary and cinematic topics and was one of the General Editors of the Rutgers University Press *Films in Print* series.

MARVIN SPEVACK is Professor of English and Director of the Englisches Seminar and the Institutum Erasmianum (Forschungsinstitut für Buchwissenschaft und Bibliographie) at the Westfälische Wilhelms-Universität Münster. He is editor of both the New Variorum *Antony and Cleopatra* and the New Cambridge *Julius Caesar*.

GARY TAYLOR, Associate Professor of English at The Catholic University of America, was joint General Editor (with Stanley Wells) of the new Oxford edition of Shakespeare's *Complete Works* (1986), in old and modern spelling, and co-author of *William Shakespeare: A Textual Companion* (1987). He is now General Editor of an edition of the complete works of Thomas Middleton, in progress.

CARL WOODRING is George Edward Woodberry Professor of Literature at Columbia University and currently is Senior Mellon Fellow at the National Humanities Research Center, working on nature and art in the nineteenth century. He is the author of *Politics in the Poetry of Coleridge* (1961), *Politics in English Romantic Poetry* (1970), and the editor of *Table Talk* in the *Collected Works of Samuel Taylor Coleridge*, forthcoming from Princeton University Press.

ROBERT F. YEAGER, Professor of English at the University of North Carolina, Asheville, is the author of *John Gower Materials: A Bibliography through Nineteen Seventy-Nine* (1981) and *Teaching Beowulf*, MLA Masterpieces Series (1984); he also has edited *Fifteenth-Century Studies: Recent Essays* (1984).

Preface

The introduction to the first volume of *TEXT* had to justify the journal's existence; the defence was based both on an interdisciplinary theory of textual scholarship and on its practice in specific cases, and it was exemplified largely by the writings of scholars associated with an "Anglo-American" school of textual scholarship (Fredson Bowers, G. Thomas Tanselle, et al.). This third volume of *TEXT* preserves a balance between theory and practice, but introduces contributions from alternative schools, particularly French and German. The theoretical essays again represent STS conference sessions. For example, Paul Oskar Kristeller's ringing defence of textual scholarship as an intellectual discipline was his address as second president of STS at the 1983 conference, Marvin Spevack's essay on the editor as philologist is a version of a paper he gave as the closing statement of the same conference, and the essays by John McClelland, John Barnard, Hershel Parker, and Jerome J. McGann were all contributions to a 1983 conference session on "The Meaning of the Text."

The French and German component in this volume (Hans Walter Gabler, Louis Hay, and Jean-Louis Lebrave) reflects a 1985 conference session on "The Continental Climate," augmented here by a version of an essay given by Klaus Hurlebusch in a different session. The fact that the continental textual critics had just come to the STS meeting in New York from attending a conference celebrating the eightieth birthday of Fredson Bowers in Virginia speaks not only to the cross-fertilization of the ideas from different schools which *TEXT* hopes to promote but also to the continued centrality of Professor Bowers' standing in the textual-scholarly community. It is therefore only appropriate that volume three of *TEXT* should also contain an essay by Fredson Bowers on a topic he has long made all his own—mixed texts and multiple authority. It is particularly appropriate since (at the time the essay was written) Professor Bowers had just begun his term as third president of STS, with a presidential address to be published in volume four of *TEXT*.

These eleven theoretical essays—on meaning, mixed texts, and so on—are balanced in this volume by the chronological sequence of essays on specific problems (from Gunilla Iversen on mediaeval tropes to Elliott Rubinstein on film). Some of these essays are practical responses to practical problems, and they deal with areas long familiar to textual scholars: bibliographical description (Elizabeth Aubrey and Jo-Ann McEachern), textual accidentals (George Killough), textual transmission (Marcia Marzec, Aubrey, and Carl Woodring), authorial revision (Gary Taylor, T. H. Howard-Hill, David Mann & William Hardesty, and Edward Mendelson), and provenance (Gunilla Iversen) . Other essays (continuing the emphasis on theory in this volume) offer a new theoretical perspective on specific media (Rubinstein on film and Rosenberg on technological artifacts), on periods (Gerald MacLean on the Restoration), or on individual works (R. F. Yeager on Gower's *Confessio Amantis*) and are particularly concerned with the nature and the ontology of the text—a topic which has recently become one of the major areas of discussion among textual scholars.

It is notable that this volume, as well as moving into theory (literary and textual) and continental textual criticism, also includes essays representing disciplines not covered in earlier volumes (e.g., the contributions on technological artifacts and on film). Frankly, the editors would like to see a good deal more of this, and, through conferences and the growing awareness of STS and *TEXT* by the scholarly community, aim to increase the representation from fields other than literature. It is a basic rationale for STS and *TEXT*, and we hope that future volumes of *TEXT* will exemplify this purpose.

That there is a third volume of *TEXT* is inevitably the result of many people's continued support and faith—most importantly, the contributors, some of whom have waited several years for their essays to be published. Our editor at AMS Press, Dr. William B. Long, has continued to offer valued advice and encouragement. Our institutional sponsors (Brooklyn College, Lehman College, Queensborough Community College, and the Graduate Center of CUNY; Fordham University and Columbia University; the New York Public Library) have maintained their logistic and financial support. The design and printing team at Queensborough (Kay Rangos and Joseph Felician respectively) have reliably continued their high standards for our conference announcements and programs. Our subscribers (most of them, anyway) have kept up their dues; and our ongoing activities (especially the conferences) have been assisted by the participation of many CUNY graduate students—Ben Sloan and Vincent Beach in particular. To all of them we give our thanks.

We offer this third volume of *TEXT* in memory of one of our valued members and contributors, Elliott Rubinstein, who died while the book was in proof.

D. C. Greetham
W. Speed Hill

PRESIDENTIAL ADDRESS

The Society for Textual Scholarship

April 23, 1983

Textual Scholarship and General Theories of History and Literature

PAUL OSKAR KRISTELLER

Ladies and Gentlemen, colleagues and guests:

First of all, I wish to congratulate the charter members of the Society for Textual Scholarship, and especially its Secretary, Professor David Greetham of the City University, and its first President, Dr. G. Thomas Tanselle of the John Simon Guggenheim Memorial Foundation, on their foresight and initiative in founding and organizing this Society, and on the immediate response given to their initiative by numerous scholars in different fields both in this country and abroad. I should also like to thank them and the other members of the Society for the great honor they conveyed on me when they asked me to serve as the second President of the Society. I gladly accepted. I cannot claim any credit for the preparation and program of this conference, or for the other affairs of the Society, for they were all conducted by our Secretary and by the committees which advised him. My only contribution is this informal address, and I shall try my best not to disappoint you by what I have to say. As you undoubtedly know, I am not a literary scholar, as most of you are, but primarily a historian of philosophy and of learning, or if you wish, an intellectual historian (I trust we are all historians, and I hope we are all intellectual). Yet I was trained in classical scholarship and in medieval history, among other subjects, have profited in my work from this training, and have always considered the precise reading and interpretation of texts and documents as an indispensable and solid foundation for anything we are trying to say about a particular author and his works, or about the schools and traditions active at a given time, or even about whole periods or about the entire history of civilization.

Textual scholarship, as I understand it, is now on the defensive, in the world at large which does not care for it or ignores it, and even in the academic world where it is often contemptuously dismissed as "traditional" scholarship. A number of new approaches have made a strenuous and widely successful effort not only to supplement traditional scholarship (which would be quite acceptable) but to discredit it and to replace it. Such new methods and trends as anthropology and psychology, sociology and social science, linguistics in its various forms, analytical philosophy, hermeneutics, new criticism, structuralism, semiotics, deconstructionism, to name but some of the better known and more influential approaches, diverse and even unrelated as they may be among each other, have this much in common that they challenge and attack traditional scholarship as antiquated and unimportant, if not wrong, and promise new and far superior insights and results in the comprehensive interpretation of our subject matter.

I cannot help being a traditional scholar, and I am far too old to learn many new tricks. I also remember that many years ago I was asked to defend traditional scholarship against some of the new critical methods, and I declined, perhaps wrongly, stating that I was too busy with doing my own work and could not spare the time to explain to others why I am doing it. I hoped at the time that the situation would get better, but it has gotten much worse, and I am now in the position of a worker whose skills and merchandise are no longer in demand and who is too old to change them. My aim has always been to be right or correct, as far as possible, and not to be fashionable, and to try to find the truth (which is not always possible and never easy) and to make it fashionable (which seems sometimes to be even more difficult). Now we are told that there is no truth, and that opinion is all there is (after more than two millennia, the sophists seem to prevail over Plato who dominated the philosophical scene until a few years ago). We are told that we should follow our creative impulse in developing opinions that are congenial to us, and persuade the public that our opinions are more in line with the needs and wishes of our present world and society than those of our predecessors. We want to be free of a tradition that has lost its meaning, of a truth that is no longer valid, and of a past that restricts our own outlook and aspirations. The study of the past for its own sake should really be abolished, so they seem to tell us, or at least it should be reshaped to suit our present needs and tastes.

I suspect that these views are shared by some of those present, but I think not by the majority, and this Society was probably founded to defend traditional scholarship, or at least some aspects of it, against the onslaught of new methods. Hence I am afraid my little lay sermon will be preached to the converted, as most other sermons are. I do not wish to make a frontal counterattack against the new methods. They still have to show whether and to what extent they are valid, and I for one am willing to learn from them if they succeed. I have read and heard a few papers written in the new style and found them interesting and plausible. I merely refuse to accept their claims and promises as valid results. I rather shall try to argue that all critical and historical theories of a general nature, however ambitious, must be tested, and stand or fall according to their agreement, not with current fashions or wishes, but with the facts established by traditional scholarship. You will be amused to hear that the history of ideas, now attacked and minimized as a mainstay of traditional scholarship, asserted itself back in the 1920s as a new approach against the narrow constraints of traditional philology. Some time had to pass before I ventured to state that there can be no conflict or rivalry between the history of ideas and traditional philology, because the history of ideas, if it claims to be valid, must be based on the results of traditional philology.

I trust there may be some difference of opinion among the founders of this Society as to what is precisely meant and comprised by textual scholarship. I should like to include under this name not merely the actual editing of texts (and documents) and the theory of textual criticism by which all editing is or should be guided, but also all or most of the other auxiliary disciplines which the trained historian and literary scholar must master and which are necessary for the textual scholar: the bibliography of manuscripts and printed editions, the technique of finding and describing manuscripts and editions, the knowledge of palæography and of the history of script, the criteria for establishing the date and the authenticity of a given text, the study of literary genres and traditions that help to understand the purpose for which a given text was composed, the grammar of its language and the rhetoric or poetics implicit in its composition, and much else. For a text must first be found or located in one or many manuscripts or printed editions, it must be transcribed and collated before it is edited according to the rules of textual criticism (which may more or less vary from case to case), and finally the text must be annotated and interpreted, determining its sources and quotations, its intrinsic meaning and its significance in relation to its time and to other texts. It is a slow and modest enterprise, but it proceeds step by step and is cumulative in its results. It consists of numerous small problems and solutions which involve skill, craftsmanship and sound judgement. Many of these methods can be learned and taught, and I know from experience that these courses are very satisfactory for the student and for the teacher, in an age that seems to discourage the teaching of the teachable, and to encourage the teaching of the unteachable. (I was once asked by a first-year graduate student in history, not at Columbia, what the difference between a text and a manuscript was; the question was not easy to answer, but it showed that the student had a lot to learn that he might better have learned in college).

When we arrive at our small textual solutions, we know very well that they are not equally certain. Evidently some of them are uncertain, but no harm is done unless we claim that something is certain or probable which is at best possible (or even impossible). However, at least some of the solutions are certain, and we are confident that a correct reading of the manuscript or printed source and a correct knowledge of the grammar and vocabulary of the language in which the text is written help us to establish some readings as certain and to eliminate others as wrong or impossible. From the fact that some solutions are uncertain we should never conclude that all of them are uncertain. We should cling to what is certain and patiently try, as in a puzzle, to expand the area of certainty and to reduce the area of uncertainty. To reject what is certain is as uncritical as to accept what is uncertain. Objective validity is our goal which we try to approximate even when we cannot fully attain it. And accuracy is the standard of our conscience as scholars, or if you wish, as pedants, and I venture to think that accuracy has its aesthetic and also its moral implications.

At this point, we are often confronted with the objection that what we attain may be certain but is in fact trivial and unimportant whereas the really important matters remain uncertain even after we have completed our work. We should reply that our concern is with what is certain, and that in expanding the area of certainty we hope to include also some problems that are important. What is claimed to be important but not susceptible of a precise investigation is not a part of our enterprise. Many problems proclaimed to be important are not really as important as they are claimed to be, or are badly formulated, or are incapable of documentation. In such cases, the historian, just as the scientist, has the right and duty to say: I do not know, or I do not yet know. This does not mean that he knows nothing, or that what he knows is worthless as compared with what he does not know.

The task of editing and studying texts in many languages, from many periods and of different form and content is still very large, in spite of the work done by previous generations of scholars. Our work along this line consists partly in applying the tested methods of our predecessors to areas and materials that did not interest them but that interest us. Even in this respect, the field of textual scholarship is wide open and may occupy many more generations of scholars, provided that they are properly trained and genuinely interested in what they are doing. New ideas and new problems will constantly emerge, and they will necessarily lead to new research. Recent concern with economic and social history has drawn attention to documents previously neglected, and recent interest in linguistics and rhetoric, in Neolatin literature or in Neoplatonic thought have led to the increased study and editing of many forgotten texts. The methods of dealing with these texts will be basically the same, though modified by their peculiar characteristics in form, content, language and transmission.

Traditional textual scholarship is based on solid and tested techniques and has led to many firm results. It deals with details, many of them minor, and thus operates as it were on a lower and more modest level. We must distinguish from it all those attempts, in history as well as in literary criticism, that attempt to establish general laws valid for all historical or literary developments. They operate, as it were, on a higher level. They may be original or interesting, but they are usually speculative, conjectural and uncertain. In my view, they cannot replace traditional scholarship or dispense with it, but they must agree with it and build on it if they wish to prove their validity. A general theory, however plausible or appealing, may be refuted by one or two contrary details. For if there is a contrast between a fact or text and a scholarly opinion, however widely accepted and applauded, the text wins and the opinion loses. It is the old epistemology of Epicurus (not of Plato or Aristotle) that shows its validity for all branches of empirical knowledge, whether scientific or historical. We may be inclined to think that a text may be interpreted on more than one level, and take as our model and justification the medieval (and ancient) method of allegorical interpretation. Yet we should remember that the allegorical meaning was always added to the literal meaning, but never contradicted it. I also find, and this is another epistemological observation, that the proponents of many general theories in history and literature fail to make the important distinction between necessary and sufficient causes. The fact that economic, social, and political developments are necessary conditions for many or even all cultural or intellectual developments of the past is easy to prove, but this does not mean that they are sufficient causes that would adequately explain the concrete texts and documents with which we are concerned, or their specific form and content.

I should like to emphasize still another point that seems to be implied in current debates on history and criticism. As historical and literary scholars, we are interested in the past and in its literature and thought, in spite of the fact that it may be very different from our present world and culture. We even believe that the past, just where it differs from the present, may be valuable, may enrich us and add something to our outlook. Just as we travel to see other countries and their monuments, and as we enjoy works of art and of music that have come to us from other periods and countries, we are also trying to appreciate the products of their writing and of their thought, which seems to involve a greater intellectual effort. As we try to overcome our provincialism by traveling to other places, we might do the same by traveling in time to other periods and cultures. The excessive preoccupation with the present time and its problems, recently labeled as "presentism," is a kind of provincialism. It may lead to a complete ignorance of the past, and it often does. It may also prompt us to impose our own preferences and fashions on the past, to misread and falsify and even to destroy it. We should cultivate a more modest attitude towards the past, and try to understand it in its own physiognomy, learn from it where feasible, criticize it where necessary, but not distort or falsify it. I have always been suspicious of interpretations that cater to our own wishful thinking or fit too well our modern preconceptions. I repeatedly attempted to refute certain conceptions of the Renaissance that were too congenial to Romanticism (my results are now either taken for granted, or they have been overthrown rather than refuted by a new wave of Romanticism). I suppose this was easy once the preconceptions of Romanticism had lost their hold on us, or at least on me. The same will happen with those current theories that are more in agreement with fashionable assumptions than with the historical facts. This may be compared with the fate of art forgeries. They always cater to the taste of the time of the forger, and therefore they appeal to his contemporaries and are successful for a while. They are immediately exposed when the taste has changed and when the original work of art is viewed from a different perspective.

The current faddism in historical and literary theories is also nourished by the widespread and exaggerated cult of novelty, originality, and creativity. When applied to historical investigations, this attitude encourages novelty at the expense of truth, and also laziness and slipshod work at the expense of the industry and hard work that has to go into real scholarly research. Many highfalutin historical and literary theories, of yesterday as well as of today, represent at bottom what I should like to call the sophistry of laziness, or at least assume that function among their less talented followers.

We should also be suspicious of all attempts to apply to the past certain concepts and methods that originate in the discussion of contemporary events and literature. In writing about contemporary subjects, we cannot easily detach ourselves from our own interests and preferences, and we cannot really judge what is and will remain valuable or important among the things that surround us, and on the other hand, we can take the background and context of our discourse for granted since it is familiar to us and to our readers. Every such writing is close to journalism, in the literal sense of the word. When we deal with past history and literature we still have our preferences, or sympathies and antipathies, but we are far more detached, and better able to pursue, if not to attain, a certain degree of objectivity. On the other hand, in dealing with the past, we lack the background and context from which our texts and topics ought to be understood. It is our job, often slow and painful, to acquire this background, by studying languages different from our own (including older English), and by learning to understand conceptions and institutions different from our own. This effort slows us down in our work, and it should make us pause and think twice before we begin to generalize on the basis of our own ideas and preconceptions.

In other words, there are two layers of historical scholarship, the textual scholarship which we pursue and which is more modest but more certain, and the general theory of history and of literature which is more ambitious but also more conjectural. I see no reason why the two should not coexist. Social history, the general theory of literature and of its place in society, the changing reception of a work of literature in later criticism, these are very interesting topics worthy of much study and investigation. But they are no substitute for the ground work of textual scholarship which should be pursued by other scholars and perhaps even by the same scholars who are interested in general theories, for they cannot succeed in establishing their general theories unless they are in agreement with the method and results of textual scholarship.

To conclude, I gladly admit and even welcome the fact that each generation sees the past in a new perspective and discovers new facets in it that had escaped its predecessors. This is as it should be, but it does not do away with all past insights, let alone with the facts firmly established by previous study. We textual scholars should patiently continue our work and not be discouraged by fashionable attempts to disparage it. It is we who are bringing about a slow and modest but sure and steady progress in the expansion of knowledge and of learning. We are the ants, and they are the birds. We do not want to clip their wings, for they may arrive at valid insights, but they ought to learn that they will ultimately fail in their attempts, as many of their predecessors did in the past, unless they comply and keep up with the solid evidence which we are trying to assemble and to build up. Their beautiful theories will collapse if they are wrong, and even turn out not to be so beautiful. I have heard statements that texts are only pretexts, and that the great texts of world literature must no longer be read by students since they have all been decoded by contemporary critics. These remarks are ridiculous, and they only show, not what modern criticism can do at its best, but how its methods can be misused at its worst.

Finally, I do not think that knowledge and scholarship should improve the world, as many people now demand, should improve the quality of life, as the NEH demanded a few years ago, or should be useful, as the American Philosophical Society founded by Franklin proclaims in its very name. I rather think that we should take such terms as "improvement" and "usefulness" in a broader and higher sense, and assert that any progress in valid knowledge, whatever its scope or content, is intrinsically important and useful, and by definition improves our human world and the quality of our life.

Text, Rhetoric, Meaning

JOHN McCLELLAND

The three terms of my title have been burdened by so many definitions and applications that they risk becoming semantic supernovae. It is virtually impossible for anyone to take account of all the meanings that have been discovered for "meaning," "rhetoric," and "text"; and literally impossible in an essay such as this adequately to review even a significant part of the literature on these subjects. Yet those who teach and reflect on the non-ephemeral forms of communication—writing, painting, sculpture, music, architecture—must have at least some working definition of "text" and "meaning" (i.e., they must have some methodology, however "unscientific"). And, as Stanley Fish has pertinently reminded us, the persuasive art of rhetoric is the very foundation of the scholar-critic's activity (Fish 1980:365). Perhaps not unnaturally, then, perhaps even not undesirably, the humanist academic is obliged to discover his own way out of the labyrinth of "text, rhetoric, meaning." Unless he is very fortunate, there will be no one single Ariadne perfectly equipped to show him the way. He is in constant danger of being devoured by the Minotaur of books and articles which claim to pertain to the solution of his intellectual problems. In what follows I shall attempt to show how I think meaning is generated by rhetoric out of text. I make no pretense at originality in any particular segment of my argument, though I hope that the argument itself, to the extent that it conflates positions which have often been treated autonomously, will offer some stimulus to thought. Definitions will arise as they are needed, as will the acknowledgements of debts incurred.

A text resides in the actual material representation, in the form of a quantifiable entity, of the mental concatenation of two or more signs. As a result of this concatenation, the sum of the signs is intended, or believed, to have more meaning than the signs taken

11

individually.[1] The mental conjoining of the signs may take place in the mind of their inventor (in the rhetorical sense of that term), who then gives them material form ("invented" texts). Or it may occur in the mind of an observer who believes that he has perceived signs and that, taken together, these constitute a text ("found" texts). The ancient haruspex discovered meaningful propositions about the future in the set of signs he found in the entrails of chickens. The modern pathologist adds up the signs he detects in tissues and excreta and thereby creates a text whose content is the etiology of his patient's condition.

In the case of both invented and found texts there is presumably some significance to the order in which the signs are conjoined. There may also be some hierarchy among the signs, but it is obviously the intention of the inventor that all the signs should be read and equally the intention of the pathologist, at least, that he discover all the signs that are there.[2] It is clear that the haruspex and the pathologist are analogous to the literary critic whose activity, it is thought by some, "brings texts into being and makes them available for analysis and interpretation" (Fish 1980:368). Whether it is equally clear that invented texts do not really exist *as texts* or have no meaning until a Berkeleian reader comes along is another matter. But it is nonetheless indisputable that unless the conjunction of signs has some physical form, i.e., unless it exists in measurable space and time, then there is nothing to read and no meaning to be deciphered or created.[3]

Because a text can exist only as a physical object, it is in very significant ways the servant and not the master of the materials available. Sumerian cuneiform is rectilinear because wax and stone tablets do not lend themselves to the incision of curved lines. The ready availability and malleability of papyrus allowed Egyptian writing to acquire the intricate visual mystery which non-Egyptians since before Plato have found to be characteristic of hieroglyphic.[4] The material support on which the text is written or drawn has always offered some form of resistance to the scribal act, whether physical or economic. Typically, harder, more costly materials have been chosen to receive texts whose content has been more highly esteemed: Hammurabi's stone tablets of the law, the *res gestae* of Roman emperors wrapped in bronze around a column, or the way we imagine the ten commandments.

For a large part of the Renaissance the printed book was less highly esteemed than the richly illuminated manuscript. Printing being a German invention, the first type faces used were variants of the so-called Gothic or black letter which remained common in Germany through the 1930s. But as the printed book became the medium used by the Italian and French humanists, new founts of type were cast which imitated the various italic and Roman styles of handwriting that had evolved in the Italian chancelleries. Much labour went into the design and carving of these beautiful new type faces, and their use was generally restricted to editions of the classics, while books of a more popular nature continued to be printed in Gothic (see Gaskell 1972:17–20).

Typically, too, the tendency has been for texts to be preserved in progressively cheaper and less durable substances: medieval vellum gave way to rag-content paper, which in turn yielded to cellulose paper, and that to the insubstantial phosphors of the Visual Display Terminal. This trend toward the material depreciation of the text is not merely a question of technology and economics; the ethos of the Romantics, who sought to make written language a more exact replica of the fluidity of thought (Rosen 1975), has led inevitably to the creation of ephemeral books and to theories of text which seem to reject as inadequate the actual inscription of messages on a material surface (Martens 1971).

The notion that there is an equation between the resistance of the material and the level of signification has carried over into the domain of language: in Antiquity and in the vernacular Middle Ages literature was defined as being written in the "hard" medium of poetry, whereas the "soft" medium of prose could be used for the less exalted chronicle and the novel. Later, as Latin became a genuinely foreign language, it was reserved for what seemed most important, while vernacular productions were thought to be ephemeral. Montaigne said, "I write my book for few men and for few years. If it had been durable matter, it would have had to be committed to a more stable language," by which he meant he would have chosen to write his essays in Latin.[5] The evolution of the formats of the published *Essais* is also revealing. The early editions and reprintings (1580–87) were small octavos and duodecimos, perhaps intended to fit into a traveller's pack. In the true second edition (1588) they appeared as more prestigious quartos, and by the third edition (1595) they had graduated to the coffee-table format of the folio. The typography of the title page also reflects this evolution. In 1580 the word "essais" was in small italic, but by 1595 it was in roman and by far the largest word on the page.

It follows that the interpretation of texts must begin with a knowledge and consideration of the socio-economic and cultural status of the materials and language in which they appear.[6] Now it may be argued that to study texts from the bibliographical point of view is more properly the domain of aesthetics than of semantics, but I do not think that any clear-cut boundary can be drawn between the two.[7]

During a writer's lifetime several texts may be published bearing the same title but varying among themselves more or less significantly. The University of Chicago Press has advertised an edition of Mary Shelley's *Frankenstein* in "the 1818 text," in distinction to that of 1831. In 1978 John Fowles issued a "revised version" of his 1965 novel, *The Magus*, and in the foreword specifies that "This is not, in any major thematic or narrative sense a fresh version of *The Magus*; it is rather more like a stylistic revision" (Fowles 1978:5). Later he speaks of "this revised text" (p. 7) and "revising the text" (p. 10). At least one Fowles scholar has, however, characterized the new version as "quite simply another novel."[8]

In addition to the manuscript of Balzac's *Le père Goriot* and its original serial publication, the novel appeared in some eight editions (not counting reprints) between 1835 and 1843. These were done by five different French and Belgian publishers, in formats ranging from in-8° through in-12° to in-16° and in anywhere from one to four volumes. The differences among these are sometimes quite significant—the hero's name is changed from Massiac to Rastignac, the roles of some characters are considerably modified—yet there seems no doubt in people's minds that in spite of these avatars we are still talking about different texts of the same novel. Conversely, Voltaire's *Dictionnaire philosophique* (1764) changed its title, without changing its content, to *La raison par l'alphabet*, "reason in alphabetical order" (1770), then in 1771 was completely reworked as *Questions sur l'Encyclopédie par des amateurs*, "Some Questions on the *Encyclopaedia* from non-professionals." Even though the articles in this last version bear virtually no resemblance to those of earlier editions, the title *Dictionnaire philosophique* is generally still applied to it, presumably because the format and many of the headings are identical to those of the earlier work.

A more serious example is afforded by the publication history of the novels of F. Scott Fitzgerald. All editions have appeared under the Scribner imprint, though in various formats, but there is no warning to the unsuspecting reader that there are significant differences among the publised texts of, e.g., *Tender Is the Night*. According to Matthew J. Bruccoli (1972), these differences are such as to affect the critical interpretation of the novel, but no critic has yet taken them into account.[9]

The first point to be made of these examples is obviously that if there is to be any meaningful discourse about an utterance, there has to be some consensus as to which text of that utterance is to be the basis of discussion. Since meaning is necessarily a matter of communication, the confusion that may exist with respect to the relative authority and validity of texts must be resolved by a close study of the extant documents and the consequent establishment of a commonly accepted hierarchy among them. If the "interpretive communities" (Fish 1980) are to perform their function, then there must be agreement among the members as to which text of whatever work will be the object of interpretation.

More importantly, however, these examples sustain my central thesis. If disagreements as to a work's meaning can arise from the different versions in which it has been studied, then meaning must reside, at least initially, in the text as I have defined it, which is to say, in the physical embodiment of its signs. Meaning is thus primarily a function of the text as it exists independently of both author and reader. To approach a text at this elementary level may not seem very interesting, but the material signs of the text are the only signs we have which will give access to other levels of meaning. It therefore behooves the scholar to get the material aspects of the text right before venturing into deeper waters.

The establishment of precedence and hierarchies among competing texts is in some respects a mechanical task which may not even require a very sound knowledge of the language involved. One can quickly spot differences among books and typographies and notice quantifiable variations between two ostensibly identical pages. Emendation of readings deemed by whatever criteria to be faulty requires, of course, a much more sophisticated level of competence. Let us assume, however, that the critic has at last before him a thoroughly reliable text, one that is generally agreed to be *the* text of, let us say, *Don Quijote* or Mallarmé's *L'après-midi d'un faune*.

By what process or in virtue of what perceptions are we persuaded that the former is not just an amusing tale about a loony Spaniard, or that the latter may be some kind of allegory for artistic creation?[10]

George Steiner places the sense that there is more than literal meaning in a text at the level of intuitive trust. His description of the process deserves to be quoted at length.

> We venture a leap: we grant *ab initio* that there is 'something there' to be understood, that the transfer will not be void. All understanding, and the demonstrative statement of understanding which is translation, starts with an act of trust. This confiding will, ordinarily, be instantaneous and unexamined, but it has a complex base. It is an operative convention which derives from a sequence of phenomenological assumptions about the coherence of the world, about the presence of meaning in very different, perhaps formally antithetical semantic systems, about the validity of analogy and parallel. The radical generosity of the translator ('I grant beforehand that there must be something there'), his trust in the 'other', as yet untried, unmapped alternity of statement, concentrates to a philosophically dramatic degree the human bias towards seeing the world as symbolic, as constituted of relations in which 'this' can stand for 'that', and must in fact be able to do so if there are to be meanings and structures. (Steiner 1975:296)

My own belief, however, is that the locus of the sense of meaning lies in the text's rhetorical dimension.

In the classical, Aristotelian, sense, rhetoric is the *technê* of persuasive communication. It is a holistic art, in that it hopes to operate on both hemispheres of the brain: the apparent logic of the enthymeme and the orderliness of the arguments are balanced by the emotional appeals to mass psychology and the aesthetic affect of the figures of speech. Unlike poetic, rhetoric purports to mediate directly between the subject and the object without resorting to poetic veils. The rhetoric of many novelists is of this sort. Sterne and Stendhal tell us in an ironical vein what meaning we are to discover in their texts, while more sober-sided authors (e.g., Balzac and Trollope) intervene in many instances to make it perfectly clear. As Wayne Booth has shown (1961), other forms of narrator-based rhetoric may be more subtle but are no less direct.

A second level of rhetoric can be extrapolated from the Aristotelian theory of the *koinos topos* or commonplace. Though most analyses of common places have been either logical or stylistic (see Curtius 1948, Ong 1958, Lechner 1962, Felman 1975), it is possible to see in the commonplace a standard component of communication. To the extent that all communication, except for purely phatic utterances, tells the listener something he or she did not know (or was thought not to know) before, the transmission of such information necessarily includes the desire on the part of the speaker to be believed. One of the guarantees of the validity of new information is that its transmission is accompanied by old information, something the speaker believes that the listener knows and accepts as true (McClelland 1977).

To a large extent a text's rhetoric consists of making the unfamiliar, the unknown, or the initially unacceptable, familiar, known, and acceptable. This is accomplished in essentially two ways, metaphorically and metonymically.[11] What is unknown, i.e., the unknown or unacceptable content the speaker wishes to communicate to his audience, is compared or juxtaposed to what is known and acceptable. What is known has meaning for the audience and hence is a commonplace where the minds of addresser and addressee may meet. Rhetorical arguments, as analyzed by Perelman (1958), are in fact that: the casting of contentious propositions into a form or into a verbal context which is part of the audience's mental set and which will therefore, it is hoped, eliminate the contention. Consequently rhetoric, in its more important sense, is *inventio* and *dispositio*, the discovery of commonplaces and their conflation with an unfamiliar content in order to constitute a significant text. Texts that use rhetoric in this way fall, I would imagine, into Barthes's category of the *lisible* (Barthes 1970:10ff). If we are to find more meaning in them than is immediately apparent, then we must resort to Steiner's "act of trust."

There is, however, a large body of texts—literary texts for the most part—where rhetoric functions in the opposite way, and it is these texts ("textes scriptibles," Barthes would say) that are customarily the objects of the critics' solicitations. For in them the unknown and the unfamiliar are not brought into the realm of our understanding by the commonplaces, but rather they produce the contrary effect and defamiliarize what we thought we knew.[12] Thus in Balzac seemingly innocuous provincial houses are revealed to be the repositories of monstrous passions, and in certain kinds of detective fiction—e.g., *The Murder of Roger Ackroyd*—the character we thought harmless proves to be the assassin.

Defamiliarization may occur at the most material level of the signs. The combination of three typographies in *L'après-midi d'un faune* (1876) makes the standard roman in which most of the text is printed abruptly and retroactively strange. Our investigation of that text's meaning starts at the very basic level of non-interpretive perception; our first questions have to do with the purpose of juxtaposing italic and roman and the function of the sporadic words printed entirely in upper-case.[13]

In *Don Quijote* defamiliarization begins with the episode of the windmills. Up to that point the "caballero de la triste figura" has amused us with his fantasies, and we are not surprised that his mind has so deformed his perceptions that he has mistaken the denizens of a crummy roadhouse for noble lords and ladies. However, when he perceives windmills as giants, a qualitative displacement has occurred which ought to indicate that he has become either incurably insane or sensorily dysfunctional. Neither, in fact, is the case, but we do not, as we read further into the novel, equate the windmill episode with what precedes and follows. Rather, we are obliged to re-evaluate the seemingly commonplace episodes in terms of the encounter with the windmills.

In spite of all this, I would still hold that meaning is a function of rhetoric, even when rhetoric operates in reverse. The reason is this. The rhetoric of a text, i.e., the places where the text clearly relates to our experience and rationality and to the powers of our imagination, is, like the material signs of the text at another level, the only access we have to areas of the text's meaning which are there but not clearly apparent.

Having said what I mean by "rhetoric," it is perhaps now appropriate that I go on to define how I understand the notion of "meaning." We may wish to think of meaning in terms of illocution and perlocution, i.e., as the communication of knowledge and will respectively, or in terms of reference, denotation, and connotation, i.e., as the capacity to relate an utterance to an entity, a class, or a set of properties. Perhaps meaning resides in ideas or behaviour or syntax. It may be generated by speech acts, and its process may involve the two inseparable faces of a sign, the three apices of a triangle, or the four corners of a square.[14] But whatever the theories we subscribe to, meaning is ultimately the connection we are able— or may feel constrained—to make between signs. By which I mean that we relate the signs of the text to other mental or material representations of intra- and extra-textual realities. The determination of the entities whose relations to the signs will produce the text's meaning is obviously a function of the "interpretive community" to which we belong by choice or by necessity. If we are reading the text on a literal or a narrative level, or if we are analyzing its form or structure, we connect its signs among themselves and find meaning in the perfection of their syntactic and/or logical coherence. We may, with certain French critics, try to link the signs to those in other texts and so practice intertextuality or paratextuality or hypertextuality.[15] Or with the Germans indulge in the arcane arts of *Hermeneutik* and *Rezeptionsästhetik*.[16] Or find meaning by relating the signs of the text to those of the author's biography or of Freud's theories or what have you. Whatever the role of the interpretive community in establishing the perimeters and parameters of our search for meaning in texts, the text itself and its imbedded rhetoric limit the set and the direction of the connections that can legitimately be made.[17]

Mark Antony's famous speech (*Julius Caesar* III 2) will both illustrate my point and conclude my argument.

> Friends, Romans, Countrymen, lend me your ears:
> I come to bury *Caesar*, not to praise him:
> The evill that men do, lives after them,
> The good is oft enterred with their bones,
> So let it be with *Caesar*. The Noble *Brutus*,
> Hath told you *Caesar* was Ambitious:
> If it were so, it was a greevous Fault,
> And greevously hath *Caesar* answer'd it.
> Heere, under leave of *Brutus*, and the rest
> (For *Brutus* is an Honourable man,
> So are they all; all Honourable men)
> Come I to speake in *Caesars* Funerall.
> He was my Friend, faithfull, and just to me;
> But *Brutus* says, he was Ambitious,
> And *Brutus* is an Honourable man.
> He hath brought many Captives home to Rome,
> Whose Ransomes, did the generall Coffers fill:
> Did this in *Caesar* seeme Ambitious?
> When that the poore have cry'de, *Caesar* hath wept:
> Ambition should be made of sterner stuffe,
> Yet *Brutus* says, he was Ambitious:
> And *Brutus* is an Honourable man.
> You all did see, that on the *Lupercall*,

I thrice presented him a Kingly Crowne,
Which he did thrice refuse. Was this Ambition?
Yet *Brutus* sayes, he was Ambitious:
And sure he is an Honourable man.
I speake not to disproove what *Brutus* spoke,
But heere I am, to speake what I do know;
You all did love him once, not without cause,
What cause with-holds you then, to mourne for him?
O Judgement! thou are fled to brutish Beasts,
And Men have lost their Reason. Beare with me,
My heart is in the Coffin there with *Caesar*,
And I must pawse, till it come backe to me.[18]

Materially this speech, as presented in the First Folio, is marked by the use of italic for all proper nouns (*Caesar, Brutus, Lupercall*) and by the capitalization of certain key words: not only "Ambitious" and "Honourable," but also "Captives, Ransomes, Coffers, Kingly Crowne," etc. It is also marked by being in verse, whereas Brutus's speech, delivered immediately before and structurally linked to this one, was in prose. Typographical signs are, of course, less important in a text composed to be delivered orally (unless we take the typography as a set of acting indications), but the prose/poetry opposition clearly determines some part of the meaning of the two speeches.

Rhetorically, several kinds of commonplaces are present in this speech. First, there are various verbal figures of repetition and contrast ("the evill/the good," "Ambitious/Honourable," "For *Brutus* is an Honourable man"). The second is the figure of irony, which in argument has been the commonplace mark of the subtle mind ever since Socrates defeated the Sophist Gorgias. The third commonplace is the conventional association of honour with telling the truth ("Yet Brutus says he was ambitious, and Brutus is an honourable man"). Antony sets this metonymically against the equally commonplace but extrinsic argument of personal experience and testimony ("You all did see, that . . . / I thrice presented him a Kingly Crowne, which he did thrice refuse"). And this figure is transformed into the figure of interpretation ("Did this in *Caesar* seeme Ambitious? . . . / Ambition should be made of sterner stuffe, / Yet *Brutus* sayes, he was Ambitious"). Later Antony will resort to the anti-rhetorical commonplace: "I am no Orator, as *Brutus* is."

Shakespeare's intended meaning, of course, is intended for the audience, not for the characters in the play. And on this level the meaning derives from the metaphorical and metonymical equation of Antony and Brutus. The latter's speech relied largely on the ethical appeal. Antony's speech consists of reversing the ethical appeal into *ad hominem* arguments. Even if the spectator did not know the story of *Julius Caesar*, he would grasp at this point the meaning that Antony is a subtler man than Brutus and will therefore defeat him. And because the rhetorical devices are so clear and so copious, we sense that we must extrapolate to derive a more general meaning concerning not only the relative advantages of honesty and guile, but also the need to develop a more variegated eloquence to survive in the political arena.

The blatancy of Antony's rhetoric is also, however, a refutation of the tragedy's commonplaces up to that point. Shakespeare's modern audience presumably brings to the play some mental baggage—or at least hand luggage—derived (at how many removes?) from Plutarch and Suetonius. To the extent that the spectators believe in advance anything about the main characters, it is probably that Brutus was the "noblest Roman of them all," that Antony is but a prefigure-ment of the Duke of Windsor, a mere "strumpet's fool," and that Caesar, like the biblical kings Saul and David, belied the promise of his early achievements. Antony's speech imposes on us a re-eval-uation of all that. It is not merely the structural and narratological turning point in the play, it also marks the point where interpretation must begin. And the major axis of that interpretation must be, I think, the relation of language to action and reality. To begin the search for the meaning of *Julius Caesar* in any other place would be aberrant.

I suspect it is obvious that what I have been arguing for is a pragmatics of meaning. Texts are concrete objects; the disembodied analogues which they in turn generate in the minds of their audience are not merely functions of the concepts produced by the words or pictures but of the total sensory experience. Such an experience and consequently such meaning as may be produced must, if it is to be other than mere fantasizing, be founded on organized knowledge of real facts, on a physical text. But meaning is also—and paradoxi-cally—ephemeral and transitory. It is (as Mark Antony knew), what an author can get away with and yet control at a particular time and place.

With the passage of time, however, the control weakens and the text that articulated that control becomes corrupt. The critic may therefore create—may therefore *have* to create—new meanings for old texts. However, he is not free to do so with a whimsical disregard for the text's rhetorical norms. And he must not do so without due consideration for the efforts of those who labor to re-establish the text in its material integrity.[19]

NOTES

1. This definition of "text" derives literally from the etymological meaning of *textum* "something woven together." It attributes some autonomous value to the text *per se* and stands midway between the position of scholars such as Martens (1971), who locates "text" within its originator's creative processes, and Barthes (1970), who locates it within the reader's imaginative re-creation. George Steiner (1975) makes the fundamental point that all understanding is translation. Which is to say that every text generates in the mind of every reader a holistic analogue of itself, something equivalent to the text but not in any case identical to it. Until and unless the text's analogues are made communicable, I do not believe they should be called texts. One further point might be made: any single communicated sign, e.g., "Go!", is a text because its material support—gesture, tone of voice, punctuation, typography—constitutes a second sign conjoined to the first.

2. On the other hand the haruspex, like the modern critic (see below), may have wanted to find only those signs that suited his or his master's purposes.

3. I have made it clear elsewhere (McClelland 1984) that I believe the intentions of a text's author to be usually unavailable or inaccessible (see also Wimsatt and Beardsley 1946). Of course even when we think we know these intentions, we may still wish to decipher the text in a different way. No one could accuse Champollion of perfidy, but the text he found in the Rosetta stone was probably not intended by the scribe.

4. This point was forcibly made by the exhibition entitled "La naissance de l'écriture" held in Paris from May to August 1982.

5. Montaigne, *Essais* (1588), III 9, "De la vanité," quoted in Donald Frame's translation (Stanford University Press, 1957). The original French reads, "J'escris mon livre à peu d'hommes et à peu d'années. Ci ç'eust esté une matière de durée, il l'eust fallu commettre à un langage plus ferme."

6. We note in passing that until the advent of Propp (1928), Parry and Lord (1954), Lord (1960), and others, literary scholars tended to dismiss the work of those who studied folk tales, detective fiction, popular romances, and other texts which had not received the cachet of a proper hardbound edition.

7. See Hospers (1946), Panofsky (1955), and Meyer (1956, 1967) for discussions of aesthetic meaning.

8. Private communication.

9. A cursory survey of the editions of Gide's *Les caves du Vatican* (1914) revealed that although all were published by Gallimard, there are differences among them that are not attributable to Gide.

10. For the view that *L'après-midi d'un faune* is not an allegory for artistic creation, see Weinberg (1966:127-69).

11. I use these terms in the way Roman Jakobson does (1956, 1960): metaphor is paradigmatic synonymy (i.e., based on some sort of equivalence), metonymy is syntagmatic synonymy (i.e., based on contiguity).

12. The concept of "defamiliarization" was first enunciated by Viktor Shklovsky of the Russian Formalist School. See Todorov, ed. (1965) for a selection from Shklovsky's writings and Jameson (1972:50-79) for an analysis of the principle.

13. The same poet's *Un coup de dés jamais n'abolira le hasard* (1897) combines eight typographies, thereby depriving the reader of any visual commonplace and plunging him into the domain of pure information.

14. References for the foregoing theories of meaning are: Austin (1962), Searle (1969), Alston (1964), Pratt (1977), Saussure (1915), Ogden and Richards (1923), Greimas (1970).

15. See Genette (1982:7-17) for a synopsis of all these (and other) "-textualités."

16. See McKnight (1978) and *Poétique*, 39 (1979) for reliable general accounts of hermeneutics and reader reception theory.

17. I say "legitimately" in the sense that if we are to expect others to accept as valid our notion of the text's meaning, then our interpretation must be based on more solid ground than the pursuit of "some mysterious inner exploration" (Norman Holland as quoted by Fish 1980:346). Stanley Fish knows perfectly well that his ironically fanciful interpretation of Blake's "The Tiger" (1980:348-50) not only violates the norms of the interpretive community but also those of the text itself and of the conventional codes of metaphor.

18. I quote the text in old spelling, for obvious reasons, as found in Shakespeare (1953), which gives "the text and order of the first folio." Antony's speech is really much longer; I quote it here only as far as the first interruption.

19. I am grateful to Donald Reiman, Peter Shillingsburg, and Sheldon Zitner for their pertinent comments.

WORKS CITED

Alston, William P.
1964 *Philosophy of Language*. "Foundations of Philosophy Series." Englewood
        Cliffs, NJ: Prentice-Hall.
Austin, J. L.
1962 *How to Do Things with Words*, ed. J. O. Urmson and Marina Sbisà.
        Oxford: Clarendon Press (2nd ed. 1975).
Barthes, Roland
1970 *S/Z*. Paris: Le Seuil.
Booth, Wayne
1961 *The Rhetoric of Fiction*. Chicago: University of Chicago Press.
Bruccoli, Matthew J.
1972 " 'A Might Collation': Animadversions on the Text of F. Scott Fitz-
        gerald," in Francess G. Halpenny (ed.), *Editing Twentieth-Century Texts*.
        Toronto: University of Toronto Press.
Curtius, Ernst Robert
1948 *Europäische Literatur und lateinisches Mittelalter*. Bern: Francke.
Dewey, John
1934 *Art as Experience*. New York: Minton, Balch.
Felman, Soshana
1975 "Modernité du lieu commun: En marge de Flaubert: *Novembre*,"
        Littérature 20: 32–48.
Fish, Stanley
1980 *Is There a Text in This Class? The Authority of Interpretive Communities*.
        Cambridge, Mass., and London: Harvard University Press
Fowles, John
1978 *The Magus, a Revised Version*. Boston: Little, Brown; New York: Dell,
        1979; 5th printing, 1981.
Gaskell, Philip
1972 *A New Introduction to Bibliography*. Oxford: Clarendon Press (reprinted
        with corrections, 1974).
Genette, Gérard
1982 *Palimpsestes: La littérature au second degré*. Coll. "Poétique." Paris: Le
        Seuil.
Greimas, A. J.
1970 *Du sens*. Paris: Le Seuil.
Hospers, John
1946 *Meaning and Truth in the Arts*. Chapel Hill: University of North Carolina
        Press.
Jakobson, Roman
1956 "Two Aspects of Language and Two Types of Aphasic Disturbances," in
        R. Jakobson and M. Halle, *Fundamentals of Language*. "Janus
        Linguarum," 1. The Hague: Mouton, 55–82.
Jakobson, Roman
1960 "Closing Statement: Linguistics and Poetics," in Thomas A. Sebeok (ed.),
        Style in Language. Cambridge, Mass.: The M.I.T. Press, 350–77.

Jameson, Fredric
1972 *The Prison-House of Language: A Critical Account of Structuralism and Russian Formalism.* Princeton: Princeton University Press
Lechner, Sr. M. J.
1962 *Renaissance Concepts of the Commonplaces.* New York: Pageant; repr. Westport, Conn.: Greenwood Press, 1974.
Lord, Albert B.
1960 *The Singer of Tales.* Cambridge, Mass.: Harvard University Press.
Martens, Gunter
1971 "Textdynamik und Edition. Überlegungen zur Bedeutung und Darstellung variiender Textstufen," in G. Martens and H. Zeller (ed.), *Texte und Varianten: Probleme ihrer Edition und Interpretation.* Munich: C. H. Beck
McClelland, John
1977 "Lieu commun et poésie à la Renaissance," *Etudes françaises* 13:53–70.
McClelland, John
1984 "Critical Editing in the Modern Languages," *TEXT, Transactions of the Society for Textual Scholarship,* I, 201–216.
McKnight, Edgar V.
1978 *Meaning in Texts: The Historical Shaping of a Narrative Hermeneutics.* Philadelphia: Fortress Press.
Meyer, Leonard B.
1956 *Emotion and Meaning in Music.* Chicago: University of Chicago Press.
Meyer, Leonard B.
1967 *Music, the Arts, and Ideas: Patterns and Predictions in Twentieth-Century Culture.* Chicago and London: University of Chicago Press.
Ogden, C. K. and Richards, I. A.
1923 *The Meaning of Meaning: A Study of the Influence of Language upon Thought and of the Science of Symbolism,* repr. New York: Harcourt, Brace & World, n.d.
Ong, Walter, S. J.
1958 *Ramus, Method and the Decay of Dialogue.* Cambridge, Mass.: Harvard University Press; repr. New York: Octagon, 1979.
Panofsky, Erwin
1955 *Meaning in the Visual Arts.* Garden City, N.Y.: Doubleday.
Parry, Milman, and Lord, Albert B.
1954 *Serbo-Croatian Heroic Songs.* Cambridge, Mass.: Harvard University Press; Belgrade: Serbian Academy of Science.
Perelman, Ch., and Olbrechts-Tyteca, L.
1958 *Traité de l' argumentation: La nouvelle rhétorique.* Paris: PUF.
Poétique
1979 "Théorie de la réception en Allemagne," *Poétique* 39.
Pratt, Mary Louise
1977 *Toward a Speech Act Theory of Literary Discourse.* Bloomington and London: Indiana University Press.
Propp, Vladimir
1928 *Morfologija skazki.* Leningrad: Akademia; 2nd ed. Leningrad: Nauka,

1969. Eng. trans., *The Morphology of the Folktale*, Austin: University of Texas Press, 1968, 1971.

Rosen, Charles
1975
"Romantic Documents," *New York Review of Books*, 15 May: 15-20.

Saussure, Ferdinand de
1915
Cours de linguistique générale; repr. Paris: Payot, 1971.

Searle, John R.
1969
Speech Acts, an Essay in the Philosophy of Language. Cambridge: Cambridge University Press.

Shakespeare, William
1953 *The Complete Works.* 4 vols. London: Nonesuch Press: New York: Random House.

Steiner, George
1975 *After Babel: Aspects of Language and Translation.* London and New York: Oxford University Press.

Todorov, Tzvetan (ed.)
1965 "Théorie de la littérature: Textes des formalistes russes". *Tel Quel.* Paris: Le Seuil.

Weinberg, Bernard
1966 *The Limits of Symbolism: Studies of Five Modern French Poets.* Chicago and London: University of Chicago Press.

Wimsatt, W. K., Jr., and Beardsley, Monroe C.
1946 "The Intentional Fallacy", repr. in W. K. Wimsatt, Jr., *The Verbal Icon: Studies in the Meaning of Poetry.* Lexington, Ky.: University of Kentucky Press; New York: Noonday Press, 1954.

Bibliographical Context and the Critic

JOHN BARNARD

The following passage on the hidden oppressions of the "definitive" text needs to be read with professorial gravity:

> . . . our tradition [of textual editing] is unwilling to allow multiple textual authorities to rest as a simultaneous set of existential entities to be encountered absurdly by the reader. . . . Editors do not—and so readers *cannot*—go in for the *infinitive* text . . . a polymorphous set of all versions, some part of each of which has a claim to substantive status, and possibly represents, by whatever independent means of transmission, an element of [for example] Shakespearean dramaturgy.[1]

Random Cloud, the aptly Redskin persona under whose name this statement appears in a recent issue of *Shakespeare Quarterly*, makes it unnecessary to describe the starting point of this paper. Cloud's parody demonstrates what happens when deconstructionists and post-structuralists invade the traditionally Paleface colony of textual criticism. Editors labour to create "definitive," "authoritative" or CEAA "approved" texts embodying "authorial intention" with all attainable possible accuracy: the deconstructive critic, denying the relevance of the writer's intentions, sets about destabilising what has been so carefully constructed. What the one creates, the other undoes.

The Folger Projector's mock-argument for the pleasures of polymorphous textuality neatly undercuts its deconstructive pretensions by holding to the notion of a "substantive status" representative of "Shakespearean dramaturgy." The authorial ghost has slipped back into the textual machine. (In any case, the *apparatus criticus* of a scholarly edition, in theory at least, allows for the kind of free play advocated: economic considerations would prevent a Derridean text of *Romeo and Juliet*, the somewhat opportunistic site for Cloud's Little Big Horn, even if it were desirable.)

Nevertheless the question of relativity of meaning (and of text) as

27

against determinacy of meaning is a real one. The point was made by
W. W. Greg:

> We have in fact to recognise that a text is not a fixed and formal thing,
> that needs only to be purged of the imperfections of transmission and
> restored once and for all to its pristine purity, but a living organism
> which in its descent through the ages, while it departs more and more
> from the form impressed upon it by its original author, exerts, through
> its imperfections as much as through its perfections, its own influence
> upon its surroundings. At each stage of its descent a literary work is in
> some sense a new creation, something different from what it was for an
> earlier generation, something still more different from what it was when
> it came from the author's hand.[2]

But for Greg's emphasis upon the "authorial hand"·this sounds
strikingly contemporary, and his remarks on the influence had
"upon its surroundings" by successive imperfect texts is an oddly
phrased recognition of the fact that each reader also creates texts in
"some sense new." But Greg's primary concern is with the *physical*
text and with the symbols on its pages. "None but the bibliographer,
trained in the material analysis of books and the signs that fill them,
can be trusted to extract from their silent record the full testimony
for the determination of the text" (Ibid.). His remarks threaten to
open up an abyss of relativity, yet what Greg observes is undoubtedly
the case. Every edition of a work differs from another, and is,
indeed, in some sense another text. Polymorphous textuality then
might appear to exist in the multiplicity of earlier texts even before
the individual reader sets to work. Yet does it really?

While it is impossible to deny Barthes's point that readers of books
cannot be stopped from reading what they like into a text—from
Thomas Rymer onwards it has been apparent that they can—there
are constraints on what they can do with responsibility. Greg's real
focus is on the signs that fill material texts, but those symbols are
part of a larger sign, the physical text itself, which, because
intentionally produced, is meaningful within a specific historical
context. This applies as much to a twentieth-century book or reprint
as to an Egyptian papyrus or a medieval illuminated manuscript.
Each text is the physical product of a series of transactions between
creator(s), copyist, publisher, and the intended audience(s). The
individual text, of whatever kind, is created to fulfill a specific
communicative function. Further, the function of written texts varies
from period to period—a manuscript Bible created for Alfred did

not have the same function as those printed for the SPCK: technology and the spread of literacy ensure that. What is common is the wish to preserve a text, otherwise transient or unavailable, for some kind of performance, mental or otherwise, on another occasion. All this is obvious enough. The reason for insisting upon it is that as members of a book-culture we take the book-as-sign for granted, reading the meaning of that sign with an ease approaching the unconscious. Nevertheless, the book-as-sign provides a delimited context of possible meaningfulness. Similarly, changes in *bibliographical* context alter meaning. In what follows I want to use examples of texts with differing bibliographical contexts to consider the "influence" which these contexts may exert upon the reader, and to draw out some of the consequences this kind of influence may have for both critic and bibliographer.

"Easter 1916," is a text familiar to any teacher of twentieth-century British poetry, and it comes in a variety of forms. In the *Norton Anthology* (1962)[3] it appears ballasted with double-column footnotes and line numbers, printed on thin paper in a small typeface, a balance between legibility and economy. The editorial notes clarify allusions and background; the dates of composition and first publication are given (the latter inaccurately). This is, with no difficulty, recognised as a classroom text: equally clearly, the manner of printing announces that Yeats is a significant poet worth studying in an academic syllabus. The *Variorum* text differs by placing the poem in the volume in which Yeats positioned it in 1921, individual line numbers are given to the left, item numbers assigned, collations are given at the foot of the page, and the whole set out on a spaciously designed page. As the elaborate formulaic structure and the obvious expense on typography indicate, this is a text for the initiate who assumes Yeats's canonisation. Yeats's *Collected Poems*, like the *Variorum*, places the poem in its proper sequence in *Michael Robartes and the Dancer*: here we have the poet's chosen format— a plain text for the poetry-reading public, with no footnotes, no line numbers and a carefully designed page set in an unobtrusive traditional typeface.

These three distinct forms, all of which might be said to mean slightly differently, present no difficulty for the informed reader, and any teacher of the poem will have at least two of these versions together with various alternative appearances in anthologies. The situation is perfectly normal for a poet accepted into the syllabus, and each text possesses an immediately recognisable function and validity. They present no problems for the practising critic or reader, whatever difficulties they might pose for the theoretician. Readers, publishers, and various bodies of readers all have a specific relationship to each text. Before arriving at the page on which "Easter 1916" occurs, the reader knows what kind of bibliographical context is involved, and, hence, has a precise way in which to regard the poem. All three books are meaningful signs reflecting a structure of literary and poetic values in which Yeats has his place.

If "Easter 1916" provides a normal example of how the manner of publication frames our reading of a major poem, its earlier publication history usefully gives an example of how changes in bibliographical context can affect meaning. The poem, although written in 1916, first made its public appearance in two periodical printings—in the *New Statesman* on 23 October 1920 and in *The Dial*, November 1920, where it is one of "Ten Poems" which form the nucleus of *Michael Robartes and the Dancer*.[4] The *New Statesman*'s text has, in the environment of a left-wing weekly currently attacking the Black and Tans and arguing for England's withdrawal from Ireland, a single very important variant (unrecorded in the *Variorum*). Appearing in an issue with articles on "Repression in Ireland" and "The History of Repressions in Ireland," "Easter 1916" was published *without* its date of composition, 25 September 1916. Thus Yeats's poem is transformed into a *retrospective* celebration of the failed 1916 Uprising and seems to belong to the battle for self-determination taking place in 1920. The importance of this to the critic is perhaps a moot point, but it clearly bears on the issue of how far Yeats's poem is divided or undivided in its attitude to the revolutionary "heroes"—and while I do not know whether or not Yeats was responsible for the *New Statesman*'s omission of the date of composition, there is evidence that he did not publish the poem earlier for fears of censorship.[5]

In all these instances the context of publication is a frame which seeks to determine meaning: historical context is always specific. To understand a particular occurrence of a text we need to know the reasons for its publication. Thus we need to answer the questions, (1) What was its intended function (sermon, play, political pamphlet, etc.)? and (2) Who was its intended audience? To a greater or lesser extent the answers to these are built into the physical text-as-sign. Little attention is usually paid to these matters because we normally decode the sign, frequently a complex one (e.g., the *Norton Anthology*) with no difficulty. Yet contexts are central to understanding. Contexts and texts create readers as much as readers create texts.

This need not lead to a profound anxiety about determinacy of meaning. As the text embodies traces of the reasons for and manner of its production, an analysis of the physical nature of a text can allow us to infer something about the nature and circumstances of production. This is a long-established procedure in the case of texts, such as medieval ones, which lack much of the contextual evidence a post-medieval critic normally takes for granted.

What are now called the *N-Town Plays* cannot be assigned to any precise place of origin or any exact date in medieval England, nor is it certain who produced the unique manuscript version or why. The plays clearly bear a general resemblance to the mystery plays of Townley, York, or Chester, but evidence of the *N-Town Plays'* contemporary context or function can only be inferred from their manuscript appearance in Cotton Vespasian D.VIII. Two kinds of evidence only are available: internal linguistic evidence and that provided by the manuscript's physical construction. The information given by dialect, spelling, and word forms, when related to the larger body of linguistic knowledge of medieval English, show the manuscript to come not from Coventry, as nineteenth-century editors thought, but from East Anglia.

Analysis of the physical construction can take us further but will not supply a full context. However, it can delimit speculation and exclude some possibilities. Clearly the mere fact of transcription involving the expense of the scribe's time and paper indicates the importance which the plays held for some person or institution (the latter being the more likely in the Middle Ages). The N-Town text is carefully written, rubricated, and neatly laid out. Its handwriting dates from the late fifteenth or early sixteenth century. Examinations of the manuscript by K. S. Block and, more recently, by Peter Meredith and Stanley Karhl,[6] show that the first scribe was attempting to create a compilation from a collection of play texts and that he or his employer were trying to edit and stitch together a text as they went. Unlike other texts of mystery plays, then, the *N-Town Plays* do not derive directly from craft-guild performance—the York sequence, for instance, is preserved in a manuscript, more elaborately produced than the *N-Town Plays*, which was made for the city

corporation and represents a record of the pageants performed by
the various guilds. By establishing the original collation it is possible
to demonstrate that the Marian (*Contemplacio*) group (plays 8–11,
13) was a separate and self-contained Mary play and that the first
Passion sequence (quires N, P, Q, R) was undoubtedly from a
separate manuscript. It is also clear that reviser B's activities were an
effort to regroup the plays for a theatrical performance. As first
compiled, then, the Cottonian manuscript was not intended as an
acting text or as a record of a performance but was meant to create
a composite version of a number of plays from different sources. It
was probably the product of a religious institution (hence the
appearance, otherwise unique in England, of something approaching
the European Passion play). It was certainly not produced by a town
corporation memorialising the plays created and acted by its craft
guilds.

   The physical evidence cannot give a full answer to the problems of
context and intention, but it does allow us to know *something* about
the play-texts' origins, their relationship or nonrelationship to any
performance, and the importance in which at least some part of
literate society held them. Further, it is clear that the N-Town
manuscript was produced for reasons and by an institution which
both differed from those which led to the creation, for instance, of
the manuscript of the York sequence. That is, the function of texts
not only differs from period to period depending upon available
technology and levels of literacy, but can also differ within periods.
The difficulties set by the *N-Town Plays* will seem normal and
unsurprising to medievalists. However, for those whose work is on
post-Gutenberg texts they are a reminder that the printed text, like
the manuscript text, is created with specific function. Without the
bibliographical and textual work of Block, Meredith, and Karhl, the
N-Town Plays would be more obscure and less accessible to the
unsuspecting twentieth-century reader. While bibliographical context may be impossible to recover in anything approaching fullness,
even an incomplete recovery of such knowledge affects our understanding of the text.

   The critic of medieval literature cannot function anachronistical-
ly: linguistic, palaeographical, and bibliographical knowledge are
prerequisites to any literary assessment that may be made. But the
use of the book as a sign in the late seventeenth century can also
propose questions of relevance to the critic, although the publishing

history of these works usually gets relatively little attention, even from editors with an otherwise historical approach. Thus what Alastair Fowler has to say about the publication of *Paradise Lost* in the Longmans Annotated Poets edition raises more questions than it answers, and this in a series committed to providing the reader with the relevant contemporary background. The following facts are given under "Printing History": Milton's contract with the printer Samuel Simmons is dated 27 April 1667; the poem was licensed "after some difficulty, according to John Toland," on 20 August; two editions appeared in Milton's lifetime, both printed by Simmons, the first having six issues with different title pages between 1667 and 1669; the first quarto edition had ten books, the second of 1674 twelve; other kinds of change are accurately noted; details of Milton's earnings are given; finally, we are told: "After a slow start, *EdI* went quickly selling 1300 copies—a large sale for the period. . . . After Milton's death there were three unimportant editions (1678, 1688, 1691), then a sixth with full-scale commentary by Patrick Hume (1695)."[7] This is a great deal more than most editions give, yet what is the reader expected to do with this information— does it have any relevance to the understanding of the poem? Apparently not. In this form it tells the reader little more than that there *may* have been some difficulty over licensing and that the poem became steadily more popular after a slow start.

A number of questions are raised if one comes to this from other late seventeenth-century books. (It may well be that Milton scholars have already supplied the answers, but my interest lies in the fact that this kind of reporting of the early publication of an important literary work is, if dealt with at all, treated as part of a routine, almost antiquarian, notation of the main facts.)

The most obvious bibliographical peculiarity is the six issues, but that is closely related with what I take to be another peculiarity— namely that Milton's contract was with a printer, not with a bookseller. Neither this, nor the names of booksellers involved, nor the fact that Samuel Simmons was the son of Matthew Simmons, a noted printer of radical literature during the Interregnum who printed some of Milton's works, is mentioned by the Longmans editor. As far as can be judged from checking Morrison's *Index* against Wing, Samuel Simmons's main occupation was as a printer: his ventures into the ownership of copy are infrequent. Certainly this is the only time his name is associated with original poetry.[8] More usually, he was involved with nonconformist works, though the Royalist Peter Heylyn also appears.[9] On the other hand, the involvement of booksellers in the six different issues suggests that Simmons, whose name does *not* appear at all on the first issue, had considerable difficulty in marketing 1300 copies. Three issues, dated 1667, 1667, and 1668, were sold by Peter Parker, Robert Boulter, and Matthias Walker, none of whom is recorded as a bookseller before 1664. As an entrepreneur, the printer seems to have turned to relatively new business ventures conveniently spread about the city (Aldgate, Bishopsgate Street, and Fleet Street), allowing the booksellers to ask for copies as needed. With the fourth issue, dated 1668, Parker's name disappears, and his place is taken by two booksellers, S. Thomson in Duck Lane and H. Mortlack in Westminster Hall. The former died 26 October 1668, though Mortlack, whose main sales were of theological works, continued in business until 1707. Nevertheless, his name along with every other bookseller's name given on previous issues, disappears on the title pages of the fifth and sixth states: their place is taken by T. Helder "at the Angel in Little Britain," whose first recorded activity dates back only to 1666. Presumably this edition was exhausted before Simmons printed the second under his own name in 1674.

Unfortunately Dryden's *Annus Mirabilis*, published in the same year as Milton's epic, does not provide as neat a comparison as might be hoped since it was pirated in 1668. Nevertheless, the fact that Dryden's poem was not republished until 1688 and that Herringman's first edition was still on sale in 1679[10] indicates that Dryden's topical poem enjoyed an immediate success while Milton's work made its way with the public over the remainder of the seventeenth century.

By setting *Annus Mirabilis* against *Paradise Lost*, the following points can be made. Dryden's volume, licensed, with its elaborate dedication to the city, its letter to Sir Robert Howard, and the complimentary poem to the Duchess of York, is structured to set up a specific relationship with its readers and to carry a clearly Royalist socio-political meaning. Sold in the normal octavo format by Henry Herringman, the bookseller of Court-centered literature, from his shop in the fashionable New Exchange, Dryden's work creates a precise set of relationships between author, producer, dedicatees, and audiences (City, Court, and England at large).[11] Milton's poem, carefully printed in the rather unexpected dress of a quarto, with an altogether chaster title page that names its author as plain "John Milton" (as against Dryden's status-conscious "Esq;"), was available only through a series of swiftly changing city booksellers. The Simmons family's strong link over the Interregnum with the printing of radical literature, and the fact that Robert Boulter, whose name is on the title page of the first four states, also appears on that of Marvell's *Miscellaneous Poems* of 1681, all suggest that Milton's epic was at least non-Establishment, that its early appearance was a difficult one, and that Toland's report of Milton's difficulty with the censors is correct. Seventeenth-century book-buyers would thus have seen at once that *Paradise Lost* differed from *Annus Mirabilis*. But without examining the careers of Simmons and the other men involved, without exploring the usualness or unusualness of a printer acting as entrepreneur and owner of copyright, without mapping the locations and lists of titles for each bookseller, and without exploring the formats and house styling adopted for different kinds of volumes of poems more rigorously, this kind of point will remain a matter of hypothesis and informed guesswork.

It may be that a study of Milton's booksellers would be more valuable for a sociological and cultural study of readers and publishing patterns in the late seventeenth century than for what it does, or does not, contribute to Christopher Hill's argument for the political nature of Milton's epic. But the early editions do have a bearing on another subject of importance, the question of how Milton's epic entered the canon of "official" literature, regardless of its author's Cromwellian background. The second and third editions remain within the same kind of non-Establishment publishing circle, but the fourth edition (1688) published by Bentley in partnership with Tonson, who had taken over Herringman's role as the major bookseller of court literature, was a handsome folio edition, well illustrated, and financed by the support of over five hundred subscribers drawn from the "Nobility and Gentry": the edition, with its "sculptures" by the Spanish artist, John Baptist Medina, who had recently arrived in England, claims *Paradise Lost* as a classic of English Literature.[12]

The early editions of a closely contemporary Puritan work, Bunyan's *The Pilgrim's Progress*, raise the question of canonisation more sharply, while even a cursory study of those publications refines what is meant when critics, usually in a loosely approbatory way, speak of Bunyan as a "folk" author.[13] *The Pilgrim's Progress* was an immediate publishing success on its appearance in 1678. It was an octavo selling for 1*s*. 6*d*. published by Nathaniel Ponder.[14] A bookseller with strong Independent and Puritan associations, Ponder had two years earlier been imprisoned for the publication of Marvell's *The Rehearsal Transprosed*.[15] He probably came to know Bunyan through his main author, the Puritan controversialist John Owen, D.D. *The Pilgrim's Progress* marks a change in Bunyan's publisher, and Bunyan's new bookseller took the allegory's publication seriously—he registered his ownership of copy, the first edition is said to have been set from new Dutch type, and the "Dreamer" plate was commissioned from Robert White and added to early editions. Clearly *The Pilgrim's Progress* belonged with nonconformist and puritan "Divinity" (it is so classified in the *Term Catalogues*) and was intended for a literate book-reading public. Ponder very quickly found his highly profitable new work being pirated, and the subsequent lawsuits give an indication of the numbers of copies being sold—editions of four and even ten thousand are referred to, and by 1692 it was said that a hundred-thousand copies had been sold in England alone quite apart from editions sold in New England or in translations in French, Dutch, and Welsh.[15] It also appears that by 1688 the belief that Bunyan was the author of ballad-sellers' wares helped sales among the uneducated literate readers outside London.[16]

This sketchy evidence could be fleshed out by identifying early editions which have their owner's signatures,[17] but an unusual publishing venture in 1692 does much to clarify Bunyan's contemporary standing and readership. The first volume of what was publicised as a two-volume folio edition of Bunyan's *Works* appeared in that year.[18] The imposing newly engraved portrait of Bunyan by John Sturt that appears opposite the title page and the folio format show that the publication was meant to establish Bunyan alongside the great Puritan and Anglican divines. But other features are peculiar. Although the bookseller, William Marshall "at the *Bible in Newgate-street*," "dealt chiefly in divinity, and at the time of the Popish plot published several pamphlets on the Protestant side" (Plomer), he did not finance the project himself or look for a partnership with other booksellers to put up the capital needed for a book of over four hundred sheets. Instead the money came from some four hundred subscribers "whereof about thirty are ministers" (sig. 5U1ʳ), and the titlepage says the volume was

"Collected and Printed by the Procurement of his Church and Friends, and by [Bunyan's] own Approbation before his Death: That these his Christian Ministerial Labours may be preserved in the World. . . ." Although the books' instigation stems from a sectarian church, which left the practical labour of arranging for its publication to one man, the Southwark combmaker Charles Doe, it was intended for a broader audience. The prefatory epistle by two ministers, John Wilson and Ebenezer Chandler (the latter Bunyan's successor at Bedford), is sprinkled with Latin tags and directs the "Serious, Judicious, and Impartial Reader" to Bunyan's virtues. Aiming to forestall criticism, the two men argue that Bunyan, despite his lack of education and learning, should not be dismissed by the educated reader—Bunyan was truly inspired and his "familiar style" has its own kind of power. They also reassure the orthodox about Bunyan's theological views: "We grant, that in respect to some circumstances . . . the Author's Sentiments are different from ours . . . yet in the Great Truths of the Gospel, we judge him to be very sound. . . . Some things he treats of, are Doctrinal and Controverted. . . . The rest of his writing (and they the greatest part, are Practical . . .)" (sig. A2ᵛ). The 1692 *Works* aimed at preserving Bunyan's writings, published and unpublished, "whereby it may be said in the Pulpit, The Great Convert *Bunyan* said so and so" (sig. 5T3ᵛ) and was possible only because of increased toleration—"By the late Act for Liberty of Conscience, it is now lawful to print the Works of Dissenters though it was not so formerly. . ." (*ibid.*). Strikingly, the only volume published contains none of Bunyan's most famous works, but for a very good reason: their copyright owners would not assign them to Doe (Sig. 5Ulʳ); Nathaniel Ponder was undoubtedly the stumbling block. Charles Doe makes one further point almost incidentally: some Anglican priests seem to have "cavilled" against *The Pilgrim's Progress* to their congregations.[19]

It would be possible to extend this examination through a detailed study of imprints, editions, translations and so on, but certain things are clear. Bunyan's allegory, which avoids too explicit deployment of the tenets of his version of Calvinism, immediately appealed to a wide literate nonconformist audience of devout readers. This appeal extended swiftly to a broader less well-educated body. It was an audience made up of a number of interrelated religious sub-cultures, cutting across class and educational background. As the work of an

"enthusiast" the allegory was clearly frowned upon by some Angli-
cans, and the effort to print the *Works* in 1692 is the expression of
a counter-culture opposed to the polite literature being published by
men like Tonson. Whatever "folk imagination" may mean when
used of Bunyan, it is no simple matter.

Unlike *Paradise Lost*, Bunyan's allegory was not thought of as
"literature" at this point. The twentieth-century problem of discussing as literature what was intended as divinity exercises many of the
contributors to Newey's recent collection of essays on *The Pilgrim's
Progress*. One practical answer, adopted by the *Norton Anthology*,
is to represent the work by passages, excising the theology and
eliminating the marginal glosses.[20] Interestingly, the Penguin English
Library's edition (1965), which, judging by the number of reprints by
1980 must have sold over 36,000 copies and must (because the work
is rarely set in its entirety for degree courses in English) be reaching
a readership outside the universities, not only restores the marginal
glosses, which are essential to a grasp of Bunyan's play between
allegory and meaning, but is essentially an historicist text. Roger
Sharrock's introduction is followed by a reproduction of the first
edition's title page, gives the author's apology, and restores earlier
more colloquial readings. It is not possible to read the Penguin
edition without a sense of Bunyan's historical otherness, while the
work's appearance in the Penguin *Library* asserts its contemporary
vitality. Sensibly, the publisher's cover-note avoids the problem of
the work's literary status, calling it simply "a work of imaginative
literature." It is the academic, not the publisher or reader, who has
difficulty in placing *The Pilgrim's Progress*. From the beginning
Bunyan's allegory has made its way outside what was "officially"
defined as literature. The case for its inclusion in the Penguin English
Library depends upon a consensus reached by readers and public
over the last three centuries and reflects the extent to which the work
has entered into the English cultural and literary imagination. This
implies both that the increasingly narrow definition of "literature"
since the late nineteenth century has been unduly constricting and
that the canon is not made exclusively in the classroom. Anxieties
about canonic hegemony stem in part from the blinkered or hubristic
assumption that it is the academic critic and the university syllabus
which determine the canon of English literature. This is certainly not
the case, for instance, with contemporary fiction; nor has it been the
case with earlier literature.

The essential point for the bibliographer is that made by D. F. McKenzie and David Foxon in their discussions of seventeenth- and eighteenth-century texts: we need a greater "historical understanding of the [publishing] trade and its practice . . . before the facts of physical bibliography and textual criticism can be seen in perspective."[21] Thus, the format, physical appearance, and the method of setting out act and scene divisions in Congreve's 1710 *Works* are clear typographical statements of the dramatist's neoclassical structuring of his plays and are part of a wider effort by Tonson, lasting over two decades, to find an appropriate form for the classics of English literature.[22] Jerome McGann's recent essay on the importance for the critic of the bibliographical, social, and cultural matrices for an understanding of Keats makes a similar case, though on a more ambitious theoretical level.[23] The examples of Milton, Dryden, and Bunyan suggest that we need to know more about the publishing trade and its place in seventeenth-century England on a number of fronts: which booksellers published what kind of books and which authors? Did they work with particular printers or with particular partners when printing a larger work? What proportion of total output was devoted to what we would define as literature? To what extent did printers depend upon the printing of books and to what extent upon jobbing printing for their income? Who bought what kind of books?

Since it is clear that particular booksellers and printers were involved, as modern publishers are, with a particular line of books, what, through the study of imprints and booksellers' advertisements, can be reconstructed of this kind of specialisation? What were the effects of censorship and proscription? Further, who was writing dedications and prefatory material and to whom? Given the importance of patronage in these years, surprisingly little is known on a general scale about them. It is quite obvious that from the dramatist's and public's point of view the dedication of a play, for instance, was a matter of considerable importance. Only in this fuller context would it be possible to make valid comparison between, say, Tonson as a publisher of court literature and the publishers of Milton or Bunyan. The work of D. F. McKenzie on books published in 1668, that of Keith Maslen on the size of editions of Defoe's *Robinson Crusoe*, that of Pat Rogers on Pope's subscribers, Margaret Spufford's study of "little books," and Peter Holland's analysis of the make-up of libraries collected by individuals—all indicate the possibilities for research, though they also indicate the limits of possible knowledge.[24] The relative paucity of information in the later seventeenth century will limit what can be done compared with the eighteenth century. There, quite apart from the greater wealth of extant documentary evidence, the British Library's computerised ESTC will greatly facilitate work on specific booksellers and on the provincial trade. Both the textual critic and the literary critic who believes in the historicity as well as the contemporary vitality of a work need to be alert to ways in which inadequate knowledge of the production and circulation of texts may deprive either of essential information.

In many cases increased knowledge may be impossible, or may offer only substantiation to what can be extracted from the book as sign. This is because those critics not programmatically opposed to considering a text's historical origins have always taken such factors into account where they are obviously relevant—as in the serial publication of Victorian novels. Nevertheless, the book-as-sign poses its own challenge to ahistorical approaches to literature. With McKenzie and McGann, I believe that bibliographical evidence and bibliographical contexts are of importance to editor and critic and that we cannot read a text without a sense of its place in history. But here we come back to Greg's point—only the bibliographer can extract the full meaning from the physical signs. If critics are to pay more attention, bibliography needs to widen its aims. The kind of analysis described above really belongs to publishing history and impinges upon social, economic, and cultural history as well as upon literary criticism. Yet if bibliography is to contribute to these areas, bibliographers ought not leave the field to amateurs.

Finally, I want to press the argument into a more problematic area. All of the texts so far discussed are ones 'fixed' either by a scribe or by the printing press, the kinds traditionally dealt with by the bibliographer and textual critic. But both bibliography and textual criticism are surely involved in any attempt to make a permanent record of the fluid text of a performed oral "literature." Here their role is not to establish a text and infer a context from insufficient evidence (for example, the manuscript of the *N-Town Plays*), but to report as accurately, and with as full a contextual sense as possible, a version or versions of the performed work. My example is non-European, involves several media, and is necessarily a 'polymorphous' text, yet it fully bears out Greg's recognition that a text is 'a living organism . . . in its descent through the ages.'

J. P. Clark, the Nigerian poet, has attempted to record his people's saga of Ozidi. The Ijo are a minority ethnic group from the Niger Delta who speak their own language. The story of their hero Ozidi, traditionally told and performed in separate four-hour sessions spread over seven successive nights, is accompanied by dance, mime, music, and ritual. Its age is unknown and there is no fixed text. When performed in an Ijo village an individual story-teller acts simultaneously as poet, composer, producer, and performer, creating a participatory group enactment of the story. The saga combines Ijo religion, myth and history, but, while belonging to the people as a whole, it is felt to be the particular property of one clan, the Tarakiri in Western Ijo, to whom the story was first revealed. Strikingly, despite the variations in each performance, the adult members of the audience interrupt the story-teller to correct or modify his version by citing tradition. As J. P. Clark says, each performance is "a dynamic process in the permanent act of recreation of an ancient art form in contemporary terms and idiom to satisfy present needs."[25]

Clark's labours to record the saga in print go back to his verse play *Ozidi* published by Oxford University Press in 1966, a version created to be acted on the Western stage (and the form in which I first encountered the saga). Over a ten-year period Clark produced three further texts: a full-length colour film of a performance at Orua, which is available only in a 45-minute 16mm. version, entitled *The Tides of the Delta*; an album of three long-playing records, *Songs from the "Ozidi Saga"*; and, finally, a printed volume published in 1977 with Ijo transcript, English translation, introduction, notes, and appendices. None of these four published forms can recreate even a single performance for the non-Ijo, while the printed text produces further oddities. J. P. Clark chose to print what he considered the fullest and most accurate version: this was not, as he had expected, the performance he had filmed in the Delta at Orua in 1963, but a version he recorded in 1963/4 from Okabou of Sama performed with the Ijo community resident in Ibadan. There was also a third performance taped, this time among the Ijos in Lagos. However, the story-teller, Mr. Afoluwa, a retired merchant seaman from whom Clark had first heard the story as a child, had been exiled from the Delta community for some twenty years. He could no longer remember the script in its proper sequence of cause and effect.

Clark's efforts to preserve the Ijo's saga makes a number of points with some vividness. First, even in an oral culture we find one clan within the people having a proprietary attitude to the story, an attitude respected by other clans; second, despite changes in detail and emphasis, each community believes that there is an essential and meaningful central story—even though the conditions of oral trans- mission ensure inevitable changes; third, the saga is a festival which asserts the whole community's sense of itself in moral, religious, and historical terms; fourth, J. P. Clark's efforts make it possible even for outsiders to understand *something* of the force and meaning of a very different form of literature in an alien cultural and linguistic idiom. It can further be said that Clark's verse play in English allows non-Ijo Nigerians and non-Africans to experience a stage version importantly and recognisably deriving from the parent.

It would be idle to pretend that the non-Ijo can ever enter into the full experience of the *Ozidi Saga*. But the printed text, though one of its functions is to serve as a memorial of a single story-teller's version, does allow the English-speaking reader to perform a mental version through an act of attention which depends upon Clark's whole apparatus of contextual and explanatory aids. What that reading reveals is an epic story which has a beginning, middle, and end, which answers in its own terms Aristotle's definition of an epic, and which has an understandable, if foreign, morality, dignity, and and meaning. Essential to that measure of understanding is a sharp sense of its severe limitations and partiality. Without a recognition of the limitations there could be no meaningful understanding or valuation of that meaning.

I am aware that Clark's scholarly text might be thought to belong not with English Literature, the classification given it by the Univer- sity of Leeds Library, but with folklore or anthropology. It is also possibly the case that as Nigeria's oil wealth hastens the process of urbanisation, the Ozidi saga will cease to be known even to the Ijo people. Indeed, there are signs in Clark's edition that the communal life in the Niger Delta is already ceasing to support the continuing life of the saga. Does the publication of the saga merely relinquish it to a shadowy non-life in some deracinated museum of the Western mind?

I think not. It is possible and worthwhile to try to understand, and to value, what is preserved by Clark's various versions, even though that means an empathic effort to go outside our limited racial, linguistic, and cultural experience. At the same time, while no one can prevent Random Cloud's free play with an infinitive text of the *Ozidi Saga*, it would clearly be absurd. Our limited understanding of the saga depends upon J. P. Clark's explanations and contextualising. A corollary is that an understanding of texts which lack full bibliographical and cultural contexts are likely to be subject to partial and inaccurate understanding. In approaching the *N-Town Plays*, a twentieth-century understanding must be based on the effort to extrapolate from the physical and other evidence as much contextual information as possible of the kind which J. P. Clark was in time to record. So too, in varying degrees, does our understanding of Milton, Dryden, Bunyan, and Yeats.

NOTES

1. "The Marriage of Good and Bad Quartos," *Shakespeare Quarterly*, 33 (1982), 422; this paper was delivered April 1983 at the second STS Conference.

2. "Bibliography—An Apologia," W. W. Greg, *Collected Papers*, ed. J. C. Maxwell (Oxford, 1966), p. 259. The paper was first given as a presidential address to the Bibliographical Society on 21 March 1932.

3. The choice of the 1962 edition is arbitrary: it is one I happen to own.

4. For further detail, substantiation, and references, see my "Dryden: History and 'The Mighty Government of the Nine'," *University of Leeds Review*, 24 (1981), 25–26, 40nn.

5. Yeats's fear of censorship is recorded in Nancy Cardozo, *Maud Gonne: Lucky Eyes and a High Heart* (New York, 1978; London, 1979), pp. 314–15. Maud Gonne did not believe that Yeats's anxiety had any grounds.

6. My information is taken from *Ludus Coventriae or The Plaie called Corpus Christi Cotton Vespasian D.VIII*, ed. K. S. Block, E.E.T.S. Extra Series, 120 (1922), and *The N-Town Plays: A Facsimile of British Library MS Cotton Vespasian D.VIII*, intro. Peter Meredith and Stanley J. Karhl, *Leeds Texts and Monographs, Medieval Drama Series*, IV (Leeds, 1977), esp. pp. vii–xiv, xxii–iv.

7. *The Poems of John Milton*, ed. John Carey and Alastair Fowler, 2nd impression with corrections (London, 1980), pp. 423–26. For an important analysis of the complexities of the first edition of *Paradise Lost* (unavailable

when this paper was delivered in April 1983), see Hugh Amory, "Things Unattempted Yet," *Book Collector* (Spring, 1983), 41–66.

8. Simmons was the son or nephew of Matthew Simmons and shared his address "Next door to the Golden Lion, Aldersgate Street" with Mary, Matthew's widow. L'Estrange's survey of printing houses in 1668 identifies her as the "Custom House printer," and she is recorded as having thirteen hearths in 1666. An establishment of this size must have needed a considerable flow of work, which could not have been supplied by the number of books having either Samuel or Mary Simmons's name in the imprint. I can only identify twenty-two books with Samuel Simmons's name in the imprint, and in most cases he seems to have been the printer not the publisher. The nearest any of these come to poetry is a reprinting of Sir John Mennes's *Recreation for Ingenious Head-Pieces* . . . (1667). The British Library copy has an additional engraved titlepage for *Witt's Recreations . . . Printed M. and S. Simmons 1663* (C.116.b.22). One of the possibly Royalist-inclined books, Hugh Davis's *De jure ecclesiasticae . . .* (1669) is in fact related to Buckingham's efforts in 1668 to create greater toleration (Davis was his chaplain). In addition there are a further twelve works printed by "S. S." in the relevant period.

9. The notable nonconformist writers are John Caryll, Thomas Goodwin, and Thomas Lye. Peter Heylyn's *Theologia veterum . . .* (1673) was printed "By S. Simmons, for A. S., to be sold by Henry Brome, and Benj. Tooke, and Tho. Sawbridge."

10. See the advertisement present in the Brotherton Collection's copy of Marie Desjardin's *The Unfo[r]tunate Heroe* (1679) (University of Leeds).

11. Further, see *art. cit.*, pp. 19–22, n. 4 above.

12. Further, see Kathleen M. Lynch, *Jacob Tonson: Kit-Cat Publisher* (Knoxville, 1971), pp. 126–29.

13. See, for example, contributions in *The Pilgrim's Progress: Critical and Historical Views*, ed. Vincent Newey (Liverpool, 1980), esp. S. J. Newman, "Bunyan's Solidness": *"The Pilgrim's Progress* . . . is the last significant product of religious folk vision, it is the most important focus of English folk life between Shakespeare and Dickens . . ." (p. 226).

14. The information on Bunyan is from two main sources, an examination of his publications through Morrison's index to Wing, and F. H. Mott's article, "Nathaniel Ponder: The Publisher of *The Pilgrim's Progress*," *The Library*, 4th series, xv (1934), 257–94.

15. Ponder had to enter into a £500 bond "with 2 sufficient Sureties" on 26 May 1676 before obtaining his release (F. H. Mott, *art. cit.*, p. 262). Marvell's book had appeared in 1672.

16. F. H. Mott records Ponder's complaint against ". . . certain ballad sellers about Newgate and on London Bridge, who have put the two first letters [J. B.] of the Author's name and his effigies to their rhimes and ridiculous books, suggesting to the world as if they were his" (*art cit.*, p. 285).

17. For instance, a copy of the first edition was owned by "William Readding at Greene fordge in the parish of Wamborne 1679" and at one point belonged to the Marsom family (*The Pilgrim's Progress*, ed. J. B. Wharey [Oxford, 1928], p. xl). This William Reading was probably the iron refiner, father of William (1674–1744), who went to Oxford and became library keeper at Sion College.

18. *The Works of that Eminent Servant of Christ, Mr. John Bunyan, late Minister of the Gospel, and Pastor of the Congregation at Bedford. The First Volume* . . . (1692). The complications of the volume's financing are plain from a note at the foot of the title page: "Whereas it was proposed to the Subscribers, that this book would contain near a Hundred and Forty Sheets, they are hereby certified, that by reason of the smallness of the writing of the Manuscripts, it could not be so exactly computed; so that it is now about 155 Sheets, which additional sheets advance the price to about 1*s.* 6*d.* more in a Book, of which only one Shilling more is Required of the Subscribers, with which it is hoped they will not be displeased." The British Library has a copy of the subscription proposals, 816.m.21(5).

19. In his account of *The Pilgrim's Progress*'s wide circulation, Charles Doe says, "none but Priest-ridden people cavil at it: it wins so smoothly upon their affections; and so insensibly distills the Gospel into them . . ." (Sig. 5T4ᵛ).

20. Again, my reference is to the 1962 edition. See also the brutal job effected by W. T. Williams and G. H. Vallins in Methuen's English Classics' *Selections from Bunyan* (1927, etc.).

21. "The London Book Trade in the Later Seventeenth Century: Sandars Lectures 1976" (n.d., n.p.), p. 1. Mimeographed copies of McKenzie's important lectures are on deposit at Cambridge, Oxford, and Leeds. A version of David Foxon's Lyell Lectures (1976) is deposited in the Bodleian.

22. See William Congreve, *The Way of the World*, ed. John Barnard (Edinburgh, 1972), pp. 10–12, D. F. McKenzie, *op. cit.* pp. 35–54. See also Peter Holland, *The Ornament of Action: Text and Performance in Restoration Comedy* (Cambridge, 1979), pp. 125–33.

23. "Keats and the Historical Method in Literary Criticism," *Modern Language Notes*, 94 (1979), 988–1032.

24. D. F. McKenzie, "The London Book Trade in 1668," *Words: Wai-te-ata, Studies in Literature*, 4 (Wellington, N.Z., 1974), 75–92; Pat Rogers, "Pope and his Subscribers," *Publishing History*, 3 (1978), 7–36; K. I. D. Maslen,

"The Printers of *Robinson Crusoe*," *The Library*, 5th series, vii (1952), 124-31, and "Edition Quantities for *Robinson Crusoe*, 1719," *The Library*, 5th series, xxiv (1969), 145-50; Margaret Spufford, *Small Books and Pleasant Histories: Popular Fiction and its Readership in Seventeenth-Century England* (1981); Peter Holland, *op. cit.*, pp. 114-16, 265-66nn. See also John Barnard, "Dryden, Tonson, and Subscriptions for the 1697 *Virgil*," *Publications of the Bibliographical Society of America*, 57 (1963), 129-57.

25. My information is drawn from seeing the film and from J. P. Clark, *The Ozidi Saga: Collected and Translated from the Ijọ of Okabuo Ojobolo* (Ibadan, 1977), and *Ozidi: An Epic Play* (Oxford, 1966).

'The Text Itself'—Whatever That Is

HERSHEL PARKER

The New Critics, dismissing information about the author as extrinsic and therefore irrelevant, located literary authority in "the text itself." That phrase has haunted all subsequent literary criticism and literary theory up through Tzvetan Todorov ("What exists first and foremost is the text itself and nothing but the text"). Recently many literary theorists such as Wolfgang Iser have located authority not in the author and not in the text alone but in "the text and the reader." Others have located literary authority in the subjective reader. Jonathan Culler has recommended a French vacation for Americans, a pleasure tour of the text in which what counts is how sybaritic the pleasures are, not how authorially contrived they are. Others have located literary authority in themselves and a small circle of friends ("the authority of hermeneutic interpretive communities"). Deconstructionists acknowledge without regret the reported death of the author at some indeterminate time during his long exile from New Critical explications, then go on to shatter into as many fragments as possible the illusion that any authority resides in "the text itself," except as that text authorizes readers, such as themselves, to play at a game of unravelling meanings which will always be, like the moment of the death of the author, indeterminate. Yet Jacques Derrida takes as given "un texte déjà écrit, noir sur blanc," thereby starting his process of deconstruction with "an already written," and therefore previously constructed, text. That is not living dangerously—that is like camping, as it were, in your own backyard.

Editors and editorial theorists have sounded curiously like literary critics and theorists. G. Thomas Tanselle in his 1976 *Studies in Bibliography* essay suggests that in making editorial decisions the editor, like the critic, "will be turning to the text itself as his primary evidence." Asking how "the author's intended meaning" is to be discovered, Tanselle says that "one is inevitably drawn back to the work itself as the most reliable documentary evidence as to what the author intended." According to Tanselle, the editor will recognize "that the most reliable source of information about the author's intention in a given work is that work itself"; "the work itself is the controlling factor in statements made about its meaning, whether or not those statements aim at elucidating the author's intended meaning"; "there is a specific and clearly defined aspect of the broad concept of 'intention' which is the appropriate concern of the scholarly editor—the intention of the author to have particular words and marks of punctuation constitute his text and the intention that such a text carry a particular meaning or meanings"; finally, "the scholarly editor will amass all the evidence he can find bearing on each textual decision: but, whenever the factual evidence is less than incontrovertible, his judgment about each element will ultimately rest on his interpretation of the author's intended meaning as he discovers it in the whole of the text itself." Implicit in all these quotations is the assumption that editorial problems usually come in a sprinkling of variant readings and a few cruxes and that everyone pretty much agrees what the rest of the text is. This way of thinking about the text is not very far, I would say, from the New Critical notion of a literary text as a verbal icon.

But in many familiar American novels (and I restrict myself to my own experience, though the application of what I say is broad), the textual situation is such that an editor might not be able to resolve textual issues under the guidelines Tanselle suggests. An editor will confront readings in the standard text which are nonsensical—a failure of agreement, for instance, where the rest of the familiar text would offer no clue as to how the disagreement could be resolved. In editing *The Red Badge of Courage* Fredson Bowers follows the Appleton edition in lack of agreement and in lack of referent instead of going outside the boundaries of the text itself to see that the blunders occur only in the printed text, not in the author's surviving manuscript. The end of Chapter 17 of *Maggie* in the Appleton edition is also literally nonsensical—tall buildings, for instance, leap from the start of the last block down to the edge of the river—all because the editorial concern at Appleton's was merely to keep the text from meaning what it had all too plainly meant as Crane wrote it, not to make it mean *something else*. Yet, once the variant forms were identified, literary critics concentrated on wresting a coherent interpretation from a nonsensical text, and, as editor, Bowers did precisely what the critics tried to do, at considerable length—to wrest meaning from a meaningless text, on the basis of the expurgated form of the text itself. Thus an editor will often confront textual situations in which passages have, or seem to have, meaning merely because something was omitted from the text the author wrote. No one tried seriously to edit *Sister Carrie* before the Pennsylvania editors, but anyone who *had* tried would have gone seriously awry in trying to resolve a textual problem in one paragraph by reference, say, to the preceding paragraph which (as Dreiser wrote it) might have stood several paragraphs away.

An editor will often confront such textual situations in which there is only *part* of the text itself in what is widely accepted as being the text itself, the case with *The Red Badge of Courage* just as with *Sister Carrie*. An editor will confront passages which because of some rearrangement of sections have gained, or seemed to gain, meaning which is merely adventitious, not possibly intended by the author. Only by closing his eyes did Malcolm Cowley manage to avoid confronting many such adventitious meanings in the reordered *Tender is the Night*. An editor will confront situations in which the author never *had* an intention for each word in relation to all the other words in the text he was authorizing: *Pudd'nhead Wilson* is an example where the author did not even read through the text itself. An editor will confront situations in which the intended meaning was merely local, the result of a temporary phase of the composition, and is not explicable in terms of the whole of the text itself: examples are in *Pierre* and *Billy Budd, Sailor,* as well as *Pudd'nhead Wilson.* An editor will find problems whenever an author does something so simple as adding a passage, as Melville did on the cook, Old Coffee, for the English edition of *White-Jacket*. Will the addition be considered as part of the whole of the text itself when the editor makes his judgments on the addition in the light of the whole of the text itself? An editor will confront situations in which cuts have wholly removed the evidence that a major theme was once present and (when present) controlled other passages which still survive in the standard text, more or less drained of intentionality. This happens in Mailer's *An American Dream.*

I am not suggesting that Tanselle did not know that such textual complexities exist. I am using a great essay rather than a routine one to emphasize how we as editors have tended to follow the literary

critics in simplifying the notion of the text itself. We simplified the
notion of the text with a vengeance when we championed W. W.
Greg's rationale of copy-text as all but universally applicable.
Tanselle always stresses Greg's modesty. Modest he was, but arbitrary: if you decide that a later reading is authorial you incorporate
it into the earlier copy-text whether you think it is an improvement or
not, and you do not worry about what the change does to any
functions of the parts of the text as the author composed it. The goal
was a new, eclectic, critical text (in Bowers's more mystical terminology an "ideal" text) which anyone could create by following
Greg's formula. In applying Greg we had to loosen the copy-text,
only to tighten it up again when we finished. Some of us tended to
simplify the notion of the text itself in another somewhat contradictory way, starting at a late point in its history: James Thorpe and
Donald Pizer declared that the text itself is whatever got published,
while others declared that the text itself is whatever got *re*published.
The notion of the text as what got published or what got republished
seems to merge with the contradictory Gregian doctrine in Bowers's
editing of *The Red Badge of Courage* and *Maggie*: that is, editors
could follow the deathbed-edition school of editing, looking to the
last form as a source for readings rather than looking back toward
the text as the author originally wrote it.

Our generation of editors, armed with the magical wand of Greg's
rationale, may have been committing or countenancing the "Novel-
istic Fallacy" on a scale undreamed of by Bruce Harkness in the late
1950s. Harkness took on his New Critical colleagues for their
assumption that "a few mistakes" (being "swallowed up in the vast
bulk of the novel") "damage neither novel nor criticism."
Harkness's heart was in the right place and his non-specific suspicions were well justified, but the examples available to him were
pretty meagre, for the most part only single-word corruptions. In the
intervening decades we have assembled textual data in an abundance
and diversity that would have overwhelmed anyone in the late 1950s.

It still overwhelms those of us who have worked on CEAA and
CSE editions, for in our confusion we have strained out gnats and
swallowed camels. We agonize over a rationale for emending standard forms into dialect, or dialect forms into standard forms, or
dialect forms into other dialect forms (as in *The Red Badge of
Courage*) without worrying about the possible effects on the text
itself of the omission of three sensational chapter endings and an

entire chapter. Might Crane in the original Chapter 12 have intended particular words and marks of punctuation to constitute his text and might he have intended that the text so constituted to carry a particular meaning or meanings? Might such a chapter even constitute—Oh, boldness of the thought!—a part of the whole of the text itself? Whenever under Greg's rationale we have printed texts shortened or rearranged or otherwise altered according to someone's whim, suggestion, or command (even the author's), we have been acting as if whole sentences, long passages, and even whole chapters do not matter in a novel—even when it happens to be so short that there is no "vast bulk" to be swallowed up in or hollowed out of. Often we have repudiated at the outset any attempt to recover the text itself as it emerged from the creative process, if indeed it did result from a single, completed creative process.

In our New Critical mind-set we as editors have tended to forget that many literary works are *not* the result of a single, completed creative process in which there was a pervading thought that impelled the book. *Billy Budd, Sailor* is incomplete—radically unreadable, to the point that nothing final can be said about the character of Captain Vere. *Pierre* may have been completed in a short version according to a pervading thought that impelled it all the way through, before a new impulse drove Melville to add what amounted to some 150 printed pages. The author's intended meaning cannot be found in the *whole* of the text itself, for one must not talk about Melville's intention in *Pierre* but his intentions, sometimes distinct and sometimes overlapping, as when he imperfectly salvaged material written under one intention for passages dominated by a later intention. *Pudd'nhead Wilson* was a great heap of pages when Mark Twain thought up the changeling plot and began to subordinate (not eliminate) the Siamese twin plot. (He wrote some Siamese twin scenes after inventing Roxy.) He never harmonized the manuscript with itself, and he never harmonized with itself what he extracted from the typescript months later. Here we have two incomplete creative processes and one careless salvage job, followed the next year by a second salvage job for *Those Extraordinary Twins*. As Mark Twain wrote it, *Huckleberry Finn* is the result of a series of pretty disparate creative impulses. As Mark Twain published it *Huckleberry Finn* embodies that series of processes, except that one of them was sabotaged by the agreement, commercially motivated, to scrap the raftsmen episode, a reduction which turned one section into partial nonsense. We do not have the text itself of *The Red Badge of Courage* as Crane completed it—parts are probably lost forever. The best we can do is to restore the parts that survive and run in pieces of rough draft (when *they* happen to survive) to eke out something which will approximate "the text itself" as Crane completed it. *An American Dream* was the result of a coherent creative process, and Mailer's revisions of it for the book version were mainly those of a writer still in the throes of the original process. But at some late stage of the revisions he removed a handful of passages, the absence of which severely damaged the book, leaving us with a coherent "text itself" discoverable in two printed documents, legally non-conflatable by anyone but Mailer himself. (I am working on him.) As this handful of examples suggests, again and again we need to move away from any lingering New Critical notions of "the text itself," for very often the text itself as we normally think of it may be most misleading as a means of elucidating the author's intended meaning, may constitute quite unreliable documentary evidence as to what the author intended.

Instead of defending the sacredness of the text itself (in whatever form that was published or was authorized or became established or in the ideal form we have created), we should be celebrating the sacredness of the creative process and the product of the creative process. But the truth is that as editors, editorial theorists, literary critics, and literary theorists we have shied away from the creative process (since the 1930s, really) and have tended to fix our attention on the product at too late a stage, after it has been casually rearranged, censored, or otherwise altered, or else we have fixed our attention on the writer at too late a stage, after he has passed out of the creative process. We act as if John Dewey were irrelevant, as if authority were not something built into the text itself, phrase by phrase, as the writer proceeds, but something the writer can bestow retroactively, like a blessing, without the bother of retrofitting anything. We have all, it seems to me, ignored the creative process, or else we would not have exalted an editorial theory, Greg's irrational rationale of copy-text, which is incompatible with what we know of the creative process. We have sworn allegiance to a theory which holds that an author retains authority over his text as long as he lives, while research into creativity and the testimony of any number of creative writers shows that the creative process is a process like any other—meaning that it begins, continues (continues, in fact, with varying admixtures and varying sequences of excitement, arousal, boredom, ecstasy, anxiety, and determination), then *ends*, if the writer lives to finish it, *ends* with such stubborn finality that a writer can rarely regain authority over a text once he has passed out of the creative phase. Greg does not work perfectly, I am saying, except in the simplest cases of authorial correction and restoration of the original readings. "The text itself" is a notion which makes sense as a guide to editorial decision-making only in relation to the creative process and only if it respects the determinacy of that process—the fact that (contrary to Greg) authors can lose control of their literary works, and in fact do so all the time.

Most editors are committed to the notion of authorial intention. Probably we are all prepared to smuggle a text into the classroom, despite the members of authority-wielding hermeneutic communities who may lurk in the halls, exercising their right of free speech and trying to check the contents of our bookbags as we enter. But what do you have to carry to class when you really *want* to have a text in the class, when you *want* to teach the text itself of a literary work? Knowing what I know, I cannot just carry *Pudd'nhead Wilson* into class and teach it—according, for instance, to James M. Cox's influential reading of it as a sustained investigation of slavery—not when I know that some middle chapters were written when slavery was not a theme at all and were never revised to *contain* the theme of slavery. I can carry in a photocopy of the manuscript (which has juicier though more incoherent stuff about race and slavery than the "book" has), and carry in the serial version, and the first printing of *Pudd'nhead* and *Those Extraordinary Twins* together. With that material I can do a great job of teaching the interconnectedness of biography, textual theory, editorial theory, literary criticism (how have the critics been able to celebrate the coherence of the text itself?), literary theory, and creativity theory. (The students may still go off complaining that the professor made them buy the text and then did not teach it.) But in all honesty I cannot teach what we have always known as the text itself. For a simpler example, I cannot teach the Dial and Dell version of *An American Dream*, either, but all I really have to carry in, extra, is a few passages from the *Esquire* version in order to have a coherent, readable, teachable (if a little ragged) text, though it is not embodied in one volume.

The upshot is that while Stanley Fish is traveling light, leaving his texts at home, we may have to buy bigger bookbags in order to carry

into class the components of an expanded notion of the text itself.
And I think as we absorb more of the aesthetic implications of the
new textual evidence which is appearing all around us we will have to
accept the duty of instilling in the classroom a little skepticism about
the notion of the text itself. Maybe we do not have to pass out
Melvillean warnings—book-markers with the motto NO TRUST—but
we should start alerting our students to the possibility that (at the
least) in any text an apparent anomaly may be a real anomaly and
that (at the worst) for many familiar texts the situation is such that
the text cannot be taught honestly from any single available form of
the text itself, or sometimes from any single form we could create,
according to Greg's rationale or any other rationale.

   This paper is printed as I read it at the 1983 STS conference. Those
who did not attend should know that my quotations from Tanselle's
1976 *Studies in Bibliography* essay did not sound quite so contentious when I read them in his presence and when I read aloud to him
and the rest of the audience a tribute then forthcoming in *College
Literature*: "an essay extraordinarily important as the first attempt
to reconcile notions of intention held by editors, literary critics,
aestheticians, philosophers, speech–act theorists, and others." Fuller
development of the ideas in this talk are in these recent essays: "The
'New Scholarship': Textual Evidence and Its Implications for Criticism, Literary Theory, and Aesthetics," *Studies in American Fiction*, 9 (Autumn, 1981), pp. 181–97; "Norman Mailer's Revision of
the *Esquire* Version of *An American Dream* and the Aesthetic
Problem of 'Built-in Intentionality,' " *Bulletin of Research in the
Humanities*, 84 (Winter, 1981), pp. 405–430 (published in January
1983); "The Determinacy of the Creative Process and the 'Authority' of the Author's Textual Decisions," *College Literature*, 10
(Spring, 1983), pp. 99–125; "Lost Authority: Non-sense, Skewed
Meanings, and Intentionless Meanings," *Critical Inquiry*, 9 (June,
1983), pp. 767–74; and "The Lowdown on *Pudd'nhead Wilson*:
Jack-leg Novelist, Unreadable Text, Sense-Making Critics, and
Basic Issues in Aesthetics," *Resources for American Literary Study*,
11 (Autumn 1981), pp. 1–26. All of these essays except the first are
revised, expanded, and reprinted along with four new chapters in my
Flawed Texts and Verbal Icons (Northwestern, 1984).

Interpretation, Meaning, and Textual Criticism: A Homily.

JEROME J. MCGANN

Dearly Beloved,

Our text today is taken from the Gospel According to Matthew, chapter 5, verse 13:

> Ye are the salt of the earth: but if the salt have lost his savour, wherewith shall it be salted? it is thenceforth good for nothing, but to be cast out, and to be trodden under foot of men. (King James Version)

What is the meaning of this dark saying, this mysterious text lifted out of that most profound of all our texts? And how shall we ascertain its meaning?

Thus have we often begun our quest for the meaning of our culture's various written deposits. In the conventional mode of expression, "We take a certain passage for our text" and we elaborate, at the "rhetorical level" (to borrow John McClelland's term), "the meaning of the text." Behind all such acts of exegesis lies the assumption that "The Text Itself" (*whatever* that is) locates a determinate and even a determinable meaning. We may "take this passage for our text" because *this* text is a reed on which we may lean with confidence: an everlasting arm, the Word of God.

My brothers and sisters, I am happy to say that we here constitute a saving and saved remnant. I am not alone escaped to tell thee that this way of *having* the text (you will excuse the profane metaphor) is not our way. We are fallen from that New Critical Paradise (or Bower of Bliss), for we know the text to be historically indeterminate. And we take comfort in the knowledge that we are escaped as well from the illusions of the Poststructuralists, the imaginations of whose hearts are evil continually. We are escaped because we are not only historical creatures, we are materialists as well. (I shall not here

pursue the question whether we are, therefore, historical materialists.)

Neither shall I pursue any longer this (entirely too) seductive mode
of address. As Byron once said—in the midst of *Don Juan*—"I now
mean to be serious."

And I think the passage from Matthew locates some serious and
interesting problems for persons concerned about the meaning of the
text. This passage in fact contains a famous crux in New Testament
studies, one of hundreds of textual problems which biblical scholars
have labored for centuries, and in vain, to solve. No one knows what
this strange passage means. Or rather I should say that no one any
longer *believes* he or she understands what the passage means. Even
more to this mordant point, everyone now knows that the passage
will and must escape all original elucidation until as yet unantici-
pated documentary evidence alters the status of the text (e.g., the
discovery of an illuminating parallel in the Qumran scrolls).

Thus we must say that a passage like this text from Matthew
prevents "interpretation." Yet the passage still has "meaning." Let
me explain why.

This passage was always mysterious to scholars of the New
Testament. But not until the development of the Lower and Higher
Critical Methods were scholars given the means to illuminate the
contours of mysterious passages like this one. Textual criticism today
knows that this passage is corrupt—corrupt at McClelland's
"textological" level. Collation of the various documents reveals the
presence of corruption, largely through the history of the variants,
emendations, and glosses which editors and scholars have produced
to elucidate the text. The textual history of this passage exposes its
"meaning," that is, its most generally applicable and acceptable
meaning, its most important "rhetorical" meaning: that it is a text
whose meaning and significance lie in its specific and explicable
mysteriousness. It represents a mystery of a determinate type and
character. Part of its "meaning," therefore, is that it cannot be
rationally or persuasively interpreted.

To know this about the passage is to know a good deal (both in the
way of facts and in the way of theory). To be *able* to know these
things—to have the practical skills for developing such knowledge—
is to be possessed of an "armed vision," as Stanley Edgar Hyman
once called critical knowledge. This room is populated by people
who have spent some time developing such historical skills, which is

why I am pleased to be here. If I could, I would persuade all "interpreters," hermeneuts, and reader respondents to go back to school and reexamine the scholarly disciplines which alone can bring the redemption to knowledge to their creative endeavors.

But today I am not talking with those gentiles who go whoring after their strange gods. The passage from Matthew is a text which bears as well a meaning for the initiate here.

We textual scholars often take it for granted that our most basic methodology—tracing back the historical development of texts in their received material forms—has as its end and aim the recovery of the authoritative text: the original meaning, the author's original (or final) intentions, and so forth. We have various formulations. Hershel Parker's essay is an eloquent plea for the importance of such a quest.

In my view, however, this quest for a primal text or a primal meaning is only one of the functions of textual criticism. In certain cases this is a wholly peripheral function, and the passage from Matthew helps to explain why. Classical scholars cannot hope to elucidate the sort of text which Hershel pursues, for classical scholars cannot retreat further back in time than to the Alexandrian period. The best text of Homer or Thucydides we can hope to have is an imitation of the Alexandrian text, and a similar historical limit is raised against the work of all biblical students.

The passage from Matthew calls attention to an important fact about *all* texts, including modern texts which can be traced back to extant authoritative manuscript states as in the cases of Mailer, or Mark Twain—or Byron. That is, the Matthew passage dramatically reveals the social character which all texts must assume. Texts are the products of cultural institutions—this is true even of the most renegade text-producers, like William Blake—and the *meanings* of these texts are equally the product of people who live and move and have their being in the dialectics of society and its institutions. Hershel's work—the *meaning* of this work—is critical: it is a critique of certain institutionally sanctioned ideas about texts, scholarly methods, and literary meanings.

Creativity has most to do with individuals, meanings have most to do with society. Textual criticism investigates the history, deposited in literary works, of the specific interactions which took (and are taking) place between determinate individuals in determinate social circumstances. What emerges from this investigation is a more or less

coherent knowledge about texts, their many producers and repro-
ducers, and their many and various meanings. Interpretations of
texts are not the "meanings" of the texts; rather, they constitute a
part of the data we require in order to elucidate the meanings of the
texts. In some cases, as for example those instanced by Hershel, the
"author" is present to *the* text (or to *a* text) in relatively unambig-
uous and unmediated forms. But this situation does not always
obtain. Whatever the status of the author in the history of our texts,
however, certain specific documents, certain material forms, remain
with us. And it is these *things* and their material histories which we
study, extend, and reproduce.

In his paper John McClelland asks for a "pragmatics of meaning," a method for elucidating what he calls "the total sensory
experience" which underpins the study and production of texts at all
levels. In fact, I think that such a request can be fulfilled, and the
following offers a schematic outline of what I would propose.

A. The Originary Textual Moment

   1. Author
   2. Other persons or groups involved in the initial process of
       production (e.g., collaborators, persons who commissioned
       the work, editors or amanuenses, etc.)
   3. Phases or stages in the initial productive process (e.g., distinct
       personal, textual, or social states along with their defining
       causes, functions, and characteristics)
   4. Materials, means, and modes of the initial productive process
       (physical, psychological, ideological)

This schema may be summarized in a brief set of instructions to
the student of literary works. The elementary maneuvers for studying, understanding, and finally teaching such works involve, first, an
elucidation of the textual history of the work, and second, an
explication of the reception history. Neither of these operations can
be performed independently of the other because the two historical
processes are dialectically related. (This is why no textual criticism,
however specialized, can be produced without at least an implicit
reference to certain more broadly established social phenomena
which impinge on a work's various textual constitutions.) Nonetheless, in textual criticism the attention will focus, necessarily, on a

work's shifting verbal forms on the one hand and on its changing bibliographical states on the other.

These general remarks can introduce the methodological schema which I would propose as a model for a procedure in textual criticism. This program is an analytic outline of the subjects and topics which are essential to textual criticism, whether it is viewed as a program of study or as an operational (a practical) event. The specific subjects and topics placed under each of the general categorical headings call for an elucidation of their circumstantial character, i.e., a socio-historical analysis of each element in the heading. These specific analyses, in combination, constitute an analytic presentation of the category, and the character as well as the adequacy of any act of textual criticism will be a function of the range of textual material which is critically examined.

My view is that a critical presentation of all the material ranged under categories A (above) and B (below) constitutes a finished program of historicist textual criticism. Such a program gains what I should call a properly historical character when the material ranged under cateogry C (below) begins to be brought into the critical analysis. The material in this category must of course be a part of any exercise in textual analysis; it need not be made a part of the *critical* (i.e., self-conscious) analysis, however, and in fact most of the material in this category is not material that is critically studied by textual scholars.

B. Secondary Moments of Textual Production and Reproduction (Individual and Related Sequences)

1, 2, 3, 4 as above ranged under two subsets:
 a. Before the author's death
 b. After the author's death

This material should be ranged under two periodic subsets: a period of reproduction carried out during the author's lifetime; the periods of production and reproduction which begin after the author's death. The elements to be ranged under each of these subsets are the same as those set out under category A above.

In the critical study of this material certain shifts of emphasis take place. Most obviously, the author is studied as he or she is a critical and historical reconstruction. The first heading, "Author," then, will comprise a range of ideas or concepts about and of the author which have emerged in the minds of various people and the ideologies of different classes, institutions, and groups. Reciprocally, the critic will necessarily bring to the center of attention not the author himself, but those "Other persons or groups" signaled in A.2.

Similarly, the influence of the work's own production history on the work itself grows more important with the passage of time. Works descend to our hands in certain concrete and specific forms and along a series of equally concrete and specific avenues. The textual history of literary works reflects the influence of these factors even as the specific texts give a visible (if unanalyzed) form to the meaning and significance of that history. The critical analysis of texts discovers one of its chief intellectual justifications in that set of circumstances. Certain patterns of history are literalized in complete and finished forms in such texts; consequently, the critical analysis of such forms is an invaluable key to understanding those most elusive types of human phenomena, social and historical patterns.

Categories A and B are chiefly to be studied under the historian's milder (and preliminary) rubric "What does this mean?" rather than under the more severe polemical question "Is this right or is this wrong?"

C. The Immediate Moment of Textual Criticism

1, 2, 3, 4 as above, with "author" now replaced by "critic"

This category calls for a critical analysis of the immediate critic's own programmatic goals and purposes. This is probably the most demanding of all critical tasks, since it involves a critical presentation of events which do not lie in a completed form of pastness, but which are coincident with the entire act of analysis itself.

This moment appears as a specific act of criticism—as a particular bibliography, edition, set of glosses, or critical commentary of one form or another. The particular bibliographers, editors, or commentators may approach their subject matter critically (categories A and B) without approaching their own work in a critical spirit. The heuristic model for such a case would perhaps be an edition undertaken by a technically skilled scholar as a set task.

The governing model for a criticism which fulfills the obligations of this categorical imperative might well be either Thucydides and his *History of the Peloponnesian War* or Trotsky and his *History of the Russian Revolution*, depending upon whether one wanted an experimental or a polemical model. In textual studies I would instance the Kane and Donaldson edition of *Piers Plowman* as a model of an experimental critical edition and Bowers' edition of *The Dramatic Works of Thomas Dekker* as a model of a polemical sort; and I would set these beside F. A. Wolf's *Prolegomena ad Homerum* (1795) and Joseph Bédier's "La Tradition Manuscrite du *Lai de L'Ombre*" as similar models of textual criticism carried out in the form of commentary.

Works which exhibit a high degree of critical expertise in this aspect of their analysis will almost necessarily appear as controversial in their immediate scholarly context. Such works may display more or less serious deficiencies in their critical grasp of their subject matter (categories A and B). Whatever the case, they approach their own projects under the imperative query: "Is this right or is this wrong?"

What do we get from such a program? Interpreters and hermeneuts in the past fifty years or so have fought shy of any historical methodology of this kind, which is customarily seen as a mere excuse to escape into the past—at best an aesthetic indulgence in the remote, at worst the reification of a philosphic illusion. "Let the dead bury their dead," we are told.

Of course, my brothers and sisters, I think this view is quite mistaken. In *my* reading of my text, the function of what McClelland calls the "organized knowledge of real facts" is not primarily to *re*cover the past, but rather to *un*cover and correct our present quests for knowledge through literary texts. It is a program which means to elucidate and perhaps even improve how we are at present using our culture's literary works.

I began with a passage from sacred scripture. Let me conclude with a classical text which seems peculiarly relevant. Thucydides, after his narrative of the plague at Athens, begins his summary with the following anecdote.

> Such was the nature of the calamity which now fell on the Athenians; death raging within the city and devastation without. Among other things which they remembered in their distress was, very naturally, the following verse, which the old men said had been uttered long ago:

'A Dorian war shall come and with it death.'
A dispute arose whether dearth [*limos*] and not death [*loimos*] had not
been the word in the verse; but at the present juncture it was of course
decided in favour of the latter; for the people made their recollection fit
in with their sufferings. I fancy, however, that if another Dorian war
should ever afterwards come upon us, and a dearth should happen to
accompany it, the verse will probably be read accordingly.

The scholarship in this commentary does not lie in the recording of
a textual dispute, and it clearly has nothing at all to do with
adjudicating between the two received readings of the line, nor even
with explaining what each version means. Thucydides' mordant eye
is not directed toward the "original version" of the line but toward
the versions produced by later "editors" and interpreters; and his
interest lies in the meaning of scholarship and criticism rather than in
the meaning of a line of ancient verse. To that extent the passage
illustrates a textual criticism which has raised and answered
Collingwood's historicist question: "What does it mean?" But the
passage pushes beyond that question in order to ask the further and
more demanding one: "Is this right or is this wrong?" Nor does
Thucydides ask this question merely as a matter of technical
accuracy, as editors today might perhaps ask such a question of the
texts they will study. What is "wrong" here is not a *textual* but a
critical deficiency.

I think much the same kind of judgment might be passed on a
good deal of the work we produce, whether as textual scholars or as
literary interpreters. The weaknesses seem to me critical rather than
technical, and they can often be traced to a failure of theory—a
failure to begin the inquiry at fundamental levels. To whatever
degree this is true, to that degree does Thucydides' scholastic satire
remain an important model and resource. It may be that we shall
never know whether the original Greek word was *limos* or *loimos*,
and that we shall fail forever to cross the boundary of the Greek New
Testament or to pass beyond the Masoretic wall and the Alexandrian
limits; it may be that we shall never hear the uncorrupted word of
God or see Homer, or even Shelley, plain. In this fate , however, we
may grieve not but rather

find
Strength in what remains behind . . .
In the faith that looks through death,
In years that bring the philosophic mind.

Mixed Texts and Multiple Authority

FREDSON BOWERS*

So long as no fresh authority enters at any stage, texts may exist in single or in multiple editions without affecting editorial procedures in any significant manner.[1] When they are in a monogamous tree, these multiple editions will necessarily derive one from another although not always in chronological order, as when the third edition of Fielding's *Tom Jones* was set from the first and not from the second edition, or the Folio skipped the fourth and fifth Quartos of Shakespeare's *Richard II* and used the third as its copy. Textually all that happens in reprints is a diminution of authority as transmission succeeds transmission and errors accumulate at a faster pace than they are corrected. Such a series of derived editions may also be called pure *single-text* editions, which should mean only that despite normal transmissional corruption the text that started with the first edition continues until the last in its initially intended form as a work, although not necessarily in every original detail.

To be precise, at no stage has the author intervened to change the text in any way nor has some document with an ultimate link to a manuscript by this author been consulted or conflated to alter the original intention of the earliest edition. From its first appearance in the Folio of 1623 up to the latest modern edition, Shakespeare's *Measure for Measure* has had its verbal details refined, its initial accidentals of spelling, punctuation, and the like modernized; but its unitary or single authority remains unchallenged. No more documentary evidence as to its text is available in 1985 than was printed in 1623. Using the term critically, and loosely, we could say that the 1985 text is more authentic than the 1623 in that stages of editorial emendation have brought it nearer to what with good reason we believe to have been the author's intentions; but restricting the sense of authority, as I shall do, to pure documentary evidence, it must be said that all editorial movements toward restoring authorial intention in *Measure for Measure* have been unauthoritative because they lacked an authoritative documentary basis (which, outside of press-variation, would have to be a link to a collateral or to the original manuscript source) for any alteration of the 1623 text. In the strict documentary sense, then, the 1623 text is more authoritative than the edited 1985 although in any critical sense the 1985 is more correct.[2] In bibliographical work, which must prepare the ground for the critic, authority is based on physical facts and must not be confused with correctness or with error, with improvement or with retrogression.

A single-text edition within itself may have some internal conflicts of authority, although sufficiently minor as not to interfere with the concept of single-text. That is, in hand-printing some proofreading was done while the earliest sheets of a gathering were being printed. After the press was stopped and the marked alterations made in the type, the remaining copies of the sheet (of the forme to be precise) were run-off, producing various copies of that forme with some readings different from its earliest readings. Appealing again to the general concept of documentary authority, we must grant that both sets of readings have that authority in the strictest sense as being an integral part of the printed document, although the circumstances of production may divide this double authority into primary and secondary. The original readings were framed by the compositor setting in type what he thought his copy read, rightly or wrongly. These readings, then, have a direct link with the source-document and so must have primary documentary authority. Nevertheless, the proofreader may have marked the forme for alteration as a result of his comparing doubtful readings with the manuscript copy (not very frequent in early times and especially for popular literature) or at least of consulting this manuscript if he suspected compositorial error he could not unravel.[3] Editorial estimate of such direct consultation is seldom strictly demonstrable; yet critical analysis of the total evidence of changes in the forme may suggest the strong probability (certainty would always be questionable) of partial or complete authority in the proofreader's variants. If it could be strongly suspected, on the basis of special evidence, that the author himself had attended the press and acted as his own proofreader, then his corrections would have superior authority; but his real revisions, although necessary to accept, would not affect the authority (to the copy) of the original printed words.

Nevertheless, in dealing with the less seriously regarded seventeenth- and eighteenth-century books the proofreader may have marked alterations according to his own standards of correctness or improvement without bothering to scan the manuscript to see what had actually been inscribed. Any form of collation would of course be out of the question except for the most weighty and important books. In the usual proofreader's variants, therefore, the critical authority is suspect since a link of the altered reading with the manuscript cannot be established. However, whether the reader corrected error or introduced readings differing from the copy,[4] it is a documentary fact that certain readings appear in some copies and other readings in the rest, no matter how they are critically viewed in whole or in part. Indeed, we may find that this is only the first of other critical selections that an editor must make between conflicting documentary authority at two levels within the same single-text work, especially in its later printings or even editions. As for press-variants, it might take the collation of more copies than are in existence to reveal all of the uncorrected and corrected formes produced during the printing of a book[5] and usually scattered somewhat at random through various bound copies. Nevertheless, by extensive collation an editor may attempt to discover the majority of such proof-alterations in the types so that he can make a critical judgment as to the authorial intent (if any) between the variant readings. This process is the more necessary on the widest scale if critical analysis points to authorial proof-correction instead of professional: naturally, authorial alterations relieve some of the pressure on editorial choice since they have the latest documentary link with authority.[6] But even so, the documentary authority of the original readings set from copy by the compositor is not infringed in any bibliographical sense if a critical choice rejects some of them.[7]

At least in seventeenth–century play printing, proofreaders' alterations have secondary authority at best: they are part of a disjunct operation in the continuum of production by the compositors of the primary documentarily-established text. An agent has been introduced as an attempted corrector who need have no documentary link with the primary source used by the compositor. If one could prove no link with authority in a proofreader's alterations (even though accepting some as necessary corrections) one could, indeed, deny even secondary textual authority to them, just as one might deny alterations in a manuscript by a strange hand that seem to have been personally motivated without documentary recourse, and not print them in an edited text.[8] It is chiefly the uncertainty and lack of demonstrable evidence for or against a link (such as consultation) that leads to any question even of secondary authority in a casual, or an over-finicky, proofreader's variants.

Proofreading alterations in early books may readily be accepted without modifying the concept of single-text, since they occur during the initial production of that text and do not materially affect its character, certainly never to the extent of forming a different work. In early books the second edition may be set from a copy of the first containing a mixture of corrected and uncorrected formes, thereby affecting some details of its transmission; but since in either case the reprinting from one observed documentary state of the forme instead of another has no independent authority, no problem arises.[9]

In later times the concept of single-text is not greatly affected, either, by authorial or publisher's changes made within stereotype plates between the various printings in series within the same edition-typesetting. Although made at different times and in different printings, these changes in their purpose and method do not differ essentially from pre-printing proof alterations but in effect carry on the correction of overlooked points in the proofs by placing these within the period of post-publication. As an example, between the first printing in 1890 and the printing in 1910, the year of his death, 164 plate changes were made in William James's classic *Principles of Psychology,* not all by the author, and indeed 13 of the 164 changes created errors. James rushed in nine corrections for the second printing in 1890, but for the third printing in the same year he made 118 changes after observing how careless he had been in marking proofs. By 1905 enough other observations had accumulated for him to make 17 fresh plate changes. These alterations corrected errors, both typographical and factual, occasionally they improved the style, but in no sense could they be said, even accumulated, to alter the textual tradition. We may rate these, like Elizabethan press-changes, as documentary variants within the single-text edition. Multiple of course they are since they offer more than one documentary reading, and documentary they are since each was printed within the plates of the originally typeset document. But since they appear within printings of the same edition, they differ in their 'multiple authority' from revisions (and errors) in different editions within the single-text tradition.

To cite Tanselle's useful distinction,[10] there may be texts and there may be works. It may clear the air, thus, if for our present purposes we throw out of consideration the kind of discrete multiple authority that is present in such rewritten works as Wordsworth's *Prelude* or Sir Philip Sidney's *Arcadia*, so altered as to intention and to circumstances of rewriting and revision and passage of time, as well as production, as to bear little or no relation to the editorial problems of the different forms of a work in a single-text edition that has been revised. One major distinction, although perhaps not the only one, is the fact that a conflated eclectic text will ordinarily be impossible to construct from a true rewritten two-tradition work, whereas a single-text tradition present in a series of derived or monogamous editions retains the framework for a series of revisions: a copy-text can be chosen and identified revisions even though in different series can be introduced into its texture.[11]

In considering multiple authority, let us start, then, with the concept of a mixed single-text that has gone through a series of revisory improvements at the hands of an author, or of some agent referring to authority, during the course of its various editions; nevertheless, it remains recognizably the same work. A powerful influence on the retention of its essential identity is the derivation of the text of each new revision from a previous identifiable edition in some direct line of the stemma.[12] When an agent revises a text by consultation of some authority, we have in varying degrees— depending upon the thoroughness of the comparison—the begin- nings of the different problems of forming an eclectic text from two or more collateral multiple authorities. Fresh authority entered the text of the Folio *Merchant of Venice* when in a minor way the editors clarified and corrected certain speech-prefixes and altered a few stage-directions in the Quarto copy given to Jaggard. A larger number of promptbook text readings and directions were transferred by hand from the promptbook to modify the Third Quarto of *Richard II* used as the Folio setting copy.[13] As compared with authorially revised copy, it is an important difference that the critical authority of such changes becomes diluted by passing through the hands of an agent and that—as in *Hamlet*—the manuscript on which the agent based his changes might itself have been partly corrupt and unauthoritatively altered in certain readings (posing more of a critical problem as to their acceptance). On the other hand, within *Troilus and Cressida* the copy for the Quarto was at firsthand authoritative and the annotations that turned this typesetting of the text into that of the Folio also came from another firsthand authoritative manuscript, but each manuscript represented a different stage in the authorial development of the play's text. The editorial problems of such a mixed text, even though partly derived one from the other through the prints, differ notably from John Locke's revising and perfecting various editions of *An Essay Concerning Human Understanding* or Henry Fielding's entering his second thoughts in successive editions of *Joseph Andrews*.[14]

Under ordinary circumstances in these single-text editions revised by interpolated authority, Greg's rationale is likely to hold.[15] That is, separate authority is given to the accidentals and to the substantives. The edition is chosen as copy-text that by derivation is closest to the author's lost manuscript; it follows that no matter how altered by the compositor(s) of the print, the accidentals of this copy-text have the only direct relation as a whole to the lost authority. In revised editions derived from this chosen copy-text edition it is assumed that the author concentrated on interpolating additions, and making deletions and substitutions mainly in the substantives, and that he paid little or no attention to altering the accidentals.[16] Logically, Greg then recommended the insertion from a revised edition of the identifiable substantive authorial alterations by their transfer into the accidentals texture of the earliest edition, or copy-text.[17] By this means, he argued, one achieved an eclectic combination of the authorially altered substantives with the other best authority, the accidentals of the originally set edition. Greg was dealing exclusively with the Elizabethan drama where a revising author's concern to alter the printer's styling of his accidentals was minimal indeed. But his rationale remains perfectly sound for works of any period whenever an editor can show that the author was so relatively unconcerned with the general run of the accidentals in a print he was revising that on the whole those in a substantively revised derived edition set from this print should carry less authority than those of the original typesetting.[18]

Occasions may arise, of course, when the example of revised substantives but generally unrevised accidentals does not hold. An author marking copy for a revised edition may indeed be so concerned about his accidentals that an editor can come to feel that the two forms of revision are so associated that it is easier to accept as a whole the variants from a revised edition and to discard only those accidental variants created by the transmission[19] than it is to substitute for all accidental variants the readings of the first edition less those that he suspects to be authorially revised. Under certain conditions, then, a revised edition may make a better and more convenient copy-text than the original edition.[20]

To sum up, it would seem that so long as the basic transmission of the copy is linear, from one edition to another, no matter how marked up by interpolated substantive revisions short of a thorough major rewriting, the Gregian distinction of double authority—of accidentals versus substantives—will rule and the editorial treatment is thereby shaped by what is appropriate for texts governed by their derivation in line one from another. When for special reasons a later revised edition is selected as the copy-text, though its substantives and various of its accidentals have been marked up by annotation, its physical derivation still keeps it within a single-text authority. That means that a modern eclectic edition can be formed from a later edition, not essentially different except in inscrutable details from an editorial text manufactured from using the earliest edition as copy-text and treating it appropriately. The only difference is that one looks back for some emendations supposed to carry authority instead of forward.[21]

Multiple authority is simultaneously *shared* as a whole between two or more basic texts by their direct derivation from different sources. In contrast, in a single-text mixed authority is created when a second authority is *inserted* as an occasional substitute for previously existing authority. Again in contrast to the overall multiple authority caused by radiation or divided stemma, a revised single-text edition possesses no alternative authority in any of its parts not affected by the inserted or substituted revisions. The accidentals, especially, are more or less fixed in their documentary authority as of the first edition. With a first edition we recognize that there is a direct relationship to the lost manuscript source, even though we may have only speculative notions about the nature of its printer's copy, including its distance and means of transmission from the author's original. If, for special reasons, we adopt a later revised edition as the copy-text, we have a less pure documentary authority for the accidentals because their overall relationship to the author is no longer fixed as the best we have, whatever its defects.[22] Instead, the relationship is not fixed but created by conjecture whether or not the author did indeed mark a substantial number of the accidentals alterations in the copy for the printer. At best there are gray areas of indifferent variants (a few substantive but mainly accidental) where authorial origin cannot be determined by any positive evidence on a critical or bibliographical basis. These variants must remain a matter of opinion, often subject to general opinion which may be influenced by what has been called 'the tyranny of the copy-text' but here transferred to a later edition with a more tenuous relationship to the lost source. An editor here plays the odds, of course. In a first-edition copy-text he has no choice but to accept unitary authority (subject to necessary correction). On the other hand, in adopting a revised edition as copy-text in the general belief that the author has overseen accidentals alteration in sufficient quantity to justify the choice,[23] an editor can discard obvious printer's restyling; but he must close his mind to the possibility that the indifferent variant is only transmissional: he must accept it not by necessity (as in a first edition), but as an act of faith devolving from his deliberate choice of general authority in the later copy-text. Nothing could more clearly demarcate the Gregian distinction between the authority of accidentals and that of substantives, accentuated—one may say—by the lesser ability of critical powers to detect authority in accidentals than in substantive variation.

A second point in textual criticism springs from the first. The interpolation of fresh authority occurs in time since the initial authority has been established before the second or substitute originates between the intervals of publication (or between a manuscript and its print with intervening revised proof). Moreover, since the unitary nature of the single-text is usually preserved in the main, authoritative revision may occur only sporadically, or else in defined sections, in which case the possibility exists that some areas of initial authority may have been left relatively unaffected except for some minor alterations, if any. Editorial problems of authoritative alteration in the accidentals of those areas may be in part nullified, but not entirely eliminated, when for special reasons a revised edition is chosen as copy-text, or a first edition over a manuscript, since this choice implies a general acceptance of its entire accidentals texture, subject only to emendation. This emendation (except for editorially originated correction) must be confined in terms of authority only to a return to the readings of the original edition (or manuscript) as the true authentic corrupted by transmissional error in the revised copy-text. For example, if textually we treat the printer's-copy of

Hawthorne's manuscript of *The House of the Seven Gables* as the original and the typesetting made from it for the first edition as a partially revised edition because of Hawthorne's lost proofreading alterations, we may feel justified at 90.27 of the Centenary Edition in retaining the more idiomatic copy-text manuscript phrase 'barndoor fowl' and rejecting the book's 'barnyard fowl' as a printer's sophistication overlooked by Hawthorne in proof instead of an authentic authorial revision.

One may not leave this subject of the single-text with its unitary authority (even though revised by interpolation) without remarking on three points: (1) the authority of interpolated variant readings, (2) the effect on editorial practice of the preservation of pre-printing forms of the text, (3) situations in which the transmission may introduce an earlier instead of a later stage of authority in an edition following the first.

One of the most serious critical problems is to attempt to identify, disentangle, and finally evaluate the authority of interpolated revisions when they are not made directly by the author but by an agent utilizing a document that derives from the author, whether immediately or at a distance. It is believed that the editors of the Shakespeare First Folio used the theater's promptbooks to make sporadic alterations in many of the printed Quarto texts they were handing over to Jaggard to print. The problem of separating normal transmissional variance, which may be extensive at this period, is here added to the difficulty of evaluating the evidence for the nature of the manuscript from which conjecturally identifiable 'authoritative' substitute readings were drawn, of estimating the authorial nature of the variants as they may have been affected by the inscriber's carelessness in misreading his copy or his memorial error in transferring the readings, and especially taking account of any penchant for independent alteration of what he thought in error or in need of improvement or clarification. The conjectural nature of the manuscript may suggest that even though the annotator correctly transferred the reading, this reading may itself have been corrupted in the transmission from Shakespeare's original manuscript to whatever copy—perhaps at several removes and itself doctored up in unauthoritative ways—that the annotator used. Into the labyrinth of this process, as in *Hamlet*, we must not wander or we shall never emerge with the purpose of this paper intact.

When we come to the effect of pre-printing forms of the text, especially on an editor's choice of copy-text from examples of mixed authority, we must again forgo any attempt at adequate enumeration. A great deal depends upon the distance of the preserved document from the actual first printing. A draft or sketch of what was later to be printed in different form, like the manuscript of Stephen Crane's "A Detail," may be useful later in emending some printed accidentals but the difficulties of basing an edition of a full-fledged worked-out printed composition on a draft manuscript copy-text will usually prove the procedure to be impracticable. If the holograph manuscript or an authorial typescript were the printer's copy, the problem of copy-text vanishes and the variants of any kind in the first printed edition resulting from changes in the lost proofs may be treated as if they were interpolated revisions, and hence variant substantives may be separated from accidentals with more confidence. If the manuscript or typescript cannot be identified as the actual printer's copy but must be in a direct line of ascent to the print (not in some collateral line), then ordinarily it may make a better copy-text than the mixed print, provided the editor is prepared for purposes of emendation to evaluate the differences in the print as typist's straying from copy, as unknown authorial revision of the lost printer's copy, unobserved stages of proof-correction, or else simple transmissional error. Usually the greater problem will occur with the substantives than with the accidentals, and thus the question of copy-text may be less complicated, although it is difficult to generalize the wide variety of these situations.

Nevertheless, an authorial manuscript may by no means be consistent in an accidentals sytem (or even invariably correct), and an editor will need to make occasional adjustments if he is producing a critical edition and not a diplomatic reprint. Without any discernible system William James might or might not put a comma before a dash, and whether he liked a dash after a colon introducing an inset quotation is problematic in view of his erratic usage in the same manuscript. Even if a professional typescript has been worked over by the author to form the printer's copy, it cannot be said to match a holograph manuscript or authorial typescript in the authority of its accidentals; yet the authority would be superior in all respects to variance in the derived print after allowance is made for authorial proofreading in the interval. If such a typescript were not the printer's copy but of the same typing, assumedly, like the carbon of a lost ribbon copy, much the same holds, although any revision of substantives (and perhaps of some accidentals) both in the lost ribbon typescript and in the proof set from it cannot be distinguished. However, there is no special editorial problem in such truncation: an editor must treat the two stages as one, which they are in the evidence. Unmarked proofsheets collated against the print will show the extent of at least one stage of proof-correction but otherwise have no superior authority to the print unless another lost set had been corrrected by the author. One must always guard, of course, against proof-reader's tinkering in still another set, or else mixed in the author's marked proofs, which if detected in the print can affirm the earlier authority of the proof. Worked-over proofsheets, on the other hand, will confirm the authenticity of the same altered readings in the print if the markings are authorial; but proofreader's markings that do not imply reference to lost copy and are unnecessary 'improvements' can be eliminated from the authority of the print when they are not useful corrections.[24]

Usually when a copy of the proof figures in the transmission, the question will arise whether it is corrected, uncorrected, or even a revise. When in derived editions proof is used as copy for the later, instead of printed sheets, some odd situations may develop. For instance, Hawthorne's *Marble Faun* was typeset in England, where Hawthorne was living at the time. Owing to the copyright laws by which editions had to be published simultaneously in England and the United States or American copyright was lost, the American edition was set up in batches as English proof was received by steamer. At first the copy was either the finished run-off sheets or else the final proofs, but as time grew shorter and whenever Hawthorne had delayed returning his corrected proofs to the English publisher, from time to time a batch of uncorrected proof would be sent and would become the setting copy for the American edition. By comparing the English edition, printed of course from corrected proof, with those American sheets printed from the uncorrected, and checking with the preserved manuscript, an editor can gain valuable information about Hawthorne's proofreading, and that of the English publisher or printer, and even can correct one mistake that Hawthorne made in his marking of a compositor's error when he misunderstood the sense because of the misprint and either did not have the manuscript to refer to or did not trouble to leaf through it to find the reading.

The second example is rather amusing. Before modern technology took over, proofs were the favorite way of transmitting copy across the Atlantic for simultaneous publication in both countries, although if prior negotiations had not been started, a ribbon typescript and its carbon might provide the duplicate copy required by the author's agents. In the case I have reference to, Stephen Crane's sketch "The Scotch Express" was set up in England for *Cassell's* magazine, a first proof being pulled and mailed to *McClure's* in the United States. Subsequently the Cassell's editor worked over the proofs, made some cuts, anglicized some of the diction, and when it came to a paste-up of his pages before the press took over he found that a large illustration he had ordered took up so much space on the last page that no room was left for Crane's conclusion, which was accordingly deleted. In these respects the earlier and purer, as well as the only complete, text of the sketch may be found in *McClure's*, despite the fact that it is a derived second edition.[25]

If we discard from our consideration works that exist in two such completely different versions that no eclectic single text can be formed by conflation—works like Pope's *Dunciad* or Henry James's *Roderick Hudson*—our other source of multiple authority is that created by what we may call *radiation*, which is sometimes accompanied by derivation, with or without authorial interpolation. Between revised *single-text* multiple authority (perhaps better named texts of *mixed authority*) and *radiating* multiple authority the difference is as night and day. Multiple, or mixed, authority in a single-text comes only through revision, or interpolation, since the series is monogamous. The authority is mixed not only because the original edition was presumably set from an authoritative document[26] and inherits that authority, but also because fresh authority has entered as a series of interpolated substitutes in a later edition. Without such alteration of the text, there might be multiple editions but not multiple authority. In some respects, it must be recalled, the revised edition may not be entirely authoritative, especially in the accidentals, so that a critical editor is almost necessarily bound to make use of the original authority as well as that of the revised. The term 'multiple' derives from the selective mixture of documentary authority in more than one edition or manuscript that is required when an editor creates an eclectic text that endeavors to reproduce the author's *full* as well as his *latest* intentions in some situations, insofar as the preserved evidence permits. (I use *latest* intentions as an agreeable substitute for the conventional 'final intentions,' which carries overtones a critic does not always intend.)

In contrast, radiation ordinarily produces two or more competing and often equal authorities of the same text without *revision* necessarily entering into the question of the multiplicity of authority. It may happen that derivation and interpolated revision do indeed enter into one leg of the radiating, or polygamous, stemma, so that this leg in part reproduces the conditions of multiple single-text authority with original and revised texts. However, this variation is no part of the fundamental principle of multiple authority created by the radiation of two or more texts from an identical document or its equivalent. An extraordinary number of different forms may be found in the radiational transmission of texts, but in the end they boil down to only two major varieties. In the first, two different typesettings are made from only one document, or its equivalent, whether or not one form of the document may have been altered before printing. In the second, the typesettings of the two lines of the radiation are made, instead, from two different documents, one derived from the other as in a copy made of the original typescript. In this variety authority is at one further remove than in the first. Unique alterations may occur, of course, in either leg or in both legs of the stemma. Especially in simple radiation, the problems of determining the authority of the accidentals may be more acute in their variance than that of the substantives despite the difficulties that, as usual, indifferent verbal variants may create.

In single-text situations the editor, at best, can attempt only to reconstruct the markings in the copy of the edition from which a revision was set; if there is no revision, there is nothing he can do to alter the documentary evidence of the first edition except by conjectural emendation. Without revision he has only single authority. On the other hand, with multiple authority stemming from radiation he has at least two sets of independent documentary evidence from which an attempt may be made to reconstruct the original lost source document. A case of simple radiation comes to hand in Stephen Crane's Civil War story "A Grey Sleeve," which was syndicated in a number of newspapers, all deriving from an identical lost document, the Bacheller proofsheets pulled from a typesetting made from Crane's lost manuscript. Given a sufficient number of texts, the original proof can be reconstructed with fair accuracy both in respect to accidentals and to substantives. In this reconstruction we are still at one remove from the manuscript itself, just as we are in a first edition set directly from manuscript; but any single piece of documentary evidence that we have, such as an individual newspaper text, is at two removes.[27] In a situation like this the *post hoc* reconstructed proof is in a manner of speaking itself the copy-text; and indeed G. T. Tanselle[28] has suggested that the apparatus of such variants may reflect this fact by being keyed to no one arbitrarily selected example as copy-text: in documentary terms no single example is superior in authority to another since all are at an equal remove from their source. Nevertheless, if he chooses, an editor—simply for convenience—can select some single example that conforms most closely in its accidentals to his reconstruction of the proof and arbitrarily make it his copy-text, simply as a peg on which to hang a conventional form of apparatus instead of the fluid apparatus that Tanselle has suggested.[29] Either method works so long as the reader is made aware of the peculiar situation and the means evolved to handle it.

But another form of copy exists that may serve as the basis for simple radiating texts with two identical documents as their source. Before the days of photoduplication a typescript and its carbon were the common means of providing printer's copy for two different publications when proofs of one were not practicable. Because each example of the typescript could be owned by a different agency, all sorts of opportunities existed for unauthoritative pre-printing interference with the copy either by marking the typescript or in proof, and it is always possible for the author's own intervention to be present in one of the printed results, especially in his own country. However, one of various demonstrably pure cases may be cited where external circumstances prevented any authorial intervention. Stephen Crane wrote the short story "The Price of the Harness" (1898) while he was in Cuba. He mailed the manuscript to his agent in New York, who had a professional typescript and carbon made. One copy the agent sold to the *Cosmopolitan* magazine; the other copy was sent to England where an agent sold it to *Blackwood's*. In wartime Crane was in no position to read proof on either; hence we have a pure case of radiation from an unworked-over common original (the typescript and carbon copies) printed independently in two places with no authorial intervention.[30]

Sometimes when there is apparent radiation but with serious variation in one leg of the stemma, an editor may be fortunate if the basic document is preserved from which the radiation started, for a great deal of conjectural reconstruction in such situations can go wrong. One of the most unusual examples I know is represented by Crane's novel *Active Service* (1899). The manuscript is lost but a messy ribbon typescript, full of misspellings, made by his common-law wife Cora is preserved, this typescript being the printer's copy for the edition published by Heinemann in England. An edition was published in the United States that must have had as its ultimate source this same typescript before Heinemann received it, no carbon apparently having been made. But Cora's typescript was so badly typed that whereas Heinemann was prepared to struggle with it, the American publisher Stokes did not wish to entrust it to his printer and hence before returning it he had a fresh typescript copy made from which setting of the American edition was started. Whatever authority might have been supposed to inhere in other circumstances in the accidentals of the radiating American edition is effectively dispelled by the interposition of this unauthoritative copy but chiefly of course by the preservation of Cora's original. Moreover, in this case the various important substantive differences between the English and American editions are to be accounted for, almost demonstrably, by the thorough editing with some rewriting that Stokes gave the American copy before it was typeset. (No evidence is preserved that Crane read American proof, an unlikely event anyway.)

All this might have been conjecturally established without the preservation of Cora's typescript, although certainly with some difficulty. Yet one anomaly would have remained quite inexplicable. In actual fact it is odd enough. Most curiously, Chapter V of Cora's ribbon typescript used as setting copy by Heinemann is replaced by a professional typescript made with a different ribbon and on paper manufactured in the United States. Cora's Chapter VI is preserved but added to it is a Chapter VI of the same American manufacture as Chapter V, placed and numbered by Heinemann ahead of Cora's Chapter VI. The Heinemann edition set Chapter V from the only copy there was, but when the printer came to Chapter VI by bad luck he continued, as paged, with the American Chapter VI before (skipping the duplicate) he returned to Cora's typescript with Chapter VII. In mirror image, the American Stokes edition prints its Chapter V from what must have been Cora's typescript, thus furnishing what is the only evidence we have for what this contained, and also Cora's Chapter VI, which can be checked from Cora's preserved chapter in the Heinemann typescript. With Chapter VII the Stokes edition continues with the American typescript as copy. This happy switch, explicable only by an error when, after retyping and the start of the American typesetting, the copy was returned from the United States to Heinemann for the English edition, provides us with the physical evidence for the unauthoritative retyped copy as the immediate source for the American edition. Certainly, without the preservation of the American typescript for these two chapters (apparently made without a carbon), the marked switch in the nature of the copy between the chapters in the two editions would have remained subject only to puzzled conjecture.

Simple radiation, in the literal sense, can occur only when two prints are made from the same document, which may be a typescript and its carbon (or photocopy), or identical proofsheets as in syndication, or in what must be very rare cases the actual manuscript. To remain simple, each print should have been subjected to no more than normal editing or compositorial styling. Although the technicalities of the situation are not altered, if one or other line of the stemma radiating from X exhibits fresh authority marked in the setting copy or the proofs what may be called complex or mixed radiation will result. The document in that variant radiation line is also in itself a single-text, as has been suggested above, even though the editorial situation has become more complicated. It will be understood that in ordinary course of radiating authority some document by necessity intervenes between the author's holograph manuscript and the printed results.[31] A curious exception is Stephen Crane's sketch "The Snake," for which the holograph is preserved marked for the printer. This must be the copy from which the Bacheller syndicate in June of 1896 ordered typesetting and proofs for newspaper syndication. However, in August of the same year Bacheller republished the sketch in his *Pocket Magazine*, oddly using the same manuscript instead of a set of the syndicate proofs. Thus the magazine is at only one remove from the manuscript whereas any individual newspaper print is at two removes; nevertheless, the common proof behind the syndication can be partially reconstructed and this text, like the magazine, would be at only one remove. In this case there was no authorial intervention in either leg of the radiation.

The more usual case of radiation is from a document that is itself at one remove from the author's manuscript, like a professional typescript and its carbon. But oddities can occur that mingle radiation with unauthoritative single-text derivation. A curious mixed case comes in Crane's novel *The O'Ruddy* (1903). A ribbon copy and three carbons were made by Cora from Crane's manuscript. One of these Crane's agent Pinker sold to the English magazine *The Idler*, which started to set it into type and to publish serial installments. Another copy of the typescript was used by the Edinburgh printer employed by Methuen to set the book. After several *Idler* installments the book typesetting caught up with the magazine serialization, and thereafter for convenience the *Idler* printer switched his setting copy to book proofs. The early part of the book's text radiates from the same basic copy as that of the magazine, but after the switch the *Idler* version becomes a mere reprint of the book proofs, with some cuts and censorship alterations made by its editor. At this point, of course, the derived magazine text loses all general authority and its variants must be viewed with caution. Even though in this problem the preservation of most (but not all) of the manuscript provides the natural copy-text, yet the radiating sections offer in theory the opportunity to analyze book variants from magazine and manuscript as possible authorial alterations in proof. And even thereafter, the *Idler* was not necessarily set up entirely from fully corrected proofs.

What may be regarded as a normal case of radiation from a lost professional typescript with authorial intervention in one leg may be found in Crane's novel *The Third Violet* (1897). This novel was syndicated before publication in six identified newspapers. With a few exceptions, from these six a pretty exact reconstruction can be made of the underlying proof set from one copy of the typescript. The book appears to have been set from the typescript's other copy, but Crane made a number of revisions that are of considerable importance. So far as the newspaper's proof-copy may be recovered, its accidentals are at the same distance as the book from the ultimate lost authority, the manuscript by way of the intervening typescript. In some respects the syndicate proof appears to have been less heavily styled than the book version. As a result, even though the book proved to be the most convenient documentary copy-text, the radiating syndicate proof was drawn on freely when its accidentals seemed more characteristic of Crane's habits than the smoothed-over book's. The editorial lesson is clear. If the newspaper syndicated texts had not existed, only one authority as to the nature of the underlying typescript would have been extant and in the book we should have had the standard single-text situation. But the existence of radiating second authority not only improved the editorial ability to evaluate the documentary evidence for the relation of the accidentals to the lost typescript but also provided the opportunity for critically evaluating the work in its original and then in its revised form. The partial reconstruction of many features of the typescript from a second source of documentary authority confirmed in some part the accidentals of the book but in others offered superior evidence to modify the book's documentary evidence and thus enabled an editor to penetrate one step in back of any single authority in the direction of the author's manuscript. In this case, as in most, the derived typescript was as far back as one could penetrate, and an editor is fortunate to be able to go that far in a search for authority behind a printed text.

In some special circumstances, however, from the evidence of the prints an editor can continue the backward voyage of discovery and partially reconstruct the author's lost manuscript behind a lost typescript. I have given this illustration before but cannot resist the temptation to repeat it, for it is unusual. Crane's short story "Death and the Child" was initially published in March, 1898, in England in the magazine *Black and White* and a fortnight later in the United States in *Harper's Weekly*. The copy was manifestly a typescript and its carbon. Later in the year the story appeared in the collection *The Open Boat* set and published by Heinemann in England and also by Doubleday, McClure in the United States, the copy for each being a second typescript and its carbon independently made up from the original manuscript with no reference to the printed magazine texts or their discarded typescripts. The full details of the production of an eclectic text are too complex to be narrated here, but the principle is obvious. From the two magazine texts one can recover the principal features of the typescript from which they radiate. Correspondingly, from the two radiating book versions the principal features of the second typescript can be reconstructed. A certain amount of cross-comparison of authority between magazines and books in cases of unequal variance can be attempted. That is, the odds favor the reading if the two magazines agree with one book against the other book, or the two books with one magazine. There is something to be said for the authority (except in conventional styling) even if only one magazine agrees with one book, English versus American.

However, an editor must make his choice on less mechanical evidence if the second magazine and the second book agree with each other against the common reading of their national opposites. And of course there are some instances when the two books agree against the two magazines. Nevertheless, an editor can find a not-to-be-despised authority whenever the reconstructed magazine typescript agrees with the reconstructed book typescript. The odds are certainly very strong that in such a case both typists had faithfully copied the readings of the manuscript. Indeed, by matching and evaluating the multiple dual evidence, an editor can make enough progress so that he can choose as the copy-text for an edition of this story what is in effect the majority of the readings of the reconstructed manuscript. This, I submit, is an authentic case of editorial legerdemain and of plucking a copy-text out of thin air or from behind an onlooker's ear.[32]

NOTES

* When in 1972 I wrote about problems of multiple authority, I did not define my terms so precisely as I should have done, nor did I distinguish clearly enough between single-texts with interpolated revision, rewritten single-texts, and radiating authority with or without revision. (See "Multiple Authority: New Problems and Concepts of Copy-Text," *The Library*, 5th ser., 27 [1972], 81–115, followed by "Remarks on Eclectic Texts," *PROOF*, 4 [1974], 15–58, both reprinted in my *Essays on Bibliography, Text, and Editing* [University Press of Virginia, 1975], pp. 447–487 and 488–528 respectively.) The present paper is a small step in that direction with, I hope, a few additional conclusions even though various of my examples will be familiar. I may say at the outset that I am considering only printed books and that I doubt my distinctions will be helpful for medieval-manuscript study. My ultimate concern is with the problems of copy-text and editorial method posed by the variable authority of different texts of the same work that have been preserved, even though I do not discuss this matter formally at any length. I may add that the methodology for the conjectural reconstruction of the transmission of lost documents in the pre-printing history of a text is almost neglected here except for a few concrete examples drawn from my experience. Pre-printing transmission is of singular importance for the evaluation of multiple authority. Nevertheless, limitations of space prevent me from venturing far into these quicksands, especially as variously analyzed in Shakespearian textual criticism. However, I do mention several illustrations of instances in which no single documentary authority offers a reliable copy-text but instead an editor may be advised to contrive a copy-text by the reconstruction of a lost document from the evidence of preserved multiple-authority documents.

1. Usually a series of editions, even though derived, is more useful to an editor than a single one despite the labor caused by the necessary collation and recording of variants. Unauthoritative as these may be, they serve as a useful source for recording the earliest corrections: it may be of some small comfort to an editor that an early reprint recognized an error and corrected it in a manner that could escape McKerrow's warning against the influence of preconceived notions based on modern sensibility and possibly incomplete knowledge of early idiom and the sense of an allusion. McKerrow suggests that "the emendation of a contemporary has at least a claim to consideration, for it will almost certainly be something that made sense at the time and *might* be the correct reading," and he is amusing about the dilemma of an editor a hundred years hence struggling with what he would regard as a necessary attempt to emend the statement "Yes, we have no bananas" (*Prolegomena for the Oxford Shakespeare* [Oxford: At the Clarendon Press, 1939], pp. 6, 38n). More in general, the substantive variants in later editions can form an object lesson in how texts of the time may change in unauthoritative ways during transmission. Philologically there may be some interest in the successive modernization of the accidentals as well as substantives of a series of editions.

2. It is hard to resist the lure of adding to documentary authority whatever authority may be generated by common acceptance of a critical emendation that manifestly seems to restore authorial intention. McKerrow writes, "I shall use then 'authoritative reading' for any reading which may be presumed to derive by direct descent from the manuscript of the author" (p. 12); and, later, "However much a modern editor may wish for some infallible objective test of what is correct in the texts which have come down to us, there is and can be no such thing. . . . If then we decide that a certain word or passage in our copy-text is corrupt and cannot represent what the author wrote, what follows? As I have already suggested, an editor who aims at reproducing his author's text not as it was actually printed, but as nearly as possible to what *would* have been printed if the printer had followed his copy correctly, must evidently try to emend it by substituting for the faulty passage what he supposes the author to have written. In deciding what to substitute he will naturally make use of any evidence that he can find as to the author's intentions" (p. 35).

3. For example, in *The Two Noble Kinsmen* (1634), I.iv.18 we cannot be positive that the proofreader's 'smeerd' for compositorial 'succord' blood is not his guess what the nonsense phrase should read or else his consultation of the manuscript. At least, no modern substitute of superior value has been proposed, and the proofreader's variant has the merit of paleographical possibility and of at least partial documentary authority.

4. It is quite probable that early proofreaders did not consult the manuscript for every change that they ordered, whether in substantives or especially in accidentals. The early reader's job was, first, to weed out obvious misprints and typos, and, secondly, to make the text read smoothly and in an apparently orderly manner. Especially with punctuation and other accidentals variants he

was accustomed to relying on his own judgment, and it is true that often the usual sketchily-punctuated manuscript would furnish him no authority for a necessary or at least for a desirable change. Most editors of Elizabethan plays are conservative in the question of accepting the proofreader's variants instead of the original save in the correction of obvious error or in the necessary repair of inadequacies. If the proofreader misunderstood the import of the text, serious error could be introduced, as when the really extraordinary reader who corrected the formes of Thomas Dekker's *Match Me in London* (1631) changed the original (and correct) Queen's 'Father' in III.ii.51 to 'Father in law', a non-existent person in the play.

5. Since proof-correction was often made in a forme at an early stage of its printing, if only a few sheets were run-off of the original, collation of preserved copies might not turn up the uncorrected state and the forme would appear to be invariant. Also, in some printing procedures the invariant mate to a variant corrected forme may exist only in a corrected state since proofreading and type-correction had been completed before the forme was placed on the press. It follows that without knowing it an editor may be reproducing the proof-reader's and not the compositor's version of some detail of the text. Critically, of course, one would always like to be in a position to assess the primary as well as the secondary forms of such documentary authority.

6. It may be argued that in his *Match Me in London* Dekker himself made the initial alterations in half-sheet A since it contained an important dedication to his patron which he wanted to be perfect in its details. If so, he would also have been responsible for a stage of correction in half-sheet L, which was printed with half-sheet A, inner A and outer L in one forme as usual. For the rest of the play it seems critically certain that he took no part in the proofing. Some of the corrections made in successive printings of F. Scott Fitzgerald's novels (corresponding in modern times to press-variation in Elizabethan) were a mixture on the same page of authorial and publisher's alterations.

7. I am not sure that 'documentary authority' can be successfully and completely defined, and indeed it is a difficult term. The 'documentary' part is easy enough since it refers only to the forms taken by the impressed types or by scribal inscription in some document, thus preserving physical evidence that is demonstrable as to the fact of its existence. The problem comes when 'authority' is suffixed, for 'authority' is a slippery word. If we may refer to a document as a whole, 'authority' certainly implies its close relationship to the author, the closer the better. Thus a simple reprint edition has its own documentary authority in respect to the readings it contains, which are physical facts. But as a simple reprint, at a further remove from the author, in a critical sense it has lesser documentary authority than its source; and indeed this lesser documentary authority may be said to dwindle to no textual authority at all when that alone is in question. Or else a revised holograph manuscript intended for the press is, as a document, more authoritative than an earlier draft, just as an authorially revised carbon copy is more authoritative than its unrevised

ribbon original. Textually viewed as to authority, such a setting copy is usually more authentic than the print made from it, which is at one remove since it has gone through the hands of one or more compositors, to say nothing sometimes of intervening publisher's copyreaders and proofreaders. Yet this print cannot be regarded as wholly derived from the manuscript and therefore without textual authority whenever the author in proof may have altered readings at his pleasure, both substantive and accidental, so that in some not always well-defined or identifiable respects the print may exhibit certain of his later intentions not found in the manuscript—although in other respects it may exhibit none of these intentions when the transmissional process alone has altered the manuscript readings. If an editor can establish that the author never saw proof and so could not have made any changes, then of course the first edition has no authority against the setting copy, just as a second printed edition published without the intervention of the author, like the Shakespeare Second Folio, has no critical authority. Yet it would be absurd to suggest that the fourth edition of *Tom Jones* is not, *as a whole,* an authoritative document (at least verbally) for it contains a text that was revised by Fielding with some thoroughness. Nevertheless, I think one could argue that unless the fourth edition were set from a fresh authorial manuscript (which it was not, being in some considerable part a derived edition reprinted from the third), its authority should be called 'mixed.' Whereas the authority of the first edition of *Tom Jones* (the manuscript not preserved) is complete and unitary, the revised fourth possesses authority only in respect to the identifiable alterations that Fielding made in the copy of the third edition given him by his publisher. Derivation with or without revision, therefore, affects authority, and that authority is purest and most certain as a whole which has the most direct link in its origin with the author. Other documents that are taken to possess authorially revised or corrected readings either directly or by an agent's conflation from some other document itself possessing authority from a separate authorial link, like the Folio text of *Richard II* and—more complicatedly—*Hamlet*, must be taken to be authoritative as a mixed document although certainly not more authoritative in respect to every variant reading. This brings us to the uncomfortable fact that the authority as a whole of a revised derived document would vanish if we could be certain that we had isolated and removed from it the precise and complete set of alterations that the author (or a trustworthy collator) had inserted. The choice between substantives is difficult enough; but when the accidentals are also theoretically involved, the authority of a derived document becomes even more watered down except for the critical choice of verbal readings, which is admittedly imperfect. Documentary authority as a whole, then, must be distinguished in the original from the kind of documentary authority in a textual sense found in a derived mixed edition where the application is only to certain readings, with others left in a limbo of uncertainty. In a different situation, however, any two radiating texts deriving at the same remove from the same lost source are of equal documentary authority, although if one leg of the radiation has undergone revision but not the other, or if both have been unequally or independently revised, critical choice alone can decide the exact final authorial readings just as it must in revised single-text derived editions. This complicated subject can only be touched on in a footnote, of course.

8. Such cases could range from censoring by the Jacobean or Caroline Master of the Revels, or the bookkeeper's annotations in a promptbook, to a modern copyreader's markings.

9. In theory it is quite possible for a forme of a second edition exhibiting variant text to have been set from an unknown state of the corresponding forme of the first (almost certainly uncorrected) that had not been identified in the collation of copies. If the evidence were sufficient, an alert editor might try to evaluate and use in his text what he regarded as the preferred readings of the hypothesized variants not known in the first edition. Although this reasoning is bibliographical, the facts on which bibliography should operate could not be present except in conjectural form, and whatever documentary evidence might be ascribed to the variant readings of the second edition could not compare textually with the documentary authority of the first. Still, the situation is always a theoretical possibility and in the editing of early books must be kept in mind. A somewhat different case I overlooked to my cost. In *Tom Jones*, Book VIII, part of the Man-of-the-Hill's narrative is invariant in the reprint second edition without authority, but it differs remarkably in the otherwise unauthoritative third edition, also set from the first, principally in the added vehemence of the Man's political opinions. It was an anomaly that no other part of the third edition showed any signs of revision and also that the revised fourth, set from the third, returned the text to the version in the first. However, it seemed possible to build a hypothesis—this being an important expression of Fielding's beliefs—that in the third edition his anger had overcome his discretion and he had exploded but without troubling, or perhaps having the time, to alter anything else. The agreement of the fourth edition with the original version of the first would then need to be conjectured as the return of discretion (perhaps after criticism of friends) following what had been an extremely intemperate outburst. This was a pretty explanation, but it was wrong. Dr. Hugh Amory's expertise observed the vital bibliographical evidence that to my shame I had overlooked ("*Tom Jones* Plus and Minus: Towards a Practical Text," *Harvard Library Bulletin*, 25 [January 1977], 101-113). It is perfectly clear from the watermarks and the unique setting of the running-titles that sheet O, containing all of the variant text, was a cancellans in the first edition. The toned-down version thus represented Fielding's later intentions, not his original ones. By mischance the third edition had been set from a copy with a state of sheet O in its uncancelled original, not now known to exist and probably preserved from the in-house copy of the first used to set the third. Otherwise we should never have been aware of Fielding's original concept, now preserved only in the third edition, and his wiser second thoughts.

10. "The Editorial Problem of Final Authorial Intention," reprinted from *Studies in Bibliography*, 29 (1976) in Tanselle's *Selected Studies in Bibliography* (University Press of Virginia, 1979), especially p. 321.

11. It is probably true that the insertion of major new authority that would in part either substitute for or expand (or contract) the form of the text in previous editions would ordinarily require a fresh typesetting and thus a new revised edition even if it could be said sufficiently to continue the single-text tradition of the work as demonstrated by the ability of an editor to make an eclectic text from the two or more authorities. Such a materially revised new edition would continue to be in part derived, and therefore, mixed, if a previous edition had been marked up as printer's copy. But if the new edition had been set from an independent source, then its text would have been formed by radiation. Of course an eclectic text can still be made, usually, from two radiating documents as well as from two mixed, but the editorial problems will differ. In Elizabethan times the so-called 'Bad Quartos' when superseded by a text set from a more authoritative source certainly create two textual traditions. Whatever use is made of these corrupt texts in editing the authoritative text would certainly resemble the selection process in working from two radiating editions, as recently illustrated by Gary Taylor's edition of *Henry V* (1982) in the Oxford Shakespeare series. Radiating as they are, Bad Quartos (although without documentary link) derive ultimately from the same source as the good edition, that is, the author's manuscript, even though the derivation is indirect, the Bad Quarto having been filtered through one or more actors' memories. The good edition, thus, is not a revised edition (usually) of this common source but the two prints are collateral although of unequal authenticity. The editorial situation somewhat changes when a Bad Quarto was annotated to serve as printer's copy for a good edition, as in *Richard III*, since then in the Folio one has a mixed text owing to the documentary link of the two. The latest fashion argues for *King Lear*'s Quarto not as a 'Bad Quarto' but as a legitimate edition in its own right with a direct link to an early draft manuscript. This change in view, if it holds, will have some effect on any future eclectic reading text based on the Folio, although at present its proponents have contented themselves with advocating separate editions of the two authorities. The fact would remain, nevertheless, that since it is generally accepted that the Folio was set from an annotated Quarto (whether Q1 or Q2 is in some dispute), it is technically a mixed edition although perhaps with an unusual source that was annotated for the print.

12. Retrogression as well as progress can exist. For example, by an oversight, in 1945 the fifth edition of Willa Cather's *Death Comes For the Archbishop* was set from a copy of the first (1927) instead of from the revised edition of 1938 (the 'Autograph Edition') and all subsequent reprintings have therefore perpetuated an inferior text. (See Joan St. C. Crane, *Willa Cather: A Bibliography* [University of Nebraska Press, 1982], pp. 143–144.)

13. For the latest examination of the authority of the *Richard II* Folio readings, see John Jowett and Gary Taylor, "Sprinklings of Authority: The Folio Text of *Richard II*," *Studies in Bibliography*, 38 (1985), 151–200.

14. Any literal comparison of Locke or Fielding with Shakespeare would be misleading because it would imply that behind whatever manuscript was the source for the promptbook from which the Folio variants derived, Shakespeare in it had revised the readings of the different manuscript used for the Quarto. In such a case of certain Folio readings accepted as of superior authority, some would be taken as corrections of Quarto errors but also some as revisions of perfectly correct Quarto readings. Not all critics are prepared to accept Shakespeare as a purely literary reviser of a manuscript that he believed to be finished and ready for the theatrical attention of the company (*vide* Harold Jenkins in the New Arden *Hamlet*). But the Quarto copies of *Richard II* or of *Hamlet* may not have been set from such a finally approved manuscript. After he had completed his working-papers, how much attention Shakespeare gave to altering the literary verbals of a play in its documentary progress to promptbook form is one of the most difficult and still relatively unsolved questions of Shakespearian textual criticism. In my own private view, Shakespeare as a verbal reviewer of his working-papers (the so-called 'foul-papers') is inevitable if for that play he himself made the fair copy that would lead to the promptbook. However, if for any given play he merely turned over his foul-papers to a scribe (or the bookkeeper), it may seem likely that he would feel shut of them unless certain theatrical alterations were suggested by the company such as we may see in the doubling of parts in *Julius Caesar* and in *1 Henry IV* made at a stage later than the working-papers. But this is a different matter from tinkering with individual words like *enurn'd* or *interr'd*, or *What's Hecuba to him, or he to* Hecuba, and *What's* Hecuba *to him, or he to her.*

15. "The Rationale of Copy-Text," *Studies in Bibliography*, 3 (1950-51), 19-36; reprinted in *The Collected Papers of Sir Walter Greg*, ed. J. C. Maxwell (Oxford: At the Clarendon Press, 1966), pp. 374-391. For an analysis and some modifications, see Bowers, "Greg's 'Rationale of Copy-Text' Revisited," *Studies in Bibliography*, 31 (1978), 90-161.

16. Even if the author made a few accidentals changes, they would be unrecogniz-able in the midst of the other accidentals variants created by the compositor of the new edition, alterations which were themselves an overlay of the individual compositors' changes of the manuscript in the first edition. For a practical example, see Bowers, "Current Theories of Copy-Text, with an Illustration from Dryden," *Modern Philology*, 48 (1950), 12-20; reprinted in *Essays in Bibliography, Text, and Editing* (1975), pp. 277-288.

17. One may not remark too often the ingrained misuse among some scholars of the term *copy-text*. McKerrow invented the term and meant by it that early edition which a modern editor selects as the basis for his own. It is quite improper to use it as a synonym for printer's copy in general.

18. Idiosyncratic or otherwise identifiable authorial accidentals characteristics in a revised edition (and especially accidentals connected with revised substantives) can always be used as emendations of the copy-text, just like the revised

substantives. It is all a question of authority. For example, in the passages that William James directly revised for his *Briefer Course* by annotating pages of his *Principles of Psychology*, statistically the majority of punctuation changes occur in the *Briefer Course* pages where the substantive revision is high, whereas very few indeed, in comparison, appear in *Briefer Course* pages that are simple reprints of the *Principles* text. An editor is justified in assigning superior authority to those accidentals changes in the annotated areas and rejecting the variants in unannotated pages. See *Psychology: Briefer Course* (Cambridge, Mass.: Harvard University Press, 1985), pp. 488–490.

19. Some transmissional variants present in a revised edition are the more easily recognizable, in part, if an author has revised for the printer a copy of, say, the third instead of, say, a copy of the first edition. In a revised second edition any accidentals variation from the first may or may not be authorial. In a revised fourth edition which used as printer's copy a purely derived third set from the second, all fourth-edition accidentals that follow the third against its copy of the second edition are automatically classifiable as unauthoritative and can be discarded in favor of a return to the first unless in turn some are further altered in the fourth edition, in which case they may or may not represent authorial marking of copy.

20. William James is an author whose habit of marking accidental changes in typescripts and in proofs shows such concern that on a number of occasions an editor may be led to select as copy-text his collected book version instead of the original journal setting, or even a print instead of his manuscript even though the manuscript had been the setting copy. A particularly interesting case is found in the essay "The Will to Believe" in the book of that title as edited for the Harvard University Press (1979), pp. 312–321 of the textual discourse. The general problems often raised by strictly applying Greg's rationale to works other than the Elizabethan drama are surveyed with illustrations in Bowers, "Greg's Rationale of Copy-Text Revisited," *Studies in Bibliography*, 31 (1978), 90–161.

21. Indeed, if an editor were omniscient so that he could positively identify every authorial revision, both of accidentals and of substantives, and then substitute them in the texture of a first-edition copy-text according to Greg's rationale, in theory such an eclectic text would be identical with the one this omniscient editor would form by adopting the revised edition as copy-text and rejecting every reading that he knew to be non-authorial. In accidentals, at least, by this procedure he would return these variants to the 'authority' of the first edition as emendations of his revised-edition copy-text, in effect exactly reproducing the authorially marked-up copy of the first edition that (in this hypothetical case) served as setting copy for the revised. Sound as this procedure would be in theory as producing an identical text in either case, omniscience is an attribute that a merciful deity has withheld from editors in order to foster the differences of opinion that preserve their livelihood. Greg quite rightly pointed out the pull that the copy-text exerts for the retention of indifferent variant

readings not susceptible of critical analysis. For a modification of his view as applied to the indifferent readings in more modern texts, see Bowers, "Greg's 'Rationale of Copy-Text' Revisited."

22. This is not to say that the transmission from copy to first edition has been accurate or even especially similar, particularly in early books; instead, it is the only game in town—all antecedent authorities being lost, the first edition is the one text we have that is not derived from some other extant source. Thus in practical terms documentary authority begins there.

23. Some critics argue that the author's approval of its accidentals is indicated by the fact that in a revised edition he passed and did not alter the readings and thus that they acquire his authority. As a general propositon this I deny, even for a revised typescript.

24. This can be a tricky business. In several places in the trial proofs which Miss Alice Johnson, of the Society for Psychical Research (London), corrected before distribution of revises to the authors of "A Case of Psychic Automatism," *Proceedings*, 12 (December 1896), 277–297, to which William James contributed an introduction, in the midst of her own styling she sometimes restored the accidentals of the original (preserved) copy from compositorial variation and a few times she restored substantives which the printer had plausibly altered. She must have collated proof against copy—but in itself that case would be unusual for the ordinary proofreader except when reference would be needed to solve some puzzle.

25. *The Marble Faun* transmission is analyzed in the Ohio State Centenary Edition of Hawthorne, where some attention should be called to the problem of the variant endings. The illustrations from Stephen Crane may be found in the textual discussions in the University of Virginia edition of his *Works*. Textual problems in William James are discussed in the various volumes of his *Works* in the almost completed ACLS–Harvard University Press edition. Henry Fielding's textual problems are discussed in the *Works* published by Wesleyan University–Clarendon Press.

26. Even when the document is of very inferior authority like a Shakespearian 'bad quarto,' it may yet retain some true readings somehow corrupted in a substitute edition.

27. The further history of this story is interesting as publishing history but produces no new authority. Bacheller followed by reprinting it in his *Pocket Magazine*, 2 (May 1896). It next appeared in *Frank Leslie's Weekly*, 82 (May 28, 1896), this text being reprinted in *Demorest's Family Magazine*, 32 (September 1896) with the same illustration first added in *Leslie's*. Its last publication was in the *English Illustrated Magazine*, 14 (January 1897). All except *Demorest's* radiate from copies of the Bacheller proof. These help the newspaper evidence in the

reconstruction of the Bacheller proofs, this reconstruction forming the most authoritative copy-text.

28. "Some Principles for Editorial Apparatus," *Studies in Bibliography*, 25 (1972), 41–88; reprinted in his *Selected Studies in Bibliography* (1979), pp. 403–450.

29. Most unusually, where fluidity would normally be expected in dealing with a large number of medieval manuscript texts, the selection of one particular manuscript as copy-text that most closely conformed to his reconstruction of the lost holograph, and the recording of variants based on this single copy-text was positively required in D. C. Greetham's treatment of Hoccleve's *Regiment of Princes* in his article remarkable for its methodology, "Normalisation of Accidentals in Middle English Texts: The Paradox of Thomas Hoccleve," *Studies in Bibliography*, 38 (1985), 121–150.

30. As is usually the case, the version printed in the author's native land may have more characteristic spelling and other accidentals than a version printed elsewhere, and thus in practical terms may require less emendation if chosen as copy-text.

31. Several variations are possible, of course. The case must be rare where an author's own typescript and carbon served as radiating copy, except in international or serial publication. In some complex examples one leg of the text might be set from the author's holograph but another from a copy of it; the commonest, and the usual procedure, is to make up a professional typescript (and carbon) ordered by the author's agent or publisher as setting copy. In a simple situation each might serve as copy without authorial revision not common to both. But the odds are good that in some manner an author might revise one leg of the radiation either in the copy or in proof while leaving the other relatively or completely untouched. This procedure would result in complex radiation.

32. The full evidence may be observed in the University of Virginia edition of Crane's *Tales of Adventure* (1970). Another case of editorial reconstruction of more than ordinary interest concerns "The Revenge of the *Adolphus*," in *Tales of War* (1970), pp. cxxix–cl. However, do not pity the editor of a single-text because of his limited and imperfect authority: if it binds him in ignorance, nevertheless it authenticates his results. But secure as he may feel in his simplified documentary authority, he has traded security for the excitements of the blue-sky adventures when working with multiple authority in radiating texts.

The Editor as Philologist

MARVIN SPEVACK

The times require a word or two about my title. When the idea for this paper came into my mind, I deliberately chose an old-fashioned term, *philologist*, to describe one role—perhaps the all-embracing one—of the editor. By *philologist* I mean not so much the etymological launching-pad—one who loves the "logos" (speech, word, reason)—nor, a bit farther on, one who loves learning and literature, but mainly one who deals with the science, especially historical and comparative, of language or languages. I consciously avoided more stylish designations, like historical or comparative linguistics, since they summon up, for some, an exotic landscape composed of surface structures and deep ones, of trees productive and unproductive—all foreign and forbidding. I wanted something more recognizable and more comfortable. (And if I also use the adjective *linguistic*, it is mainly to supply some variety in vocabulary, not in substance.)

But, to my dismay, I find the *Gemütlichkeit* threatened by currency. A short while after settling on my title, I picked up a copy of the *TLS* (of 10 December 1982) and found that *philology* was back in style: a review of two biographies of George Borrow was headlined "A philologist in the wild" (p. 1353) and a contribution (in a special section called "Professing Literature") by Paul de Man was entitled "The return to philology" (pp. 1355–56). Not to worry: I do not intend to move toward that kind of exotic landscape. But before the modishness of the word *philology* twists it beyond recognition—before chic semantics converts or perverts my title—let me say that it is the traditional "grand old term" which I mean. For it unites us all.

We are editors but we were not editors to begin with. We come from no Department of Editing. We are philologists by profession, editors by choice or chance, by nature or necessity. As philologists and editors we practice philology: we deal with language in texts. We

91

are professionally engaged in all the types of linguistic organization: phonology, which includes phonetics; orthography or graphology; lexicology, which includes semantics and lexicography; and grammar, which includes syntax and the inflections of morphology. Our orientation is essentially analytic and historical. Like it or not, our statements and deeds have philological implications. Not always consciously and not always well, we are nevertheless always, inescapably, philologists.

Let me illustrate on the map of our activities: the printed page of a typical critical edition. Like all good things, it usually consists of three parts: text, collation, and commentary. Each is philologically motivated, informed, and describable.

A text is a rendition of what an author wrote. It may involve editing by an editor, which may be a code name for the author himself, for a friend or colleague who gives advice, for a professional reader employed in a publishing house, for a compositor or his modern-day manifestation, a computer/word processor, and—*pace* deconstructionists and others—for a reader. Igor Stravinsky was a meticulous author: he produced scores so immaculately set down that they could well have served as copy for photo-offset production. Professionally (if not personally), that is the way he was, composer and editor and everything else in one. In such a rare case, there is relatively little employment for a conventional editor or compositor: the work is transferred almost "bodily" from one surface to another. The linguistic implications of the production of the text are similarly nil: the movement from textology to textography is simple, involving little more than, perhaps, syllabication when a difference in format calls for a difference in line-justification. Other linguistic concerns—grammar, semantics, orthography—exist, of course, in all texts: authors make errors, change their minds, heed advice. But these remain relatively stable as long as the author is alive and can assert which version is "authoritative" or as long as a computer can store all the versions and "re-versions."

Older texts, however, are different from modern ones in numerous ways, not the least of which is, as in the case of my employer, Shakespeare, the absence of the author himself. If the author is dead, or distant from his work (or a work ascribed to him), then the editor has employment. For he may have to re-construct, in the manner of an archaeologist, and not mainly transfer. This involves decisions which are almost totally philological. The editor must base his actions on his understanding of the grammar, semantics, orthography, and phonetics of a time and language gone by. In other words, his practice derives from the larger, theoretical areas: grammar, lexicology, graphology, phonology. He makes linguistic utterances, follows linguistic concepts and rules, however curiously stated. W. W. Greg's seven "main principles or rules . . . which should govern the procedure of an editor of Shakespeare," formalizing the "lines laid down in McKerrow's *Prolegomena*,"[1] are linguistic assertions or, at least, assertions which may be phrased and understood linguistically. Greg himself illustrates the presuppositions and implications. After stating Rule 1—"The aim of a critical edition should be to present the text, so far as the available evidence permits, in the form in which we may suppose that it would have stood in a fair copy, made by the author himself, of the work as he finally intended it" (p. x)—he goes on to say that "an editor should of course remove so far as possible all errors and imperfections for which there is reason to believe either a scribe or compositor responsible; indeed, he may be allowed to rectify any blunder which it is certain the author would have recognized as such had it been pointed out to him, provided that neither the nature of the blunder nor the form of the correction is open to doubt" (p. xi). McKerrow's *Prolegomena* provides the details.[2] A philologist *malgré lui*, he attempts to define and illustrate what he calls the "meaning" of the term "certainly corrupt": i.e., "any form which, in the light of our knowledge of the language at the time when the text in question was written, was 'impossible', that is, would not have been, in its context, an intelligible word or phrase" (p. 21). And he proceeds to treat specific examples of orthographical and grammatical "irregularities" and compositorial "abnormalities."

Both Greg and McKerrow and most others agree on presuppositions and intention. They assume the existence of an author's manuscript (or "fair copy") which they attempt to re-construct after it has either gone astray or been manipulated by careless authors, bumbling compositors, "iniurious impostors," or what-have-you. They assume a larger linguistic context—usually call it the "language of the time or author"—which enables them to recognize and treat the "irregularities" and "abnormalities." Although admitting "there is no recent period of the language of which we have so little precise knowledge,"[3] they nevertheless—albeit cautiously—attempt to restore a text through a process which very much resembles normalization, if it is not normalization *per se*: that is, the "irregularities" and "abnormalities" are made into regularities and normalities. Linguistically, if not logically, this is quite a risky procedure. All editors would doubtless agree. And they would also agree with Alice Walker that "the two great fallacies of twentieth-century editorial theory have been, (1) the assumption that fuller knowledge about transmission would establish which readings were right and which were wrong, and (2) that palaeography would serve as a main tool in emendation."[4] But there is work to be done. All are unanimous in saying that we need but lack the essential philological knowledge, and all are equally unanimous in continuing anyway—no, not *any* way but one way in particular: a concentration on "irregularities" based on turning mechanically to a historical reference work, like the *OED*, and on what must be called an "intuitive" sense of an author's style or idiolect. For individual lexical questions, consultation of the *OED* or some other lexical reference work suffices. For the rest—and that would have to be perhaps 95 per cent—the automatic adoption, as a linguistic backdrop, of the rules and patterns of *modern* English is the practice. The resulting overattention to the irregular—to, say, palpable errors or an unusual vocabulary—proceeds from the unspoken assumption that every thing else remains the same. This procedure is superficial and distorting.[5]

Illustrations are abundant. Dover Wilson's assertions in his edition of *Antony and Cleopatra* (The New [Cambridge] Shakespeare, 1950, pp. 124–25) are not untypical.

> In an Introduction to the facsimile of this text issued by Messrs Faber and Faber in 1929 I suggested that the copy for F., the only original we have of the play, was Shakespeare's own manuscript. F. certainly contains a number of spellings of an unusual or, by 1623, of an archaic character, such as are either found in 'good' quarto and other F. texts, or are of similar type to those found therein. Here are a handful: one (on) 1.1.39; how (ho!) 1.2.114; to (too) 2.5.8, 3.1.15; too (to) 5.1.56, etc.; reciding (residing) 1.3.103, 2.2.37; hard (heard) 2.2.223; arrant (errand) 3.13.104; in (e'en) 4.15.73; triumpherate (triumvirate) 3.6.28. The last two look like misprints. Yet 'in' (e'en) occurs again in *Merch.* (Q1) 3.5.20, *Rom.* (Q2) 5.1.24, *Err.* (F.) 2.2.101, and *All's Well* (F.) 3.2.18; and so can hardly be anything but a Shakespearian spelling. As for the remarkable 'triumpherate', *L. L. L.* (Q1) which like *Antony and Cleopatra* was almost certainly printed from a Shakespearian MS. lends its support in 'triumpherie' for 'triumviry'. Equally noteworthy is the spelling or perversion of the classical names. Working presumably with

North under his eye, Shakespeare was nevertheless restrained by no habits of 'correctness' or consistency so long as the names sounded all right on the stage. Thus he spells 'Sicyon' 'Scicion' (1.2.115, etc.), 'Taurus' 'Towrus' (3.7.78, etc.), 'Actium' 'Actiom', which is not unnaturally printed 'Action' (3.7.51). 'Medena' for 'Modena' (1.4.57) and 'Brandusium' for 'Brundusium' (3.7.21) are probably simply misreadings, while misreading and inconsistency will account for variations like 'Camidius', 'Camidias' and 'Camindius' for 'Canidius' and the occurrence twice of 'Ventigius' for 'Ventidius', a name which assumes even stranger forms in *Timon*. Sometimes a variation is, I think, deliberate. 'Anthonio' for example, an acceptable spelling of the period as the quotation in note 1.1.10 shows, seems to suggest familiarity or intimacy on the part of the speaker at 2.2.7 and 2.5.26. And a form in which I think we are bound to follow Shakespeare is 'Thidias', the name he gives to Caesar's emissary who gets a good thrashing, possibly because the 'Thyreus' he found in North was so difficult for an actor to speak. For 'Thyreus', though all editors read it, has no authority, since the name in Plutarch is 'Thyrsus'. Similarly I follow Shakespeare and read 'Dercetus', which is the form he gives to Plutarch-North's 'Dercetaeus' at 4.14.111, and not like Pope and later editors 'Dercetas', which lies half-way between North and the spelling 'Decretas' that crops up in F. at 5.1.3 S.D. and 5.1.5, and is in fact the sort of conflation that pre-Pollardian editors loved.

His thesis is "that the copy for F. . . . was Shakespeare's own manuscript." His main evidence is orthographic and phonetic; his supporting evidence is distributional: "F. certainly contains a number of spellings of an unusual or, by 1623, of an archaic character, such as are either found in 'good' quarto or other F. texts, or are of a similar type to those found therein." The first part of the statement implies orthographic norms: else, how is "unusual" to be defined? It also implies changing norms: else, how is "archaic" to be defined? The statement is obviously based on observation and intuition; it is an educated guess, of course. It must be respected: good editors work this way, and Dover Wilson was extremely well read and experienced. But since the method of inquiry is being scrutinized as well as the conclusions, it is a guess nevertheless; for there is very little in the way of empirical evidence for any changes, any unusualness (again, the emphasis on the irregular), in the first quarter of the seventeenth century. This is not to say that there was no change; this is just to emphasize that there is very little precise detail about what did change and how and when. Linguistically, the detailed evidence is likewise insufficient. Dover Wilson offers a vague "handful" of spellings. A "handful," however, is not nearly as accurate a measure as a foot or even a span. Against a total of some 900,000 tokens in the Shakespeare corpus, it is hardly a measurement at all. But the shortcomings are not merely statistical. The examples are indeed a "handful" in that they lack differentiation. True, the pairs may all represent possible phonetic renditions (with the exception perhaps of *in/e'en*). Yet there is a world of difference between, say, *to/too* and *triumpherate/triumvirate*. This first—*to* for *too*—is hardly "unusual" or "archaic," and is too frequent to be an error, or a sign of carelessness, or an idiosyncratic sign of a particular writer or author. The second—*triumpherate* for *triumvirate*—is indeed remarkable: it is an ignorant spelling. It is most unlikely that Shakespeare—even with small Latin (which incidentally was really quite good)—could have so misunderstood the etymology, especially when writing plays featuring the three men.[6] The same might be said for *reciding* for *residing*: phonetically, English interchangeables perhaps, but not to one who had ever read or heard elementary Latin.[7] The *one* for *on* example is likewise interesting but for different reasons: for one thing, it is evidence that the two were possibly homophonic; for another, there is at least a slight chance of a genuine misunderstanding of the sense of the passage since both forms are to a point grammatically acceptable.

Dover Wilson's assertions about the "spelling or perversion" of classical names are similarly a "handful": statistically inadequate, qualitatively obtuse. Time permits only one or two examples. If *Taurus/Towrus* "sounded all right on the stage," then why attribute "misreading and inconsistency" to a pair which are as phonetically alike, *Ventidius/Ventigius*?[8] Can we accept the statement that "Shakespeare was . . . restrained by no habits of 'correctness' " in the spelling of these names when we know that a consistent spelling of names is only a relatively modern development? Why should *Medena* for *Modena* be a misreading and not a phonetic rendition? Surely, Dover Wilson's statement on variation (or, as some would call it, register)—" 'Anthonio' . . . seems to suggest familiarity or intimacy"—is linguistically and statistically hard to prove, if not untenable.[9] A metrical consideration—the extra syllable—achieved through a morphological variation, seems not unlikely. And just as surely, Dover Wilson is mistaken not merely in saying that Plutarch has *Thyrsus*—all contemporary editions of North's translation have *Thyreus*—but, more important, in asserting that *Thyreus* was somehow "so difficult for an actor to speak" (as is Ridley, who feels "it was the other way round"), when a slightly trilled *r* (Elizabethan or modern) will make it sound all but indistinguishable from *Thidias*? It is no wonder that such assertions are matched by similar ones about the manuscript as a whole. All agree with Greg in finding "a very carefully written copy, elaborately prepared by the author for the stage" (p. 148). And yet all agree with Greg in finding it "full of Shakespearian spellings and misprints," containing "few cruxes but many errors" (p. 147). Shakespeare's errors? Compositor B's? Perhaps not errors at all? The paradox is fitting for one who writes scenes which are tedious and brief, merry and tragical.

There are conclusions to be drawn. First, the experience of the editor is essential. The more he reads of the language he is editing, the more knowledgeable and sensitive his philological conclusions will be. So, *inter alia*, our debt to great readers of the literature of the period they were editing, like Kittredge or Rollins. Second, it is not enough simply to admit, as does Greg in discussing normalization, that "our present philological equipment is inadequate to the task" (p. li). It is, of course, but it need not always be so. The awareness is important, as is attention directed to the overall linguistic situation of a time and the particular linguistic situation of an author. In the mean time, a certain caution is advisable and a heightened awareness of the implications, philological and otherwise, of assertions made regarding language.

This may sound rather negative to those eager to get down to work. Let me therefore delineate the possible concrete effects of what I would call philological sophistication rather than resignation. They may be seen in the collation and the commentary.

These sections present the work of the editor in high relief. He and they are exposed. The particular arrangement of the collation and commentary—the one like files of single soldiers, the other like massed platoons or companies—highlights a semiotic intention. An entry in a collation or a commentary note signals the reader that something is being said, something more than nothing (else the space would be blank), something selected from a larger body and so deemed special. In short, we must observe what is selected, what it says, how it is said, and how much is said—all philological duties of the first rank.

The collation consists, as a rule, of substantive and semi-substantive variants. Let me concentrate on substantive variants, those which would be expected to appear in both full and select collations. As I have written elsewhere,[10]

> theoretically the definition of 'substantive' would seem to be clear enough. McKerrow's rule has been generally accepted: true variant readings 'as between a later edition and an earlier one on the same line of descent may be defined as not merely readings which differ from one another, but readings the later of which cannot have been derived from the earlier by the normal process of modernization: or to put the matter in another way, a reading in a later edition can only be considered as a "variant" in respect of an earlier reading if it implies an attempt to emend that reading.' Accordingly, the *Shakespeare Variorum Handbook* specifies *substantive* (as distinct from semi-substantive) variants as 'all verbal changes that affect meaning—i.e. all changes, substitutions, omissions, additions, and reordering of words, phrases, lines or scenes.' 'Meaning' is not explicitly defined, but practice implies that it involves in the main 1) lexical aspects—the change or substitution of words differing in sense and reference, as in *gift-guest, Henry-Thomas*, etc; 2) inflectional and morphological aspects—as in *sings-singeth, horse-horses, who-whom, go-went, unfortunate-infortunate, cheerily-cheerly, innocence-Innocencie*, as well as interesting phenomena like older forms of strong verbs (*wan-wonne*), of the genitive (*Calchas-Chalcas his*), and of adverbs (*toward-towards*) and adjectives (*momentary-momentany*); 3) certain syntactical aspects—word order, repetition, addition, and omission.
>
> The criterion of 'meaning' is not entirely fortunate, however, for it may lead to overinterpretation or overrefinement of nuances. What is most often a concentration on the isolated lexical instance may well suit the literary critic but it can handicap the textual editor: the divergence between them is reflected in the different aims of the commentary or explanatory notes and the textual notes. For the editor normally proceeds from the assumption that his copy-text is 'correct,' that it 'makes sense,' that it is unambiguous—that, in short, 'interpretation' is all but unnecessary. In a modern-spelling edition, the editor modernizes: that means that he is compelled to limit alternatives, for orthography is restrictive. The same is true for any editor who must determine which forms are to be given in a collation of texts.

Theory, of course, is not practice. An analysis of the way Dover Wilson's examples are treated in the collation of three other modern editions of Shakespeare—Kittredge's (1941), Ridley's *Arden* (1954), and Mack's *Pelican* (1960)—reveals that no one edition agrees entirely with another: Dover Wilson gives all nine; Kittredge gives only two; Arden, four; Pelican, three. They agree only on *in/e'en*. My Variorum collation gives only two and agrees with all the others only on *in/e'en*. If, however, we omit Dover Wilson, who is committed to illustrations of what he considers "Shakespearian spellings," then the picture looks considerably better. The remaining four editions still do not agree entirely, but they do agree on *in/e'en* and on *to/too, too/to,* and *arrant/errand.*

The reasons for the agreement, as well as for the disagreement, are not always stated or clear. But it is certainly worthwhile to attempt them in order to discover their causes. Obviously, the orthographic versions are ambiguous: seemingly homophonic, they seem to present two possible "meanings." In order to disambiguate, we apply linguistic criteria: first, grammatical and syntactical, I would say, and, if that is not enough, semantic. This would account for the unanimity on *to/too, too/to, arrant/errand.* Strangely enough, *hard/heard* is retained in the collation by Pelican, *triumph-erate/triumvirate* by Arden, although the first offers no genuine grammatical, syntactical, or semantic alternative, and the second no semantic alternative. Unfortunately, the editors do not elucidate; fortunately, we can engage in speculation. I would guess that both were thought "interesting," though perhaps for different reasons. What these reasons are is not as important as the fact that the very appearance of the pair suggests something special. From a phono-logical point of view, they are no different from the scores of homophones of the *hart/heart* variety that are not recorded. From a semantic and grammatical point of view, they are of little interest too. *One/On* and *how/ho* are more "interesting," to be sure. Both are phonologically interesting, but in essence no more so than *hart/heart*. Grammatically, they are interesting because they present alternatives—*how/ho* more than *One/On*—which are especially attractive because of the change of word class. But semantically only *how/ho* is satisfyingly ambiguous, a surmise supported by the fact that no source after F1 has retained or even attempted to explain *one*, whereas *how/ho* has checkerboarded its way through textual history.

Linguistically, the procedure thus far may be described as follows. In an Elizabethan context of orthographic and grammatical lati-tude—Baugh describes it with notable understatement as marked by a "considerable variety of use"[11]—homophones with apparent grammatical and/or semantic alternatives are abundant. Since it is to be assumed that only one is "correct"—that as a rule no deliberate multiplication is intended—a process of disambiguation takes place:

the lexical items are subjected to various grammatical and semantic filters to determine whether or not they "make sense." At this point most of the cases are "solved." Those that remain are usually those that not only "make sense" but—as an added and necessary criterion—have a history during which disambiguation takes place, that is, a time when orthography and grammar become more rigidly established, as the efforts of Shakespeare's eighteenth-century editors testify. This procedure of course is not new: it is the customary linguistic procedure of all editors.

In practice the better editors, I would venture to say, are those with perhaps more discipline and less fantasy. Disambiguation is mandatory in almost all instances. It is self-indulgence to give disinformation by including orthographic alternatives as if they were grammatical or semantic ones. What editor can refrain from giving F1's "sixteene" although reading with Q2 in *Hamlet* (5.1.162), "I have been sexton here, man and boy, thirty years"? Discipline does not mean lack of flexibility and imagination. Recognizing the "word" requires following the strait and narrow path just described. But it also requires more than a mechanical recourse to the *OED*. Sensitivity to the nature of word-formation, for example, may lead to a small but truly interesting group of words not recorded but nevertheless "well formed"—i.e., look like words—and thus possible (I am not saying probable): e.g., *composion, connectural, conspicuate, festuant, gentletie*. Sensitivity to historical development may likewise prevent us from making naive remarks, as when one reviewer reprimands a spelling like *hane* (as a verbal inflection and not just a misspelling of *haue* brought about by a turned *n*) because the *OED* does not happen to list it for the sixteenth century, although he admits to finding earlier and later examples.

Linguistic discipline and sensitivity are likewise essential for the commentary, which is at once the most attractive and the most discouraging part of an editor's work: attractive because it enables the editor to display his understanding and knowledge in an at-times virtuosic manner—Fredson Bowers once complained of the editor who "is content to have any kind of a text, because what he really wants is only a peg on which to hang his annotations";[12] discouraging because it is often viewed condescendingly by scholars who cannot count on the royalties to be had from set-texts and is rarely noted by reviewers, except now and then for an objection to a particular interpretation, present or missing, of a certain crux. In any case, serious discussions of the nature of the commentary have been sparse and sporadic.

A good part of many commentaries consists of encyclopedic information, about which there is time for only a brief mention of two points which apply as well to the philological areas I have been focussing on. The first and all-embracing one is, naturally, the assessment of one's audience—i.e., what to give and how much: is Sicilia to be located? is Waterloo to be dated? is Mars to be identified? The second and more limited one is the occasional linguistic implications behind certain of these notes. Perhaps one example will suffice before I turn to the more prevalent instances of notes directly involving philological matters.

The name *Agincourt* (*H5* PR.14) receives no comment in the four not untypical editions referred to earlier—Kittredge, New [Cambridge], Arden, and Pelican—presumably because the editors felt it was well known or because it had been dealt with in the general introduction. A more recent edition, however, provides a gloss: "*Azincourt* in modern French; but the English spelling is well established." I am not sure I understand the point, linguistic and otherwise, of the note. One could just as well say, "*Rome: Roma* in modern Italian; but the English spelling is well established." I do know that an interesting point and an opportunity have been missed: the linguistic point—the relationship of the English *g* to the French *z*; the opportunity—the formulation of the kind of note which not merely informs but explains.

I have dealt in some detail elsewhere with the notes on language in editions of Shakespeare.[13] Perhaps I may be permitted to summarize the essential philological assertions and implications. Most linguistic commentary in older texts consists of dictionary-like "definitions," usually in the form of synonyms, and paraphrases, usually following the ubiquitous "i.e." Underlying this semantic attempt is a belief in synonymy. Leaving aside (but not ignoring) the fact that synonymy is by no means an accepted notion although much practiced, the method as such suffers further from at least two deficiencies. For one, the defining words are modern words: consequently, there emerges a kind of superimposition of one set of semantic conditions upon another. This is unavoidable: we know we are not native speakers of the languages we are editing. But we do not always realize that there is as much a certain and automatic blurring of focus in the very employment of synonyms as there is in the blunt and at times cruel prose paraphrases. Defining *greets* as "addresses" or *measureless* as "extremely" is as obtuse as saying "How goes the night?" means "What time is it?" This is obvious, of course. But it is not always recognized that the blur is increased even as the attempt is made to "define" more precisely by giving not one but several "synonyms," often without a full consideration of the intricacies of such concerns as polysemy and hyponymy. What we have is the interesting situation in which a reader who presumably does not know the "meaning" of a particular word or expression is asked to choose the "best" one or even to select the "best" ingredients from the assembled choices. He will, of course, choose from the words he knows, thus obliging the editor to provide definers which are simple, which reduction of definers to modern and simple words increases the difficulty of defining accurately. Furthermore, the defining words themselves, more often than not a loosely arranged group, may be even more diffuse in effect than a single definer. In most instances they cannot be said to constitute a kind of semantic field, for they usually come about without sufficient attention to semantic categories, conceptual and affective meaning, and other aspects of the ongoing linguistic discussion.[14]

The focus is further blurred by the fact—the experience of all practicing editors—that the editor often chooses alternatives with an eye not on his semantic target nor even on his audience but on his competition, other editions of the same work, lest he repeat their alternatives. Thus, among all too numerous examples, commentators on *meetly* ("You can do better yet; but this is meetly," *Ant.* 1.3.81) over the past hundred years range from "pretty well" (Wordsworth, ed. 1883) to "reasonably well" (Ridley, ed. 1954) to "well" (Irving & Marshall, ed. 1889) to "very well" (Case, ed. 1906). Or, if you wish, a chronological march through a dozen leading editions over the past thirty or so years reveals: "tolerable" (Wilson, 1950), "not bad" (Alexander, 1951), "fairly good" (Phialas, 1955), "well suited to the occasion" (Mack, 1960), "moderately well acted" (Wright, 1961), "properly, well done" (Troy, 1961), "not too bad" (Houghton, 1962), "suitable" (Everett, 1964), "pretty fair" (Walter, 1969), "quite good" (Ingledew, 1971), "pretty good" (Evans, 1974), and "you are doing quite well" (Jones, 1977). In short, starting from the questionable notion of synonymy, proceeding through the inevitable traps of historical myopia, modern oversimplification, and not so elegant variation, the editor moves or is moved inexorably away from the center to a peripheral area called semantic fuzziness.

As if this were sensed, the editor often employs other semantic devices. He seeks clarity in authority. If he is an Anglist, then he is in the enviable position of being able to turn to the *OED*. And if he is really fortunate he will be able to assert that the *OED* cites the very work and the very instance he is dealing with. This is obviously a kind of semantic incest, a circular definition with historical contour—or, if you wish, a ceremonial demonstration of buck-passing. The *OED* does locate the word historically, but so does the text being edited. And its definitions are still dictionary definitions—that is, subject to the same limitations just mentioned, though more professionally formulated. As if sensing the inadequacies of this procedure, the editor reaches into his semantic bag for a related practice: defining by parallels or illustrations, with the not uncontroversial assumption that one instance is the same as another, be they in the same author and even in a different one, not to mention the additional acceptability if the other author or work is renowned and respected, like Homer or the Bible.

To the inherent semantic limitations may be added a final kind of linguistic assertion found in the commentary: distributional information, a form of statistical statement as casual and widespread as it is misleading and dangerous. It deals in the main with frequency: such-a-word occurs so-many times in such-an-author; or such-a-word occurs very frequently, rather frequently, fairly frequently, frequently, not infrequently, not so infrequently, not too infrequently . . . in such-an-author. And what is more dramatic than the precision of "This is the only instance of such-a-word in such-an-author" or "Such-an-author uses such-a-word once"? Notes of this kind are dangerous for a variety of reasons. For one thing, they impart an importance to a particular word which it may not have; the information may be correct but it is unlikely to match the expectations it arouses. For in most cases there exists no complete statistical picture of a corpus, and so weighting is meaningless. Where a statistical picture is available, as in the case of Shakespeare, any assertion of uniqueness of this kind may have to be modified by the fact that 43.29 per cent of all his words (types) occur only once. Potentially even more dangerous is the view of language, poetic and otherwise, which helps shape such assertions. It tends to measure effectiveness according to highs and lows, as is obvious in the inordinate attention paid to word-coining and hapax legomena. It is ironic that Shakespeare, who makes such practitioners comic butts, should himself be celebrated as the master of the art. Such an assessment, be it of literature or language in general, is simply wrong. It calls to mind Edwin Denby on ballet: "To a number of people ballet means toe dancing, that is what they come to see, and they suspect a dancer only gets off her 'pointes' to give her poor feet a rest." How happy the editor who can combine many of these ingredients, as does Case in the Arden *Antony and Cleopatra* commentary on *lank'd* (1.4.71): "became lank, lost its fulness. The *New English Dictionary* gives no other instance of the verb in an intransitive sense." How blissful he who can add: "now obsolete," "the adjective occurs three times in Shakespeare," "the transitive verb is to be found in Horman's *Vulgaria* (1519)," etc.

Professor Greetham said he was looking forward to an "inspiriting" address. I fear I may seem to have come to bury not to praise. For ample discussion and concrete results would require a conference in itself. Yet it is worthwhile to repeat the admonitions, for they serve in their own way to emphasize the importance of the task of editing—the scholarly and imaginative re-creation of a bit of the past. But you will want more than a pep talk. And you will want more than a list of caveats, although it is never wrong to repeat that the language of the text you edit is not the same as the language you yourself manipulate or encounter daily; that it has its own rules and conventions which it is your task to discover and employ; and that in many practical instances more is achieved by saying less. In other words editing involves a sound philological preparation and mental set, hardware and software, to connect the past with the present. The work of editing is not a translating of the past into the present but a rendition of it on its own terms. Ideally, the edited text is a moment of time past, but is also beyond time in the hermetic unity of the re-creation: it looks neither like a work of its time, nor a work of this time. It is a pure feat of philological re-construction.

Still, you will want to carry away something more than "it is time to begin the serious discussion." But life's "time's fool." Therefore since philology is fond of rules and laws, the sweet fruition of the earthly philologist, allow me to leave you with Spevack's textogenic law: textology recapitulates philology.

NOTES

1. W. W. Greg, *The Editorial Problem in Shakespeare*, Third Edition (Oxford: Clarendon Press, 1954), p. ix.

2. Ronald B. McKerrow, *Prolegomena for the Oxford Shakespeare* (Oxford: Clarendon Press, 1939).

3. McKerrow, p. 3.

4. Alice Walker, "Principles of Annotation: Some Suggestions for Editors of Shakespeare," *Studies in Bibliography*, 9 (1957), 96.

5. It is interesting that Alice Walker, in her worthy discussion of "Principles of Annotation," calls a more sensitive use of reference works like the *OED* and Elizabethan works "literary means." This signifies a kind of lay philology, and her procedure is not without the flaws which are typical of such "literary" investigation. When she suggests (p. 100) that attention be drawn to *lowering* (*Ant.* 1.2.122) as "the first recorded use of the adverb as a verb," she attempts to illustrate the "norm" not the "oddity" as the "hall-mark" of Shakespeare. This utterance is to be welcomed. Ironically enough, however, her well-intended suggestion misses the point. Putting aside the fact that the verb derives from the adjective (not the adverb) and that the *OED* is very selective in giving adverbs lemma status, and that the use of the "adjective" as a transitive verb is recorded earlier and fully, the main point here is not the first recording, which would be an instance of that emphasis on "oddity" which Walker would refute, but the nature of the adjective-verb conversion. The existence of the phenomenon itself is relatively less important than an assessment of, say, its productivity in the English language and/or in Shakespeare's idiolect. If it is common, there is as little reason to mention it as there is to mention noun-verb or verb-noun conversions.

   Interestingly, too, authorship studies, however diverse and often unsatisfactory, quite rightly search for "regularities"—concentrating, in matters of vocabulary, on function words and other high-frequency lexical items.

6. Wilhelm Franz, *Die Sprache Shakespeares*, Fourth Edition (Halle, 1939), p. 583, regards *triumpherate* as a blending of *triumvirate* and *triumph*. But this is unlikely because Shakespeare seldom practices this kind of invention and, when so, usually in comic characters.

7. For contemporary Latin pronunciation see, for example, Bror Danielsson, *John Hart's Works on English Orthography and Pronunciation* (Stockholm, 1955), 1:214 ff. For Shakespeare's Latin, see J. W. Binns, "Shakespeare's Latin Citations: The Editorial Problem," *Shakespeare Survey*, 35 (1982), 119–128.

8. See J. C. Maxwell, "Shakespeare's Manuscript of *Antony and Cleopatra*," *N&Q*, 196 (1951), 337. Fausto Cercignani, *Shakespeare's Works and Elizabethan Pronunciation* (Oxford, 1981), p. 323, cites other and perhaps unnecessarily complicated explanations: "The readings of *Ventigius* and *Ventidgius* may be either scribe's misspellings (cf. Arden edn. xx–xxi) or author's inconsistencies not properly revised (cf. Bullough, vi, 225)."

9. Cleopatra uses it this once (2.5.26) to the Messenger; she uses *Antony* (35 times) to everyone else, including Antony. Enobarbus uses it this once (2.2.7) to Lepidus; he uses *Antony* (22 times) to everyone else, including Antony. That is, they do not use *Anthonio* directly as an indicator of intimacy: Cleopatra, dying, calls "O Antony!" (5.2.312); Enobarbus's dying words are "O Antony, O Antony!" (4.9.23).

10. *A Complete and Systematic Concordance to the Works of Shakespeare, Volume IX: Substantive Variants* (Hildesheim, 1980), pp. vii–viii.

11. Albert C. Baugh, *A History of the English Language*, Second Edition (London, 1959), p. 303.

12. Fredson Bowers, "Some Relations of Bibliography to Editorial Problems," *Studies in Bibliography*, 3 (1950–51), 61.

13. "A New Shakespeare Dictionary (SHAD) and the Notes on Language in Editions of Shakespeare," *Studien zur Englischen Philologie*, ed. Herbert Mainusch and Dietrich Rolle (Frankfurt, 1979), pp. 123–134; and "Shakespeare Synchronic and Diachronic: Annotating Elizabethan Texts," *Festschrift für Karl Schneider*, ed. Ernst Dick and Kurt R. Jankowsky (Amsterdam, 1982), pp. 441–453.

14. In Onions's *Shakespeare Glossary*, as I have shown elsewhere ("Notes on Language," pp. 127–28), "the word *nice*, for example, is admitted to be 'of somewhat vague use in the 16–17th cent. and freq. variously explained by comm. on S.' Onions nevertheless assigns it ten 'meanings' (in Schmidt there are but eight; in the *SOED* there are twelve). They are listed in no particular or logical sequence; the illustrations do not account for all occurrences. And it may take some very 'nice' distinguishing to draw the line between meaning 2 ('not able to bear much, delicate') and meaning 7 ('slender'); or to reconcile meaning 1 ('wanton, lascivious') with meaning 3 ('shy, coy'); or meaning 8 ('unimportant, trivial') with meaning 10 ('accurate, exact, precise')."

The Text as Process and the Problem of Intentionality

HANS WALTER GABLER

For well over a decade now, I believe, we have seen a productive process of critical reorientation of editing. This has been a reorientation towards the foundations of textual studies and editorial practice in criticism, and a critical—or meta-critical—reflection on the definable—or perhaps not always so easily definable—concepts of 'work', 'author', 'text' or 'intention' in their implications for the pragmatic operations of our discipline, and their results. Seen as problematical, these concepts have gained in critical contour, although the complexity in which they stand revealed as relevant to textual analysis and editing has not necessarily made them easier to handle—and not at all easy to handle, it would seem, within the framework of the conventional model of the critical edition, hierarchically structured and designed, on a copy-text basis, to establish a stable reading text of unquestioned privilege. Hitherto, this model has been least affected by the process of critical reorientation, understandably so, for its assumed inviolability has provided the heuristic stepping-stone in the restructuring of the conceptual background of critical editing that we have been engaged in. Yet the point may now have been reached when our conceptions of the nature, the aims, and the potential of a critical edition, as well as those of the functional relationship of edition and editor, come into question. In this context, I venture to offer some reflections on the text as process and the problem of authorial intention.

Jerome McGann's *Critique of Modern Textual Criticism* of 1983, as we are all aware, is quite specifically a critique of the high functional role assigned to 'authorial intention' and 'final authorial intention' in current Anglo-American textual thinking.[1] Recognising that role as a post-Greg ramification of the methodology erected on

the foundations of Sir Walter Greg's "Rationale of Copy-Text,"
McGann insists on severing again the connection, meanwhile fairly
ingrained, between Greg's reasoned recommendations of how, in the
face of divergent textual materials, to arrive pragmatically at editorial decisions, and the subsequently-posited ideal of the critical
edition as the global fulfillment of an author's intention. Thomas
Tanselle, in his 1976 essay in *Studies in Bibliography* entitled "The
Editorial Problem of Final Authorial Intention," assumes a general
agreement on this ideal.[2] "Scholarly editors may disagree about
many things," he opens his essay, "but they are in general agreement
that their goal is to discover exactly what an author wrote and to
determine what form of his work he wished the public to have." The
statement falls into two parts. Following McGann's cue, we may
consider that the second part " . . . and to determine what form of
his work [the author] wished the public to have," if it means "to
determine what form of his work, *so as to establish it as the critically
edited text*, the author wished the public to have," does not follow
inevitably from the first. Observance of the public form of the work
and the intentionality implied in the act of publication carry considerable weight with McGann and Tanselle as, perhaps, with most
theorists in the field. Implied in my subsequent argument is the
contention that the published form of a work need not categorically
be an editor's main, and overriding, point of orientation. Under
given conditions, rather, a critical edition *qua* critical edition may
legitimately claim the privilege of bringing into focus a form or
forms of the work not attained in publication.

My immediate point of departure, however, is the first part of
Tanselle's statement. Holding that the goal of editors is "to discover
exactly what the authors wrote," it addresses the editorial problem
of establishing a text in every single and individual detail. Specifically, it would seem, 'to discover exactly what the author wrote'
involves considering intention when what the author wrote in fact
needs to be discovered because it is not evident, that is, when what he
wrote is not at all, or at best mediately, documented. This, clearly
enough, marks the point of entry of the notion of authorial intention
into the methodological rationale of critical editing as we currently
know it. To assess and determine the author's intention is deemed
necessary or desirable, basically, in respect of individual readings.
Here, in passing, and unless we hold it an axiom that the whole of a
text is merely, and nothing but, the sum of its textual parts, we may

well concede to McGann's critique the point that to raise the notion of authorial intention from such basic application to the level of an overriding editorial principle is, at the very least, fraught with theoretical difficulty.

On the basic level of constitution of critical texts, to assess and determine authorial intention in respect of individual readings may be recognised as a rule of editorial procedure analogous to Greg's rule of following the copy-text for indifferent readings. For indifferent variants encountered in an editorial situation, follow the copy-text; for invariant, yet suspect readings, follow the author. Thus paired, these rules are designed to avoid or eliminate potential or manifest transmissional error when establishing a stable critical text from documents that, however manifestly or inferrably corrupt, essentially provide only a single substantive basis.

At a further level, authorial intention is invoked in situations where, according to current editorial practice, two or more substantive bases call for procedures of eclectic editing. What defines each basis as substantive is the manifest or inferred fact of authorial revision. The variants relevant to the act or acts of revision stand opposed no longer as 'erroneous' and 'correct'—that is, 'wrong' and 'right'—but as 'invalid' and 'valid.' Thus it is here that the extended notion of 'final authorial intention' properly comes into play. Yet since the editorial concern remains with 'exactly what the author wrote', the 'final authorial intention,' too, is assessed properly only in respect of individual readings in pairs or series of authorial variants.

It should also be noted, however, that the construing of 'authorial intention' as a common point of perspective seems to overshadow the appreciation of a difference in kind between authorial variants and transmissional errors: the common manner of dealing with authorial variants reveals no fundamental change, even hardly a ripple of adjustment, in editorial thinking and procedure. 'Valid' and 'invalid' become subsumed under the categories 'correct' and 'erroneous' (or 'right' and 'wrong'). In establishing a critical text, the final one among revisional variants is admitted as the right reading because it would—obviously—be wrong to retain its antecedent, thereby annihilating the act of revision. What is near-to-annihilated instead in the established critical edition is the superseded authorial variant, relegated as it is to apparatus lists in footnotes or at the back of the book, together with the bulk of rejected transmissional errors. This mode of editorial procedure is naturally furthered by the circumstance that revisional situations to be dealt with in acts of eclectic editing appear always embedded in surroundings from which the critical text must be established against transmissional corruption. The editorial approach levels out the categories of variants that differ in their nature, and the desired result remains the stable critical text.

An edition that, in providing a stable reading text, relegates superseded authorial variants much as it rejects transmissional errors may in a sense claim to be modelled on the result of an author's endeavour to arrive at the form of the work he wishes the public to have, in a text of "final authorial intention." That result is always the result of revision, and revision—from the author's point of view—implies rejection. But authorial rejection cannot be equated with editorial rejection. Authorial revision and rejection spring from willed, and essentially free, choice. Editorial rejection, by contrast, results from critical assessment and is pre-determined by the textual materials on which the critical sense is exercised. What the editor rejects—what it is an important part of his critical business to reject—are extraneous elements of textual corruption. Under this category, however, authorial rejections—that is, superseded authorial variants witnessing to the authorial acts of writing and the text's development—cannot properly be subsumed. Yet they are tendentially so subsumed in a type of edition that emulates a text of final authorial intention in the form of a stable critical text. It appears, therefore, that the underlying edition model does not answer adequately to the process character of the text under the author's revisional hand.

What the edition model implicitly posits is an editor vicariously assuming an authorial role. This shows as much in his trained focus on a stable text (oftentimes termed an 'ideal text') as it does in his claim to be fulfilling the author's intention. To attempt, in search of a viable alternative edition model, to recast the editor not in an authorial, but in a properly editorial role involves therefore trying to define a specifically editorial perspective on the questions of textual stability and of authorial intention.

A work revised in successive stages signals the author's free intentional choices at any given textual stage, and the aggregate of stages may justifiably be considered to embody his final intentions with regard to the work as a whole. Yet, since the author's choices are in principle free, the aggregate of stages is also always in principle open to further modification through continued revision. This means that the text of a work under the author's hand is in principle unstable. Instability is an essential feature of the text in progress. Nevertheless, the author who is always free to continue to revise is also free by an act of will to close the process of revision, which he does by publishing or otherwise leaving the text. This may appear as an achievement of textual stability by a performative act of final intention. However, the stability achieved—barring transmissional corruption by which it remains threatened—is strictly that of a specific textual version. It does not cancel out the instability of the text in process, which the author can at most set aside, but never undo. Nor can the editor undo it, and, regardless of the author's attitude, he may choose—indeed, he has the freedom—not to set it aside. Since the instability of the text in process is not cancelled out by the final or any other authorial textual version, it can and should not be editorially neglected—though this is what happens in a critical edition hierarchically oriented towards a stable critical text.

Yet textual instability that is an expression of free intentional choice from the authorial angle takes on a different aspect under editorial perspective. Whereas for the author the text is open and indeterminate, for the editor it is determinate. Its instability is confined within the complex, yet closed system of the words and signs on paper that convey the author's revisionally stratified text. The author's rejections and revisions are in the nature of events. They leave a record when, though only in so far as, committed to paper. As events they are tied up and ramified in contexts, yet as records they appear particularized and localised as variant readings. The variant records thus do not constitute the authorial acts of rejection and revision themselves. Rather, they represent them as written deeds of textual invalidation and validation. It is these localised written deeds that the editor is confronted with and that he—and the critic to whom he ministers in preparing an edition— must in turn analytically read. The text in the determinate record of its instability falls to the editor therefore not for the fulfillment of its real or assumed teleology, but for the description and analysis of its documentary existence. It is because the record is determinate that it becomes amenable to editorial scrutiny and treatment at all. Yet underlying the text recorded are the intention-guided processes that cause its instability. The process–character of the text is thus ultimately due to the process–nature of authorial intention. Hence authorial intention cannot rightly provide a constitutive basis, statically conceived, for editorial performance. Instead, being the constitutive base of the text (as is implied in the record of willed textual changes), authorial intention, as the dynamic mover of textual processes, requires to be editorially set forth for critical analysis. So viewed, authorial intention is not a metaphysical notion to be fulfilled but a textual force to be studied.

It were a task beyond the scope allowed me today to pass at this point from the general to the specific and to develop in all its relevant features of design an edition model that would answer to the theoretical demand. It is likely, indeed, that no single model would answer, but that, with the shifting of 'authorial intention' from an absolute to a relative position in the theory of editing and, hence, within the conceptual design of a critical edition, one would look to different forms of editorial realisation to present, and be capable of presenting, authorial intention as a textual force to be studied.

I will refer only very summarily to the critical edition of James Joyce's *Ulysses* as an edition realised on the theoretical assumptions I have outlined.[3] Its innovative synoptic apparatus notation analysing the genetic progression of the work is designed precisely to lay open the records reflecting the operation of the author's intentions in the making of the text. But it also draws editorial critical conclusions from that operation. As a consequence—and this should not be overlooked—the edition provides a reading text, extrapolated from and, as it were, merely accompanying the synoptically notated edition text, whose shape and apparent stability are explicitly of editorial critical making. What it makes explicit, however, has always been implicit in the acts of editing. The stability of a critical text conceived and presented wholly as a reading text is equally of editorial making. Hence, too, a critically edited text can never claim to be definitive; indeed, the notion of 'definitiveness' would seem logically incongruous with the precepts of scholarly critical editing.

These realisations may appear daunting, and it might be considered 'safer' in their light not to aim at providing reading texts at all, but instead to define apparatus formats only as properly equivalent to the process-character of texts. This is a concept quite seriously entertained by some theoreticians and practitioners of editing for example, in Germany.[4] It emphasises the presentation of textual matter over the critical establishment of text, or texts. If ultimately untenable, in my opinion, for the editing of texts from a multi-document basis ("Textedition"), it is arguably justifiable in the specialised field of "Handschriftenedition," i.e., the editing of manuscripts as manuscripts. Here, in specific editorial situations, presentation may well be given precedence over critical editing, and editorial judgement firmly relegated to apparatus sections devised for the purpose. An extremely interesting case in point has been developed by the Brecht scholar and editor Gerhard Seidel, who in a recent article has offered an apparatus model expressly designed for the study and discussion of Brecht's shifting intention in the course of versions of a poem reacting to the implied political stance taken by the poem's addressee, Karl Kraus, toward the coming into power of the Nazi regime. The salient feature in this apparatus model is a discursive apparatus section explicating the contextual implications of the authorial rejections and revisions as displayed in the sequence of discrete versions—each a text to be read, but none the edition's reading text—that make up the textual section itself of the edition.[5]

The devising of a discursive apparatus section is a telling indication that an edition opening up 'authorial intention' as a subject for study is itself situated at the systematic point of intersection of editing and literary criticism. It is a point of intersection that 'critique génétique,' such as it has been developed in France—and into which the contributions of Dr. Hay and Dr. Lebrave give further insights, approaches from the critical angle. Critical discourse and editorial presentation always run close, and are often interdependent. In the extended version on my 1981 STS paper recently published in *TEXT* 1,[6] as you may recall, I develop a critical discourse from the synoptic notation of a passage in *Ulysses* for which I might not have found the critical clues had I not first edited the text. To end my paper today, I wish, on a mainly descriptive level, to sketch out a 'critique-génétique'-type of approach to some textual materials for which an editorial presentation format has not yet been developed. The work concerned is Ezra Pound's *Canto LI*, whose preserved manuscript materials I have quite recently happened to encounter. They permit some fascinating glimpses of authorial intentions in progress.

Two or three segments into the published text, we get involved in a section concerned with fly-fishing. It culminates:

12 of March to 2nd of April
Hen pheasant's feather does for a fly,
green tail, the wings flat on the body
Dark fur from a hare's ear for a body
a green shaded partridge feather
 grizzled yellow cock's hackle
green wax; harl from a peacock's tail
bright lower body; about the size of pin
the head should be. can be fished from seven a.m.
till eleven; at which time the brown marsh fly comes on.
As long as the brown continues, no fish will take
 Granham

Juxtaposed to it is the next segment beginning

That hath the light of the doer, as it were
a form cleaving to it.
Deo similis quodam modo
hic intellectus adeptus
Grass; nowhere out of place. Thus speaking in
 Königsberg
Zwischen die Volkern erzielt wird
a modus vivendi.

A quotation in an approximation of German? and Königsberg? Are
we to think of Immanuel Kant? A source note reveals a wholly
different point of initial reference:

"Es ist die höchste Zeit, das endlich eine wirkliche
Verständigung zwischen den Völkern erzielt wird.

 Rudolf Hess, Königsberg
 8 July 1934"

In the typed note possibly excerpted from a newspaper report,
Pound encircles the opening phrase and emphatically repeats in
pencil "Yah es die hoschste Zeit ist." In a draft fragment, the
excerpt is raised to the tone of incantation and attracts philosophical
reflection:

"O Grass, my uncle, that are nowhere out of place!"
Es ist die hochste
Die hochste Zeit das endlich
Endlich eine Verstandigung
Zwischen den Volkern erzielt wird. Konigsberg July 8
(anno dodici, Rudolf Hess)

light that is the first form of matter
that hath the light of the doer,

> as a form cleaving to it
> from "possibilis et agens" is the intellect adept,
> est intellectus adeptus compositus
> Deus similis modo, and to know what all desire,
> this is felicity contemplativa.

On several separate sheets of typescript, whose temporal relationship is not readily discernible, variations are played on this collocation of ideas, while on other sheets, and independently, as it seems, the fly-fishing motif is elaborated. In the draft fluidities, then, the two complexes at some point merge, most remarkably so perhaps in the amalgamation achieved in these lines from one draft fragment:

> Das Endlich, said Hess, a means of understanding
> together
> shd be found between nations. Toiling over the booty
> Fish to be caught with cunning;
> small or fly
> dry hackle. etc

Here the contextual yoke permits us to recognise a significant transposition to metaphor of the fishing image. The explicit directness is transitory, as the printed version shows. But it holds a clue to the background of intentions and meaning governing the wording as well as the juxtaposition of segments in *Canto LI*. A marginal note added in ink to the incantatory (first?) draft would appear to signal the impulse from which the poem's meanings changed direction. It reads: "Follows lgty murder of Dollfuss." The act of *Realpolitik* perpetrated in late July 1934, by which Nazi Germany callously turned the course of neighbouring Austria's politics to its own ends, dampens the enthusiasm with which the invocation of an understanding between nations was first greeted. The public phrases stand revealed as baits of oratory cunningly held out to the unwary. Implicit in the work, then, is political meaning, and evident from the fragments of the work's genesis are the dramatic shifts of intention that control the utterance in the recorded endeavours to infuse such meaning into the poetry.

An edition of Ezra Pound's *Cantos* is nowhere yet in sight. If and when it is undertaken, it cannot merely aim at establishing a text. It can hope to be an adequate response to the work only if it lays open the text in process as moved into multiple directions and dimensions of meaning by force of developing and shifting authorial intentions.[7]

NOTES

1. Jerome J. McGann, *A Critique of Modern Textual Criticism*. Chicago & London: The University of Chicago Press, 1983.

2. G. Thomas Tanselle, "The Editorial Problem of Final Authorial Intention." *Studies in Bibliography*, 29 (1976), 167–211.

3. James Joyce, *Ulysses. A Critical and Synoptic Edition*. Prepared by Hans Walter Gabler with Wolfhard Steppe and Claus Melchior. 3 vols. New York & London: Garland Publishing Inc., 1984.

4. See especially Gunter Martens, "Textdynamik und Edition." *in:* Gunter Martens und Hans Zeller (eds.), *Texte und Varianten*. München: C. H. Beck, 1971, pp. 165–201.

5. Gerhard Seidel, "Intentionswandel in der Entstehungsgeschichte. Ein Gedicht Bertolt Brechts über Karl Kraus historisch–kritisch ediert." *Zeitschrift für Deutsche Philologie* 101 (Sonderheft: *Probleme neugermanistischer Edition*), 1982, 163–188.

6. Hans Walter Gabler, "The Synchrony and Diachrony of Texts: Practice and Theory of the Critical Edition of James Joyce's *Ulysses*." *TEXT* 1 (1984 for 1981), 305–326.

7. Interest in text processes and their exploration through critical theory are beginning to make it possible to think of editing Ezra Pound's *Cantos*. A preliminary discussion, though not often very close as yet to the hard, if elusive, textual facts, is gathering momentum. A recent installment is the "Coda" to Jerome J. McGann, "*Ulysses* as a Postmodern Text: The Gabler Edition." *Criticism*, 27 (1984–85), 283–306. Highly stimulating in its theoretic implications is the monograph by Christine Froula, *To Write Paradise: Style and Error in Pound's* Cantos. New Haven and London: Yale University Press, 1984.

This paper is substantially unchanged from the version delivered at the STS conference in New York on 26 April 1985. I wish to thank the Deutsche Forschungsgemeinschaft for a travel grant out of funds of the German Foreign Department to aid my attendance at the conference.

Genetic Editing, Past and Future:
A Few Reflections by a User

Louis Hay

Translated by J. M. Luccioni
and
Hans Walter Gabler

The questions raised by genetic editing—the kind of editing that aims to offer readers a "work in progress"—cut across most of the themes of this convention, and first of all its main topic, the limits of pluralism and the limits of uniformity. The breadth of this questioning is itself a token of current renewals in editorial debate. Starting from some highly technical research about how to reconstruct and present the genesis of a text, the debate now abuts onto some fundamental questions, both in scholarly and in cultural terms, concerning the objectives and aims of editing. The trend is still a recent one, but it revives an old tradition springing from the very beginnings of the editing of modern texts. Thus it may be useful to take a second look at some of the lessons the history of our subject has taught us.

The Genesis of Genesis

The premisses on which every present-day enterprise is predicated were first laid down more than a century and a half ago, in the wake of a vast stirring of change both in politics and in the world of ideas. The study of national literatures took new flight from the awakening of patriotic feeling in early modern times, and it is not by accident that the first critical editions were published between the French revolutions of 1830 and 1848. History thus reminds us that editing has always embodied the main ideological and cultural concerns of its day. Current events on both sides of the Atlantic point the same way: I need only mention the part played by manuscripts and by editorial ventures in the National Heritage Year which France organised in the early eighties; or again the recent decision by ten European and Latin-American governments to join in promoting a great series of contemporary Latin-American writing.

Institutionally, the past has left a mark which is equally plain to see today. In the nineteenth century it was the "Springtime of nations" which set the works of each nation's great writers on a plane with those of the ancient classics. This gave their manuscripts right of entry into the state archives and libraries, and this vast influx of collections has been gathering momentum ever since. It is these that have come to form the foundations for the new "genetic criticism"; without them, it would be just another theory. From the outset, critical editing ran parallel with the growth of collections, and its crowning achievement (though in fact more in a symbolic than in a scholarly sense) was the celebrated Sophien-Ausgabe of Goethe's works. This edition, produced by the accumulated labours of some seventy scholars, appeared from 1887 to 1919, as if to bridge the turn of the century, and it may be considered a prototype for any exhaustive, definitive edition of an author's complete works. The impact of the ambition it betokens may be felt to this day.

Thus at the turn of the century manuscripts and editions had become the acknowledged symbols for a culture; they shared its monumental quality: the great editions of Goethe and Herder were contemporary with the erection of the "Goethe- und Schiller-Archiv" in Weimar, and with Victor Hugo's vast bequest to the Paris Bibliothèque Nationale which, he said, "will one day be the library of the United States of Europe." But in spite of the remarkable achievements of a few forerunners in the twenties and thirties, not until the half-century mark did editing and manuscript really come together in such a way as to give birth to a common offspring of their union, a new kind of scholarly object: the text as it grows. This conjunction is generally thought to date from the great edition of Hölderlin's works by Friedrich Beissner, starting in 1943. By making the temporal dimension of the process of writing visible through the way he presented the variants, Beissner at a single stroke initiated genetic editing and thus, in short, modern European editing. From then on, in fact, the history of editing and that of the treatment of variants are essentially one and the same thing. For several decades after that, the great editions of German-speaking authors have been, as it were, the laboratory in which this new editorial way was being worked out.

The Germanic Laboratory

We shall not here retell the history of that period, fascinating though it is; a number of studies have already been written about it. For my purpose it will be enough to offer a few quite general remarks.

The first is about the cultural implications of such enterprises. For they are still revealed by editors' thought processes, even if the debates in the twentieth century are mainly about theory. Take F. Beissner's "stepped" apparatus: the observation could not fail to be made that it implies a teleological view of the author's working methods, in keeping with Goethe's concept of the writer "working unremittingly towards what is better." Fifteen years later, Hans Zeller adopts and perfects the same type of apparatus, but his perspective is appreciably different: the stress is no longer on the author's intentions but on the structure of the text; the whole set of permutations of variants is taken into account with all its potential for textual filiation and convergence; and synoptic display assumes its position alongside lemmatized listings, or "steps."[1]

Another fifteen years later, the edition of Klopstock's works takes its departure from a theoretical frame of reference of yet another kind. It tries to show that genesis has both a communicative function and a function as a means of aesthetic articulation. To that end, its apparatus displays what you might describe as a semiotic figuration of the speech act.[2] Many more examples could be brought to bear confirming the importance of the theoretical (even sometimes ideological) attitudes assumed by successive editors. The main point is after all obvious: the scholars in charge of the editions are literary historians and critics by training, and their editorial practice also expresses the results of their thinking on theory. In fact, for that same reason, the fast-moving theoretical evolution of contemporary criticism tends to question the very model of a canonical, *ne varietur* edition. We shall see in a moment that this model is being undermined in several ways.

For the nonce a second remark is to be made: the growing significance of genesis shows through every shift of theory, to the extent of forming as it were a connecting thread. Though F. Beissner's apparatus shows variants only as "steps" toward the "definitive" text, Hans Zeller's apparatus already displays them in their own right and only presents (in bold type) the final state of each version; in turn, the Klopstock edition reproduces the process of genesis as a continuous one and, in certain of its volumes, disclaims any attempt at a distinction between genesis and definitive text; finally, of the latest editions—Hölderlin for instance and Kafka as well—each in its way only strengthens the same trend.[3]

Thus the Germanic laboratory has shown the way for genetic criticism. But, and this is one of those paradoxes that stand out here and there in the history of our subject, genetic criticism has not fully benefitted from its editions. This is partly for technical reasons: genesis presented in apparatus typography does not always lend itself easily to analysis. But there is also here a quirk of history: just when the editing of German texts was taking this turn, German-language criticism was mainly preoccupied with problems of a sociological nature. Only from the early seventies, and at first only in France, has there been a concentration of interest upon the processes of writing. This development has its own reasons and its own history, but they cannot be discussed here. I only point to the outcome: the appearance, from the early seventies onwards, of a new trend in criticism, new types of editions and new exchanges between editors from different countries.

Current Problems and Models

The latest genetic editions appear clearly definable by their common outlook: aimed at a public interested in genesis itself, they respond to the new scholarly and commercial possibilities that such an interest offers. So they often publish *manuscripts*, that is manuscripts by themselves, in editions which no longer work toward a *printed* text. Their common aim marks out these editions as a sharply-defined class; but their techniques and procedures vary considerably.

The simplest and oldest mode is, of course, that of facsimile reproduction. For more than a century this kind of edition has served a public of autograph lovers, only we may observe that the collector is now offered a choice extending from the neat hand-written fair copy to the most scribbled-over draft. But the decisive fact is that now this kind of edition is given a new lease of life by appealing to an altogether different public, that of researchers, to whom it makes available reproductions of documents scattered over many places or otherwise difficult of access. The recent example of the *James Joyce Archive* is an excellent illustration of the speed attained through modern reproduction techniques, and also of the sales success which may attend a very large facsimile edition, even at a high price.[4]

On this basis, after such an important technical investment, one is tempted to follow up with a philological achievement of the same magnitude, by adding to the reproduction a transcription of the manuscript, especially when the facsimile or even the original is exceptionally difficult to read. Figures 1 to 3 exemplify that kind of work, in this case by an Italian team on a Flaubert manuscript for a French publisher.[5] The system of diacritics used would in itself deserve a technical discussion which, however, cannot be entered into here; moreover, it is well known that the typographic transliteration of complex manuscripts often allows only approximate solutions. However, what must be stressed is the extraordinary feat of deciphering accomplished by the editors, which probably explains the commercial success of their enterprise. As a result, other editions of that kind are currently being prepared, primarily devoted to particularly difficult documents; the facsimile often figures only as a selection of representative samples.

In this field a new experiment was recently undertaken in the re-editing of Joyce's *Ulysses*.[6] H. W. Gabler and his international team took advantage of the specific structure of the genetic documentation in this case, consisting of numerous distinct documents: they applied to it, in an original fashion, both the method and the technique used by modern editions of mediaeval texts. That is, computer treatment was used to establish automatically a classification of those various textual elements and to present side by side a view of the genesis and an "archetypal" reconstruction of the text (see Figures 4 and 5).

Finally, another kind of experiment was performed in the editing of Proust, also by using the characteristics of the manuscript documents, which are quite different from Joyce's. The documents were the notebooks for *Le Temps Retrouvé* (the final part of *Remembrance of Things Past*), which allow for fairly continuous reading. H. Bonnet and B. Brun have edited those manuscripts with a simplified apparatus (Figures 6 and 7), in a purely literary, widely-sold series.[7] Their project (to allow the general public to follow a writer's working processes) achieved significant success: the edition sold out swiftly and had to go into a second printing.

SIGNES EMPLOYÉS
DANS LA TRANSCRIPTION

italique : variantes interlinéaires

$\uparrow$ variantes en interligne supérieur, 1ère campagne

$\uparrow$ variantes en interligne supérieur, 2ème campagne

$\uparrow$ variantes en interligne supérieur, 3ème campagne

$\uparrow$ variantes en interligne supérieur, 4ème campagne

$\int$ variantes en interligne inférieur, 1ère campagne

$\int$ variantes en interligne inférieur, 2ème campagne

$\int$ variantes en interligne inférieur, 3ème campagne

$\hookleftarrow$ ce qui précède le cran est en marge

$\hookrightarrow$ ce qui suit le cran déborde de la marge

<...>   ratures

l/sa   surcharge

[...]   reconstitution, entière ou partielle, d'un mot

[...]   crochets remplaçant ceux de Flaubert

*   lecture conjecturale

‖   fin de ligne

GIOVANNI BONACCORSO ET COLLABORATEURS
CORPUS FLAUBERTIANUM
.I.
UN CŒUR SIMPLE

SOCIÉTÉ D'ÉDITION «LES BELLES LETTRES»
95, Boulevard Raspail · 75006 PARIS

Figure 1

UN CŒUR SIMPLE					285

---

†aucun changemt mais			A. dut renouveler toute la provision de charbon>. l'été <de
c'était une diversion			1827> †suivant <M• ‖ Aubain> offrir le pain bénit. <†en x M' B
D'autres petits				un hiver tout cela †les occupait> ∫avait l'importance d'un <[ill.]>
événemts				∫événemt, <faisait entre ‖ la maîtresse α la servante des sujets
					de conversation> ∫a faisaient des dates où l'on se reportait quand
qui faisaient des dates			on voulait se rappeler qque chose. – <Ou bien au ‖ printemps
où l'on se reportait			on parlait des jours qui commençaient à s'allonger[8] ‖ à l'au-
					tomne de la nuit qui arrivait †tombait plutôt. on attendait ‖
					les g^dᵉˢ fêtes. Noël, le jour de l'an, Pasques, la ‖ Fête-Dieu,
					les processions>

> 1 L'ajout est à l'interligne précédent.
> 2 Terme en surcharge.
> 3 Le morphème du singulier surcharge celui du pluriel.
> 4 Ce dernier terme est plus bas.
> 5 L'ajout, de la seconde campagne, est au niveau de la ligne.
> 6 Trois traits obliques barrent, en outre, tout ce paragraphe.
> 7 La ligne reprend ici un degré plus haut.
> 8 Cette ligne et la précédente sont en outre barrées par une douzaine de traits obliques.

171. VI. Ib.[1] (321v).

α^a elle s'accusait ‹affr›			†‹de trouver un moyen de la cacher› ensemble ‖ alors ils cherchaient à
voulait la g/reprendre			voir la pl †‹une cachette †de la cacher †*porter› ∫qque part

‹affr› constitut[ion] de			Le désespoir de M• Aubain fut illimité, profond †[<α *violent,
la sienne				violent †âcre> persistant.
					D'abord elle se révolta contre Dieu, †le trouvant injuste
‹de lui›				[†<*son que la Providence ‖ l'eut punie |†d'> avoir pris †sa
					fille à elle qui jamais n'avait fait l/de mal| α dont la conscien-
ψ^a gémissait				ce ‖ était si pure.
criait, la nuit				<Puis elle s'accusa. †*aurait du moins †[2 ill.]> ∫Mais non. Elle
					aurait dû †‹peut-être la mener †conduire ∫conduire> †conduire
il^b y avait ‹bien peut-			tout de suite <en Provence> †dans le Midi – ‖ < *s'irritant [de]
être †des d'autres› †d'au-			s'empêtrer dans des conditions accessoires. Peut-être que d'au-
tres ∫‹des				tres †des> ‖ médecins †‹de Paris ∫plus forts l'eussent> ∫l'auraient
il^b devait y avoir› des			sauvé[e]. ∫<car Il y ét des [ill.] à Paris †il y avait d'autres †d'au-
remèdes ‹certains› ∫cer-			tres> †remèdes ∫bien sûr, mais †<α> non puisque ‖ la pauvre
tains					enfant tenait <sa mauvaise constitution> †cette <affreuse santé>

Figure 2

PLANCHE XXI   f. 171. Désespoir de Mme Aubain, premier brouillon.

Figure 3

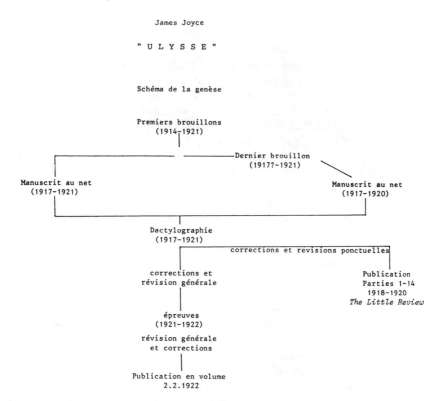

James Joyce

" U L Y S S E "

Schéma de la genèse

Premiers brouillons
(1914-1921)

Dernier brouillon
(1917?-1921)

Manuscrit au net
(1917-1921)

Manuscrit au net
(1917-1920)

Dactylographie
(1917-1921)

corrections et revisions ponctuelles

corrections et
révision générale

Publication
Parties 1-14
1918-1920
The Little Review

épreuves
(1921-1922)

révision générale
et corrections

Publication en volume
2.2.1922

Figure 4

By its very diversity, this "new generation" of genetic editions casts a light upon the multiplicity of requirements which condition such productions, including the nature of the source documents, of the chosen public and of the techniques used. To these factors which in every case act in the here and now, must be added the historical transformations we mentioned at the outset. Collections have become richer at an increasing rate in the course of the last quarter-century, so much so that most reference books need to be recast, whether they be editions or histories of literature. As for the evolution of ideas, the debate about the most basic concepts: text, oeuvre, writing process, is lively enough to foreshadow the likely changes in editorial practice which will follow.

We are thus led to wonder if the discussion about the limits of pluralism and the limits of uniformity is not taking on a different meaning. Hitherto it used implicitly to stay within a frame of reference provided by the century-old model of the *ne varietur* edition, first appearing in an exhaustive version for scholars, then in

Afterwit. Go back.

The dour recluse still there ⌐(he has his cake)¬ and the douce youngling, minion of pleasure, Phedo's toyable fair hair.

Eh ... I just eh .... wanted ... I forgot ... eh ...

5 —Longworth and M'Curdy° Atkinson were there ...

⌐(B)[Buck] Puck(B)¬ Mulligan footed featly, trilling:

—*I* *hardly hear* ⌐*[a] the*¬ *purlieu cry*
Or a Tommy talk as I pass one by
Before my thoughts begin to run

10 *On F. M'Curdy* *Atkinson,*'
The same that had the wooden leg
And that filibustering filibeg°
That never dared to slake his drouth,°
Magee that had the chinless mouth.'°

15 ⌐*Being afraid to marry on earth*
They masturbated for all they were worth.¬

Jest on. Know thyself.

Halted,° below me, a quizzer looks at me. I halt.

—Mournful mummer, Buck Mulligan moaned. Synge has left off wearing

20 black to be like nature. Only crows, priests and English coal are black.

A laugh tripped over his lips.

—Longworth is awfully sick, he said, ⟨about that⟩ after what you wrote about that old hake Gregory. O you inquisitional drunken jewjesuit! She gets you a job on the paper and then you go and slate her ⌐[book] drivel¬ to

25 Jaysus. Couldn't you do the Yeats° touch?

He went on and down, ⌐mopping,¬ chanting with waving graceful arms:

—The most beautiful book that has come out of ⌐[Ireland°] our country¬ in my time. ⌐One thinks of Homer.¬

30 He stopped at the stairfoot.

—I have conceived a play ^for the mummers^, he said solemnly.

The pillared Moorish hall, shadows entwined. Gone the nine men's morrice with caps of indices.

⌐(B)[With] In(B)¬ sweetly varying voices Buck Mulligan read his tablet:

---

5 M'Curdy] (aW):tC; McCurdy aR   7-14 *I--mouth.*] aC; *NU* aR,tC   10 *M'Curdy Atkinson,*] (aW):tC *(NU)*; McCurdy Atkinson aR   12 *filibeg*] STET aR,(aW):tC *(NU)* 13 *drouth,*] a2; drouth aR; *drought,* tC-aC   14 *mouth.*] aR *(NU)*,a4; *mouth* ... (aW):tC-aC 18 Halted,] aR; Halted tC; *TD:* Malted 1; Halted a1   25 Yeats] aR,1932; Yeats' tC 28 Ireland] *TD: PHRASE ABSENT* 1

SIGLES

R⁰ : Recto (ou Folio avec F⁰).
V⁰ : Verso.
MR⁰ : Marge d'un Recto.
MV⁰ : Marge d'un Verso.
PR⁰ : Recto d'une paperole.
PV⁰ : Verso d'une paperole.
| | : entre crochets (pour les mots qui manquent ou pour les titres proposés).
  * : astérisque (après le mot au-dessus de la ligne) : interprétation douteuse.
...... : Lacune ou interruption.
*** : Mot non déchiffré (les signes sont placés sur la ligne).
**** : Plusieurs mots non déchiffrés.
  / : Point de départ d'un autre folio dans un texte continu.

L'*italique* est utilisé pour les indications données en tête des textes, notamment dans les « Notes pour *Le Temps retrouvé* ».

ABRÉVIATIONS

R.T.P. ou la Recherche pour *A la Recherche du Temps perdu.*
T.R. pour *Le Temps retrouvé.*
B.M.P. pour *Bulletin de la Société des Amis de Marcel Proust et des Amis de Combray.*
B.I.P. pour *Bulletin d'informations proustiennes.*
R.H.L.F. pour *Revue d'Histoire littéraire de la France.*

Figure 6

162   *Matinée chez la Princesse de Guermantes*

passent au fond de notre cœur, le premier [1] jour où la
jeune fille que nous aimons nous a parlé, celui où elle
nous a appelé par notre prénom, celui où elle nous a
laissé l'embrasser — nous ne cherchons pas à les

V° 17   connaître[2], | à élever à la lumière, à préserver du
néant ce qu'elles contiennent d'original, de si nouveau et de si doux, nous *** du résultat obtenu, nous

MR° 18   nous attachons au fait seul[3], | nous en détour-
nons les yeux, nous nous attachions tellement au
fait lui-même[4], purement utile et sans élément qua-
litatif ni durable, comme à un échelon que nous
avons réussi à saisir *[5] et qui nous rapproche d'un
bonheur plus grand où demain peut'être nous par-
viendrons. Nous reproduisons pourtant parfois en
nous par le souvenir le plaisir que nous avons eu sans
chercher à le voir plus clairement de sorte que quand

V° 17   nous n'aimons[6] | plus la jeune fille ces moments
sont anéantis alors que nous aurions dû en déga-
ger la réalité éternelle de l'amour qui a passé en nous

F° 18   grâce à elle[7]. | Quand Maria[8] m'avait pour la pre-
mière fois appelé par mon prénom, semblant ainsi
me dévêtir de toutes mes écorces et coques sociales,
et prendre ainsi mon être, avec délicatesse, entre ses
lèvres, qui lui faisaient éprouver le plus intime attou-
chement, avais-je cherché à éclaircir, c'est-à-dire, à
me rendre maître, de ce que cette joie avait de si
nouveau et de si doux. Non![9] ravi des espérances que
pouvait me donner ce premier succès je ne retenais
que le fait lui-même, ce rapport nouveau * existant

1. En chiffre.
2. La suite au Verso 17 (indiquée par un rond entourant une croix).
3. Proust ajoute dans une parenthèse non refermée : « voir en face la
suite. » Et nous revenons au texte situé en marge, Folio 18.
4. Renvoi au Verso 17 pour les sept mots qui suivent.
5. Mots douteux.
6. La suite au Verso 17.
7. Retour au texte principal, Folio 18.
8. Maria est une jeune fille en fleurs de la première version de la *Recherche*.
Son nom disparaît quand apparaît Albertine, en 1913.
9. Nous ajoutons le point d'exclamation.

Figure 7

a simplified version for a larger public, but still meant to last as a definitive production (and of course a printed one). Now during the latest period, which already has a long history behind it, other ideas have come forward to compete with the original model. These appear especially in the field of genetic editing, in which the thrust of new ways and new techniques is felt most directly.

Questions for the Future

Technological perspectives

The impact of modern technology upon genetic editing is felt on two levels. First, it concerns the concrete analysis of manuscript documents. In this field the gap between possibilities and actual applications is particularly wide. Though the Anglo-American school has developed the technical history of printing—"analytical bibliography"—into a fully-fledged auxiliary discipline in textual criticism, with brilliant results, the material analysis of manuscripts still does not always follow widely-agreed procedures. This explains how it is possible for some large editions now being published by world-famous scholarly institutions to carry inaccurate, even occasionally ludicrous descriptions of their documentation, together with all the consequent mistakes in interpretation. Of course there are positive counter-examples, from the annotated classification of paper in H. Zeller's edition of C. F. Meyer's works, to the trenchant paper analysis carried out by M. Pasley in the apparatus to Kafka's *The Castle* (to speak only of the two editions I have mentioned as situated at the beginning and end of the period). Still, on the whole, neither the analytical techniques (fairly simple though they be in most cases), nor the principles of the historical interpretation of their results, nor the methodology of how to use them in editing, are yet mastered with enough efficiency. Therefore their application is only gradually going to modify our approach to problems of classification (and consequently of establishing a text), localisation, and dating; the concrete documents of the work's genesis will be seen in a new light. This is even more true of the analysis of handwriting, upon which editors are only just now beginning to bring to bear the power of present-day optical and data-processing instruments. Here again the "archaeology of written documents" lags behind the techniques of archaeology proper. Here again, contemporary technology may help us resolve problems beyond our present reach: how to discover whose handwriting we are reading, untangle the puzzle of a date, map out the stages of a writer's creative activity. On this plane, briefly, the new techniques will bring information that is both additional and objective, information through which the editor's work can be checked and filled out. For us, a positive gain in knowledge will be the end result.

On another level, the textual one, there will be a parallel gain in expertise. This will be brought by the new applications of computer science, the two functions of which are shown by the example of the *Ulysses* edition. These functions are: a) the treatment of textual data (here, the classification of the various versions of the text that are extant); b) the reproduction and duplication of the results (here, the computerized printing program). In both fields the uses of the computer are becoming more numerous.

As regards the processing of data, the computer first makes it possible to gather data (such as variant loci, for instance) too numerous to be reasonably collected "by hand." But it can also *analyse* these data from various standpoints, thus transforming a quantitative count into a piece of substantial qualitative information. I will not dwell upon examples of this, since there are many such studies. As regards reproduction, the computer is a kind of gearing device which extends both in range of power, from the printer-assisted mini-computer to industrial-size machines controlled by programs for scholarly editing, and in range of applications, including not only printed texts but also on-screen presentation, not only for the book trade proper but also for the electronic dissemination of texts.

This is after all much more than a mere matter of machines. Yoking together text-processing and text-reproducing technologies will reverse the traditional editing process. Instead of starting from a certain idea of the *object* to be made—an edition of a work to which anyone may then refer—it will stem from a reflection about a certain type of *demand* (scholarly or cultural) to which the editor will tool the appropriate response. It is no longer a matter of technical possibilities, but of a whole set of intellectual problems.

Intellectual perspectives

I have just now sketched the logic of a "demand-led" editing process. It involves, of course, a whole train of practical consequences. It will especially answer the objection which some, in good faith or not, have been making against traditional editions, on the grounds that, the more specialised their public, the more exhaustive they must be, coming out in an ever-larger number of volumes for an ever-smaller number of readers. This paradox will be resolved by a wider application of contemporary techniques. For these will process any particular corpus in the particular way or ways required for any particular use, all the more so as research in genetic criticism seldom investigates thousands of pages at a time. The results of such analysing processes may be then reproduced on a printer (or shown or broadcast on a screen) whenever needed; the circulation figure may range, according to each new demand, from one to several hundred copies.

As far as genetic studies are concerned, it is probably in this field, that of specialist working tools, that the difference between traditional and computerized editing shows most sharply. This does not mean that the former will soon be replaced by the latter. Too many scientific, technical, and commercial factors come into play and make it impossible to forecast anything but the rise of new possibilities.

This is even clearer at a lower level, that of students' editions designed as reading texts. They illustrate a genesis without producing the materials which might allow the reader to reconstruct it on his own. Here, the mode of the discursive commentary will gain increasing importance. It provides the reader with a significant synthesis of the editor's factual observations, and experience confirms that such information is most likely to arouse the interest of students. According to the nature of the various manuscripts, such a presentation is completed by a simplified genetic apparatus (an aim already set out by H. Zeller a quarter of a century ago) and by a range of facsimiles selected for their illustrative value. By sketching such possibilities I do not mean to take sides in the controversy about objectivity, about the purported obligation on the editor's part to allow the reader to check his every choice and decision. This controversy has no relevance outside of scholarly editing, whereas I am now concerned with more widely-available student texts.

At the next level, that of editions meant for the general public, our experience does not go back very far yet. The example I have shown (see Figures 6 and 7) provides a lay-out (other lay-outs could certainly be proposed) through which one may, if the writer's working processes lend themselves to it, offer to satisfy anyone who

is curious enough to want to read the manuscripts. If I have any
doubts, it is how far we may at this moment forecast the extent of
such curiosity. In literary studies, and beyond them in the whole field
of the social sciences, there is a growing interest in what is sometimes
optimistically called the "science of creativity." Will this change
people's reading habits? Will future readers wish to follow a text as
it becomes itself? Does Julien Gracq speak for them when he writes:
"what we want is literature on the move, caught at the very moment
when it seems to be astir still . . . "? Upon such questions the future
of genetic editing will eventually depend.

Here we are back at our starting point: editing only confronts such
problems as are posed by the culture of the day; over a century and
a half it has produced ever-new solutions. In that regard, genetic
editing undoubtedly offers an excellent point of vantage from which
we may descry the outline of the changes that lie in wait for us
between now and the end of this century. In this future span, editions
will probably follow each other faster, take more varied forms, make
use of new technologies. But the very newness involved by such
mutations is a guarantee, if one were needed, that the editor's
function is a function with a future.

NOTES

1. Conrad Ferdinand Meyer: *Sämtliche Werke*, historisch-kritische Ausgabe,
   besorgt von Hans Zeller und Alfred Zäch, Bern, 1958 ff., Benteli-Verlag.

2. Friedrich Gottlieb Klopstock: *Werke und Briefe*, historisch-kritische Ausgabe,
   begründet von Adolf Beck, Karl-Ludwig Schneider und Hermann Tiemann,
   herausgegeben von Horst Gronemeyer, Elisabeth Höpker-Herberg, Klaus
   Hurlebusch, Rose-Maria Hurlebusch, Berlin, New York, 1974 ff., Walter de
   Gruyter.

3. Friedrich Hölderlin: *Sämtliche Werke*, 'Frankfurter Ausgabe', historisch-
   kritische Ausgabe herausgegeben von D. E. Sattler, Frankfurt, 1975 ff., Verlag
   Roter Stern. Franz Kafka: *Schriften, Tagebücher, Briefe*, kritische Ausgabe,
   herausgegeben von Jürgen Born, Gerhard Neumann, Malcolm Pasley und Jost
   Schillemeit unter Beratung von Nahum Glaser, Rainer Gruener, Paul Raabe
   und Marthe Robert, Frankfurt, 1982 ff., S. Fischer.

4. *The James Joyce Archive*, general editor Michael Groden, associated editors
   Hans Walter Gabler, David Hayman, A. Walton Litz, Denis Rose, New York
   and London, 1977, Garland Publishing, Inc.

5. *Corpus flaubertianum*, 1 *Un Coeur simple*, en appendice édition diplomatique et génétique des manuscrits, édité par Giovanni Bonnacorso, Maria Francesca Davi-Trimarchi, Simonetta Micale, Eliane Contaz-Sframeli, Paris, 1983, Belles-Lettres.

6. James Joyce: *Ulysses*, a critical and synoptic edition, prepared by Hans Walter Gabler with Wolfhard Steppe and Claus Melchior, New York and London, 1984, 3 vol., Garland Publishing, Inc.

7. Marcel Proust: *Matinée chez la Princesse de Guermantes*, Cahiers du *Temps retrouvé*, edition critique établie par Henri Bonnet en collaboration avec Bernard Brun, Paris, 1982, Nrf Gallimard.

Rough Drafts: A Challenge to Uniformity in Editing

JEAN-LOUIS LEBRAVE

Dealing with rough drafts (*brouillons*, *Arbeitsmanuskripte*), and more generally speaking, with documents that are part of the *"avant-textes,"* such as plans, preparatory notes, sketches, rough drafts, and so on, raises specific problems related to the nature of the material. Notions inherited from the tradition of textual studies are here misleading. As was shown once by Louis Hay,[1] the traditional concept of *text* is based upon two oppositions: one between text and comment (or translation), the other between text and existing copies of that text. The main purpose of criticism is to establish or re-establish the text itself through the multiple deformations it encountered in its historical life. This implies that the text by itself exists, as an object the uniqueness and perfection of which is not affected by change and history. Historical change starts beyond the text itself. Confrontation of this object to the data shown in avant-textes led Hay to the provocative statement that "the text does not exist": the text has a history, it is the result of a series of complex temporal processes. Textual production is discontinuous, heterogeneous, imperfect.[2] Similar statements can be made upon writing, which, instead of aiming primarily at reproducing existing textual material, becomes a tool to produce text that did not exist before and is ruled by original functions like going backwards or correcting. As such, writing can no longer be considered as just an extension of human memory for textual treasuries of the past: it becomes also a memory for the process of text production itself. How can this 'genetic memory' be read? What kind of a model can be built to represent these original characteristics? Which results can be expected from such a study? Such are the points which I would like to develop briefly.

Rough drafts contain textual data and as such show the one-dimensional linear structure of normal texts, which corresponds to the structure of standard spoken language.[3] But at the same time, they bear witness to the concrete temporal structure of writing and text production, which allows pauses, interruptions, corrections, and can literally break text into pieces. As a result, the written page is two-dimensional, and the main problem arising is to reconstruct how the chronology of writing interferes with the sequential structure of text, and to separate those two temporal lines so as to make the genetic time visible through the textual data.

Basically, two solutions can be thought of, depending upon the complexity of the genetic process. If one has to work with 'late' stages of text production, like typescripts, proofs, various editions—in other words, if one does not have to deal primarily with complex rough drafts—it is possible to use a one-dimensional model, where the text simply contains embedded variants. Such is, for example, the solution adopted by Hans Walter Gabler for his edition of *Ulysses*. It has many advantages, mainly because it does not break the linear structure of text and allows continuous reading. But conversely, it implies that the text can be used as a "red garn" to organize the material, or that there is such a thing as a final text to which all data can be referred. Unfortunately, this is generally not the case with more complex genetic material, in which not all textual fragments can be related directly to a final version and the number of variants is so high that having them embedded within the text would lead to a rapid decrease of readability. In that latter case, one has to find a more specific model, where the two dimensions of text genesis are taken into account.

The system I am using[4] is based upon reconstructing the basic writing operations from their traces in the manuscripts and ordering the results of these operations according to the chronology of text production. As a result, the genetic data are treated as a stream of text—corresponding to continuous writing—which is interrupted every time a different genetic operation occurs—like adding, suppressing, or replacing. From a technical point of view, it can be seen as extending the linguistic concept of substitution through chronological ordering. Once the data have been given that structure, they are fed into a computer in machine-readable form and submitted to various treatments, the first of which produces an edition of the rough draft. Figure 1 shows a sample from Marcel Proust's early drafts for what will become *A la recherche du temps perdu*. Figure 2 shows a so-called diplomatic transcript of this material. Last comes in Figure 3 the output of the editing program.

Figure 1. A rough draft by Marcel Proust. (Paris, Bibliothèque Nationale, N.A.Fr., 16643l. Cahier 3. Folio 8 recto).

"J'avais du m'endormir assez brusquement, et sans garder avec§
"moi le plan de la chambre§
  "m'endormir assez brusquement§
"j'avais du§ "être supris§ "par§ le sommeil et§ "sans avoir le§
"temps de§ "oublié de§ "J'avais du m'endormir assez brusquement§
"Le sommeil avait du me prendre assez brusquement à un moment où j'avais laissé un instant "xx§ tomber de ma pensée le plan du lieu où je me trouvais; quand je m'éveillai je l'avais perdu; je ne savais pas où je me trouvais

Figure 2. Diplomatic transcript of the rough draft shown in Figure 1.

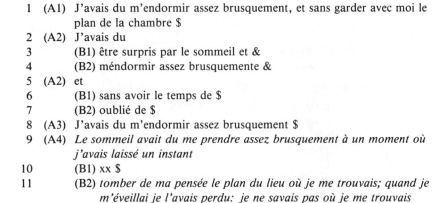

```
 1  (A1)  J'avais du m'endormir assez brusquement, et sans garder avec moi le
          plan de la chambre $
 2  (A2)  J'avais du
 3        (B1) être surpris par le sommeil et &
 4        (B2) méndormir assez brusquemente &
 5  (A2)  et
 6        (B1) sans avoir le temps de $
 7        (B2) oublié de $
 8  (A3)  J'avais du m'endormir assez brusquement $
 9  (A4)  Le sommeil avait du me prendre assez brusquement à un moment où
          j'avais laissé un instant
10        (B1) xx $
11        (B2) tomber de ma pensée le plan du lieu où je me trouvais; quand je
          m'éveillai je l'avais perdu: je ne savais pas où je me trouvais
```

Figure 3. Output of the editing program for the manuscript above.[5]

The main purpose of this work is not to bring out another system for just editing rough drafts—even if an edition can be a useful intermediate result—but to take into account the structure of genetic data in order to master the complexity of the material and produce specific hypotheses on writing. From this point of view, chronologically ordered substitutions provide a useful tool in that they represent an acceptable generalization and can be easily computed. I would now like to indicate briefly what kind of results can be expected from such a treatment.

Once the heterogeneous data contained in rough drafts have been filtered and organized in form of substitutions, the next step is to extract those and build up a dictionary which contains all 'variants' of a given group of rough drafts, sorted in alphabetical order. Figure 4 shows a sample for such a dictionary: it shows substitutions as they appear in the 'avant-textes' of H. Heine's *Lutezia*.

```
----------------
1: ha< $
2: besitzt $
5700936-5700937
----------------

----------------
1: habe &
2: trage &
8900056-8900057
----------------
```

```
1: haben &
2: gewinnen &
9200812-9200813
--------------
--------------
1: haben &
2: in der Brust tragen &
5501380-5501381
--------------
--------------
1: haben &
2: besitzen &
8800239-8800240
--------------
--------------
1: haben &
2: kennen &
3: besitzen &
8800275-8800277
--------------
--------------
1: hat &
2: besitzt &
0400251-0400252
--------------
--------------
1: hat &
2: besitzt &
6100627-6100628
--------------
--------------
1: hat &
2: findet &
5200015-5200016
--------------
--------------
1: hat &
2: hat &
8600878-8600879
--------------
--------------
1: hat &
2: bietet &
3300458-3300459
--------------
```

Figure 4. A page from the dictionary of substitutions for *Lutezia*. [6]

How can such a dictionary be used? Of course, it can be used simply for documentation purposes, such as finding out where a given variant takes place or looking up all substitutions involving a given word. This minimal use does go beyond standard applications in processing machine-readable texts. Moreover, it forms a base for a more specific analysis where variants are compared to each other and sorted out according to the change they represent (for example, changes in tense, in mood, replacement of a word by the same, etc.). Furthermore, it gives insight into phenomena that would remain invisible in a normal approach to the data. I would like to describe briefly such a case, as it appears in H. Heine's drafts for *Lutezia*.

If one goes through the dictionary of variants corresponding to those drafts, a striking fact appears that would remain invisible without the coding and automatic processing of the data: whereas most lexical items involved in substitutions appear only a few times (mostly one or two items) in the dictionary and are indifferently replacing another item or being replaced by a new item, there are a few items, like *gross, haben, sein, bilden*, etc., that appear with a relatively high frequency (from 50 to 100 times) and are most likely to be replaced by another word rather than being replacement words themselves. From a semantic point of view, it is obvious that *gross, haben*, etc. have a very vague and general meaning, whereas the words by which they are replaced, like *ausserordentlich, frappant, genial*, have a much more specific meaning and are quite adjusted to the context in which they fit. The substitution involving these words appears to be non-symmetrical.

One could object that the fact I am describing simply reflects another obvious fact: *gross* or *haben* are very common words in German, so the chances of their entering a substitution have to be much bigger than those of less frequent items. But this would explain only why *gross* or *haben* occur so frequently in Heine's writing, not why the corresponding variants are non-symmetrical. Various answers can be thought of: one can imagine, for example, that Heine, like a mediocre student, tends to use many vague and improper words and that he has hard work eliminating those items. A more flattering hypothesis would be the following: in the first stage of text production, Heine—who is known for writing directly "from scratch," without prior plans or sketches—writes a text which is not equally elaborated in all its parts: it contains elements that are simply markers for an adjective or verb-to-be and could be interpreted as: "here, a verb of existence has to come," or "this noun has to be qualified by an adjective meaning high degree," etc. In the next stage—re-reading and correcting—Heine fills out those empty places and puts an appropriate word. Such an explanation is not contradictory to what we know of Heine's writing techniques: for example, his manuscripts quite often contain sentences that appear twice: once as a scratched fragment, and a second time, a few lines (sometimes a few pages) later, as definitive text. It does not seem that they just appear 'too early', it is more likely to suppose that Heine wrote them down first, as a text-to-be, then worked on the intermediate text, and scratched the first occurrence of the sentence once he reached his 'aim'. I do not know if this writing device is specific to Heine or if it is more general, but according to A. Levine it seems that Byron also used to write things "in advance."[7]

This example shows what can be looked for in *avant-textes*: an insight into the process of text production itself; and as such they are of unique value, since they contain information which no text will ever contain. But it also shows what price one has to pay in order to find something in *avant-textes*. In many respects, *avant-textes* are too rich, too heterogeneous, too complex to be accessible all at once. Critical editions intend to make them available and allow anybody to read and analyze the material, but I think it would be a utopia to hope that an edition—as precise and perfect as may be—could support any kind of research or analysis. It operates like a filter: every time it selects something in the manuscript, some information is retrieved and becomes part of an abstract interpretation of the data. So it is a step toward the analysis of the data. But at the same time, it loses part of its original complexity in order to fit into that specific construction which aims at a specific result, and it is not available any further for different research unless one goes back to the original. In that sense, rough drafts raise a problem for any kind of textual criticism, as can be seen in the fact that for most purposes, one needs not only an edition, but also a facsimile and a transcription of this facsimile, and even facsimiles happen to be far from an exact reproduction of the original. So what should be done?

A solution would be to have many different editions available, that is, many readings of the data, each one corresponding to a specific construction and aiming at a specific purpose. Something like an apparatus of apparatus. This is certainly impossible under traditional book form. But it might be considered with recent computer technology: a multi-media data base, giving access to facsimiles, to various transcriptions, to interpretational tools, like dictionaries or programs for automatic comparison of textual fragments.[8] Such a pluralistic system would allow any reader to construct his own reading according to the hypothesis he wants to build up. It may sound like another dream of technological utopia, but are these dreams not the only possible answer to the challenge launched by *avant-textes*?

NOTES

1. Louis Hay, "Le texte n'existe pas," *Poétique* 1985. The opposition between text and commentary can be best exemplified by the text of the Bible, as seen in the following definition, quoted by L. Hay: "Text is technically applied to any passage quoted from the text of the Scripture, as a subject of discourse or sermon."

2. Since "*avant-texte*" contains the word "text," its use can be misleading. On the evolution of the concept of text, see L. Hay, op. cit. For a discussion of the concept of text as discontinuous material, see J. L. Lebrave, "L'écriture interrompue: quelques problèmes théoriques." To appear in 1985.

3. For European languages, transposing this structure into a graphical form "consiste à disposer les lettres de chaque mot et les mots de chaque ligne de gauche à droite, les lignes de chaque page de haut en bas, et les pages de chaque volume de gauche à droite" (Beauzée, *Grammaire générale*, p. 127 of the 1819 edition).

4. See J. L. Lebrave, "Le traitement automatique des brouillons." *Programmation et Sciences Humaines*, 3 (special issue). Paris, 1984.

5. 'xx' stands for undeciphered letters. Incomplete words are terminated by '<'. '$' indicates immediate correcting, '&' a correction which occurred after the main writing phase. Final text is italicized. Lines are numbered for reference purposes.

6. The numbers refer to the lines of the editing program output.

7. A. Levine. Paper presented at the Third STS Conference: "Policies and Procedures in Editing the Manuscripts of the Younger Romantics."

8. An experimental version of such an editing system has been presented by R. Laufer and the *Paragraph* group of the Paris VIII University for all editions of the *Maximes* published before La Rochefoucault's death. Four windows contain different versions of a single maxime. The software also compares the text of these versions and underlines differences.

"Relic" and "Tradition": Some Aspects of Editing Diaries[1]

KLAUS HURLEBUSCH

It is a well-known fact that diaries, as far as their contents are concerned, represent a very flexible kind of literary genre. Their various forms can only roughly be described by stressing certain more predominant internal aspects, like *journal intime*, diary of events and experiences, diary of works in progress.[2]

In this paper I am mainly concerned with the type of diary for which Friedrich Gottlieb Klopstock's *work journal* (*Arbeitstagebuch*) can be taken as a good example. In my critical edition[3] I have called Klopstock's diary (which is part of the Klopstock papers deposited in the State and University Library in Hamburg, West Germany) a *work journal* because almost three quarters of its contents are devoted to notes on literary works and to text sketches. The diary does not give any evidence of self-examination, of confessions, confidences, or reflection, usually found in diaries of a contemplative nature. The 72 folios of notes form a genuine diary in the sense that they show the author's unmistakable intention of recording something for each day of the period covered. The entries are partly report—often no more than a single word or a stereotypically unfinished sentence like "Changed," "Into town," "Started XI canto"—and partly sketches of literary texts; and report and sketches are interchanged daily or spread over several days. And although Klopstock's *work journal* is no intimate document, it was a private one, a document not intended for publication. The private sphere, however, was not confined to Klopstock alone, it included at least his wife Margareta. To prevent uninitiated intelligence of certain topics, these had to be recorded in code. There are several examples of this in the diary.[4] Certain editorial problems of Klopstock's *work journal* can surely—mutatis mutandis—be found in other diaries with similar characteristics, e.g. preservation in manuscript form as part of a literary estate, chronological entries according to a calendar which is an unmistakable feature of a diary,[5] definition as a diary of events and experiences or works in progress, and "privatization" of certain topics in the form of a code.[6] Generally speaking, the problems connected with diary editions— scholarly editions that is—are not confined to diaries alone; they apply equally to editions of literary works and of letters, and they include the question of adequate text rendering, of text constitution, the representation of variants and versions, and of dating and commentary. The peculiarity of diary editions consists in a shifting of emphasis towards the greater importance of text rendering and text explanation and in their greater interdependence. This charac- teristic change in standard editorial procedures can go so far that new solutions may have to be found for each individual diary. Obvious measures to solve editorial tasks are even less appropriate for this form of document than for any other. Diaries are less likely to fit into usual editorial schemes than editions of literary texts or letters. For greater clarification I shall now try to differentiate between these various groups of documents.

Unpublished letters and diaries are generally considered to be related documents,[7] and editorially they do form a separate entity. Letters and diaries, supplemented by records, tracts, etc., are seen as documents of an author's life style, derived from it and destined for it. Literary and scholarly works, on the other hand, are usually given significance beyond the material and temporal limitations and experiences of an author's life span. In this context one could perhaps introduce certain critical terms, well established in German historical research, namely "relic" and "tradition."[8] These terms emphasize the purpose of the document, the intention of the person behind it. Consequently, it could be argued that unedited diaries and letters are part of the "relic" group of documents, not intended for transmission by the writer, whereas texts transmitted in printed form or in a form destined for publication belong to the "tradition" group, with the author's intention of publication beyond any doubt.

There are, of course, overlapping cases, where *published* letters and diaries gain a new importance.[9] They become part of "tradi- tion," with their original value as "relic" more or less intact. Letters and diaries are related documents in the sense that their *raison d'être* usually does not extend beyond an author's lifetime. Their main difference lies in the fact that they relate to different aspects of a person's life: letters reflect the relationship with other people,[10] diaries one's own existence. As documents of an interpersonal aspect of life, letters show their writer's relation to social norms and conventions as well as the expectations and the knowledge he presumes in the recipient. Traces of these considerations appear on every level of the document, in format, material, and type-face just as much as in the style of the text.[11] The genuine diary, on the other hand, the private one, originally not intended for public consumption, presents an altogether different case: the diarist has absolute freedom, he need consider neither a recipient nor a reader, as in the case of a literary text.

The diarist can take liberties which might cause consternation, disapproval, and even a complete breakdown in communications between the letter writer and its recipient. A diary can contain linguistic anomalies, grammatical, stylistic, and orthographical negligence and irregularities, without the diarist having to fear misunderstandings or sanctions. This freedom in contents and form is surely the reason for the immense variety of the diary as a literary genre, which has been accused of being without form and art on account of its incoherence.[12] What distinguishes diaries from notebooks, from mere collections of notes,[13] limits at the same time the possibilities of their privatization: the orientation on universally valid measures of time, especially the use of a calendar.[14] The all-important feature of the diary is the arrangement of the diary entries in chronological order, the adjustment of an individual experience of time to its universal definition. The diary cannot simply reproduce the contents and form of the individual experience of time. The necessity to reduce the period between experience and report to its minimum forces the diarist to adopt a close, recollective attitude towards his past experiences. The recollections are temporalized, and this is not without consequence for their internal coherence, for their significance in the author's consciousness. The structural tension between original and diaristic experience of time can become so considerable that the writer interrupts his entries, breaks off completely, or changes to reflection, which can even happen to exceptionally chronistic diarists like Samuel Pepys, Goethe, or Arthur Schnitzler. And Klopstock's *work journal* is no exception in this respect.

In editing diaries, how can their criteria as "relics," their freedom of expression and privatization, their chronological structuring of individual experience of time be represented by the editor? With reference to the heuristic analysis of the type of document recognized as a "diary," the editorial task can be defined as follows: private diaries must be edited in a way which preserves their individuality and uniqueness as documents of non-intended transmission while maintaining as far as possible the conventions of text rendering and readability which belong to the area of "tradition" documents.

In the second part of my paper I should like to draw attention to those problems in my work on Klopstock's *work journal* which resulted directly from the characteristics of diaries already discussed, i.e. problems of text rendition, of critical text constitution, and of commentary.

Text rendering. Nearly all entries in Klopstock's *work journal* have a proper date in the form of year, month, and day. Similarly, all passages concerning poetry and prose works are headed by a date, or more accurately, the original entries are, but not the later, sometimes manifold revisions. Often remarks about events of the day were added at a later stage, with a lesser or greater lapse of time between the date of the incident itself and its entry in the diary. In the text rendering a method had to be found which allowed the presentation of the relevant chronological findings. The genetic method of text rendering, developed for the Klopstock edition in general, seemed appropriate. This method consists of a transcription which includes all textual variations authorized by the author and given in their proper sequence of time. The conceptual foundations and editorial details of the genetic text rendering are explained elsewhere.[15] In this context I merely want to draw attention to its immense informative value. Literary texts are included in the *work journal* as integral parts, and they represent directly and in their entirety the work process to which there are references in the rest of the diary in the form of clues and quotations. We not only know how many days it took the author to write the essay 'On Expression' ('Vom Ausdruck'), we also know which paragraphs he wrote which particular day, but we cannot be sure when he made changes other than those effected during the actual writing of the text itself. He may have made certain changes the same day, or at a later date when he mentions revisions of the essay in the diary, or even after a considerable period of time. Given the complex nature of the diary manuscript it is, therefore, impossible to establish the exact stage of a text as it existed on a specific day.

The traditional editorial arrangement of a genetic homogenous text on one side (the basic text or last version) and—set apart—the variants on the other could not be used in this case because it would have led to misinterpretation. For instance, if one were to edit a text in the last version distinguishable in the manuscript, but not dated as such, with the date of its first entry in the diary, one would certainly give a very wrong impression of the achievement of that particular day, as changes were introduced later, and one would also date later versions in the wrong way.[16] The genetic text rendering liberates the editor from the impossible decision whether changes other than those made during the actual process of writing are of the same day or not. All variants are diacritically marked as additions or non-specifically datable variations, as potentially later additions. Because of the need to account for the chronological sequence of variations, this method seemed preferable to a mere diplomatic transcription. The genetic text rendering is supplemented by an apparatus of footnotes which gives information on the differences—if any—between the time for which an event is recorded and when it was actually written down, and it also records information on the manuscript and the text, such as graphical revisions, additions and their different stages, orthographical mistakes and corrections, alternative decodings and readings. In my edition I have also included a clear text version, without dates or diacritical details, for those readers who are only interested in a basic text which can be quoted.

In view of the great variety of diaries the genetic text rendering cannot be considered the only practicable method of editing. The simpler the state of the manuscript in question and—even more important—the longer the text, the easier one could opt for a simpler way. One lesson to be learned from Klopstock's *work journal*—and which may be applicable to other diary editions as well—seems to me, however, that the usual division between text rendering and the recording of text alterations ought to be rejected in editing diaries. In many cases footnotes will provide the best method to combine alterations, corrections of date, even deletions and later additions, with the established text of the diary as such. The edition of Zinzendorf's diaries, of Lichtenberg's notes in *Lichtenberg in England*, of Wilhelm von Humboldt's diaries as well as those of Georg Heym can be quoted as examples in this direction. In the Anglo-

American world one could cite the critical edition of Washington Irving's journals for purposes of illustration.[17]

Text constitution. As a document not intended for publication Klopstock's *work journal* presents the editor with fairly difficult problems, especially as far as the frequent abbreviations are concerned. These abbreviations are predominantly suspensions, adopted for reasons of speed, but sometimes they are in form of code.

In the first case the words were restored to their usual form with the restored elements in brackets.[18] Although the actual reconstruction may be a minor one, it can be crucial for our comprehension of a style that by its very nature tends to be rudimentary, and it also shows us that the task of the editor is twofold: on the one hand, he has to preserve the nature of the document and, on the other, he must present a readable text. Codes which the writer intended only for his personal use and identification have to be treated in a different way. Their decoding could be given in the footnotes or in the commentary. But the different kinds of abbreviation have to be visible in the established text. To distinguish between the different forms can be of great significance, because not only do we have diaries where large parts are written in an individual form of shorthand—Samuel Pepys' diaries are perhaps the most well-known example—there are also those where part of the contents is hidden behind cryptograms, as in Goethe's or Leisewitz's diaries.[19] Ideograms, for instance, the astronomical signs in Goethe's diaries, should be reproduced as such in the text, and their meaning—if known—must be explained in the notes. However, whole passages in a code which has been decoded should not be reproduced as code in the text, but their transcription has to be differentiated from the rest of the text. In the edition of Leisewitz's diaries brackets were used, and in addition the code itself is given in a facsimile.[20]

There are certain other problems of abbreviations which I do not want to discuss in detail—for example, in which grammatical or orthographical form a reconstruction should be given. All these questions concerning abbreviations can also be relevant in editions of letters, though perhaps to a lesser extent, because the use of abbreviations and codes in letters is a very restricted one—perhaps only in extreme situations when the secrecy of the letter is under threat of violation. Otherwise, the usual editorial procedures should also be applied in transcribing diaries. Orthographical mistakes, for instance, can be retained as long as they do not impede the comprehension of the text. This restriction may, however, be waived when a text passage needs annotation in any case. And the correct form of names can easily be given in the notes or the index.[21]

Commentary. As private documents diaries and letters not only need a large amount of commentary, but also commentary of a difficult nature. Both letters and diary entries result in many different representations of individual knowledge and experience that can be difficult to verify. As far as diaries are concerned there may be problems of chronological annotation and indirect commentary where the diary appears fragmentary. Klopstock's entries are headed by proper dates in the form of year, month, and day. In the edition this framework has been completed by indicating the day of the week and also the movable feasts of the Christian calendar, Easter, Whitsun, etc., which seemed obvious in view of the eminently religious orientation of the author in question.[22]

Another important point which needed commentary was that there are quite frequently differences between the date for which an event was recorded and when it was actually entered in the diary. These differences are indicated in the footnotes. Klopstock shows a tendency not to report day by day, but in a cumulative manner for several days together, which implies a greater or lesser degree of distance from a particular event. The idea of an immediate day-by-day recollection inherent in certain types of diaries had clearly no appeal for him. When we take into account that a diarist, as a rule, always has the possibility of reconsidering his entries, of changing, deleting, or completing them, then the time difference between recording and writing down must surely be quite a common phenomenon. Arthur Schnitzler, for example, always specifically noted when, at which precise moment, he made certain additions in his diary.[23]

A very special problem of annotation seems to me the difficulty of commenting on events and experiences which the writer has not indicated in the diary, but which did take place and which he participated in beyond any doubt. In a biographical summary, information gained from diaries could be given parallel to information deduced from other sources. It is only a question whether there is enough material for such a summary, and it is only worthwhile when a diary deals predominantly with events and experiences.[24]

One final point: I would greatly welcome more documentary illustration in diary editions. Good reproductions and facsimiles are more suitable than any amount of description to convey an idea of the material aspects of a particular document, of visible passages of writing, of space provided for additions and their arrangement on the page, of different ways of writing—in short everything that gives us further clues of the author's attitude towards his diary.

NOTES

1. The following text is an abridged version of a paper given in Paris in February 1983 under the title 'Editionsprobleme von Tagebüchern, dargestellt an Klopstocks Arbeitstagebuch' during a Franco–German conference held under the auspices of the Centre Nationale de la Recherche Scientifique and the Deutsche Forschungsgemeinschaft, 23 to 25 February 1983. The translation is by Dr. Monika Jafri (London). The complete German version of the paper will be published in *Edition et Manuscrit. Edition des Ecrits en Prose, Statut du Texte, Normalisation des Procédures. Probleme der Prosa-Edition*, ed. M. Werner and W. Woesler.

2. On the different aspects of type casting see P. Boerner, *Tagebuch*, Sammlung Metzler M 85 (Stuttgart, 1969), pp. 14–25, 47–51.

3. *Klopstocks Arbeitstagebuch*, ed. K. Hurlebusch, in: Friedrich Gottlieb Klopstock, *Werke und Briefe. Historisch-kritische Ausgabe*, ed. H. Gronemeyer et al., sect. Addenda, vol. II (Berlin, New York, 1977).

4. *Klopstocks Arbeitstagebuch*, pp. 9, 10, 20, 23, 35, 101.

5. See P. Boerner, p. 11.

6. Among the great number of books on diaries the following merit special attention: *English Diaries. A Review of English Diaries from the Sixteenth to the Twentieth Century with an Introduction on Diary Writing*, ed. A. Ponsonby (London, 1923); G. R. Hocke, *Das europäische Tagebuch*, (Wiesbaden, 1963); *Das Tagebuch und der moderne Autor*, ed. H. Schulz (München, 1965); P. Boerner, *op. cit.*; B. Didier, *Le Journal intime*, Littératures modernes, 12 (Paris, 1976); *Le Journal intime et ses formes littéraires. Actes du colloque de septembre 1975*, ed. V. Del Litto, Histoire des idées et critique littéraire, 175 (Genève, 1978); M. Jurgensen, *Das fiktionale Ich. Untersuchungen zum Tagebuch*, (Bern, München, 1979). Didier's book contains some interpretations from the point of view of diarist-author which touch upon the characteristics here analysed. (See above all the chapter 'L'emploi du temps', pp. 159–175). See also M. Walser's interpretation of Kafka's diary through the habits and conditions of its author in his essay 'Baustein beim Bau der chinesischen Mauer', in: M. Walser, *Wer ist ein*

Schriftsteller? Aufsätze und Reden, edition suhrkamp, 959 (Frankfurt a.M., 1979), pp. 7-23.

7. Letters and diaries are often edited jointly. See, for example, Goethe, *Briefe und Tagebücher*, ed. H. G. Gräf, 2 vols. (Leipzig, n.d. [1927]) and Georg Heym, *Tagebücher, Traüme, Briefe*, in: Georg Heym, *Dichtungen und Schriften*, ed. K. L. Schneider, vol. III (München, 1960).

8. See J. G. Droysen, *Historik. Vorlesungen über Enzyklopädie und Methodologie der Geschichte*, ed. R. Hübner, 7th ed. (Darmstadt, 1972), pp. 37-84. Droysen used the word "Quelle" (source) for "Tradition" (tradition) and he also distinguished a third group of historical material which he called "Denkmäler" (monuments). E. Bernheim, in his *Lehrbuch der Historischen Methode und der Geschichtsphilosophie*, unchanged reprint of the 5th and 6th ed. (München, Leipzig, 1914), pp. 252-259, developed Droysen's concept into the dichotomy "Überrest"/"Tradition" (relic/tradition). See also A. Heuß, 'Überrest und Tradition. Zur Phänomenologie der historischen Quellen', in: *Archiv für Kulturgeschichte*, XXV (1935), 134-183; A. v. Brandt, *Werkzeug des Historikers. Eine Einführung in die historischen Hilfswissenschaften*, Urban-Bücher, 33, 5th ed. (Stuttgart, 1969), pp. 58-75.

9. See, for instance, *Briefwechsel zwischen Goethe und Schiller in den Jahren 1794 bis 1805*, 6 pts. (Stuttgart, 1828-1829).

10. Letters inserted in private diaries represent a very special case; see G. R. Hocke, 'Der Brief im Tagebuch. Doppelgang im intimen Bekenntnis', in: *Deutsche Akademie für Sprache und Dichtung Darmstadt. Jahrbuch 1975* (Darmstadt, 1976), pp. 100-106; B. Didier, p. 155.

11. See A. Schöne, 'Über Goethes Brief an Behrisch vom 10. November 1767', in *Festschrift für Richard Alewyn*, ed. H. Singer und B. v. Wiese (Köln, Graz, 1967), pp. 193-229; R.-M. Hurlebusch, 'Zum Briefwechsel zwischen Klopstock und Gleim', in: *Festschrift zur 250. Wiederkehr der Geburtstage von Gleim und Lichtwer*, ed. Gleimhaus (Halberstadt, 1968), pp. 81-100; W. Woesler, 'Der Brief als Dokument', in: *Probleme der Brief-Edition. Kolloquium der Deutschen Forschungsgemeinschaft 8.-11.9.1975. Referate und Diskussionsbeiträge*, ed. W. Frühwald et al. (Bonn-Bad Godesberg, Boppard, 1977), pp. 41-59.

12. See Goethe's 'Zahmes Xenion', "Es schnurrt mein Tagebuch/ Am Bratenwender:/ Nichts schreibt sich leichter voll/ Als ein Kalender" (quoted from P. Boerner, 'Einführung zu Johann Wolfgang Goethe: Tagebücher', in: J. W. Goethe, *Gedenkausgabe der Werke, Briefe und Gespräche*, suppl. vol. II, ed. P. Boerner [Zürich, Stuttgart, 1964], p. 633). R. Musil, *Tagebücher*, ed. A. Frisé (Reinbek, 1976), p. 11, "Es ist die bequemste, zuchtloseste Form." Arno Schmidt, 'Eines Hähers: "Tué!" und 1014 fallend', in: *Das Tagebuch*

und der moderne Autor, ed U. Schultz (München, 1965), p. 116, "Das TB ist das Alibi der Wirrköpfe; ist einer der Abörter der Literatur!"

13. When dated entries alternate with entries without a date in a manuscript it may be difficult to decide whether the text in question is a diary or rather a notebook. See J. Rousset, 'Pour une poétique du journal intime', in: *Literary Theory and Criticism. Festschrift Presented to René Wellek in Honor of his Eightieth Birthday. Part II: Criticism*, ed. J. P. Strelka (Bern, 1984), p. 1220, "un journal intermittent, de périodicité lâche, longs abandons et brefs retours, est-il encore un journal? Aucun diariste (ou presque) ne respectant strictement la pratique quotidienne, à quel rythme de discontinuité faut-il fixer la limite séparant le journal d'un sous-genre qui serait le dossier de travail, le carnet de notes, les feuillets sans date, l'agenda? Et sur quel critère?" (This article has come to my notice after the completion of my paper.)

14. The time indications may even give the time of day and the exact hour, see B. Didier, p. 171-172.

15. These are discussed in detail in *Klopstocks Arbeitstagebuch*, pp. 178-225.

16. See *Klopstocks Arbeitstagebuch*, p. 179.

17. 'Zinzendorfs Tagebuch 1716-1719', ed. G. Reichel und J. T. Müller, in: *Zeitschrift für Brüdergeschichte*, I (1907), 113-191; II (1908), 81-117, IV (1910), 5-69; *Lichtenberg in England. Dokumente einer Begegnung*, ed. H. L. Gumbert, vol. I (Wiesbaden, 1977), pp. 29-120; *Wilhelm von Humboldts Tagebücher*, ed. A. Leitzmann, in: *Wilhelm von Humboldts Gesammelte Schriften*, vol. XIV and XV (Berlin, 1916-1918); Georg Heym, *Tagebücher*, pp. 6-176; Washington Irving, *Journals and Notebooks. Vol. I, 1803-1806*, ed. N. Wright (University of Wisconsin Press, 1969). See also *The Diary of Samuel Pepys*, ed. R. Latham and W. Matthews, 9 vols. (London, 1970-1976).

18. Not restored were "u" and "u." (i.e. "und") and "Sr. M." (i.e. "Seiner Majestät"), see *Klopstocks Arbeitstagebuch*, p. 174.

19. *Goethes Werke. Herausgegeben im Auftrage der Großherzogin Sophie von Sachsen. Abt. III: Tagebücher*, 15 vols. (in 16) (Weimar, 1887-1919); *Johann Anton Leisewitzens Tagebücher*, ed. H. Mack and J. Lochner, 2 vols. (Weimar, 1916-1920). In Pepys' diaries only names are usually given in longhand.

20. *Johann Anton Leisewitzens Tagebücher*, p. [197].

21. See Arthur Schnitzler, *Tagebuch 1909-1912*, ed. Kommission für literarische Gebrauchsformen der Österreichischen Akademie der Wissenschaften, Obmann W. Welzig (Wien, 1981). This edition has no commentary but a very detailed register instead.

22. Other diarists with similar attitudes, for instance Zinzendorf, Pepys, Novalis, have incorporated such characteristics in their diaries themselves. Klopstock's conception of time was surely not uninfluenced by the weekly seven-day cycle and the Christian calendar, see *Klopstocks Arbeitstagebuch*, p. 62.

23. *Tagebuch 1909–1912*, pp. 23–24.

24. In Klopstock's case only a systematic index ("Schematische Inhaltsübersicht") of the diary itself could be established.

Aspects of the Transmission of the *Quem Quaeritis*

GUNILLA IVERSEN

The dialogue known as the *Quem quaeritis* is like a precious jewel in the medieval Easter liturgy. The three Marys come to the sepulcher of Christ on Easter morning, search for his body in the grave, and are told that he is risen. This short dialogue, this jewel, is found in ever-varying and more or less ornamented settings in the liturgy of the Easter celebration all over Europe. It was preserved in manuscripts dating from the tenth century, by which time it is already established in one form or another from St. Gall in the East to St. Martial in the West and Winchester in the North. Few texts from the tenth and eleventh centuries have been the subject of so many studies, not only by musicologists but especially by the historians of drama, for they have seen in the *Quem quaeritis* the second birth of European drama. Like the Greek tragedy arose from the religious ritual of ancient Greece, so does this dramatic dialogue belong to the religious ritual of the Christian Church. "The history of the *Quem quaeritis* is nothing less than the history of the origins of the sacred drama" (. . . les origines du théatre sacré), proclaimed Léon Gautier a century ago.[1]

This is the well-known version from the St. Gall manuscript SG 484:

> Quem queritis in sepulchro christicole.
> Iesum Nazarenum crucifixum o caelicolae.
> Non est hic; surrexit sicut predixerat.
> Ite nuntiate quia surrexit de sepulchro.

> Whom do you search in the sepulcher, adorers of Christ?
> Jesus of Nazareth, the crucified, o inhabitants of heaven.
> He is not here. He has risen as he foretold.
> Go and tell that he has risen from the sepulcher.

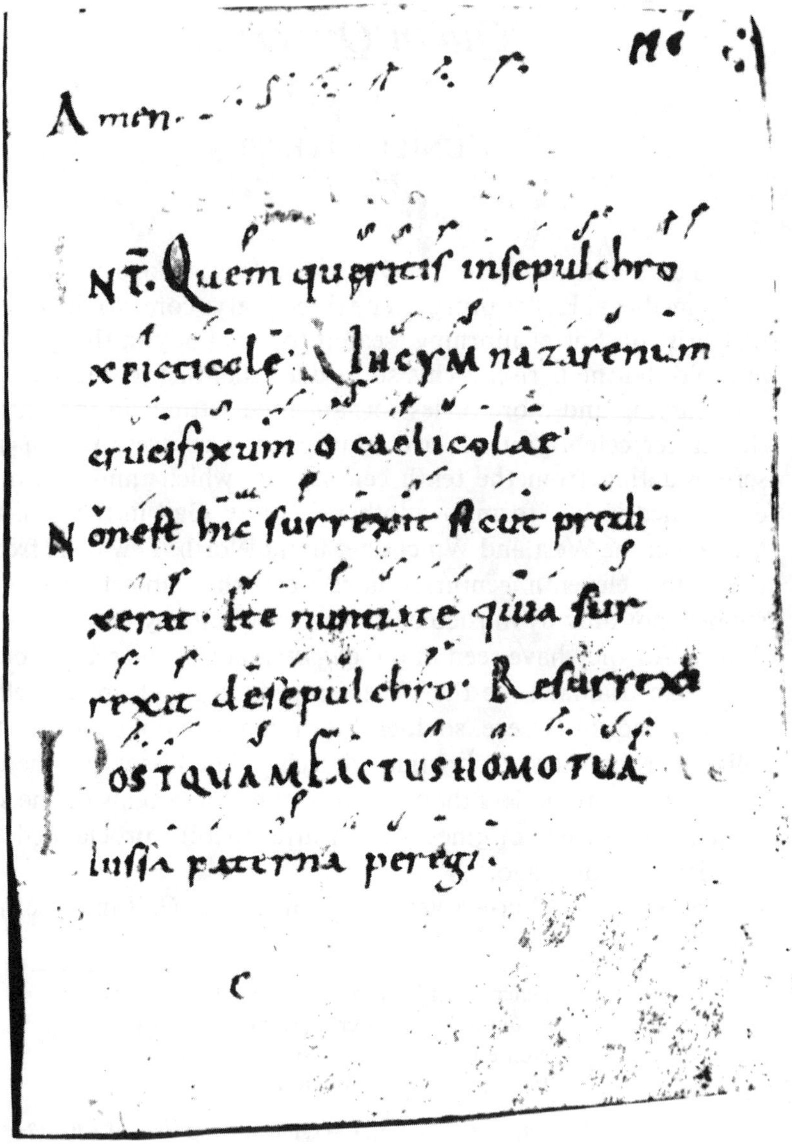

Amen...

NT. Quem queritis insepulchro
xpicticole. Ihcym nazarenum
crucifixum o caelicolae
Non est hic surrexit sicut predi
xerat. Ite nunciate quia sur
rexit desepulchro. Resurrexi
POSTQUAM FICTUS HOMO TUA
iussa paterna peregi.

Figure 1. Sankt Gallen Stiftsbibl. 484 p.111.

As an object of the study in the transmission of a medieval text, few items could be more intriguing to the scholar than the *Quem quaeritis* dialogue. And consequently the main question to which scholars have devoted themselves has been the origin of the dialogue.[2] Which was the original form of the text? What was its original function?

1. Was it a trope to the introit antiphon *Resurrexi* at Easter Mass?
2. Was it part of a procession preceding the Mass?
3. Was it an autonomous verse of the Mass, unconnected with the introit?
4. Or was it from the beginning a part of the *Visitatio sepulchri* ceremony at the end of Matins and thus followed by the *Te Deum*?

In fact the dialogue exists in all of these forms in the earliest sources. But which was the original? And what is the evolutionary history of the *Quem quaeritis*?

E. K. Chambers in *The Medieval Stage* and Karl Young in *The Drama of the Medieval Church* both expressed the theory that the *Visitatio sepulchri* ceremony developed from the *Quem quaeritis* dialogue, which in its original form was a trope introducing the introit antiphon *Resurrexi*.[3] This theory has been criticized, for example, by O. B. Hardison, Jr., who took the opposite position in his book *Christian Rite and Christian Drama*, arguing that the longer version, the *Visitatio sepulchri*, in its turn had developed within the Easter Vigil service and that the short *Quem quaeritis* dialogue was a reduced form of the *Visitatio* for the beginning of the Mass.[4] Timothy McGee argued that the *Quem quaeritis* was not originally a trope, but rather a *Collecta*, and as such part of a procession in front of the church which preceded the Mass.[5] Helmut De Boor in *Die Textgeschichte der lateinischen Osterfeiern* proposed that the *Quem quaeritis* was from the beginning an independent text which later developed two functions: one as a trope and another as part of the *Visitatio sepulchri* ceremony,[6] and Johan Drumbl in *Die Ursprung des liturgischen Spiels* also favored the theory that the *Quem quaeritis* was originally an autonomous text subsequently adapted to different functions.[7]

Thus opinions concerning the chronology of the different versions have been and still are divided. Efforts to describe an evolutionary history of the dialogue have not been totally successful, nor have they produced unequivocal results, partly because they have not been based on primary sources, have not returned to the manuscripts, and partly because they have been based on a limited number of sources or on sources from a limited number of regions, such as those of St. Gall or of Aquitania. But the most urgent question in the study of the *Quem quaeritis* is not simply to discern which was the original text form and function and which developed out of which, but to focus on a study of the dialogue in its different forms and functions in different traditions and to describe and try to understand the different liturgical—and literary—contexts into which it was placed.

In his interesting article on "the Dissemination of the *Quem quaeritis* and the *Visitatio sepulchri* and the chronology of their early sources," David A. Björk stressed the importance of studying the geographical distribution of the different versions of the *Quem quaeritis* in just this way. He wrote:

> The geographical distribution of the various versions is the best key to understanding the relationships among them, particularly among the three main types associated respectively with the Mass, the procession before it and Matins.[8]

On the map facing (based on the mss. sources investigated for the CT III)[9] are indicated where these different versions of the *Quem quaeritis* occur. We get a picture of the divergencies among the earliest sources. In northern Italy, Aquitania, and Catalonia the dialogue is mostly presented as a trope to *Resurrexi*; in northern France and the northeastern region of the Frankish Kingdom the dialogue forms part of the *Visitatio Sepulchri* ceremony; and in central and southern Italy we find examples in which the dialogue is a verse.

Although the four lines of the dialogue are found in all regions in almost identical form and although there are a few significant variants, there are considerable variations in the surrounding settings. Consider the number of surrounding texts found in in the trope manuscripts:

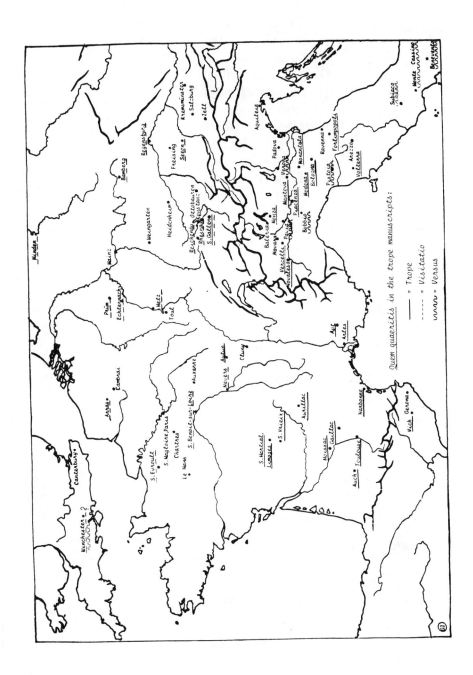

Map Manuscript 206

A   Alleluia ad sepulchrum/En ecce
B   Alleluia resurrexit dominus
C   *Cito euntes
D   *Eia carissimi verba
E   Et dicebant ad invicem
F   *Hodie resurrexit leo fortis
G   *Hora est psallite
H   Magister iam tempus est
I   *Psallite fratres
J   *Psallite regi magno
K   Surrexit Christus
L   Surrexit dominus de sepulchro
M   Surrexit enim sicut dixit dominus
N   Ubi est Christus meus
O   Venite et videte

Texts used as trope elements and combined with other trope elements are indicated by *. In the case of *Psallite regi magno* we should rather say that the *Quem quaeritis* is a trope element added to the *Psallite regi magno/Dormivi pater* in Pa 1240. (See below p. 177.) The following table records all the combinations of the *Quem quaeritis* and its surrounding texts in the investigated material.[10]

Q	SG 484 SG 381 Zü 97 Vce 146 Vce 161 Vce 162
QA	Pa 1121 Pa 909 Pa 1120 Pa 1119 Pa 1084b Pa 887 Pa 1871 Pa 779[11]
GQA	Apt 17 Pa 1118
GQBFA	Apt 18
GNQA	Vic 106
NAGQ	Vic 105
NQA	Vic 105 sec
QB	Ox 222 To 20 To 18 Ben 34 Ben 35 Ben 38 Ben 39 Ben 40
GQ	Vro 90 Vro 107 RoC 1741 Bo 2824 RoC 1343
GQB	Pst 121a Pst 121b
QBD	Cai 75 Pia 65
QBDI	Vce 56 Ivr 60
QBF	Pa 9449 Pa 1235 Ba 30 PaA 1169 Mza 76 Mza 77 Mod 7 Vat 4770
JQBF	Pa 1240
HGQBF	Vol 39
QBFOCL	Cdg 473 Ox 775
QBK	RoA 123
GQM	Ox 27

QM	SG 376 Be 11 Ka 25
EQM	Ba 5 Zu 132*
EQL	Mü 14083 Mü 14845
QL	Me 452 Pa 9448 Pa 10510 Ba 6
(*M or L?)	

The letter Q signifies the dialogue itself and the other letters signify the different surrounding verses.

Among the 95 manuscripts investigated for the *Corpus Troporum* edition of Easter tropes dating before 1200, there are in 64 mss. 22 different ways of presenting the lines of the dialogue and its surrounding texts.[12] Among the texts which are combined with the QQ dialogue there are a certain number which are also found either as trope elements to the *Resurrexi* antiphon or as additions to the QQ dialogue. These are texts of an exhorting character, such as the *Cito euntes dicite, Eia carissimi verba, Hodie resurrexit, Hora est psallite,* and *Psallite fratres.* And if we look at the sources in which these texts are given as trope elements to *Resurrexi,* we find that the predominance of Italian sources is considerable:[13]

Texts combined both with *Quem quaeritis* and *Resurrexi*:

Quem quaeritis	Resurrexi
C Cito euntes dicite discipulis quia surrexit dominus alleluia alleuia Cdg 473 Ox 775	Cito euntes dicite discipulis quia surrexit sicut dixit dominus POSUISTI *Pst 121a Vat 4770 Ben 35 Ben 38 Ben 39 Ben 40*
D Eia carissimi verba canite Christi Cai 75 *Vce 56 Ivr 60 Pia 65*	Eia carissimi verba canite Christi RESURREXI *Ox 222 Mza 76 Pst 121a Pst 121b Ben 40* Exsultemus et laetemur omnes eia carissimi verba canite Christi RESURREXI *Vce 186*

	Quem quaeritis	Resurrexi
F	Hodie resurrexit leo fortis Christus filius dei deo gratias dicite eia Cdg 473 Ox 775 Pa 9449 Pa 1235 Ba 30 PaA 1169 Pa 1240 Apt 18 *Mza 76* *Mza 77 Vol 39 Mod 7 Vat 4770*	Hodie resurrexit leo fortis Christus filius dei deo gratias dicite eia RESURREXI Pa 9448 Apt 17 Pa 1118 *Vce 186 Vro* *107 RoC 1741 Bo 2824 RoN 1343 Ben* 35 Hodie exultent iusti resurrexit leo fortis deo gratias dicite eia RESURREXI INVESTIGASTI SG 484 SG 381 Mū 14843 *Pia 65 To 20* *To 18 Pst 121a Pst 121b Ben 34 Ben* *35 Ben 38 Ben 39 Ben 40* Leo fortis de sepulchro resurrexit hodie deo gratias dicite eia RESURREXI Apt 17 Apt 18
G	Hora est psallite iubet domnus canere eia dicite Apt 17 Pa 1118 Apt 18 Vic 106 Vic 105 *Ox 27 Vol 39 Vro 90 Vro107 RoC* *1741 Bo 2824 RoN 1343 Pst 121a Pst* *121b*	Hora est psallite iubet domnus canere eia dicite *Pad 47 Mod 7 Bo 7*
I	Psallite fratres hora est resurrexit dominus eia et eia *Vce 56 Ivr 60*	Psallite fratres hora est resurrexit dominus eia et eia RESURREXI *Mza 76 RoC 1741 Bo 2824 RoN 1343*
J	Psallie regi magno devicto mortis imperio Pa 1240	Psallite regi magno devicto mortis imperio eia RESURREXI Cdg 473 Cdg 473 (sec) Ox 775 PaA 1169 Pa 909 Pa 887

Why should the *Quem quaeritis* have so many settings? What are the liturgical, esthetic, and literary needs to which they correspond? And just what are these texts that surround the central dialogue? For the purpose of answering these questions the collection of texts edited by Walther Lipphardt and entitled *Lateinische Osterfeiern und Osterspiele* is a most useful instrument;[14] we hope that the edition in *Corpus Troporum III* will also prove useful.

Four different ways to insert the dialogue into the liturgy

In the following I will illustrate by a few examples some different ways to "incorporate" the *Quem quaeritis* into the Easter liturgy. We will study the dialogue in four main versions:

1. As an introductory verse before the Mass
2. As part of the *Visitatio Sepulchri* ceremony followed by *Te Deum Laudamus*
3. As an introductory trope to the *Resurrexi* antiphon
4. As what might be called a trope to a trope of the *Resurrexi* antiphon.

The textual basis for the central dialogue

The textual basis for the central dialogue is the four Gospels—and in particular the descriptions given by the synoptics Matthew, Mark, and Luke. The first line of *Quem quaeritis* recalls *Scio quod Iesum qui crucifixus est quaeritis* (Matthew 28:5) and *Iesum queritis Nazarenum crucifixum* (Mark 16:6). The next line *Non est hic* is found in all the Gospels, the continuation *surrexit sicut predixerat* recalls the text from Matthew, Mark, and Luke, and the last line *Ite nuntiate* also recalls Matthew, Mark, and Luke.

In the QQ dialogue the past is transformed into a liturgical here-and-now, *hic et nunc*. The Christicolae are the three mourning, searching Marys but at the same time all those who are gathered to celebrate Easter, the Marys searching for their crucified Master represent all those who are searching. In biblical language, the verb used in the dialogue, *quaerere*, often signifies the *search for God*; at the same time, it has the same meaning as *lugere*, to miss, mourn for.[15] Like the Marys the Christians receive the message that Christ has risen. When the angel asks the women "Whom do you seek in the sepulcher?" the word *sepulchrum* not only signifies the tomb but also the altar.[16]

We recall that since the early centuries of the Christian tradition Christians often celebrated the mass right on the tombs of the martyrs. Later the altar, made of stone, was not only the communion table but also a sepulcher, and its form is more like a sepulcher than a table. Relics of saints were kept within the altar in a cavity called the *sepulchrum*. Thus was the altar ritually transformed into the sepulcher of Christ. At the same time it was the focal point for the presence of God in the celebrating assembly, the place where Christ appears in Glory *in gloria*. In its short and condensed form the dialogue expresses the very essence of the Easter liturgy:

1. The seeking for God
2. The victory over Death, "Why do you seek the living among the dead?" *quid viventem quaeritis cum mortuis*
3. and the exhortation "go and tell," *Ite nuntiate.*

1. THE *QUEM QUAERITIS* AS AN INDEPENDENT VERSUS

Our first example is the *Quem quaeritis* as an independent versus before the Mass from Monte Cassino 127:[17]

> *Dominicum sanctum Pasche*
> *Finita tertia vadat unus sacerdos ante altare*
> *alba veste indutus et conversus ad chorum dicat alta voce*
> Q Quem queritis
> *Et duo alii clerici stantes in medio chori respondeant*
> Iesum Nazarenum
> *Et sacerdos*
> Non est hic. Surrexit
> *Illi vero conversi ad chorum dicant*
> B Alleluia.
> Resurrexit dominus
> *Post hec incipit Tropos. sequitur Introitus*
> RESURREXI ET ADHUC TECUM SUM ALL.
> POSUISTI SUPER ME MANUM TUAM. ALL.
> MIRABILIS FACTA EST SCIENTIA TUA > ALLELUIA

And from Benevento 40:[18]

Dominica sancte Pasche

Q   Quem queritis in sepulchro, christicole.
     Iesum Nazarenum, o celicole.
     Non est hic. Surrexit sicut predixerat;
     Ite nuntiate quia surrexit.
B   Alleluia
     Resurrexit dominus.

Tropos
Hodie exultent iusti.
Resurrexit leo fortis.
Deo gratias dicite omnes.
RESURREXI ET ADHUC TECUM SUM.
Lux mundi dominus resurrexit hodie.
POSUISTI SUPER ME MANUM TUAM.
Manus tua domine salvavit mundum hodie
et ideo
MIRABILIS FACTA EST SCIENTIA TUA.
Scientia domini mirabilis facta est hodie.
ALLELUIA

In the Benedictine tradition of Montecassino, represented here by Beneventan ms. Ben 34 [See Figure 2, below][19] and from the Benedictine MC 127 and Ben 40, the dialogue is performed by the altar, which also represents the sepulcher.

When "*Tertia* is finished one priest goes in front of the altar, dressed in an alb, a white dress, turns to the Choir and sings *Quem quaeritis* . . . For whom are you searching in the sepulcher adorers of Christ? And two other clerks standing in the middle of the choir answer '*Iesum Nazarenum* . . . ' And the priest says 'He is not here; he has risen . . . .' And they turn to the choir and say 'Alleluia the Lord has risen.' Then there is the indication: '*Post hec* . . . .' After this the trope begins and the introit antiphon follows." (The *Tertia* mentioned as an indication of when the dialogue should be performed is the office that precedes the Mass in the liturgical day.)

In the Beneventan tradition the *Quem quaeritis* precedes the Introit without being totally incorporated with the antiphon itself.

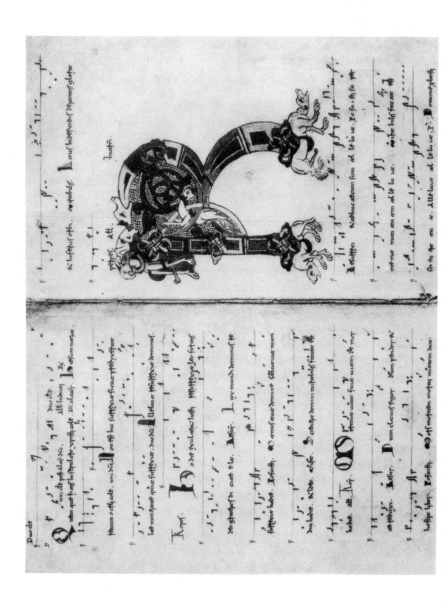

Figure 2. Benevento Bibl. cap. ms. 34 ff. 122ᵛ–123.

According to MC 127 it forms the *transition* between the Terce and the Easter mass, or perhaps we should say it functions as an opening or introduction to the entire Easter mass, not only to the introit. We can compare this with the indication given in the Regularis Concordia, that is, the code of monastic observance in England approved by the Winchester synod in 970 and following a modified Benedictine tradition:[20]

REGVLARIS CONCORDIA

51. Dum tertia recitatur lectio, quattuor fratres induant se, quorum unus, alba indutus ac si ad aliud agendum, ingrediatur atque latenter sepulcri locum adeat ibique, manu tenens palmam, quietus sedeat. Dumque tertium percelebratur responsorium residui tres succedant, omnes quidem cappis induti, turibula cum incensu manibus gestantes, ac, pedetemptim ad similitudinem quaerentium quid, ueniant ante locum sepulcri. Aguntur enim haec ad imitationem angeli sedentis in monumento, atque mulierum cum aromatibus uenientium ut ungerent corpus Ihesu. Cum ergo ille residens tres, uelut erraneos ac aliquid quaerentes, uiderit sibi approximare, incipiat mediocri uoce dulcisone cantare *Quem quaeritis*? Quo decantato finetenus, respondeant hi tres, uno ore, *Ihesum Nazarenum.* Quibus ille: *Non est hic. Surrexit sicut praedixerat. Ite, nuntiate quia surrexit a mortuis.* Cuius iussionis uoce uertant se illi tres ad chorum, dicentes *Alleluia. Resurrexit Dominus.* Dicto hoc, rursus ille residens, uelut reuocans illos, dicat antiphonam: *Venite et uidete locum.* Haec uero dicens, surgat et erigat uelum ostendatque eis locum, cruce nudatum sed tantum linteamina posita quibus crux inuoluta erat; quo uiso deponant turibula quae gestauerant in eodem sepulcro, sumantque linteum et extendant contra clerum ac, ueluti ostendentes quod surrexerit Dominus et iam non sit illo inuolutus, hanc canant antiphonam: *Surrexit Dominus de sepulcro,* superponantque linteum altari.

52. Finita antiphona prior, congaudens pro triumpho regis nostri quod deuicta morte surrexit, incipiat hymnum *Te Deum laudamus;* quo incepto una pulsantur omnia signa. Post cuius finem dicat sacerdos uersum [*Surrexit Dominus de sepulcro*] uerbotenus et initiet. . . .

The instructions, as well as the indication to sing *Alleluia, Resurrexit dominus*, in MC 127 recall the instructions given in the *Regularis concordia*. Still there are considerable differences. In the *Regularis concordia* the dialogue is placed at Matins and followed by the *Te Deum*. It is also accompanied by the antiphons *Venite et videte* and *Surrexit de sepulchro*. These southern Italian manuscripts are not the only ones to present the *Quem quaeritis* as a more or less independent verse, but the cases where the dialogue is presented as an independent verse are nearly all Italian.[21] There might, however, be other examples as well where the dialogue is performed either before or as an introduction to the Mass. The difficulty is that in the manuscripts the dialogue is normally presented just before the text of the introit. Sometimes this reflects a connection in the actual performance; whereas other times it can be doubted that it actually was connected closely to the antiphon.[22] This has also been remarked by Alejandro Planchart concerning the *Quem quaeritis* version of the Winchester tropers.[23]

2. THE *QUEM QUAERITIS* AS A VISITATIO OF MATINS

In the version from Nevers Pa 9449 the text is presented without any rubrics:

> Quem queritis in sepulchro, o Christicole.
> Iesum Nazarenum crucifixum, o celicole.
> Non est hic; surrexit sicut predixerat.
> Ite nuntiate quia surrexit.
> Alleluia.
> Resurrexit dominus.
> Hodie resurrexit leo fortis
> Christus filius dei
> Deo gratias dicite eia.
> TE DEUM LAUDAMUS . . .

Just as in the Beneventan version the dialogue is immediately followed by *Alleluia. Resurrexit dominus.* The *Te Deum* is followed by procession antiphons. In the Nevers version the dialogue is not at all connected with the introit antiphon. Still, the form if not the function of the dialogue might also well have been that of a trope. The *Hodie resurrexit leo* is, as a matter of fact, used as a trope element in other combinations in a number of manuscripts.

Hodie resurrexit is used as a trope in the following mss.: Pa 9448 Apt 17 Pa 1118 Vce 186 Vro 107 RoC 1741 Bo 2824 RoN 1343 Ben 35 Ben 38 Ben 39 Ben 40:[24]

> Hodie resurrexit leo fortis
> Christus filius dei
> deo gratias dicite eia
> RESURREXI

And we can also compare with the following trope element taken from the Apt manuscripts 17 and 18:

> Leo fortis de sepulchro resurrexit hodie
> deo gratias dicite eia
> RESURREXI

This illustrates how delicate the question of distinction between the different functions can be. The same textual version can be used as a verse or trope in one liturgical practice and as a *Visitatio* in another, *not because one function represents an earlier, more original state than the other, but simply because one function fits the local liturgical practice better than the other.*

We can compare this with the longer versions of the Visitatio, in which the four Gospels that form the textual basis of the dialogue all contain an account of the scene by the empty grave on Easter morning. Each begins with some indication of the time:

> 'Vespere autem sabbati quae lucescit in primam sabbati . . .'
> (Matthew)
> 'Cum transisset sabbatum, valde mane . . . orto iam sole . . .'
> (Mark)
> 'Valde diluculo . . .' (Luke)
> 'Mane cum adhuc tenebrae essent . . .' (John)

Whereas the synoptics describe the scene in the early morning at sunrise or when the sun was already risen *orto iam sole*, St. John specifies early in the morning, when it was still dark *cum adhuc tenebrae essent*. This last description is especially important for the *Visitatio*, whose *Sitz im Leben* is Matins, which took place before daybreak, and it is the version of John that forms the basis for the *Visitatio* dialogue. Here the story is made especially dramatic: the form of the dialogue is particularly clear because it is punctuated by such expressions as *'et dicit eis,' 'dicunt ei illi,' 'dicit ei Jesus,'* etc.

In the well-known version of the *Visitatio* from Saint Benoît sur Loire[25] are found all the phrases given in the gospel of St. John expressing the mourning, disbelief, and difficulty of realizing what has happened: the predicted, but still unexpected resurrection; the fright at the first meeting with the risen Christ. In the opening scene the three Marys approach to the sepulcher step by step *pedetemptim*.[26] In alternation they express their sorrow and their anger for what has happened: *O res plangenda* etc. They want to show their devotion to the dead Master by anointing his holy body. But they cannot reach him by themselves. Who will open the sepulcher, they ask? And the angel who is sitting by it asks them, "Whom are you seeking (mourning for) in the sepulcher?" etc. The angel says, "Why are you seeking the living among the dead? He is not here but has risen as he told the disciples. Remember that was told you already in Galilee, that Christ had to suffer and on the third day rise again in glory." But the women do not understand. They repeat what he says, but they continue to weep, and Mary Magdalen asks who has removed the body from the tomb. She repeats her lamentation to Peter and John. Peter is the first to understand what has happened *ut predixit vivus surrexit credo dominus*. "I believe that the Lord is alive and has risen as he foretold." Approaching the angels in the tomb, Mary once again repeats her laments.[27] "They have taken away my Lord and I do not know where they have laid him." At this moment Christ appears as the gardener and asks her simply: "Woman why do you weep? Whom do you seek?" She does not recognize him but asks if he has taken away the body. He says her name *Maria*, and not until then does she recognize him. She exclaims "*Raboni,*" wants to touch him, but he says *Noli me tangere*. He disappears and the two angels pronounce the essential words: *Venite et videte* "Come and see where the Lord was laid." *Alleluia* "Be not affrighted. Leave your sadness aside. Proclaim that Jesus lives" etc. Then, in alternation, the three women praise the resurrection. Finally Christ appears again and confirms the message of the angels: *Nolite timere* "Do not be affrighted"; *Ite nuntiate* "Go and tell my brothers that they shall go to Galilee—There they will see me as I foretold, *sicut predixi.*" The play ends with the praise *Alleluia resurrexit* etc.

All the way through it is built up as a dialogue with alternate lines. Following the Gospel of John it is possible to turn the resurrection message from *legomena* to *dromena*.

3. *QUEM QUAERITIS* AS A TROPE TO THE ANTIPHON *RESURREXI*

When the dialogue functions as a trope to the introit antiphon, its textual basis is more complicated. On the one hand there are the texts of the Gospels; on the other there is the text of the introit antiphon itself.

The text of the antiphon is taken from Psalm 38, verses 18, 5, and 6:

> 18: 'exsurrexi et adhuc tecum sum.'
> 5:   (ecce domine tu cognovisti omnia novissima et antique, tu formasti me) 'et posuisti super me manum tuam.'
> 6:   'Mirabilis facta est scientia tua' (ex me)

(18: 'I woke up and I am still with you'; 5: 'See, Lord, you know everything of late and of old; you made me and you laid your hand upon me'; 6: 'Your wisdom is wonderful'). And here is the antiphon:

> 'Resurrexi et adhuc tecum sum
> posuisti super me manum tuam
> mirabilis facta est scientia tua'

The poetic power of this psalm, in which King David sings of the incomprehensible greatness of his God, is still found in the antiphon. But it is no longer David singing: it is Christ speaking. The scene has changed, or deepened we might say, although we still hear the same text praising the Lord of David in the background. In the foreground we hear the crucified and risen Christ talking to his Father. The verb *exsurrexi* in the Psalm, which simply means 'I woke up,' is changed in the antiphon to the prehieronyman form *resurrexi*, which here and now means 'I have risen.' So the text of the Psalm has become a text about the Resurrection of Christ; this meaning acquires even sharper definition when the introit antiphon is preceded by the *Quem quaeritis* in the form of a trope or introductory verse.

As we have seen, the dialogue in the traditions of Aquitania, Catalonia, and in many Italian centers is above all used as a trope to this antiphon. In order to insert the dialogue into the context of the antiphon, additional trope elements were often added to introduce the whole complex and to form a transition between the dialogue and the antiphon.

The following is the version given in the Aquitanian troper from Apt, Apt 17:

Hora est, psallite.
Iubet domnus canere,
eia dicite.
Angelus:
Quem queritis in sepulchro, o christicole.
Respondeant:
Iesum Nazarenum crucifixum, o Celicole.
Angelus:
Non est hic; surrexit sicut predixerat.
Ite nuntiate quia surrexit.
Cantores:
Alleluia.
Ad sepulchrum residens angelus nuntiat
resurrexisse Christum.
Angelus:
Ecce completum est illud
quod olim ipse per prophetam dixerat
ad patrem taliter inquiens:
RESURREXI ET ADHUC TECUM SUM.
POSUISTI SUPER ME MANUM TUAM.
MIRABILIS FACTA EST SCIENTIA TUA.

The time is come, O sing!
The master orders us to sing!
Hurray! Sing!
Whom you are looking for in the sepulcher, O you
    who adore Christ?
Jesus of Nazareth who was crucified, O you who live
    in Heaven.
He is not here:
He is risen, just as he had foretold;
Go and announce that he is risen.
Alleluia!
Sitting by the grave the angel announces
    that Christ is risen.
See, that is fulfilled
    which he himself once had said quoting the prophet
    speaking these words to his father:
I AM RISEN AND I AM STILL WITH YOU.
YOU LAID YOUR HAND UPON ME.
YOUR WISDOM IS WONDERFUL.

In this version the whole song is introduced by an *Aufforderung*, an
invitation to sing, as so often in the Aquitanian tradition *eia dicite*—

"Hurray! Let us sing!" With the addition of extra lines after the dialogue, namely *Ad sepulchrum residens* and *Ecce completum est*, the dramatic dialogue *Quem quaeritis* has been attached to the following introit antiphon, turning it into an introduction to the introit. These particular additional lines are found in the Aquitaine, in Apt and in Vic in Catalonia, but apparently not outside this area.[28] The introductory lines *Hora est psallite* are found in the same area: in the Apt tropers, in the southern Aquitanian troper Pa 1118, and in the tropers from Vic in Catalonia, but most frequently in the northern Italian tropers from such places as Nonantola, Verona, Volterra, and Pistoia.[29]

In the version of the dialogue given in the older of the Apt tropers, Apt 18, we find a unique combination of texts forming the dialogue:

> Hora est, psallite.
> Iubet domnus canere,
> eia dicite.
> Quem queritis in sepulchro, christicole.
> Iesum Nazarenum, o Celicole.
> Non est hic; surrexit sicut predixerat.
> Ite nuntiate quia surrexit.
> dicentes:
> Alleluia
> Resurrexit dominus.
> Hodie resurrexit leo fortis.
> Christus filius dei.
> Deo gratias dicite eia.

> In the margin the *En ecce* element is added by another hand:

> En ecce completum est illud
> quod olim ipse per prophetam dixerat
> ad patrem taliter inquiens:

This version shows a closer connection with the Italian mss. The *Alleluia resurrexit dominus* is the most frequent addition to the *Quem quaeritis* lines in Italy. Thus in Benevento, as we have seen, but also in Novalesa and Bobbio, it is the only addition to the dialogue; in Pistoia it is found in combination with the introduction *Hora est psallite*; in Piacenza, in Ivrea, and in Cai 75 from Arras, it is found in combination with *Eia carissimi verba*. But far the most frequent element combined with *Alleluia resurrexit dominus* is *Hodie resurrexit leo fortis*. This is the case in the repertories of Mza 76 and 77 from Monza, Mod 7 from Modena, Vat 4770, which may be from Subiaco, and Vol 39 from Volterra; it also appears in a few tropers from the 'transitional zone' between northern France and the Aquitaine, namely Pa 9449 and Pa 1235 from Nevers, Ba 30 from Rheims, and PaA 1169 from Autun; it also appears in the two tropers from Winchester, Cdg 473 and Ox 775, and in the intriguing version of Pa 1240.[30]

4. *QUEM QUAERITIS* AS A TROPE TO THE TROPE OF THE INTROIT ANTIPHON *RESURREXI*

This is the version given in Pa 1240:

Trop. in Pasche

Psallite regi magno
devicto mortis imperio.
Quem queritis in sepulchro o christicole.
Iesum Nazarenum crucifixum o celicole.
Non est hic; surrexit sicut ipse dixit.
Ite nuntiate quia surrexit.
Alleluia
Resurrexit dominus.
Hodie surrexit leo fortis,
Christus filius dei.
deo gratias dicite eia.
⟨RESURREXI ET ADHUC TECUM SUM.⟩
Dormivi pater et surgam diluculo
et somnus mea dulcis est mihi.
PO⟨SUISTI SUPER ME MANUM TUAM,⟩
Ita pater sic placuit ante te
Ut moriendo mortis mors fuissem
morsus inferni et mundi vita.
MIRAB⟨ILIS FACTA EST SCIENTIA TUA.⟩
Qui abscondisti hec sapientibus
et revelasti parvulis
ALLELUIA

Sing praises to the great King
As the reign of Death is broken!

Whom do you search in the sepulcher, o adorers of
   Christ?
Jesus of Nazareth, the crucified, o Inhabitants of
   Heaven.
He is not here. He has risen as he foretold himself.
Go and tell that he has risen.
Alleluia.
Lord has risen.
Today the powerful Lion has risen,
Christ, son of God.
Sing thanks to God, eia.
I HAVE RISEN AND I AM STILL WITH YOU.
I was asleep, Father, and I will wake up early
   and my sleep is pleasant to me.
YOU LAID YOUR HAND UPON ME,
For thus, Father it pleased you,
   that in dying, I should become the death of Death
   the destruction of Hell, the life of the world.
WONDERFUL IS YOUR WISDOM MADE
who have hidden this from the wise
and revealed it to the poor.
ALLELUIA

The song begins with the exhortation "Praise the great King"
Psallite regi magno and recalls Psalm 46:7:

Psallite deo nostro, psallite.   "Sing praises to God, sing praises."
Psallite regi nostro, psallite.   "Sing praises to our King, sing praises."

After this introduction comes the *Quem quaeritis*, immediately
followed by *Alleluia resurrexit/Hodie surrexit*, a combination that
we recognize from a number of versions from Italy and the transitional zone that is the Rhein-Meuse-Rhone. The reading *sicut
ipse dixit* is an *hapax* found only in this manuscript. After this
trope element we could expect to find the incipit of the antiphon
Resurrexi et adhuc tecum sum. This, however, is missing in the
manuscript, due to a lapse of the scribe, for we can see that he
has only indicated the other incipits of the antiphon by *Po*, *Mirab* in
a shortened form and without any notation. So it seems probable
that he should have written out a simple *Re*, as he did at the bottom
of the page in the following song, but simply missed it here. But
even if we assume that the *Re*-indication to the antiphon should
follow after the phrase *deo gratias dicite eia*, there is another problem here, namely the relation between the *Quem quaeritis*-complex

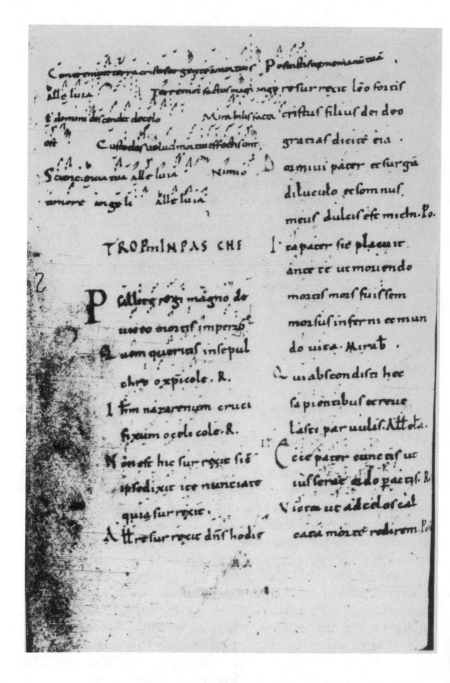

Figure 3. Paris Bibl. Nat. Lat. 1240 f.30.ᵛ

and the *Resurrexi* and its trope elements. In this case it seems as if the two are closely related.

The introductory element *Psallite regi magno* in other sources forms the first element in the suite of elements *Psallite regi magno/Dormivi pater/Ita pater* and *Qui abscondisti*, into which in Pa 1240 the *Quem quaeritis* dialogue has been inserted. Let us follow the rest of the song. Just as *psallite regi* does, the following element *Dormivi pater* alludes to a Psalm and also to Jeremiah 31:26, both expressing the theme of sleep and wakening: *Ego dormivi et soporatus sum/ exsurrexi quia dominus suscepit me* "I lie down and sleep; I wake again for the Lord sustains me"; *Ideo quasi de somno soporatus sum/et vidi/et somnus mea dulcis mihi* "I awoke and I looked, and my sleep was pleasant to me."

The trope text makes the double allusion both to the meaning of the antiphon *resurrexi* "I have risen," and to the Psalm *esurrexi*, "I woke up": "I was asleep father, and I will wake up early/ and my sleep is pleasant to me." This is then followed by the words of the antiphon, "You put your hand over me," and the next element "For thus, Father, it pleased you," citing the word of Luke 10:21: *pater quia sic placuit ante te* and Matthew 11:25: *ita pater quoniam sic fuit placitum ante te*. The second part of this element *ut moriendo mortis* etc. "that in dying I should become the death of Death, the destruction of Hell and the life of the World" refers to Hosea 13:14:

> Ero mors tua o mors   "I shall be your death, o Death"
> Ero morsus tuus inferne   "I shall be your destruction o Hell"

The antiphon continues with the phrase, "Wonderful is your wisdom" *Mirabilis facta est scientia tua*, and the final trope element comments on this by *Qui abscondisti* "you who have hidden this from the wise and revealed it to the poor." Again the trope recalls the words of Luke 10:21: *Quod abscondisti haec a sapientibus et prudentibus et revelasti ea parvulis*.

The main theme of the whole song is the victory of life over death, wakefullness after sleep, and the revelation of the news about the resurrection given to the *christicole* and to the *parvulis*. And this is exposed from different points of view in the QQ dialogue and in the trope elements: in the dialogue the protagonists are the angel and the Marys; in the trope elements Christ himself is speaking to his Father. The dialogue with the vivid scene in front of the grave is inserted as "a trope to the trope" to *Resurrexi*.

When the trope *Psallite/Dormivi* is presented in the trope manuscripts from Winchester and in Pa 887 from Aurillac, it is separated
from the QQ.[31] In Winchester the QQ-dialogue is rubricated
Angelica de Christi resurrectione, that is, "The angelical song about
the Resurrection." And after the QQ there is a new rubric, *Tropi
in die Christi resurrectioni* "Tropes on the Resurrection Day," and
after this rubric follows the group of elements *Psallite/Dormivi
pater* etc. In the Aurillac troper the order is the same, but there
are no rubrics. When QQ functions as a trope, it is always used
as an introduction to the antiphon and thus always precedes the
initial phrase of the introit antiphon *Resurrexi et adhuc tecum
sum*. Sometimes it can be difficult to identify clearly where the
QQ complex ends and the *Resurrexi* complex begins. In some cases
the two are obviously contiguous, with one trope element func-
tioning as a conjunction between them, as in the Aquitanian
and Catalonian versions in the verses *Alleluia Ad sepulchrum
residens angelus / En ecce completum est, Eia carissimi verba*, or
Psallite fratres. All of these form a transition between the dramatic
lines of the dialogue and the prophetic and solemn words of the
antiphon.

But the trope elements may also introduce the dialogue itself, as do
Hora est psallite and *Magister iam tempus est* in Volterra, where they
form a framework to the dialogue. It is as if the specific character of
the dialogue demands some sort of operation to make the "foreign
body" an organic part of the liturgical context in each particular
tradition. Whereas the lines of the QQ dialogue form an organic part
of the long *Visitatio* in its longer or shorter versions in which the
form of dialogue is maintained, there is a considerable tension
between the dialogue itself and its surrounding texts in the versions
from Apt 17 and Pa 1240, for example. There is a tension between
the horizontal dialogue of the angel and the Marys' speaking about
Christ and praising the event in the third person. Against this there
are the different points of view in the antiphon where Christ speaks
in the first person to his Father: "I have risen and I am still with
you." Thus the connection between the dialogue and the antiphon is
made by means of added transitional verses.

Conclusion

Returning to the remarks at the beginning of this survey, the question of the original form of *Quem quaeritis*, I should not be surprised if in the end we will come back to the thesis of Helmut de Boor and others that the QQ was originally an independent verse in the form of a dialogue, performed as an alternate song, an introduction to the whole Easter Mass. Today we do not know. Even if it is a thrilling challenge to trace the transmission of the text from one source to the other, what we need to do in the first place it to study the dialogue in its different versions. We should then not only see the different versions as steps in the history of the transmission of the dialogue but as texts in their own right. We should try to understand why it has these different forms, to study just how the dialogue was incorporated into the Easter liturgy according to local liturgical and literary practices and preferences, and to identify the different liturgical, esthetic and literary demands to which the *Quem quaeritis* in its various forms was made the answer.

NOTES

1. Léon Gautier, *Histoire de la poésie liturgique au Moyen Age, Les Tropes*, Paris, 1886 (1969).

2. Cf. David Björk, "On the Dissemination of '*Quem quaeritis*' and the '*Visitatio sepulchri*' and the Chronology of Their Early Sources," *Comparative Drama* 14 (1980), 46–69. Björk gives a summary of previous research, as does Clifford Flanigan in his two articles, "The Liturgical Drama and its Tradition: A Review of Scholarship 1965-1975," *Research Opportunities in Renaissance Drama*, 18 (1975), 81–102, and 19 (1976), 109–136.

3. E. K. Chambers, *The Medieval Stage*, 2 vols., London, 1903; Karl Young, *The Drama of the Medieval Church*, 2 vols., Oxford, 1933.

4. O. B. Hardison, Jr., *Christian Rite and Christian Drama in the Middle Ages*, Baltimore, 1965.

5. Timothy McGee, "The Liturgical Placement of the *Quem quaeritis* Dialogue," *Journal of the American Musicological Society*, 29 (1976), 1–29.

6. Helmut De Boor, *Die Textgeschichte der lateinischen Osterferien*, Tübingen, 1967.

7. Johan Drumbl, "Ursprung des Liturgischen Spiels," *Italia Medioevale e Umanistica*, 22 (1979), 45–96; idem, *'Quem quaeritis'. Teatro sacro dell alto medioevo*, Rome, 1981.

8. Björk, p. 63.

9. *Corpus Troporum III, Tropes du cycle de Pâques*, Studia Latina Stockholmiensia 25, ed. Gunilla Björkvall, Gunilla Iversen, Ritva Jonsson, Stockholm, 1982, pp. 8–9.

10. *Corpus Troporum III* mss. investigated:

Apt 18	Apt, Arch Bas S Anne 18 (4)	Lo 19768	London, Br Libr add 19768
Apt 17	Apt, Arch Bas S Anne 17(5)	Me 452	† Metz, Bibl mun 452
Ba 5	Bamberg, Staatsbibl lit 5	Mod 7	Modena, Bibl cap 0 1 7
Ba 6	Bamberg, Staatsbibl lit 6	Mü 14083	München, Bayer Staatsbibl Clm 14083
Ba 30	Bamberg, Staatsbibl bibl 30	Mü 14322	München, Bayer Staatsbibl Clm 14322
Be 11	†Berlin, Staatsbibl th lat IV°11		
Ben 34	Benevento, Bibl cap VI 34	Mü 14843	München, Bayer Saatsbibl Clm 14843
Ben 35	Benevento, Bibl cap VI 35		
Ben 38	Benevento, Bibl cap VI 38	Mü 14845	München, Bayer Staatsbibl Clm 14845
Ben 39	Benevento, Bibl cap VI 39		
Ben 40	Benevento, Bibl cap VI 40	Mü 27130	München, Bayer Staatsbibl Clm 27130
Bo 7	Bologna, Civico museo Q 7 (=cod. 86)	Mza 76	Monza, Bibl cap 13/76
Bo 2824	Bologna, Bibl univ 2824	Mza 77	Monza, Bibl cap 14/77
Cai 75	Cambrai, Bibl mun 75 (76)	Ox 27	Oxford, Bodl Selden supra 27
Cdg 473	Cambridge, CCC 473	Ox 222	Oxford, Bodl Douce 222
Ivr 60	Ivrea, Bibl cap 60	Ox 341	Oxford, Bodl Can lit 341
Ka 15	Kassel, Murhardsche Bibl 4° Ms theol 15	Ox 775	Oxford, Bodl 775
Ka 25	Kassel, Murhardsche Bibl 4° Ms theol 25	PaA 1169	Paris, Bibl Arsenal 1169
Kre 309	Kremsmünster, Stiftsbibl cc 309	Pa 495	Paris, BN n a lat 495
		Pa 779	Paris, BN lat 779
		Pa 887	Paris, BN lat 887
Lei 33	Leiden, Universiteitsbibl Voss lat 4° 33	Pa 903	Paris, BN lat 903
		Pa 909	Paris, BN lat 909
Lo 14	London, Br Libr Cott Cal A XIV	Pa 1084	Paris, BN lat 1084
		Pa 1118	Paris, BN lat 1118

Pa 1119	Paris, BN lat 1119	SG 378	Sankt Gallen, Stiftsbibl 378
Pa 1120	Paris, BN lat 1120	SG 380	Sankt Gallen, Stiftsbibl 380
Pa 1121	Paris, BN lat 1121	SG 381	Sankt Gallen, Stiftsbibl 381
Pa 1137	Paris, BN lat 1137	SG 382	Sankt Gallen, Stiftsbibl 382
Pa 1235	Paris, BN n a lat 1235	SG 484	Sankt Gallen, Stiftsbibl 484
Pa 1240	Paris, BN lat 1240	Stu 160	Stuttgart, Württ Landesbibl
Pa 1834	Paris, BN lat 1834		Cod brev 160
Pa 1871	Paris, BN n a lat 1871	To 18	Torino, Bibl naz F IV 18
Pa 9448	Paris, BN lat 9448	To 20	Torino, Bibl naz G V 20
Pa 9449	Paris, BN lat 9449		(1088)
Pa 10510	Paris, BN lat 10510	Ud 78	Udine, Bibl Arcivesc 78
Pa 13252	Paris, BN lat 13252	Vat 4770	Roma, bibl Vat lat 4770
Pad 20	Padova, Bibl cap A 20	Vce 56	Vercelli, Bibl cap 56
Pad 47	Padova, Bibl cap A 47	Vce 146	Vercelli, Bibl cap 146
Pad 697	Padova, Semin vescov 697	Vce 161	Vercelli, Bibl cap 161
Pia 65	Piacenza, Bibl cap 65	Vce 162	Vercelli, Bibl cap 162
Pro 12	Provins, Bibl mun 12 (24)	Vce 186	Vercelli, Bibl cap 186
Pst 119a	Pistoia, Bibl cap C 119a	Vic 105	Vich, Bibl episc 105 (111)
Pst 120a	Pistoia, Bibl cap C 120a	Vic 106	Vich, Bibl episc 106 (31)
Psa 121	Pistoia, Bibl cap C 121 a + b	Vol 39	Volterra, Bibl Guarnacci L 3
a + b			39
RoA 123	Roma, Bibl Angel 123	Vro 90	Verona, Bibl cap XC
RoA 948	Roma, Bibl Angel 948	Vro 107	Verona, Bibl cap CVII
RoC	Roma, Bibl Casan 1741	Wi 1609	Wien, Nationalbibl 1609
1741		Wi 1845	Wien, Nationalbibl 1845
RoN	Roma, Bibl naz 1343	Zü 97	Zürich, Zentralbibl Rh 97
1343		Zü 132	Zürich, Zentralbibl Rh 132
SG 376	Sankt Gallen, Stiftsbibl 376		

11. CT III, p. 222 (in the table in CT III the ms. Pa 1121 is incorrectly placed after the Italian mss.).

12. CT III, pp. 217–22.

13. In the table all the Italian manuscripts are given in italics.

14. Walter Lipphardt, *Lateinische Osterferien und Osterspiele, Ausgabe Deutscher Literatur des XV. bis XVIII. Jahrhunderts*. Reihe Drama V. 1–5, Berlin, 1975–1976. See also Susan Rankin, "Musical and Ritual Aspects of *Quem queritis*," Liturgische Tropen. Referate zweier Colloquien des Corpus Troporum in München (1983) und Canterbury (1984), ed. Gabriel Silagi, München, 1985, 181–192.

15. Åke Frid9h, "Zum Bedeutungswandel von lat. quaerere," *Eranos*, 74 (1976), 139–66.

16. Cf. Clifford Flanigan, "The Liturgical Context of the *Quem Queritis* Trope," *Studies in Medieval Drama in Honor of William L. Smoldon. Comparative Drama*, 8 (1974), 45-62: p. 56; cf. also Bernard Quint, *The 'Quem quaeritis': Its Context as Liturgical Drama*, Arizona State university, Ph.D. diss., 1976.

17. Ms. lat. Monte Cassino 127 f. 105v.

18. Ms. lat. Benevento 40 f. 20.

19. Ms lat. Benevento f. 28; ed. facs. Paleographie Musicale 15

20. *Regularis Concordia*, ed. Dom Thomas Symons, London etc., 1953, pp. 49-50.

21. Cf. CT III, pp. 222-23.

22. Cf. e.g. the *Eia carissimi verba* in the two Italian mss. Pia 65 and in Pst 121; see CT III, p. 331 and p. 333.

23. Alejandro Planchart, *The Repertory of Tropes at Winchester*, 2 vols., Princeton: Princeton University Press, 1977, I, 237-40.

24. See CT III, p. 114 and p. 133.

25. Orleans, Bibl. de la Ville, MS 201 *Colim 178*; text in Karl Young, *The Drama of the Medieval Church*, I, 393-397.

26. Cf. Susan Rankin, "The Mary Magdalene Scene in the '*Visitatio Sepulchri*' Ceremonies," *Early Music History 1:Studies in Medieval and Early Modern Music*, Cambridge, 1981.

27. Cf. Clifford Flanigan, "The Roman Rite and the Origins of the Liturgical Drama," *University of Toronto Quarterly*, 43 (1974), 279.

28. Cf. CT III, p. 218.

29. Cf. CT III, p. 117 and p. 220.

30. Cf. CT III, pp. 113, 114, 133, and 219.

31. Cf. CT III, p. 220.

Middle English Verse Punctuation: A Sample Survey

George R. Killough

Because research into medieval English punctuation has consisted mostly of single-manuscript studies, the question of the general punctuational custom has long been a puzzle.[1] This large puzzle has helped to maintain the specific puzzle of the mid-verse punctuation in the two best manuscripts of the *Canterbury Tales*, Hengwrt and Ellesmere.[2] Some scholars have been tempted to say that this punctuation is unimportant, but in the absence of knowledge about general customs these scholars are reluctant to make such a definite pronouncement, especially when the manuscripts themselves are so extremely important. Other scholars have speculated that the mid-line punctuation is an indication that Chaucer was writing a native English meter with half-line movement instead of a five-stress line adapted from the French decasyllable, which is the normal modern view.[3] If we are to know definitively why the *virgula suspensiva* (hereafter called a virgule) appears with line-by-line regularity in mid-verse throughout the poetic tales in the Hengwrt and Ellesmere manuscripts, we must survey the punctuating custom in other Middle English manuscripts.

The present survey of Middle English manuscripts suggests that mid-verse punctuation is not going to require any changes in our present ideas of Chaucer's text or meter. The evidence shows that there was indeed a limited tradition or vogue of mid-verse punctuation in Middle English, a tradition not at all tied to the native alliterative meter. There are in fact numerous manuscripts of texts in nonalliterative meters with high proportions of mid-line punctuation and even several manuscripts having mid-line punctuation to the extent and with the frequency of Hengwrt and Ellesmere. However, most manuscripts do not have this punctuation, and in the ones that do it is probably scribal, not authorial, in origin. The abundance of evidence supporting these conclusions should help to reduce the uncertainty and speculation surrounding the issue of mid-line punctuation in Hengwrt and Ellesmere.

These conclusions complement an earlier analysis of the punctuation in Hengwrt and Ellesmere, which showed that the mid-line puctuation was put in systematically according to guidelines based on syntax and the five-stress scansion, and hence not according to native meter;[4] the general purpose of the Hengwrt-Ellesmere scribe-punctuator(s) was primarily to mark the most important syntactic boundary in every line and secondarily and simultaneously to locate a metrical center.[5] Close analysis of Hengwrt and Ellesmere also showed that the marks were put in by the scribe(s) and not by Chaucer, because the rate of placement disagreement between the two manuscripts remains relatively constant from tale to tale and does not vary with textual affiliations. In sum, mid-line punctuation in Hengwrt and Ellesmere, though highly systematic, does not require us to change our ideas about Chaucer's text or meter.

The method for the present survey has been to examine as many Middle English manuscripts as possible. Although an exhaustive survey is not feasible, I have looked at manuscripts, microfilms, and facsimiles in several libraries, including the Bodleian, the Huntington, the University of Pennsylvania Library, Duke University Library, and the Hill Monastic Manuscript Library. The resources of these libraries are certainly large enough to produce a representative body of evidence. The primary objective was to find manuscripts with large quantities of mid-verse punctuation in nonalliterative English meters; see Table 1. A list was also made of manuscripts having nonalliterative poetic texts which do not contain extensive mid-line punctuation (not reproduced here). The main method of analysis was simply a determination of the proportion of the mid-line punctuation, a determination accomplished by taking counts (of all the lines if only a few leaves were available, or of the lines on sample pages if the whole manuscript was available). Counting was necessary because early experience showed that quick impressions produced erroneous estimates. Positive evidence was distinguished from negative evidence by a simple majority-minority principle: a manuscript was listed among the positive evidence if it contained texts with mid-line punctuation in more than half the lines per page and among the negative evidence if it contained mid-line punctuation in less than half the lines per page. Other factors besides proportion were recorded as well: the text, the leaves that the text occupies, the meter, the kind of mark or frequency of mark, and factors such as changes in hand or division in the text that might explain irregularities. In addition, occasional transcriptions were made of representative passages. All this information is necessary, and even more would have been useful in some cases because of the complications in texts, hands, and punctuation that can be found in Middle English manuscripts.

The survey shows (1) that *mid-line punctuation is not the exclusive possession of native meter, and there is a limited Middle English tradition of mid-line punctuation in three-stress, four-stress, and five-stress verse.* First of all, not all scribes felt obliged to punctuate the alliterative mid-point. Some manuscripts of alliterative poetry have mid-line punctuation, and some do not.[6] But more important, mid-line punctuation appears in meters other than the native alliterative meter. Several manuscripts serve as striking illustrations. The Vernon manuscript, probably produced during Chaucer's lifetime and before any of the surviving Chaucer manuscripts, had mid-line points in three-stress and four-stress poems. Cambridge Trinity College 581, containing the *Confessio Amantis*—a four-stress text—has mid-line virgules in the leaves done by Hand B, the hand Doyle and Parkes judged to be the Hengwrt-Ellesmere hand.[7] Bodleian Fairfax 16, an authoritative manuscript for some of Chaucer's minor poems, has mid-line points in four-stress and five-stress verse. Hoccleve uses mid-line virgules in substantial quantities in his own five-stress poetry; his hand, writing verses of five stresses and inserting virgules in at least half the lines, appears in Durham Cosin V.iii.9, in Huntington HM 111, and in Huntington HM 744. Finally, Table 1 reports eleven manuscripts comparable to Hengwrt and Ellesmere in extent and frequency of mid-line punctuation. These manuscripts have at least 70 leaves (that is, thousands of lines) of mid-line punctuation with line-by-line regularity. The first is the Vernon, the second is the Bodleian Fairfax 16—the above-mentioned Chaucer manuscript, and the remaining nine are manuscripts of texts by Hoccleve and/or Lydgate.[8]

Several tables show sample transcriptions to illustrate the punctuation practice in the manuscripts with mid-line punctuation. Table 2 shows lines 225–240 of *A Mournyng Song of the Loue of God* from fol. 300 of the Vernon manuscript. The line is a unit of three stresses, and the scribe customarily puts one point within this unit, not at a fixed metrical mid-point, but instead at the most important syntactic boundary—just as the Hengwrt-Ellesmere scribe(s) in the five-stress Chaucerian line. Not surprisingly, the Vernon scribe separates the alliterative half-lines in *Piers Plowman* with a point (see fol. 394), but clearly the three-stress units here are too short to be divided into half-lines. This mid-line point simply cannot be mistaken for an indication of half-line movement.[9]

Table 3 is a transcription from the Trinity Gower, Cambridge Trinity College 581, fol. 9. The text is the *Confessio Amantis*, Book III, lines 658–671. This is four-stress verse with a virgule at the most important syntactic boundary in every line. Again the line is too short to be divided into native half-lines by the mid-line mark. Notice also that the virgule does not appear at a fixed metrical mid-point; in fact, six of the lines here show a virgule after the first two syllables— hardly a likely spot for either a fixed mid-point or a native half-line division.

Lines 840-852 of Chaucer's *House of Fame*, from fol. 165[v] of Bodleian Fairfax 16, transcribed in Table 4, illustrate again, this time in a manuscript from about 1450, a mid-line virgule in four-stress verse with line-by-line regularity. This scribe is probably not as accurate as the Vernon scribe or the Hengwrt-Ellesmere-Trinity Gower scribe(s) in locating the most important syntactic boundary in every line, but he is still apparently aiming for such a position, as the lines show.

Finally, the transcription in Table 5 of the first two stanzas of Hoccleve's *Invocacio ad patrem*, written in his hand in Huntington HM 744, fol. 25, shows a mid-line virgule in five-stress meter. Notice that most lines have a virgule and that it appears at a syntactic boundary, usually at the most important one.

(2) *Most Middle English verse manuscripts do not have mid-line punctuation in any significant quantity.* In the search for punctuated manuscripts, I compiled a list of one hundred and twenty that are substantially not punctuated (have mid-line punctuation in less than half the lines per page). Most of these one hundred and twenty have practically no mid-line punctuation at all. The list contains, among other things, several manuscripts of romances, including the famous Auchinleck manuscript, and most of the *Confessio Amantis* manuscripts, which I have seen in the nearly complete microfilm collection at Duke Univesity assembled by John H. Fisher when he was

researching his book on Gower.[10] The only *Confessio Amantis* manuscript with extensive mid-line punctuation is the Trinity Gower, in which the only regular punctuator is Hand B, thought to be the Hengwrt-Ellesmere scribe himself (see above). Moreover, the vast majority of Chaucer manuscripts do not contain mid-line punctuation in any noteworthy quantity. Manly and Rickert, who make a practice of commenting on punctuation in their descriptions of the eighty-odd manuscripts of the *Canterbury Tales*, say nothing about a mid-line mark for most of the manuscripts. They note mid-line punctuation in only nine manuscripts, a small fraction of the total.[11] Even the list of manuscripts with punctuation in Table 1 may *seem* to demonstrate a greater quantity of positive evidence than there really is. It is worth remembering that only eleven out of the forty-two are known to have mid-line puctuation in the extent and frequency of Hengwrt and Ellesmere.

(3) *In Middle English nonalliterative meters, poetic punctuation is probably used first for separating verses written out in prose lineation, gains popularity in the role of separating short lines written out in a long-line format, and then appears in the syntactic-metrical role within four-stress and five-stress lines, as in Vernon, Hengwrt, and Ellesmere.* An example of English verses written as prose but separated by points is the *Bestiary* manuscript from the second half of the thirteenth century, British Library Arundel 292.[12] An example of English septenarious verse written in a long-line format and separated into four-stress and three-stress segments by punctuation is the *Life of St. Margaret* in Cambridge Trinity College 323, a manuscript from the thirteenth century.[13] Table 6 shows four lines from fol. 20. The famous Harley 2253 from about 1330–1340 also uses punctuation, this time a virgule, to separate short lines written out in long-line format. Table 7 shows the way *Alysoun* appears on fol. 63ᵛ. In the late fourteenth century, punctuation begins to appear *within* the line in *nonalliterative* meters. The Vernon mauscript from the last decade of the century is the first example I have found of this practice (see sample transcription in Table 2).

The importance of this description of development is that it shows how poetic punctuation progressed from marking verse boundaries to marking syntax boundaries within verses. The long-line format that appears in manuscripts like Cambridge Trinity College 323 and Harley 2253 gives the impression of a mid-line marking even though

the mark is really a between-line marking. English scribes who had
seen this format and some syntactically-punctuated Latin manuscripts (not to mention the native alliterative punctuation, which
would contribute to the general impression that verse lines deserve
interior marks) could easily make the next step of giving mid-line
punctuation to every four-stress or five-stress English line.[14]

(4) *Mid-line punctuation enjoys a limited vogue in England in the
fifteenth century.* The list of manuscripts with substantial punctuation suggests that from the time of the Vernon manuscript, mid-line
punctuation had a certain fashionableness for several decades. To be
sure, the fashion was not observed in most manuscripts, but it was
observed in several, especially in manuscripts associated with
Chaucer and his admirers. Hengwrt, Ellesmere, and Cambridge
University Library Dd.4.24 are all early Chaucer manuscripts with
extensive mid-line punctuation. In addition, Table 1 shows that both
John Shirley and Thomas Hoccleve used mid-line punctuation.
Moreover, texts by Hoccleve or Lydgate have mid-line punctation in
twenty-seven of the manuscripts listed in Table 1. In contrast, only
one of the thirty-six *Confessio Amantis* manuscripts that I have seen
in microfilm (including those thought to be from Gower's
scriptorium) has any significant quantity of mid-line punctuation,
and that one manuscript is the Cambridge Trinity Gower in which
the one punctuating scribe is thought to be the same scribe who wrote
Hengwrt and Ellesmere. Until more is known, we can infer that
mid-line punctuation enjoyed a certain fashionableness in the texts
of Chaucer's followers, perhaps arising out of concern for the
legitimacy of the new English poetry, but that this fashion did not
extend to the scribes of Gower's texts.[15]

(5) *Mid-line punctuation is usually scribal, not authorial, in
origin.* My earlier study showed that the mid-line virgules in Hengwrt
and Ellesmere were put in by the scribe(s) and not by Chaucer.[16] The
present study supports this conclusion by showing that mid-line
punctuation is often associated with individual hands or hand types.
The hands in Hengwrt and Ellesmere and Hand B in the Trinity
Gower, which all look like the same hand, use a mid-line virgule.
This virgule is especially noticeable in the Trinity Gower because, of
the other four hands, only Hand E, Hoccleve, uses mid-line virgules.
Hoccleve of course uses mid-line punctuation in other manuscripts
too. John Shirley's hand is another identifiable one associated with
mid-line punctuation. Two of the eleven manuscripts comparable to

Hengwrt and Ellesmere in extent and frequency of punctuation, Bodleian Ashmole 46 and Bodleian Laud Misc. 673, are now thought to be by the same hand.[17] And several manuscripts, each written by more than one scribe, show mid-line punctuation in some hands but not in others within the same text; see Table 8.

(6) *In general, scribes took a less systematic attitude toward punctuation than modern editors do.* For this conclusion the negative evidence is especially instructive. Numerous Middle English manuscripts that have little mid-line punctuation still have a few punctuated lines, sometimes five lines per fifty-line column, sometimes one-third of the lines per page. These proportions, coupled with the wide variation in proportion from page to page and from manuscript to manuscript in the total sample, suggest that most scribes had no firm commitment to punctuation, no list of rules posted on their desks or in their minds, but instead simply inserted a mark from time to time because they had seen mid-line punctuation in other manuscripts, thought it was not a bad idea, and felt especially inspired when they came to certain lines. Table 9, a selection of items excerpted in abbreviated form from the list of English manuscripts that are less than half punctuated, supports this conclusion. The salient characteristic in this list is the sporadic and casual incidence of punctuation.

More evidence of the unsystematic tendency of the scribes is found in the way that regular punctuation stops short in some manuscripts. In Cambridge Trinity College 602, for example, there is a mid-line virgule with line-by-line regularity in the first text, Lydgate's *Life of the Virgin* (fols. 1–109^v), and on the first page of the second text, Hoccleve's *De Regimine Principum* (fol. 111); then the virgule ceases until fol. 147 where it resumes through fol. 192 but fails to reach the end of the text on fol. 207^v. The hand is the same throughout, and the stopping and starting does not correspond to divisions in the text. The same kind of change in practice is found in Bodleian Fairfax 16, in which the scribe, after using a mid-line virgule with line-by-line regularity in several poetic texts for over 267 leaves, suddenly stops in the middle of fol. 268^v, half way through Lydgate's *Reason and Sensuality*, and the virgule remains absent through the end of the text on fol. 300. This lapse can be attributed neither to change of hand— it is all the same scribe—nor to division in the text; it is simply a lapse.

In addition to showing that scribes were generally less persistent with punctuation than modern editors, lapses sometimes suggest that punctuation was regarded as a special feature, something worth having at the beginning of a manuscript or text but hard to sustain (or simply remember) through a whole work. For example, Lambeth 742, containing Lydgate's *Siege of Thebes*, has a mid-line virgule in about half the lines in only the first third of the manuscript, and Lambeth 306, a collection of several texts in several hands, has a mid-line point or virgule in almost every line of the first page of the *Libeaus Desco*n*us*, fol. 73, but virtually no mid-line punctuation in the rest of this text.

One final difference between the scribal attitude and the attitude of modern editors is that, in general, scribes put less importance on the kind of mark. First of all, it is clear that the point and the virgule had equivalent value (a phenomenon for which there is no exact counterpart in modern practice). The Vernon, for example, uses points in the same kinds of positions where Hengwrt uses virgules. Moreover, the role of line-separator can be performed by the point (as in Cambridge Trinity College 323), the virgule (as in Harley 2253), or the *punctus elevatus* (as in Cambridge Trinity College R.4.26).[18] Variation in marks is probably not just the result of equivalences mandated by medieval guidelines, nor is it likely to be the result of systematic disagreement between scribes. Instead it must stem mostly from a more casual attitude than our own, because some scribes even change marks in mid-manuscript. Cambridge Trinity College 652, for example, shows a mid-line point in three-quarters of the lines per page in Lydgate's *Destruction of Thebes* from fol. 89 to fol. 152; then from the middle of fol. 152 through fol. 169 there is an equally regular mid-line virgule, put in apparently by the same scribe who used points before. Likewise, Bodleian Fairfax 16 has its first text punctuated in the first three pages (fols. 15–16) with a regular mid-line point, and then the same scribe begins using a mid-line virgule in mid-text on fol. 16^v and continues with a regular mid-line virgule through many texts for over 250 leaves.[19] These shifts and the failure to correct them (only three pages would have needed to be corrected in Fairfax 16) must certainly indicate that scribes and readers paid less attention to the exact form of the mark of punctuation than we do. It is important to recognize this difference in attitude, not because individual marks had no characteristic uses, but because modern experience may lead us to seek exclusive uses for each mark when in fact there was an overlap.

The numerous manuscripts showing a dearth of mid-line punctuation, the varying incidence of mid-line punctuation within manuscripts and from manuscript to manuscript, and the lapses and overlaps in mark usage all suggest that Middle English scribes had an attitude toward punctuation much more casual than our own—so casual, in fact, that further study of mid-line punctuation is not *likely* to lead to any new revelations about Middle English texts or meters. To be sure, not all scribes were alike in attitude or habit, and special attention to particular manuscripts may prove fruitful, but the balance of evidence from the present survey severely decreases the likelihood that scribal punctuation study will ever change our idea of Chaucer's text or meter.

The survey-catalogue method used in this study helps to solve questions about Chaucer's meter and the origin of the virgules in Hengwrt and Ellesmere. For both questions, the survey confirms the results of close analysis: (1) the orthodox theory of meter is still the best one because there is no longer any reason to associate mid-line punctuation with alliterative half-lines; and (2) the punctuation is attributable to the scribe(s) instead of Chaucer because the probable custom was for punctuation to be a matter of scribal preference and prerogative. Although mid-line punctuation can be highly systematic and enjoyed a certain vogue in the texts of Chaucer's followers, it need not change our present understanding of Chaucer's meter or text.

Table 1

English Manuscripts Containing Texts with Mid-line Punctuation in More Than Half the Lines Per Page

The entries are organized roughly by date, except that I have tried to keep manuscripts of the same text together. Because some manuscripts contain many texts that are not all written in the same meter, with the same punctuation, or by the same scribe, organization is difficult. Since it is desirable to know how many manuscripts have mid-line punctuation, every entry is listed as a manuscript, but within an entry there can be several texts, each with its own special features listed thereafter. The order of information is as follows. The first line gives the library and shelf-mark or catalogue number of the manuscript, and if I have seen only a few leaves in reproduction, those leaves. The second line gives the text and, for manuscripts that contain several texts, the leaves which that text occupies. In manuscripts of numerous texts, I list only a few texts which are significant because of their fame, length, or peculiar kind of punctuation. The line below the text shows the date of the mauscript. If I have not seen the manuscript itself, I list on the next line the modern sources where I have found reproductions. The penultimate line shows the meter of the text, and the last line tells about the punctuation.

XIVth Century

1. Bodleian Library, Eng. Poet. a.1 (Vernon)
    La Estorie Del Euangelie, Brown-Robbins no. 3194, fols. 105–105^v
    1390–1400
    English 4-stress verse
    A mid-line point with line-by-line regularity

    Northern Homily Cycle, fols. 167–227^v
    English 4-stress verse
    A mid-line point with line-by-line regularity

    The Pricke of Conscience, fols. 265–284
    English verse, mostly 4-stress
    A mid-line point with line-by-line regularity

    Þe *Prikke of Loue*, Brown-Robbins no. 974, fols. 284–286
    English 4-stress verse
    A mid-line point with line-by-line regularity

    King Robert of Cicyle, fols. 300–301
    English 4-stress verse
    A mid-line point with line-by-line regularity

    Charite is no lengor Cheere, Brown-Robbins no. 4157, fol. 410
    English 4-stress verse
    A mid-line point with line-by-line regularity

2. Cambridge, Trinity College 353 (B.15.17)
    Piers Plowman, B Text, fols. 1–130^v
    late XIV
    Hill Monastic Manuscript Library microfilm
    English alliterative verse
    Regular mid-line points

    "Crist made to man a fair present," Brown-Robbins no. 611, fol. 147
    English 4-stress verse
    A mid-line point in half the lines

XVth Century

3. University of Pennsylvania Library, Eng. 1
   Prick of Conscience, fols. 14–118
   ca. 1400
   English verse, mostly 4-stress
   A majority of lines have a mid-line point; some pages, e.g., fol. 91, have a
   point in every line.

4. Bodleian Library, Douce 157
   Prick of Conscience, fols. 1–114ᵛ
   ca. 1400
   English verse, mostly 4-stress
   A mid-line point in as many as 10 lines per 37-line page for the first 50 leaves,
   then a mid-line point or two or three or four per line in 30% to 95% of the
   lines per page for the rest of the manuscript; the increase in incidence is
   gradual and does not correspond with any textual division or change of
   hand.

5. Bodleian Library, Douce 141
   Prick of Conscience, fols. 1–129ᵛ
   first half XV
   English verse, mostly 4-stress
   Virtually no mid-line punctuation for the first 96 leaves; the new hand on fol.
   97 uses a mid-line point in two or three lines per page, increases the
   frequency, has a point in a majority of lines by fol. 105ᵛ, and then
   substitutes a mid-line *punctus elevatus* on fol. 106ᵛ, which continues with
   nearly line-by-line regularity to the end of the text; although the beginning
   of mid-line punctuation can be explained by the beginning of a new hand
   and a new quire on fol. 97, there is no such explanation for the increase in
   incidence, which occurs gradually, or for the shift to the *punctus elevatus*,
   which occurs suddenly in mid-text and in mid-page.

   Exposition of the *Pater Noster*, Brown-Robbins no. 958, fols. 130–138
   English 4-stress verse
   A mid-line *punctus elevatus* with nearly line-by-line regularity

6. Cambridge, Trinity College 581 (R.3.2)
   Confessio Amantis, Gower
   first quarter XV
   Duke University Library microfilm N/1549
   English 4-stress verse
   This is the Trinity Gower MS in which Doyle and Parkes have identified five
   hands, of which Hand B is the Hengwrt-Ellesmere scribe and Hand E is
   Hoccleve. Hand B here uses a mid-line virgule with line-by-line regularity
   and Hand E uses as many as 11 mid-line virgules in a 46-line column.

7. Cambridge, University Library Dd.4.24, fols. 177–187
   Canterbury Tales, Chaucer

ca. 1400–1420
Xerox copy circulating for *Variorum Chaucer* transcription work
English 5-stress verse
A mid-line virgule with line-by-line regularity.

8. British Library, Harley 2392 (H⁴), fol. 64ᵛ
   Troilus and Criseyde, Chaucer
   middle XV
   Robert Kilburn Root, *The Manuscripts of Chaucer's Troilus*, Chaucer
     Society, 98 (London: Kegan Paul, Trench, Trübner, 1914), pp. 29–30.
   English 5-stress verse
   27 of the 28 lines on fol. 64ᵛ have mid-line virgules.

9. Bodleian Library, Rawl. Poet, 163
   Troilus and Criseyde, Chaucer, fols. 1–113ᵛ
   XV
   English 5-stress verse
   Hand 2 uses practically no mid-line punctuation in his first stint, then has as
     many as 37 lines with a mid-line virgule per 38-line page in his second stint.
     Hand 3 has a few mid-line virgules on fols. 20–25, but then on fols.
     25ᵛ–42ᵛ, the end of his stint, he has a mid-line virgule in 60% to 95% of the
     lines per page; the increase in virgule incidence does not correspond with
     any textual division or quire boundary. Hand 1 uses practically no mid-line
     punctuation. Hand 4 has some but only on the two pages following Hand
     2, who punctuates.

10. British Library, Harleian 1239 (H³), fols. 15, 33ᵛ
    Troilus and Criseyde, Chaucer
    XV
    Root, *The Manuscripts of Chaucer's Troilus*, pp. 25–28.
    English 5-stress verse
    Hand 2 has a mid-line point or virgule in at least half the lines.

11. Bodleian Library, Fairfax 16
    The Complaint of Mars, Chaucer, fols. 15–19
    ca. 1450
    Bodleian Library, MS Fairfax 16, intro. John Norton-Smith (London: Scolar
      Press, 1979).
    English 5-stress verse
    A mid-line point with line-by-line regularity on fols. 15–16, and then a
      mid-line virgule with line-by-line regularity on fols. 16ᵛ–19

    Legend of Good Women, Chaucer, fols. 83–119ᵛ
    English 5-stress verse
    A mid-line virgule with line-by-line regularity

    The Parliament of Fowls, Chaucer, fols. 120–129ᵛ
    English 5-stress verse
    A mid-line virgule with line-by-line regularity

The Book of the Duchess, Chaucer, fols. 130–147^v
English 4-stress verse
A mid-line virgule with line-by-line regularity

The House of Fame, Chaucer, fols, 154^v–183^v
English 4-stress verse
A mid-line virgule with line-by-line regularity

Reason and Sensuality, Lydgate, fols. 202–300 (text incomplete)
English 4-stress verse
A mid-line virgule with line-by-line regularity up to fol. 268^v, where it is
    absent in the last 17 lines and remains absent through fol. 300; there is no
    change of hands nor division in the text nor anything else on fol. 268^v to
    explain the cessation of mid-line punctuation.

12. Sion College, Archives 2.23
    ABC, Chaucer (in the hand of John Shirley)
    ca. 1440
    Autotypes of Chaucer Manuscripts, ed. Frederick J. Furnivall, Chaucer
        Society, 62 (London, 1880), Part 3.
    English 5-stress verse
    23 of the 25 lines have mid-line virgules.

13. Bodleian Library, Ashmole 59, fols. 1–134 (in the hand of John Shirley)
    Fall of Princes, Lydgate, fols. 13–16^v
    middle XV
    English 5-stress verse
    A mid-line virgule in 75% to 95% of the lines per page

    Poems by Lydgate, Chaucer, and others, interspersed with bits of prose, fols.
        16^v–73^v
    English verse, most poems being 5-stress but some being 4-stress
    A mid-line virgule in 60% to 90% of the lines per page; in the long-line
        format used for the *Stabat Mater Dolorosa*, Brown-Robbins no. 1048
        (English 4-stress verse), a virgule appears regularly as a line-separator and
        occasionally within the 4-stress segment.

    Sayings of Old Philosophers, Brown-Robbins no. 3487, fols. 84^v–98
    English 5-stress verse
    A mid-line virgule in 65% to 85% of the lines per page plus an occasional
        mid-line point.

14. Cambridge, Trinity College 600 (R. 3. 20), (in the hand of John Shirley)
    Poems by Lydgate, Chaucer, Hoccleve, et al.
    1456?
    Hill Monastic Manuscript Library microfilm
    English, French, and Latin meters
    Varying quantities of mid-line virgules, more frequent on dark unfaded pages
        than faded pages and more frequent in English and Latin poetry than
        French poetry.

15. Durham University Library, Cosin V.iii.9, fols. 13ᵛ, 95 (Hoccleve's autograph)
    Dialogus Cum Amico, Hoccleve
    ca. 1419-1426
    H. C. Schulz, "Thomas Hoccleve Scribe," *Speculum*, 12 (1937), 71-81,
    plate #2.
    English 5-stress verse
    6 of the 7 lines that appear in the plate have mid-line virgules.

    Envoy to the Duchess of Westmoreland, Hoccleve
    English 5-stress verse
    All 8 lines that appear in the plate have mid-line virgules.

16. Huntington Library, HM 111, fol. 26 (Hoccleve's hand)
    Le Male Regle, Hoccleve
    ca. 1422-1426
    H. C. Schulz, "Thomas Hoccleve Scribe," *Speculum*, 12 (1937), 71-78,
    plate #1.
    English 5-stress verse
    4 of the 8 lines in the plate have mid-line virgules.

17. Huntington Library, HM 744 (Hoccleve's hand)
    Invocacio ad patrem and other short poems, Hoccleve, fols. 25-52ᵛ
    ca. 1422-1426
    English 5-stress verse
    Mid-line virgules in about half the lines.

18. Bodleian Library, Digby 181
    Letter of Cupid, Hoccleve, fols. 1-6ᵛ
    last quarter XV
    English 5-stress verse
    A mid-line virgule or point in 60% to 80% of the lines per page

    The Pain and Sorrow of Evil Marriage, Brown-Robbins no. 919, fols. 7-8ᵛ
    English 5-stress verse
    A mid-line virgule or point in two-thirds of the lines per page

    Examples Against Women, probably by Lydgate, Brown-Robbins no. 3744,
    fols. 8ᵛ-10
    English 5-stress verse
    A mid-line virgule or point in two-thirds of the lines per page

    Instructions, Peter Idle, Brown-Robbins no. 1540, fols. 10ᵛ-30ᵛ
    English 5-stress verse
    A mid-line virgule in as many as half the lines per page but usually much less

    The Complaint of the Black Knight, Lydgate, Brown-Robbins no. 1507, fols.
    31-39
    English 5-stress verse
    A mid-line virgule or point in 10% to 50% of the lines per page

    Anelida and Arcite, Chaucer, fols. 39ᵛ-43ᵛ

English 5-stress verse
A mid-line virgule or point in one-quarter of the lines per page

The Parliament of Fowls, Chaucer, fols. 44–52
English 5-stress verse
A mid-line virgule or point in 20% to 40% of the lines per page

The Fall of Princes, Lydgate, fols. 52–53ᵛ
English 5-stress verse
A mid-line virgule or point in 40% of the lines per page

Troilus and Criseyde, Chaucer, fols. 54–93ᵛ (different scribe)
English 5-stress verse
Virtually no mid-line punctuation.

19. Bodleian Library, Selden Supra 53
    De Regimine Principum, Hoccleve, fols. 1–76
    ca. 1430
    English 5-stress verse
    A mid-line virgule with line-by-line regularity

    Hoccleve's *Complaint*, fols. 76–83ᵛ
    English 5-stress verse
    A mid-line virgule with line-by-line regularity

    Dialogus Cum Amico, Hoccleve, fols. 83ᵛ–98
    English 5-stress verse
    A mid-line virgule with line-by-line regularity

    Hoccleve's *Tale of the Emperor Gerelaus*, fols. 98ᵛ–115ᵛ
    English 5-stress verse
    A mid-line virgule with line-by-line regularity

    Ars Sciendi Mori, Hoccleve, fols. 117–133
    English 5-stress verse
    A mid-line virgule with line-by-line regularity

    Tale of Jonathas, Hoccleve, fols. 134ᵛ–146ᵛ
    English 5-stress verse
    A mid-line virgule with line-by-line regularity

    Dance of Macabre, Lydgate, fols. 148–158ᵛ
    English 5-stress verse
    A mid-line virgule with line-by-line regularity.

20. British Library, Royal 17D.vi, fol. 93ᵛ
    De Regimine Principum, Hoccleve
    early XV
    F. E. Halliday, *Chaucer and his World* (New York: Viking, 1968), frontispiece.
    English 5-stress verse
    Mid-line points with line-by-line regularity.

21. Bodleian Library, Douce 158
    De Regimine Principum, Hoccleve, fols. 1–96ᵛ
    second quarter XV
    English 5-stress verse
    A mid-line virgule in 50% to 90% of the lines per page; occasional mid-line
    points and *puncti elevati* as well.

22. Bodleian Library, Ashmole 40
    De Regimine Principum, Hoccleve, fols. 1–97ᵛ
    third quarter XV
    English 5-stress verse
    A mid-line virgule with line-by-line regularity.

23. Bodleian Library, Rawl. Poet. 168
    De Regimine Principum, Hoccleve, fols. 1–58
    middle XV
    English 5-stress verse
    A mid-line point with nearly line-by-line regularity.

24. Bodleian Library, Dugdale 45
    De Regimine Principum, Hoccleve, fols. 1–96ᵛ
    late XV
    English 5-stress verse
    A few mid-line points and fewer virgules in the first half of the MS, then
    suddenly a mid-line virgule in one-half the lines per page from fol. 53ᵛ
    through fol. 67ᵛ, and then after a lapse in which the rate of mid-line
    punctuation falls to one-quarter of the lines per page, there is a mid-line
    virgule in three-quarters of the lines per page from fol. 77 to the end; there
    is no change of hand or division in the text to explain the changes in
    punctuation incidence, and the changes occur near but not at quire
    boundaries.

25. Cambridge, Trinity College 602 (R.3.22)
    Life of Our Lady, Lydgate, fols. 1–109ᵛ
    early XV
    Hill Monastic Manuscript Library microfilm
    English 5-stress verse
    Mid-line virgules with line-by-line regularity

    De Regimine Principum, Hoccleve, fols. 111–207ᵛ
    English 5-stress verse
    Mid-line virgules with line-by-line regularity on fols. 111, 147–192; the
    virgules stop and start for no apparent reasons, neither for a change of text
    nor for a change of hand—this is all one text and the whole MS is in one
    hand.

26. Bodleian Library, Bodley 120
    Life of Our Lady, Lydgate, fols. 1–94ᵛ
    second half XV
    English 5-stress verse

A mid-line virgule in 50% to 90% of the lines per page in the work of Hand 1 (fols. 1-7); Hands 2 and 3 use little mid-line punctuation.

27. Bodleian Library, Rawl. C.446
    Troy Book, Lydgate, fols. 1-174^v
    second quarter XV
    English 5-stress verse
    A mid-line virgule in 80% to 100% of the lines per column.

28. Cambridge, Trinity College 652 (R.4.20)
    Siege of Thebes, Lydgate, fols. 89-169
    early XV
    Hill Monastic Manuscript Library microfilm
    English 5-stress verse
    Mid-line points in more than 3/4 of the lines per page on fols. 89-152 and then equally regular mid-line virgules on fols. 152-169; this shift from points to virgules occurs for no apparent reason: there is no major division in the text here, and the hand, though more compact as if the pen had been sharpened, seems the same.

29. Bodleian Library, Bodley 776
    Siege of Thebes, Lydgate, fols. 1-72
    1430-1440
    English 5-stress verse
    A mid-line point, virgule, [~], or point-and-virgule in 60% to 95% of the lines per page; the most common mark as the manuscript progresses becomes the point-and-virgule.

30. Lambeth Palace Library 742
    Siege of Thebes, Lydgate
    XV
    The Medieval Manuscripts of Lambeth Palace Library on microfilm
    English 5-stress verse
    Mid-line virgules in about half the lines in the first third of the MS.

31. Bodleiam Library, Rawl. C.48
    Siege of Thebes, Lydgate, fols. 5-78
    end of XV
    English 5-stress verse
    A mid-line virgule in 50% to 85% of the lines per page

    Short Poems, Lydgate, fols. 78^v-81^v
    English 5-stress verse
    A mid-line virgule in 50% to 90% of the lines per page

    Cato Major, Benedict Burgh, Brown-Robbins no. 854, fols. 84-111^v
    English 5-stress verse (interspersed with Cato's Latin Distichs)
    A mid-line virgule in 60% to 90% of the English lines per page

    Short Poems, Lydgate, fols. 111^v-134^v

English 5-stress verse
A mid-line virgule in 65% to 90% of the lines per page.

32. British Library, Harley 2278, fol. 66^v (Wright), fol. 109^v (Watson)
   St. Edmund and St. Fremund, Lydgate
   1433
   C. E. Wright, *English Vernacular Hands* (Oxford: Clarendon, 1960), plate
   #18; Andrew G. Watson, *Catalogue of Dated and Datable Manuscripts*
   (London: British Library, 1979), II, plate #418.
   English 5-stress verse
   Mid-line virgules in more than 3/4 of the lines.

33. Bodleian Library, Tanner 347
   St. Edmund and St. Fremund, Lydgate, fols. 1–98
   XV
   English 5-stress verse
   A mid-line virgule with line-by-line regularity.

34. Bodleian Library, Ashmole 46 (perhaps the same hand as Laud Misc. 673)
   St. Edmund ad St. Fremund, Lydgate, fols. 1–96^v
   after 1461
   English 5-stress verse
   A mid-line virgule with line-by-line regularity.

   Secrees of old Philisoffres, Lydgate and Burgh, fols. 97–160^v
   English 5-stress verse
   A mid-line virgule with line-by-line regularity.

35. Bodleian Library, Laud Misc. 673 (perhaps the same hand as Ashmole 46)
   Secrees of old Philisoffres, Lydgate and Burgh, fols. 1–73^v
   XV
   English 5-stress verse
   A mid-line virgule with line-by-line regularity.

36. Bodleian Library, Rawl. C.448
   Fall of Princes, Lydgate, fols. 1–185
   middle XV
   English 5-stress verse
   Mid-line punctuation with line-by-line regularity from fol. 9, the begining of
   the second quire, to the end; on fols. 9–11 the mark is a double virgule, on
   fol. 12 the mark is a point-and-virgule, and then from fol. 12^v onward the
   mark is a single virgule except for a brief spate of double virgules on fol.
   32 and 32^v; the changes in mark occur in mid-text, mid-quire, and in most
   instances in mid-page, and the hand is the same throughout.

37. Bodleian Library, Bodley 263
   Fall of Princes, Lydgate, pp. 1–447
   second quarter XV, after 1439
   English 5-stress verse
   A mid-line virgule with line-by-line regularity.

38. Lincoln Cathedral Library 129
    Minor Poems, Lydgate, fols. 1–89
    XV
    Lincoln Cathedral Library: The Medieval Manuscripts Collection on microfilm
    English 5-stress verse
    Mid-line virgules with line-by-line regularity.

39. Cambridge, Trinity College 601 (R.3.21)
    Miscellaneous poems in English
    XV (time of Edward IV)
    Hill Monastic Manuscript Library microfilm
    English 4-stress and 5-stress verse
    Virtually no mid-line punctuation in the bulk of the MS except for a regular mid-line punctuation in the 4-stress poems on fols. 34–49^v; these points begin at the beginning of "By a forest side walking as I went" and end in the middle of another poem, "Lef lord my soule thou spare," and their beginning and ending do not correspond to any change in hand.

40. British Library, Harleian 3869
    Pageant Verses for Queen Margaret's Entry into London (1445), Brown-Robbins no. 2200, fols. 2–4^v
    XV
    Duke University Library microfilm N/1558
    English 5-stress verse
    Mid-line virgules with line-by-line regularity on these 3 leaves, which are written in a hand different from the hand that does the main text, *Confessio Amantis*, which has as many as 4 mid-line points per 46-line page.

41. British Library, Arundel 327, fols. 11, 28^v, 134^v
    Lives of the Saints, Bokenham
    1447
    Andrew G. Watson, *Catalogue of Dated and Datable Manuscripts* (London: British Library, 1979), II, plate #488.
    English verse, mostly 5-stress
    Mid-line virgules with line-by-line regularity in fol. 11, which represents Hand 1, but the other two leaves, which represent the other two hands, show no mid-line punctuation.

42. Cambridge, Trinity College 597 (R. 3. 17)
    The Romance of Earl Raymond of Poitiers in English
    late XV
    Hill Monastic Manuscript Library microfilm
    English 5-stress verse
    An average of half the lines per page have mid-line virgules; faded ink or bad filming make it hard to tell for sure.

Table 2

Bodleian Library, Eng. Poet. a.1 (Vernon), fol. 300
A Mournyng Song of the Loue of God, lines 225–240

Ful hard hit is . þi bed.
A treo . þat stondeþ stille
In wo . and weder sted.
Þ eroute . he hongeþ on hille
For beten . and for bled.
Wiþ Men . þat wolden . hem spille.
Al þus ha þloue þe led.
Þi le*m*mon . for to tille.
Þi self þou mai3t not schelde.
Ne torne . so art þou fest
Þou hast nout on . to helde.
Þin hed . on for to rest.
Al mihti kyng . to welde
Al þat is worst . and best
Hou miht I . euer þe3 elde
Þe loue . þat þus wol lest.ª

Table 3

Cambridge, Trinity College 581 (R.3.2), fol. 9
Confessio Amantis, Gower, Book III, lines 658–671

And seigh / how þat hir sely spouse
Was set —/ and looked on a book —/
Nigh to the fir / as he which took —/
His ese / for a man of age
And she bigan / the woode rage
And axeth hi*m* / what dẹuel he thoghte
And bar on hond / þat hi*m* ne roghte
What labour / þat she took —/ on honde
And seith / that swich an housbonde
Was to a wif —/ noght worth a stree
He seide / nouther nay / ne yee
But heeld hi*m* stille / and leet hire chide
And she / which may hir self nat hide
Bigan / with Inne for to swelleᵇ

Table 4

Bodleian Library, Fairfax 16, fol. 165ᵛ
House of Fame, Chaucer, lines 840–852

> Hyt seweth euery sound / p*a*rde
> Moueth kyndely / to pace
> Al vp / in to his kyndely place
> And this place / of whic*h* I telle
> Ther as Fame / lyst to duelle
> Ys set / amyddys of these three
> Heven / erthe / and eke the see
> As most conseruatyf / the soun
> Than ys this / the conclusyon
> That euery speche / or eu*er*y man
> As y the telle / first began
> Moveth vp / on high to pace
> Kyndely / to fames place

Table 5

Huntington Library, HM 744, fol. 25 (Hoccleve's hand)
Invocacio ad patrem, Hoccleve, lines 1–14

> *T*o thee / we make our*e* inuocacioun
> Thow god / the fadir / which vn to us a̶l̶l̶
> Art eueremo / for our sauuacion
> Reedy to heer*e* vs / whan we to thee ca̶l̶l̶
> In any cause / þ*a*t may happe *and* fa̶l̶l̶e̶
> As fer / as sowneth in to Rightwisnesse
> Which excede nat may thy blisfulnesse
>
> For thow fadir / art trouthe and veritee
> Thyn owne sone / þ*a*t same is also
> And syn it so is / what may bettre be
> If þ*a*t a man shal to the trouthe go
> Than preye thee / withouten wordes mo
> Fadir of heuene / in thy sones name
> Foryeue our giltes / and relesse our blame.

Table 6

Cambridge, Trinity College 323 (B.14.39), fol. 20
Life of St. Margaret, Brown-Robbins no. 2672 XIII

From asie to auntioge . bet miles tene a*n*t fiue.
For to slen c*r*istene men . he hiede him biliue.
e sei maidan maragrete . scep bi foren hire
sone wolde þe sarezin . habben hire to wiue.

Table 7

British Library, Harley 2253, fol. 63ᵛ
Alysoun 1330–1340

¶Bytuene mersh *and* Aueril . When spray biginne*p* to sp*r*inge
Þe lutel foul haþ hire wyl / on hyre lud to synge
Ich libbe in louelonginge / for semlokest of alle βynge.
He may be blisse bringe / . icham in hire baundoun
An hendy hap ichabbe yhent —/ ichot from heuene it is me sent —/
From alle wymmen mi loue is lent —/ *and* lyht on Alysoun
On heu hire her is fayr ynoh / hire browe broune hire eʒe blake
Wiþ lossum chere he on me loh / wiþ middel smal *and* wel ymake
Bote he me wolle to hire take / forte buen hire owen make
Longe to lyuen ichulle forsake / *and* feye fallen adoun / An hendy hap
etc.

Table 8

*Manuscripts Having Punctuation In Some Hands But Not In Others
In The Same Text*

1. Bodleian Library, Douce 141
   Prick of Conscience
   Hand 1 uses virtually no mid-line punctuation, but Hand 2 uses a few
   mid-line points at first, then a mid-line *punctus elevatus* with line-by-line
   regularity.

2. Bodleian Library, Rawl. Poet. 163
   Troilus and Criseyde, Chaucer
   Hands 2, 3, and 4 use a mid-line virgule in varying frequencies, but Hand 1
   uses practically no mid-line punctuation.

3. British Library, Harley 1239, fols. 15, 33ᵛ
    Troilus and Criseyde, Chaucer
    Hand 2 has a mid-line point or virgule in a majority of lines, but Hands 1 and 3 use no mid-line punctuation.

4. Bodleian Library, Bodley 120
    Life of Our Lady, Lydgate
    Hand 1 uses a mid-line virgule in 50% to 90% of the lines per page, but Hands 2 and 3 use little mid-line punctuation.

5. British Library, Arundel 327, fols. 11, 28ᵛ, 134ᵛ
    Lives of the Saints, Bokenham
    Hand 1 uses mid-line virgules but Hands 2 and 3 do not.

6. Bodleian Library, Tanner 346
    Book of the Duchess, Chaucer, fols. 102-119ᵛ
    The first hand uses a mid-line virgule in 10% to 60% of the lines per page, but the other hand uses practically no mid-line punctuation.

Table 9

Representative List of Negative Evidence
Showing Manuscripts with Infrequent or Sporadic
Mid-Line Punctuation

1. Huntington El. 26 A. 17 (*Confessio Amantis*), up to 3 lines with a mid-line tick (✓) per 46-line column

2. Bodleian Fairfax 3 (*Confessio Amantis*), up to 5 lines with mid-line points per 46-line column

3. British Library Egerton 913 (*Confessio Amantis*), virtually no mid-line punctuation, but the second of the three hands has up to 5 lines with mid-line virgules per 30-line page

4. Cambridge St. Catharine's College 7 (*Confessio Amantis*), up to 4 mid-line virgules per 47-line column

5. British Library Additional 12043 (*Confessio Amantis*), up to 5 lines with a mid-line point or *punctus elevatus* per 50-line column

6. Oxford New College 266 (*Confessio Amantis*), up to 4 mid-line points per 58-line column

7. British Library Harleian 7184 (*Confessio Amantis*), up to 5 mid-line points per 49-line column

8. Oxford Magdalen College 213 (*Confessio Amantis*), up to 2 mid-line points per 48-line column

9. Lambeth 492 (*Prick of Conscience*), a few sporadic sections of several points per line

10. Bodleian Rawl. C.319 (*Prick of Conscience*), virtually no mid-line punctuation except a spate of mid-line points and *puncti elevati* in 0 to 90% of the lines per

page on fols. 107–116; the beginning and end of this outburst occur in mid-text and mid-quire, and the end occurs in mid-leaf, and there is no change of hand to explain the difference.

11. Bodleian Rawl. Poet. 175 (*Prick of Conscience*), a mid-line point or *punctus elevatus* in as many as 3 lines per 44-line column
12. Bodleian Arch. Seld. B.24 (*Troilus and Criseyde*), a mid-line point or virgule in as many as 22 lines and as few as 5 lines per 35-line page; most pages have less than half the lines with mid-line punctuation.
13. Cambridge Queens' College 12 (*De Regimine Principum*), up to 2 mid-line virgules per 35-line page
14. Bodleian Laud Misc. 735 (*De Regimine Principum*), a mid-line point in as many as 5 lines per 37-line page
15. Bodleian Digby 185 (*De Regimine Principum*), mid-line points, virgules, or *puncti elevati* in as many as one-third of the lines per page, but the normal incidence is much less.
16. Bodleian Rawl. Poet. 10 (*De Regimine Principum*), a mid-line virgule in as many as one quarter of the lines per page
17. Bodleian Digby 232 (*Troy Book*), a mid-line virgule in 15% to 60% of the lines per column, with occasional mid-line points and *puncti elevati*
18. Bodleian Rawl. Poet. 144 (*Troy Book*), a mid-line point in 10% to 70% of the lines per page but in less than half the lines on most pages; Hand 1 shows greater incidence at the beginning of his stint, and Hand 2, which starts on fol. 332^v in this text of 404 leaves, uses virgules as well as points and maintains the rate of mid-line punctuation at 40% to 60% of the lines per page.
19. Bodleian Bodley 596 (*Life of Our Lady*), a mid-line point and an occasional virgule in 0 to 50% of the lines per page in fols. 86–95, and a mid-line virgule in 30% to 85% of the lines per page in fols. 96–174^v

Notes to the Tables

[a]This transcription and those that follow in other tables contain line-end punctuation and second mid-line marks in some lines. Line-end punctuation is not unusual in Middle English manuscripts, but I have not conducted a full-scale analysis of it because it is infrequent in Hengwrt and Ellesmere. Additional mid-line marks per line are not unusual in heavily punctuated manuscripts. Hengwrt and Ellesmere have many of them. Their occurrence cannot be predicted, except in lines with items in series, but they probably result from the difficulty in some lines of locating a *single* most important syntactic boundary.

[b]In Hengwrt and Ellesmere, mid-line attached virgules have been demonstrated equivalent to mid-line free virgules, but line-end attached virgules are almost certainly calligraphic ornament; see George B. Killough, "The Virgule in the Poetry of the *Canterbury Tales*," Ph.D. Diss., Ohio University, 1978, pp. 9–11.

NOTES

1. In addition to the normal brief comments in paleographical manuals and facsimile volumes, scholarship on Middle English punctuation includes the following articles: A. C. Cawley, "Punctuation in the Early Versions of Trevisa," *London Medieval Studies*, 1 (1937), 116-33; Peter Clemoes, *Liturgical Influence on Punctuation in Late Old and Early Middle English Manuscripts*, Occasional Papers Printed for the Department of Anglo-Saxon, No. 1 (Cambridge, England: 1952); George B. Killough, "Punctuation and Caesura in Chaucer," *Studies in the Age of Chaucer*, 4 (1982), 87-107; Peter J. Lucas, "Sense-Units and the Use of Punctuation-Markers in John Capgrave's *Chronicle*," *Archivum Linguisticum*, 23 (1971), 1-24; Margery M. Morgan, "A Treatise in Cadence," *Modern Language Review*, 47 (1952), 156-64; Elizabeth Zeeman, "Punctuation in an Early Manuscript of Love's *Mirror*," *Review of English Studies*, NS 7 (1956), 11-18. M. B. Parkes is now working on a full-length study of medieval punctuation that promises to be helpful; see also his "Punctuation, or Pause and Effect," in *Medieval Eloquence: Studies in the Theory and Practice of Medieval Rhetoric*, ed. James J. Murphy (Berkeley: University of California Press, 1978), pp. 127-42.

2. These are the familiar names respectively for National Library of Wales, Peniarth 392, and Huntington, EL.26.C.9. The punctuation in question, a *virgula suspensiva* (looks like a slash) in the middle of nearly every line of the poetic texts of both manuscripts, may be observed in Geoffrey Chaucer, *The Canterbury Tales: A Facsimile and Transcription of the Hengwrt Manuscript, with Variants from the Ellesmere Manuscript*, Vol. I of *The Variorum Edition of the Works of Geoffrey Chaucer*, ed. Paul G. Ruggiers (Norman, Oklahoma: University of Oklahoma Press, 1979).

3. See James G. Southworth, *Verses of Cadence: An Introduction to the Prosody of Chaucer and His Followers* (Oxford: Basil Blackwell, 1954); James G. Southworth, *The Prosody of Chaucer and His Followers: Supplementary Chapters to Verses of Cadence* (Oxford: Basil Blackwell, 1962); Ian Robinson, *Chaucer's Prosody: A Study of the Middle English Verse Tradition* (Cambridge: Cambridge University Press, 1971). The best summary and critique of the metrical discussion is Alan T. Gaylord, "Scanning the Prosodists: An Essay in Metacriticism," *Chaucer Review*, 11 (1976), 22-77.

4. George B. Killough, "The Virgule in the Poetry of the *Canterbury Tales*," Ph.D. Diss. Ohio University, 1978; the conclusions of the dissertation are explained and summarized in "Punctuation and Caesura in Chaucer," *Studies in the Age of Chaucer*, 4 (1982), 87-107.

5. There is debate about how many scribes wrote Hengwrt and Ellesmere. On the basis of handwriting analysis, A. I. Doyle and M. B. Parkes have argued that the two manuscripts were written by the same scribe; see "The Production of Copies of the *Canterbury Tales* and *Confessio Amantis* in the Early Fifteenth

Century," in *Medieval Scribes, Manuscripts and Libraries: Essays Presented to N. R. Ker*, ed. M. B. Parkes and Andrew G. Watson (London: Scolar Press, 1978), pp. 163–210. Roy Vance Ramsey has argued on the basis of spelling patterns and graphic and graphemic variation that Hengwrt was written by one scribe and Ellesmere by another; see "The Hengwrt and Ellesmere Manuscripts of the *Canterbury Tales*: Different Scribes," *Studies in Bibliography*, 35 (1982), 133–54.

6. For example, Cambridge Trinity College 353, containing *Piers Plowman*, has mid-line points, but Cambridge Trinity College 594, also of *Piers Plowman*, has no mid-line punctuation. Likewise, Bodleian Laud Misc. 656, containing the alliterative *Siege of Jerusalem*, has mid-line *puncti elevati*, but Lambeth 491, also of the alliterative *Siege of Jerusalem*, has virtually no mid-line punctuation.

7. A. I. Doyle and M. B. Parkes, "The Production of Copies of the *Canterbury Tales* and *Confessio Amantis* in the Early Fifteenth Century."

8. Although the Vernon manuscript, an enormous volume, has several long texts punctuated in mid-line with line-by-line regularity, there are some texts in meters other than the usual four-stress meter that lack punctuation with line-by-line regularity. For example, the three-stress text "A Preier to Vre Ladi" on fol. 114ᵛ has mid-line punctuation in only a quarter of the lines, the tail rhyme "A Preyer at þe Leuacioun" on fol. 115 has mid-line punctuation in 47 percent of the lines, and the tail rhyme " Þe Fyue Ioyes of Vre Ladi" on fol. 115 has mid-line punctuation in 75 percent of the lines. The nine Hoccleve and/or Lydgate manuscripts are Bodleian Selden Supra 53, Bodleian Ashmole 40, Cambridge Trinity College 602, Bodleian Tanner 347, Bodleian Ashmole 46, Bodleian Laud Misc. 673, Bodleian Rawl. C.448, Bodleian Bodley 263, and Lincoln Cathedral 129.

9. Neither can the mid-line points here be mistaken as clues for performance. A pause or pitch change at each of the points would only further chop up an already choppy verse form. For discussion of the performance question, see Killough, "The Virgule in the Poetry of the *Canterbury Tales*," pp. 237–246.

10. John H. Fisher, *John Gower, Moral Philosopher and Friend of Chaucer* (New York: New York University Press, 1964).

11. *The Text of the Canterbury Tales, Studied on the Basis of All Known Manuscripts*, ed. John M. Manly and Edith Rickert (Chicago: University of Chicago Press, 1940), Vol. I; the nine manuscripts are Ad[1], Ch, Dd, El, En[3], Hg, Lc, Ma, and Mg.

12. A plate of fol. 4 may be found in C. E. Wright, *English Vernacular Hands* (Oxford: Clarendon Press, 1960), plate 8.

13. The word *septenarius* is chosen over *ballad meter*, not because of any theory about the relation of English and Latin septenarius meters, but because it has often been used by editors of Middle English texts and because it emphasizes the number seven (for seven stresses).

14. Study of Latin verse manuscripts is in progress. Punctuation, which is probably syntactic, often occurs in the middle of many lines. See for example British Library MS. Arundel 244, fol. 37^v, in Andrew G. Watson, *Catalogue of Dated and Datable Materials* (London: British Library, 1979), II, plate 196; the text is Alanus de Insulis, *Anticlaudianus*, the manuscript is dated 1316, and the plate shows mid-line virgules in 20 of the 24 lines.

15. There is virtually no mid-line punctuation in the manuscripts of Gower's French and Latin works either.

16. Killough, "The Virgule in the Poetry of the *Canterbury Tales*," pp. 186–224.

17. Kathleen L. Scott, "Lydgate's Lives of Saints Edmund and Fremund: A Newly-Located Manuscript in Arundel Castle," *Viator*, 13 (1982), 335–366.

18. M. B. Parkes will have a good discussion of the history of the marks in his full-length study; an early sketch of his work, called "Medieval Punctuation: A Preliminary Survey," has been circulating in photocopies.

19. Here as elsewhere it would be desirable to have information about the quiring and the textual affiliations in order to check the outside chance that punctuation alterations depend on a change of exemplar. Future surveys should consider recording such information, even though quiring cannot be determined accurately with microfilms, and investigation of textual affiliations for numerous minor texts might not be feasible. In the Bodleian Fairfax 16, it is clear at least that alterations in punctuation do not correspond to quire boundaries—neither the change from point to virgule on fol. 16^v nor the cessation of mid-line punctuation on fol. 268^v.

The Transmission of Troubadour Melodies: The Testimony of Paris, Bibliothèque nationale, f. fr. 22543

ELIZABETH AUBREY

I

It is widely known that only about one-tenth of the surviving troubadour poems are preserved with their melodies. Modern studies bring this tragic circumstance into sharp relief by contrasting the sparse transmission of troubadour tunes with the comparative abundance of surviving trouvère melodies. Most descriptions of the troubadour *cansos* are coupled with analyses of the trouvère *chansons*, and the writers of these studies usually concentrate on the northern repertoire, even implying that the similarities between the two repertoires are close enough that separate discussions are not necessary.[1]

The troubadour art faded rather suddenly when the southern French culture was devastated in the Albigensian Crusade and its aftermath during the first three decades of the thirteenth century. To be sure, many troubadours carried on their work in other countries, especially Spain and Italy, but there can be no doubt that artistic momentum, with political momentum, shifted to the north. Furthermore, while the troubadour tradition was largely self-contained throughout its history, the trouvère art was both influenced by and contributed directly to the emerging polyphonic technique centered in Paris during the twelfth and thirteenth centuries. Perhaps because of this, the manuscript transmission of monophonic songs in the *langue d'oïl* is relatively broad. The manuscripts that preserve the trouvère corpus are generally considered to be fairly reliable witnesses to the art of the northern composer-poets, for several reasons: many of them are thirteenth-century or early fourteenth-century manuscripts of northern provenance, of the same period and region in which the trouvères were active; there are a number of concordances, making evaluation of readings more dependable; and some of the notation is early mensural, which makes possible a better understanding of performance practice.

By contrast, the troubadour music manuscript tradition is quite narrow. Not only do few melodies survive, but of the 260 or so that were recorded, nearly half are transmitted in manuscripts that were apparently produced by Italian or French scribes. Only sixty-two melodies survive in more than one reading, and the notation in almost all of the extant songs is non-mensural. The single musical source that is evidently of meridional provenance could not have been produced before 1286, a very late date for a literature that flourished from about 1140 to about 1300.

It is unfortunate that these circumstances should have caused analysis of the troubadour repertoire to be overshadowed by study of trouvère song. It is quite likely that thorough investigation of the transmission of the troubadour melodies—both its process and its testimony—will show that the troubadour repertoire is more distinct from its northern counterpart than most previous musicological research has led us to believe.

Two procedures must be followed in developing an understanding of the transmission of troubadour melodies. One is a paleographical analysis of the extant codices to determine the scribal practices and the nature of the exemplars. The other is a codicological comparison of concordant readings to discover possible stemmatic relationships, the effect of scribal editing and error, and the influence of oral transmission. Both of these areas have been neglected by scholars of the medieval Occitan music literature, even though they are the only ways in which the transmission process can be established and our understanding of the tradition increased. The present study is intended to address these paleographical and codicological questions with particular reference to the most important musical source of the troubadour repertoire, Paris, Bibliothèque nationale, f. fr. 22543.

II

Most of the poetry of the troubadours survives in manuscripts that were never intended to record melodies, since no space was allowed for music. Medieval scribes evidently took much greater care to preserve the poems than the melodies. Of some ninety-five codices and fragments of troubadour works, only four manuscripts include significant numbers of melodies.[2] Two of these four are actually trouvère manuscripts in which small sections were given over to recording songs in the *langue d'oc*: Paris, Bibliothèque nationale, f. fr. 844, fols. 188-204 and 212-213, and Paris, Bibliothèque nationale, f. fr. 20050, fols. 81-82, 84-91, and 148-150.[3] Both of these manuscripts are of northern provenance, produced in the second half of the thirteenth century. The other two music sources, Milan, Biblioteca Ambrosiana, R 71 supp., and Paris, Bibliothèque nationale, f. fr. 22543, are the only two extant manuscripts that were devoted entirely to transmitting troubadour songs with their melodies.[4] The Milan chansonnier almost certainly was compiled in Italy in the early fourteenth century, as its dialectal traits and paleographical features such as common use of six-line staves and the pre-humanistic script style suggest. Thus Paris 22543 is the only surviving source of troubadour melodies that was probably copied in southern France.

The codex was evidently copied in Languedoc or western Provence around 1300, which places it, along with Milan R 71 supp., at the very end of the troubadour era.[5] Of the nearly 950 lyric, stanzaic poems it records, only 160 are supplied with melodies (representing 158 different melodies, since two of them are found twice in the codex, with different texts); 113 of these melodies are *unica*. It was clearly the intention of the scribe to provide music for nearly all of the poems, an intention that he must have been fairly sure of fulfilling, since he used precious parchment to draw musical staves above the first strophe of most of the poems. The parchment was largely wasted, however, because the majority of the staves remain empty.

Paris 22543 is one of the largest troubadour chansonniers, measuring about 43 x 30 cm. The texts were copied by one scribe, with a few very minor additions made in scattered places by copyists working perhaps two or three decades later than the main scribe. The poems are laid out in two columns, with staff lines above the first strophe of each poem (the Appendix below contains photographs of several folios of Paris 22543). There were originally at least seventeen gatherings, most of them quinternions, of which all but one bifolio survive. At present the manuscript has an eighteenth-century binding.[6]

The manuscript lacks some of the hallmarks of a carefully planned compendium. While it is decorated and rubricated and some attempt seems to have been made to collate its contents, this attempt was increasingly abandoned as more texts were added; even the decoration became less consistent and elaborate in the latter part of the volume.[7]

The nineteenth-century philologist Gustav Gröber, in his valuable analysis of the hierarchy of the contents of Paris 22543 and of the other troubadour chansonniers, concluded that Paris 22543 was copied from several poetic exemplars.[8] He described the manuscript's immediate archetypes as "Gelegenheitssammlungen," or "chance collections" of a number of troubadours' songs, arranged by the collector chronologically, by the prestige of the author, and finally randomly. Several such anthologies served as the exemplars for Paris 22543, according to Gröber, which accounts for its somewhat disordered arrangement and the occasional recurrence of a song, assuming that the scribe did not collate his sources.

The investigations of Gröber and other philologists who have studied Paris 22543 led them to say very little about the model or models that were used for the melodies. Gröber believed that the complexity of the texts required their transmission by written means, while he thought it would have been comparatively easy to pass on the "simpler" melodies orally.[9] For this reason, he suggested, little would be gained by an investigation of musical stemmatics. However, several paleographical features, which suggest the nature of the musical exemplars and of the use that was made of them, do yield believable hypotheses concerning the transmission of the music.

As he began copying the poems, the scribe allowed room for melodies to accompany only a few texts (see Figure 1). In the first gathering after the index, staves for music were provided for only ten of seventy-two poems, with seven melodies entered (see Figure 2). From the second quinternion on (fols. 11–111ᵛ), there are staves for nearly every poem, although most of them remain blank (see Figure 3). The many empty staves after fol. 11 suggest that the melodies were not always available to the scribe and had to be supplied from

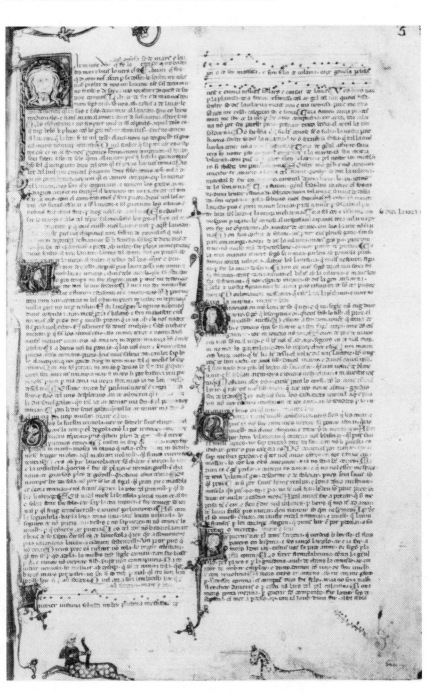

Figure 1

Figure 2

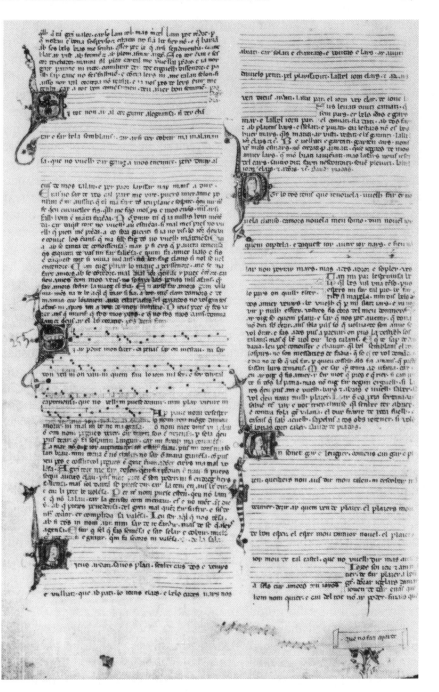

Figure 3

another source. For example on fol. 8, in the first gathering (see Figure 4), the nine strophes of Guiraut de Bornelh's poem "'S'ie-us quier cosselh bel'ami' Alamanda,'' were written in the left column and the top of the right, without notes or staves. The scribe then went on to copy another poem by Guiraut. The next entry in the right column is again the first strophe of "'S'ie-us quier cosselh bel'ami' Alamanda,'' this time with music. It seems unlikely that the scribe would have done this if the text and melody had been together before him as he copied the poem the first time. Instead, he would have measured room for the music above the first strophe, as he had already done on fols. 5–6^v. It is more likely, rather, that the text exemplar did not have the melody with the poem, and that a source for the tune was discovered (or remembered) before the scribe had finished copying fol. 8. It was soon after this space-squandering error that the scribe began adding staves regularly, whether or not he had music immediately available. This resulted in the long run in an even more severe waste of parchment, as the unfilled staves attest.

The texts of Paris 22543 were inscribed first, then the decoration added, and finally the notes entered. That the decoration should have been done before the melodies were entered is an unusual procedure that requires some comment. In general, a medieval manuscript was illuminated after all of the text and music had been copied.[10] Numerous music manuscripts show clear signs that the decorators' work followed the notators', such as initials that overlay the written notes, illuminations that circumscribe the music to avoid obscuring it, and so forth. Evidence of exactly the opposite kind is abundant in Paris 22543: notes that avoid illustrations, clefs superimposed over initials, and red and blue pen-lines covered by the black ink of the notes. In Figure 5, at the top of the right column of fol. 6^v, the feet of the dancer rest squarely on the bottom staff line and the notes are carefully arranged around her garment without reference to the alignment with the text syllables, compelling evidence that the texts and the melodies were entered as separate layers, perhaps by different scribes.

Further, the scribe failed to allow adequate space above the text for extended melismas, so several of the melodies, particularly in phrases *sine littera*, are crowded on the staves. While he measured the leaves carefully on the vertical to allow a consistent amount of room for the staff lines above the first strophes, he made little effort

Figure 4

Figure 5

to accommodate the notes on the horizontal, as if he was not looking at an exemplar with music. Certain corrections of the poetry appear to have been prompted by the entry of the music, for example in places where an omitted word or syllable was discovered as a musical distinction was written. Such corrections are not often found in poems that lack melodies, suggesting that the music was added sometime after all the texts had been copied. Similar evidence is found in songs for which the scribe abbreviated multi-syllable words, leaving less space than would be needed for the notes above such words (for example, "G." for "Guilhem," or "frāq'z" for "franquez"). The text scribe seems not to have been very sensitive to the needs of a musical scribe nor to have had a music source in front of him.

Thus it is doubtful that the music scribe and the text scribe were the same person. Unless he himself also illuminated the codex, it seems strange that the scribe would have waited until after the manuscript was decorated to have finished his job by writing in the notes. He surely would have kept the volume in his scriptorium until after he had completed his portion of the labor before sending it to the atelier. Furthermore, not all of the notation appears to have been written by the same hand. The quite rudimentary notation in Paris 22543 probably dates from no later than the first quarter of the fourteenth century (although there is no proof that later scribes did not deliberately use an archaic notational style). Six different music scribes are possible for the melodies in Paris 22543, whom I have designated scribes P, Q, R, S, T, and U in Tables I and II. There appear to be recognizable differences in the shapes of clefs, the presence or absence of *currentes*, *custodes*, and oblique ligatures, the shapes of those symbols, and the use of the *plica*. Most of the scribes drew quite long tails on *notae simplices* as well as on ligatures, with the exception of scribe R, and the ligatures assume a wide variety of forms throughout the manuscript. There are no ligatures *cum opposita proprietate*. There seems to be no consistent pattern—modal or otherwise—to the shapes of the ligatures in any of the hands.

Scribe Q entered the largest number of melodies (see Figure 6), and comparison of the other hands with his makes certain differences clear. He uses three forms of clef, notably an unusual F-clef

TABLE I: MUSICAL ORTHOGRAPHIES OF NOTATION HANDS IN PARIS 22543

hand	clefs	simplices	binariae	ternariae	larger ligatures	plicae	currentes	custodes	Bb
P									
Q									
R									
S									
T									
U									

Figure 6

(𝆏). He uses a wide variety of ligatures, some with tails, some without, some oblique, others square. He employs one form of the *nota simplex* (𝆏), with a long tail and large square note head, occasionally a *plica*, *currentes*, no *custodes*, and rarely a B♭. Scribe P used alternating *longae* and *breves*, seeming to indicate modal rhythms, but the inconsistent notation is hardly mensural (see Figure 2). His note heads are smaller than those of Scribe Q, and he uses the Roman F-clef (F). Scribes P and Q might have been the same person, since the only significant orthographical difference between them is the use or lack thereof of *breves*, perhaps a conscious variant and not part of a scribe's habitual style.

Scribe R is notable for his more modern F-clef (𝆑), *custodes* (see Figure 3), and lack of large ligatures other than those involving *currentes*. Hand S is much more compact and careless, and the ligature forms rather peculiar, suggesting less skill on the part of the scribe: see, in particular, the *currentes/plica* combinations. Scribes T and U stand out for their avoidance of oblique ligatures and for the ubiquitous tail at the end of almost every ligature, ascending or descending (see Figure 7). Scribe T uses a different type of *custos* from those of Scribe R. Scribes R, S, and T entered only one song each. As Table II shows, the hands are scattered throughout the volume, indicating rather haphazard entry.

TABLE II: DISTRIBUTION OF MELODIES AND NOTATION HANDS IN
PARIS 22543

folio	melodies	notator
5	1	P
5ᵛ	1	P
6	1	P
6ᵛ	1	P
8	1	Q
8ᵛ	1	P?
9ᵛ	1	Q
30ᵛ	1	R
36ᵛ–37ᵛ	8	Q
39ᵛ–40	2	Q
41ᵛ	2	Q
42–43ᵛ	9	Q
43ᵛ–46	8	Q
46ᵛ–47	2	Q
48	1	Q

folio	melodies	notator
48^v	1	S
48^v-49	2	Q
51^v-52	3	Q
55^v	1	P?
56^v-58	12	Q
57	1	P
61-62	6	Q
63-65	12	Q
66	1	Q
69^v	1	T?
72	1	Q
72^v	1	P?
81-81^v	2	Q
83	1	Q
84	1	Q
85-88^v	22	Q
88^v	1	P?
89-89^v	3	Q
104^v-111^v	47	Q
109	4	U?

It is always dangerous to assert a positive identification of different amanuenses, particularly of musical symbols, since the characters subject to variation are relatively few. Late medieval music notation was anything but standard, and isolation of individual scribes' orthographies is highly speculative. Nonetheless, the differences cited here, coupled with the sporadic entry and the late addition of the melodies to the codex in the overall copying process, do suggest that several notators entered music at various times, and that the sources they used were not the same as those for the texts.

This would help explain several otherwise puzzling circumstances manifest in Paris 22543. The use of different sources for text and music would account for the addition of notation some time after the manuscript had been decorated. Further, it would explain why music staves were not added regularly until after fol. 11, and why melodies were added sporadically after that. The text scribe apparently was copying from an exemplar with texts alone, and he occasionally made room for a melody when he was sure that one was available. After he had to copy a poem twice on fol. 8 in order to make that room (see above, Figure 4), he decided to allow for staff lines for every poem, trusting that sources for all of the melodies eventually would be found. Unfortunately, the music collectors were not as thorough as the text scribe.

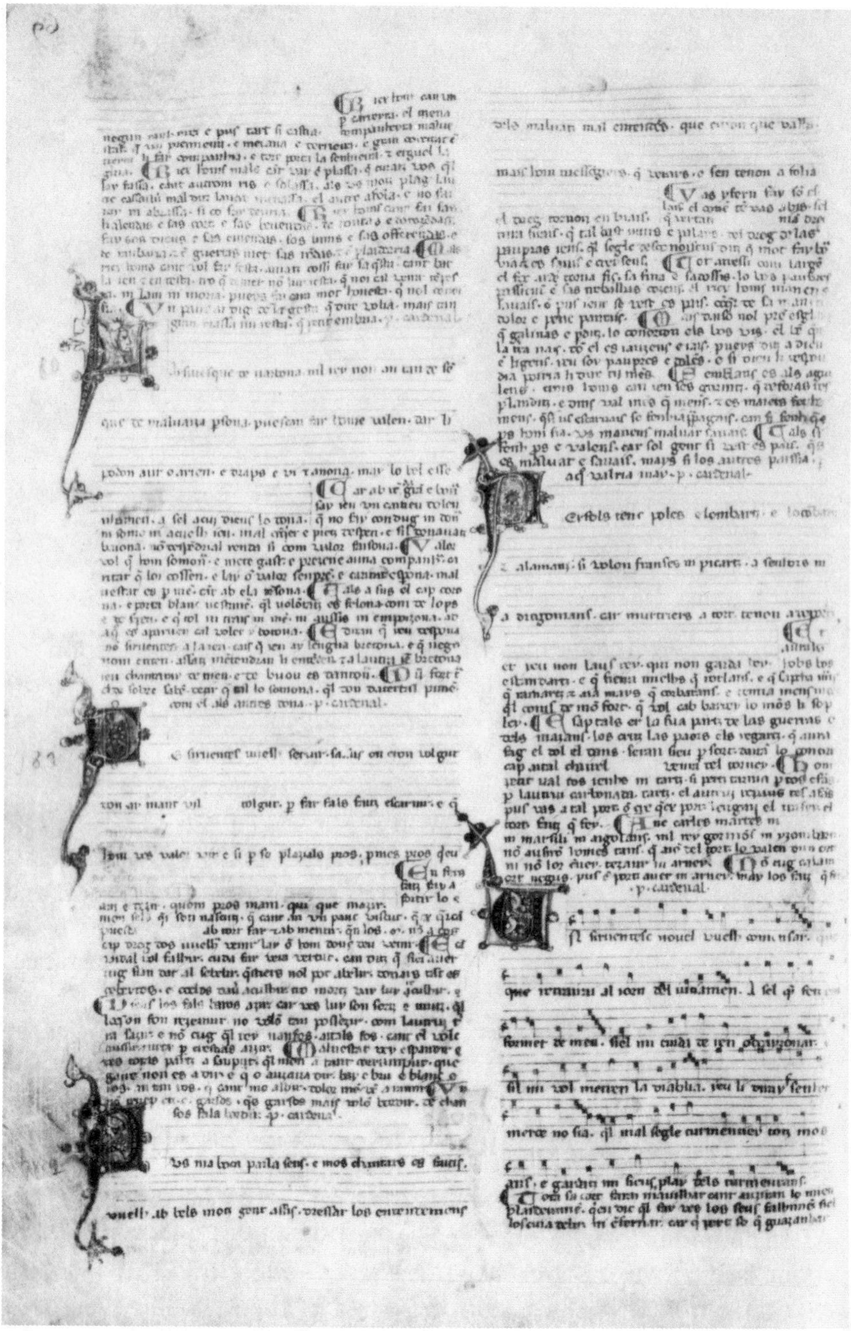

Figure 7

One section in Paris 22543 defies this description of transmission, and its unified appearance provides sɔ sharp a contrast to the rest of the codex as to seem the exception that proves the rule. It occupies the final leaves of the portion of the chansonnier devoted to lyric poems, fols. 104ᵛ–111ᵛ; in it is found a nearly complete "edition" of the works of one of the last troubadours, Guiraut Riquier. In format the layout of these folios is the same as that observed earlier, the poems written in two columns and provided with staves above the first strophes. Each song begins with the customary initial and a rubric identifying the composer. Unlike the rubrics on previous leaves, however, these all give more than an attribution: they all specify a year of composition and sometimes a month and day, and many refer to the genre of the poem, such as *canso* or *vers* (see Figure 8, where the rubric in the left column reads "aiso es la premieira canso d'en Gr. Riquier, l'an mcc.liiii.", "here is the first song of Lord Guiraut Riquier, the year 1254").[11] Of the fifty-three songs in this collection, all but six have music. It is by far the largest group of one troubadour's works in the manuscript, or anywhere else in the extant sources.

No other section in Paris 22543 compares with this one in the unity of its contents. No other rubrics are as detailed. Most significantly, no other section contains as many melodies, all *unica*. This fascicle must have been copied from a single exemplar containing both text and music.[12] In contrast with its contents, the distribution of melodies throughout the rest of the chansonnier is very uneven. Clearly the exemplars for the rest of the volume were not nearly so unified internally as for the Guiraut Riquier section.[13]

All the evidence points to the use of not one, but several music exemplars for the melodies in Paris 22543. If it is true, as most scholars believe,[14] that the poems in this codex were copied from several exemplars, then it does not seem odd that the melodies also might have come from various sources. Clearly the Guiraut Riquier section had its own coherent and self-contained model. The uneven distribution of melodies elsewhere in the chansonnier suggests that they were filled in haphazardly as sources for the music became available, by different scribes, working over an unknown period of time.

The appearance of two *contrafacta* within the leaves of Paris 22543, with some melodic differences, also implies the use of more than one music source. The two versions of one of these melodies,

Figure 8

shown in Example 1, are separated in the manuscript by only twelve leaves, which contain three tunes. There are paleographical as well as melodic differences, notably in the different forms of the F-clef and the ligatures, suggesting not only different exemplars, but perhaps also different notators. Furthermore, the rubrics ascribe these two works to different troubadours: "Ar mi puesc yeu lauzar d'amor" on fol. 72^v to Peire Cardenal and "Non puesc sofrir c'a la dolor" on fol. 84 to Guiraut de Bornelh. The rubrics were added by the main text scribe, who clearly saw no conflict in attributing these two poems to different men. The addition of a single melody to both poems, however, not only suggests a lack of comparison of the exemplars, but it also gives rise to the more troublesome question of which troubadour was the composer of this melody, a question that cannot be answered before thorough stylistic analysis of each troubadour's music has been done.

III

There is thus the possibility that there existed a manuscript tradition for the troubadour melodies separate from that for the poems, at least at the level just prior to the production of the extant codices. This might have been in the form of loose leaves that circulated among *joglars* and troubadours and which eventually fell into the hands of scribes, what Gröber called "Liederblätter," or what some musicologists refer to as "fascicle-manuscripts." The dissemination of such copies of troubadour *cansos* or of small collections of songs is reminiscent of the *pecia* system used in Bologna and elsewhere by students of legal and scholastic texts.[16] Sarah Jane Williams brought up the possibility that this pedagogical practice was imitated by disseminators of cultural artifacts as well, in her study of the "Voir Dit" by Guillaume de Machaut.[17] Even though Williams rejects the idea that Machaut circulated his works in "pièces," it is not impossible that some such practice was followed by the troubadours or *joglars*. Further study of Paris 20050, which may have been a *jongleur's* copy since it is small, undecorated, and unglamorously executed, might yield further information on the role

Example 1

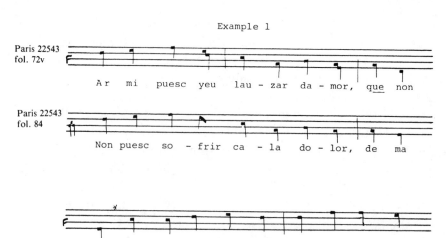

Paris 22543
fol. 72v

A r   mi   puesc   yeu   lau - zar   da - mor,   que   non

Paris 22543
fol. 84

Non puesc   so - frir   ca - la   do - lor,   de   ma

perc   man - iar   ni   dor - mir,   nin   sent   fi - gou -

den   la   len - gua   no   vir,   el   chant   a   la

ra   ni   ca - lor,   ni   non   ba - dalh   ni   non   sos - pir,

no   ve- la   flor,   lay cant vey   los   ram- els   flo - rir,

Ex. 1, continued

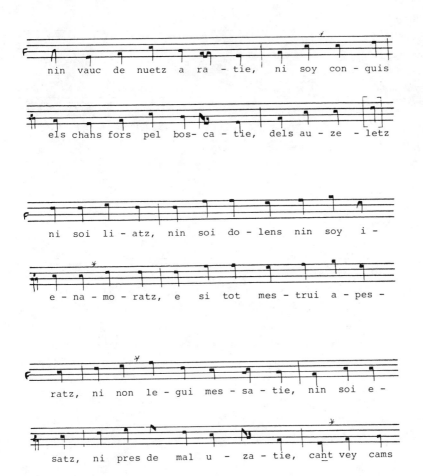

Ex. 1, continued

that performers played in disseminating the repertoires.[18]

Another stage in the transmission process might have been anthologies of melodies uncluttered by numerous strophes of text. There survive some poetic anthologies with a single strophe of each poem, such as the fourteenth-century Occitan manuscript Rome, Biblioteca Apostolica Vaticana, Chigiana, L. IV. 106, which has the first strophes of 186 poems on fols. 13–62. Another such "florilegium" is Modena, Biblioteca Estense, α, R, 4, 4, from the late fourteenth or early fifteenth century, which transmits an anthology on fols. 243–260, introduced by a rubric calling the poems "totas las cansos dels bos trobadors del mon" ("all the songs of the best troubadours in the world"). Jean-Baptiste Beck noted the strong correlation between the poems extant in these anthologies ("Blumenlesen") and the corpus of surviving melodies, suggesting that this correspondence means that the melodies too were considered the troubadours' best or most popular.[19] Perhaps there were also musical florilegia, now lost, which served as exemplars for more complete compendia of both poetry and music, like Paris 22543 and Milan R 71 supp.

IV

The transmission of troubadour melodies was largely a written tradition, and the extant codices, including Paris 22543, were copied from written archetypes, however many such archetypes there might have been. But in the interpretation of the paleographical evidence afforded by these sources, problems abound. While the criteria for evaluating copying procedures outlined recently by Margaret Bent, Allan Atlas, Stanley Boorman, and others are useful for the study of sources of medieval and renaissance polyphony,[20] there remains to be formulated a methodology for discerning scribal habits in the sources of monophonic vernacular literatures. Alejandro Planchart has examined some of the problems in discussing monophony in his recent article on the transmission of tropes.[21] As he points out, the rules of counterpoint used to identify corrupt readings in polyphony are irrelevant in monophony. Further, as with chant, the lack of rhythmic clarity in the notation of secular monophony until the fourteenth century eliminates the possibility of discovering rhythmic errors.

Planchart discusses another area yielding information on the written transmission of monophony, that of language variants. In chant, these can provide valuable evidence bearing on transmission, particularly in the peripheral layers. In the troubadour chansonniers, indeed, text variants in lexicology, syntax, dialect, orthography, word order, and even verse and stanza order, are quite common. However, if it is true that the music was drawn from exemplars different from those of the poetic texts, then the stemmatic relationships between textual readings in different manuscripts might have nothing to do at all with musical filiation.

Unlike the situation for much of chant, it is impossible to compare readings in the troubadour corpus as it survives because there are few clear-cut concordances. Yet, however difficult this may make the evaluation of extant versions, it is still one of the best ways we have of analyzing the repertoire.

Finally, the preservation of troubadour songs surely involved some combination of both oral and written transmission. Recently advanced theories that the scribes noted down melodies with which they were personally familiar[22] or that the songs were transmitted orally almost exclusively until the mid-thirteenth century, when written records appeared,[23] are difficult to support in light of the paleographical evidence. In the first place, the codices are relatively late, and it seems unlikely that the scribes would have known the earlier melodies. On fol. 8 of Paris 22543, it is easier to believe that the scribe's memory of the tune to "S'ie-us quier cosselh" was jogged by a written model rather than by a remembered one. In general, the somewhat disordered contents of the surviving sources suggests that oral transmission played a part early in the copying process, but that the songs were written down randomly and collected gradually.[24]

Some scholars have maintained that the songs were not only passed on orally, but were composed orally as well.[25] Many of the troubadours were performers, according to their *vidas*, and evidently changed their texts to suit specific situations. But whether the performers improvised intentionally or unintentionally, or whether such improvisation was expected or merely tolerated cannot now be known. Nonetheless, the critical problem remains of identifying and classifying the variants that are due to oral composition and transmission—formulas, themes, repetition patterns, overall formal schemes, and so on.[26]

Vernacular monophony was apparently a very fluid art, and there is little chance of recovering an "original" or "authoritative" reading of a melody, which in fact may never have even existed. As Bruno Stäblein has observed, "the all-too hasty restoration of a primordial version (Urfassung) of the original (which is itself a problematic concept), is utopian."[27] With no autographs extant and with all of the surviving sources apparently terminal, we must content ourselves with analyzing each reading on its own terms and offering comparisons of readings, not for the purpose of approaching a more "correct" version, but as evidence of the variability of the tradition. It is hardly possible to employ the methods of common error that are so effective in developing correct versions in other repertoires.

While we must abandon the hope of reconstructing an Urtext, it is still possible, and even necessary, to use the extant concordances to clarify the nature of the transmission process. Each reading must be analyzed separately, and not necessarily as it relates to the codex as a whole. This procedure has been adopted by a number of philologists and by a growing number of musicologists,[28] and it should be clear by now from our examination of the likely musical models of Paris 22543 that each melody might just as well have been copied from a separate source as from a collection of music. Thus each individual song might have its own stemmatic tree.

V

The four main sources of troubadour melodies share a relatively small number of concordant readings. Only one melody is found in all four manuscripts, seventeen in three of them, and thirty-four in two of them. The concordances among these four codices are shown in Table III.

TABLE III: UNICA AND CONCORDANCES OF TROUBADOUR
MELODIES

Manuscript	Melodies	Unica
Milan R 71 supp.	81	35
Paris 22543	160	113
Paris 844	51	33
Paris 20050	24	6

Melodies in two sources:

Milan R 71 supp. and Paris 22543	17
Milan R. 71 supp. and Paris 844	6
Paris 22543 and Paris 20050	5
Milan R 71 supp. and Paris 20050	3
Paris 22543 and Paris 844	3

Melodies in three sources:

Milan R 71 supp., Paris 22543, and Paris 844	11
Milan R 71 supp., Paris 22543, and Paris 20050	5
Milan R 71 supp., Paris 844, and Paris 20050	1

Melody in four sources:

Milan R 71 supp., Paris 22543, Paris 844, and Paris 20050	1

If we cannot use all of the criteria that are applied to other repertoires for evaluating these concordant readings, there are other elements that can provide clues to the transmission process. First of all, certain paleographical features might suggest a common ancestry for some readings. Some melodies common to Paris 22543 and 20050, even though one manuscript is notated in square notation and the other in Lorranian neumes, bear a resemblance to each other simply in their musical orthographies—ligatures, position of notes on the staff, choice and shape of clef, and text placement.[29] Such similarities can be found between other manuscripts as well, as in this excerpt from "Lo jent cors onratz" by Gaucelm Faidit (Example 2), one of five concordances among Paris 22543, Paris 20050, and Milan R 71 supp.

The ligatures in the latter two manuscripts, as over the words "plaz," "plaisenz," "humilitatz," "captenensa," "preiaz," and "soven" are identical or very similar, while those in Paris 22543 differ somewhat. Note the use of vertical strokes at the end of each verse in Paris 22543, absent entirely from Paris 20050 and usually from Milan R 71 supp. Note also that the scribes of Milan R 71 supp. and Paris 20050 began the second verse with "et" (Italian "e"), omitted by the scribe of Paris 22543, so that the music scribes distributed the notes slightly differently in Milan R 71 supp. and Paris 20050 than in Paris 22543.

Example 2

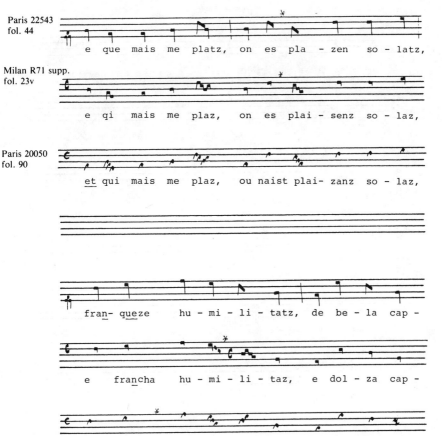

Paris 22543
fol. 44

e que mais me platz, on es pla - zen so - latz,

Milan R71 supp.
fol. 23v

e qi mais me plaz, on es plai - senz so - laz,

Paris 20050
fol. 90

et qui mais me plaz, ou naist plai- zanz so - laz,

fran- queze hu - mi - li - tatz, de be - la cap -

e francha hu - mi - li - taz, e dol - za cap -

et franche hu - me - li - taz, et be - le ca -

Example 2, continued

te - nen - sa, e gent pretz pre - zatz, me fay

ten - za,   e gais, prez pre - iaz   mi fai

te - nan - ce, et rich prez   pu - jaz,   mi fait

chan - tar so - ven.

chan - tar so - ven.

chan - tar so - vent.

These fine distinctions of musical orthographies are not proof of filial or fraternal relationships among manuscripts, particularly since there are numerous reasons for doubting such a relationship between any of the extant music manuscripts (among them differing dates, provenances, dialects, overall contents and format, and many codicological details). In fact, that paleographical likenesses are seen sometimes between one pair of manuscripts and sometimes between another proves that readings must be compared case by case and not always in the context of entire collections.

A second criterion for evaluating concordances among troubadour melodies is the general melodic shape and comparative melodic ornateness among versions. Related to this consideration is a third, that of the mode or tonal center of the readings. It is not uncommon to find songs in which the first few phrases are very similar in different manuscripts (although rarely are two readings identical), but in which the later phrases diverge in melodic direction, shape, mode, or all three. In Example 3, the song "Jamais nulh tems non poiretz far amors," attributed to Guillem de St. Leydier in Paris 22543 (fol. 41ᵛ) and to Gaucelm Faidit in Milan R 71 supp. (fol. 28), both melodies begin on D, but beginning with the fifth phrase, the melodic shapes begin to differ, until the seventh phrase, when the pitch levels (and consequently the tonal centers) diverge. The reading in the Milan chansonnier ends on the note D, while that in the Paris manuscript ends a fourth higher. This is not a case of simple transposition, since the melodies arrive at their respective pitch levels by different paths. Other "concordances" among the troubadour sources seem so mainly in text, and their melodic readings have little apparent relationship to each other.[30]

In other cases, however, the melodic differences do seem to be due to transposition, and evidently not always through scribal error. Scribes (or performers?) did not always retain the same intervallic relationships by the addition of chromatic inflections (B^b). Sometimes only a portion of a melody is transposed, and in most cases it is impossible to know which reading is correct—if indeed it can be certain that one is wrong and the other right. Paleographical orthographies might have contributed to such transposition, as seems to be the case in some concordances between Paris 22543 and 844 and between Paris 22543 and 20050.[31]

Example 3

Paris 22543
fol. 41v

Ja-mays nulh tems nom poi-retz far a-mors, qu<u>er</u> si-a fais

Milan, R 71
supp.
fol. 28

Ja-mais nulz tems no<u>n</u> pot ren far a-mors, qem si-a greu

ni mal-trag ni a- fans, car tan me fay a-ra va-len

ni mal-traiz ni af-fanz, qe tan me fai e-ra va-lenz

se-cors, que las p<u>er</u>-das me re-stau-ra els dans, ca-

so-cors, qe las p<u>er</u>-das me re-stau-ra els danz, ca-

Example 3, continued

vi-a pres a-dreg per   fo-lat-ge, e si anc iorn me fetz

vi-a pres a-dre per mon fo-la- ge, e si anc iorn mi feç

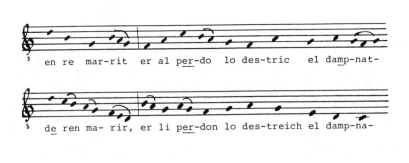

en re mar-rit er al per-do lo des-tric el damp-nat-

de ren ma- rir, er li per-don lo des-treich el damp-na-

ge, ca tal do-na fa mos precx o-be- zir, don mes-men-

ge, qa tal do-na fai mos precs a-cuel-lir, don mes-men-

Example 3, continued

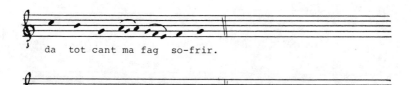

da tot cant ma fag so-frir.

dat tot qan ma fait so-frir.

Finally, the forms of the melodies can help establish a relationship or lack of one between concordances. Sometimes motivic differences necessitate different formal graphs. Such motivic diversities certainly reflect the variations common during performances of the songs, and they suggest that the troubadours themselves thought about musical form in terms other than those dictated by poetic form. Example 4 shows the two readings of "Lai can li jorn son lonc e may" found in Paris 22543 fol. 63 and Paris 20050 fol. 81^v.

The version in Paris 20050 yields the form α β α β γ δ β, while that in Paris 22543 gives a more complex $\alpha_5\beta_3$ $\gamma_5\beta_3'$ $\alpha_5\beta_3$ $\gamma_5\beta_3'$ $\delta_5\beta_3''$ δ $\alpha_3\beta_5$ '[32]. Subtle motivic interrelationships among the phrases in the version in Paris 22543, notably the musical rhyme in all but the sixth phrase, give this melody a more sophisticated structure, although the reading of Paris 20050 is obviously no less ornate. Note also the transposition of the α and β motives in the fifth phrase in Paris 22543, not reflected in Paris 20050.

There is no way of discerning whether either form is more "accurate," or is what the troubadour to whom the song was attributed, Jaufre Rudelh, intended, especially since neither source can lay claim to greater authority—Paris 22543 is of meridional provenance but is late, Paris 20050 is earlier but produced in the north. Evidently the performers of the songs, or perhaps the scribes, altered the melodic structures freely.

What conclusions can be drawn from examining troubadour concordances by these means? First, we might learn if there are stemmatic relationships among the sources, and, if so, whether they concern entire collections, smaller sections, or individual songs. Second, we can better investigate the influence oral transmission had on the melodies, specifically whether there were recurring formulas or motives, what sort of "coding" (formulas, form, musical vocabulary, poetic cues, etc.) aided memories, what sorts of changes a singer might be expected to make in the process of performance, and how accurately these changes are reflected in the written record. Next, we can develop a more realistic comprehension of the attitude of the composers towards musical form, an attitude that appears to have been more casual than the concern with sophisticated poetic forms, but which may have had organizing principles we have not yet discovered. Finally, we can better evaluate the procedures and attitudes of the scribes who were charged with preserving the troubadours' works in order to understand why they

Example 4

Paris 22543 fol. 63

Lai can li iorn son lonc e may, mes bel dos chans

Parris 20050 fol. 81v

Lan qant li ior sont lonc en mai, mest bel del chant

dau-zels de lonc, e can mi soi par-titz de lay,

dau-ziaus de long, et qant me sui par-tiz de lai,

re-men-bram un a - mor de lonh, vau de ta-lan en

mem-bre moi d'une a - mor de long, vains de ta-lant bruns

Example 4, continued

provided posterity with so few melodies yet in such great variety. Such an understanding of the transmission process as a whole— the mysterious combination of oral and written tradition—will reshape our thinking about the troubadour repertoire itself, enabling us to understand the compositional process, especially the attitude towards melody that fostered seemingly endless variation during transmission. It will help answer more of our questions about the worth of the extant tunes. Assuming that we will never identify an "original" troubadour song, is it possible to determine whether a transmitted reading is one that the composer would have approved or did approve? Put another way, are the extant readings valid, and are all surviving versions equally valid? If so, is this because any reading was performed or performable? In sum, a new set of criteria for describing and evaluating the troubadour corpus is needed, and the most reliable route to that end will involve exhaustive research in paleography, textual criticism, and melodic analysis.

NOTES

1. This is implied by Gustave Reese, *Music in the Middle Ages* (New York, 1940), pp. 205–30, where discussion of the two repertoires is intermixed and only two of the eight examples are of troubadour songs. Hendrik van der Werf, in *The Chansons of the Troubadours and Trouvères* (Utrecht, 1972), and in *The Extant Troubadour Melodies: Transcriptions and Essays for Performers and Scholars* (Rochester, N.Y., 1984), reiterates this position.

2. D'Arco Silvio Avalle lists these sources and provides much useful insight into the manuscript tradition in *La Letteratura medievale in lingua d'oc nella sua tradizione manoscritta: Problemi di critica testuale* (Turin, 1961). According to Avalle, fifty-two sources were produced in Italy, ten in Catalonia, fourteen in northern France, and only nineteen in the Midi. None can be dated earlier than the middle of the thirteenth century.

3. Paris 844 has appeared in facsimile edited by Jean and Louise Beck, *Le Manuscrit du Roi (Paris, Bibliothèque nationale, f. fr. 844)*, 2 vols. (London and Philadelphia, 1938). Paris 20050 has appeared in a facsimile edition edited by Paul Meyer and Gaston Raynaud, *Le Chansonnier français de Saint-Germain-des-Prés (Bibl. nat. fr. 20050): Reproduction phototypique avec transcription*, 2 vols. (Paris, 1892, vol. I repr. New York, 1968).

4. Diplomatic edition of Milan R 71 supp. by Ugo Sesini, *Le melodie trobadoriche nel canzoniere provenzale della Biblioteca Ambrosiana R 71 sup.* (originally published in *Studi Medievale*, XII [1939], 1–101, XIII [1940], 1–107, and XIV

[1941], 31-104; repr. Geneva, 1973). The melodies of Paris 22543 are given in diplomatic facsimile by Friedrich Gennrich, *Der musikalische Nachlass der Troubadours*, vol. II, Summa Musica Medii Aevi, 4 (Darmstadt, 1958-65), 139-67.

5. An analysis of the script, dialect, decoration, and notation of Paris 22543 is found in Elizabeth Aubrey, "A Study of the Origins, History, and Notation of the Troubadour Chansonnier Paris, Bibliothèque nationale, f. fr. 22543" (Ph.D. diss, University of Maryland, 1982).

6. Neither the origins nor the early history of Paris 22543 can be verified. The earliest record of ownership places it in the Parisian library of the Marquise d'Urfé in the eighteenth century, where it was consulted by the provençaliste Jean-Baptiste de la Curne de Sainte-Palaye. See Aubrey, pp. 51-54. His transcriptions of its texts (but not the melodies) are found as manuscripts 3094 and 3095 in the Bibliothèque de l'Arsenal in Paris. Alfred Jeanroy, in his *Bibliographie sommaire des chansonniers provençaux (manuscrits et éditions)* (Paris, 1916), p. 13, offered the theory that the early seventeenth-century poet Honoré d'Urfé, great-great-great-uncle of the husband of the Marquise d'Urfé, owned the codex—a theory implied earlier by Nicolas Thomas LePrince and Léopold Delisle. Others have suggested that the d'Urfé family owned the manuscript in the early sixteenth century. No documents, including testaments and library inventories of d'Urfé family members, corroborate any of these hypotheses (see Aubrey, pp. 67-78). The chansonnier passed from the d'Urfé library into the hands of the Duc de la Vallière by 1777, and his daughter sold it, along with many other precious volumes, to the Bibliothèque du Roi. David Fallows, in his description of the chansonnier for *The New Grove Dictionary of Music and Musicians*, ed. Stanley Sadie (London, 1980), XVII, 638, garbles the history of the codex somewhat by placing it in La Vallière's library in 1635 (the date given by Jeanroy for Honoré d'Urfé's death, which is presumably a typographical error, since he died in 1625) and in the Bibliothèque du Roi in 1783.

7. Antoine Tavera, in "Le Chansonnier d'Urfé et les problèmes qu'il pose," *Cultura Neolatina*, XXXVIII (1978), 233-50, has shown that the index, which occupies the first gathering (fols. A-C), reveals the lack of planning for the complete codex, since names of composers and song incipits were added to the index at the same time or after the texts had been copied. Many troubadours' works are found in more than one section of the manuscript, for instance those of Guiraut de Bornelh, which are found on fols. 8 (four songs), 8^v-11^v (twenty-nine songs), 35^v-36 (five songs), 41 (two songs), and 83-85 (seventeen songs).

8. "Die Liedersammlungen der Troubadours," *Romanische Studien*, II/9 (1877), 368-401 and *passim*.

9. Gröber, p. 342.

10. Excellent background on the various stages of producing a medieval book can be found in Falconer Madan, *Books in Manuscript: A Short Introduction to their Study and Use* (London and New York, 1893); Janet Backhouse, *The Illuminated Manuscript* (New York, 1979); W. Wattenbach, *Das Schriftwesen im Mittelalter*, 3rd ed. (Leipzig, 1896, repr. Graz, 1958); James Douglas Farquhar, "The Manuscript as a Book," in Sandra Hindman and James Douglas Farquhar, *From Pen to Press: Illustrated Manuscripts and Printed Books in the First Century of Printing* (Baltimore, 1977), pp. 1–99; and J. J. G. Alexander, *The Decorated Letter* (New York, 1978).

11. One of the later rubrics gives the date 1286, which is thus the *terminus ante quem non* for the manuscript. None of the rubrics, however, specifies a time of day, as Robert Falck asserts in his article on Guiraut Riquier in *The New Grove Dictionary*, XVI, 52.

12. Gröber (n. 8) called this and similar sections in the extant manuscripts a "Liederbuch," or an independent collection of one troubadour's works.

13. There is extant another manuscript with a section almost exactly like this one in Paris 22543, except that it lacks melodies, Paris, Bibliothèque nationale, f. fr. 856. This codex was also produced in the Midi, although possibly from a region slightly to the south of the one that produced Paris 22543, if we may trust dialectal evidence (See Jacques Monfrin, "Notes sur le chansonnier provençal C," *Recueil de travaux offerts à M. Clovis Brunel* [Paris, 1955], II, 282–312). A tantalizing rubric in this poetic chansonnier offers the following, which is not found in Paris 22543: "Aissi comensan lo cans d'en Guiraut riquier de narbona en aissi cum es de cansos, e de verses, e de pastorellas, e de retrohenchas, e de descortz, e d'albas, e d'autres diversas obras en aissi ad ordenadamens cum era ad ordenat en lo sieu libre del qual libre escrig per la sua man fon aissi tot translatat." ("Here begin the songs of Lord Guiraut Riquier of Narbonne, such as cansos, verses, pastorellas, songs with refrain, descorts, albas, and other sundry works; this is the order in which they were arranged in his own book, with his hand, and here fully transmitted.") Philologists have speculated both that Guiraut had a direct hand in the production of Paris 856 (and perhaps Paris 22543 as well) and that the two codices might have shared a common ancestor. A filial relationship between the two sources has been rejected.

14. Suggested first by Gröber, n. 8, above.

15. Gröber, p. 337 and *passim*.

16. See Jean Destrez, *La Pecia dans les manuscrits universitaires du XIIIe et du XIVe siècle* (Paris, 1935).

17. "An Author's Role in Fourteenth-Century Book Production: Guillaume de Machaut's 'Livre ou je met toutes mes choses'," *Romania*, XC (1969), 434–54.

18. Suggested by Jules Brakelmann, *Les plus anciens chansonniers français (XIIe siècle)* (Paris, 1870-91), pp. 80-82.

19. Jean-Baptiste Beck, *Die Melodien der Troubadours und Trouvères* (Strassburg, 1908; repr. New York, 1976), pp. 39-40.

20. Margaret Bent, "Some Criteria for Establishing Relationships between Sources of Late-medieval Polyphony"; Allan Atlas, "Conflicting Attributions in Italian Sources of the Franco-Netherlandish Chanson, c.1465-c.1505: A Progress Report on a New Hypothesis"; and Stanley Boorman, "Limitations and Extensions of Filiation Technique," all found in *Music in Medieval and Early Modern Europe*, ed. Iain Fenlon (Cambridge, Eng., 1981), pp. 295-313, 249-93, and 319-46 respectively. See also the excellent introductory study by Stanley Boorman, "The Use of Filiation in Early Music," *Text* I (for 1981), pp. 167-184.

21. "The Transmission of Medieval Chant," in Fenlon, pp. 347-363.

22. Theodore Karp, "Troubadours, trouvères, III. Music, sources," *The New Grove Dictionary*, XIX, 197, 199.

23. Van der Werf, p. 28 (see n. 1, above).

24. The rubric introducing the Guiraut Riquier section in Paris 856 (see above, n. 13) clearly indicates the use of a written archetype, and the comparable section in Paris 22543 must be assumed to have had a written model as well.

25. Such as Martín de Riquer, *Los Trovadores: Historia, Literaria y Textos* (Barcelona, 1975), I, 15. Both Gröber, p. 434, and Avalle, pp. 43-48, have argued against an oral stage in the composition of the songs.

26. I have addressed this issue in more detail in a paper delivered at the first international congress of the Association Internationale d'Etudes Occitanes at the University at Southampton, England, August 4-11, 1984, "Forme et formule dans les mélodies des troubadours," to be published in the acts of that congress. Recent studies have introduced valuable new methodological tools in the study of oral transmission. These include William A. Quinn and Audley S. Hall, *Jongleur: A Modified Theory of Oral Improvisation and Its Effect on the Performance and Transmission of Middle English Romance* (Washington, D.C., 1982); Ruth Finnegan, *Oral Poetry: Its Nature, Significance and Social Context* (Cambridge, 1977); Leo Treitler, "Homer and Gregory: The Transmission of Epic Poetry and Plainchant," *The Musical Quarterly*, LX (1974), 333-72, and "Oral, Written, and Literate Process in the Transmission of Medieval Music," *Speculum*, LVI (1981), 471-91; Donald Fry, "Oral Poetry: Some Linguistic and Typological Considerations," *Oral Literature and the Formula*, ed. B. A. Stolz and R. S. Shannon (Ann Arbor, 1976), pp. 99-126; and Albert Bates Lord, "Memory, Fixity, and Genre in Oral Traditional

Poetries," *Oral Traditional Literature: A Festschrift for Albert Bates Lord*, ed. John Miles Foley (Columbus, Ohio, 1981), pp. 451–61. An invaluable addition to modern research tools is John Miles Foley, *Oral-Formulaic Theory and Research, An Introduction and Annotated Bibliography* (New York and London, 1985).

27. *Schriftbild der einstimmigen Musik*, Musikgeschichte in Bildern, III, Musik des Mittelalters und der Renaissance, IV (Leipzig, 1975), 83.

28. Notably by Rupert T. Pickens, whose recent poetic edition, *The Songs of Jaufré Rudel* (Toronto, 1978), gives every extant reading of each poem in its entirety, with critical notes to other readings in footnotes. See also the article by Margaret Bent, pp. 298ff.

29. Aubrey, p. 202. Stanley Boorman has postulated the same theory in his study of typesetters' habits in Petrucci prints, "Petrucci's Type-Setters and the Process of Stemmatics," *Formen und Probleme der Überlieferung mehrstimmiger Music im Zeitalter Josquins Desprez (Musikwissenschaftliches Kolloquium, Wolfenbüttel, 1976)*, ed. Ludwig Finscher (Munich, 1981), pp. 245–80.

30. Such as "Eras no vei luzir solelh" by Bernart de Ventadorn, in Paris 22543 fol. 57 and Paris 844 fol. 190.

31. See, for example, Bernart de Ventadorn's "Can par la flor justal vert fuelh," in Paris 22543 fol. 56^v and Paris 844 fol. 188, in both of which the clef is placed on the second line from the bottom, but it is an F-clef in 22543 and a C-clef in 844. "Us gays conortz me fay gaya men far" by Pons de Capduelh, in 22543 fol. 55^v and Paris 20050 fol. 90^v, has the same clef difference, F-clef in 22543 and C-clef in 20050, but the latter also has a B^b in the signature, altering the mode. This concordance has major melodic differences as well.

32. The subscript numerals with Greek characters indicate musical phrases that do not correspond with complete poetic verses, and the numerals refer to the number of syllables involved. This system of graphing musical form reflects the structure more precisely than other methods, and demonstrates that musical form, far from being dependent on poetic form, often consists of interlocking and recurring motives that both accentuate the poetic form (as in the case of musical rhyme) and transcend it (as when a motive bridges two poetic verses). See Aubrey, chapter IV and Appendix 3, for further application of this system.

English, Latin, and the Text as "Other": the Page as Sign in the Work of John Gower

ROBERT F. YEAGER

For most readers, the *Confessio Amantis* is John Gower's "English" poem. Certainly the *Confessio*'s more than thirty thousand Middle English lines do justify this general classification, the more so when we recall that the remaining two-thirds of Gower's work—like the *Mirour de l'Omme* and the *Vox Clamantis*—were written in Anglo-Norman and Latin. Yet it is important to notice, for a number of reasons, that the *Confessio Amantis* is neither all English nor all poetry. Interspersed throughout are Latin hexameter headings which introduce, albeit often in a somewhat oblique fashion, the activity described in the English sections to follow [See Figure 1]; and in the margins of many manuscripts there are to be found at various intervals Latin prose lines which also comment on the English text, in the manner of glosses [See Figures 2 and 3].[1]

The mere fact that such verse and descriptive commentary appear in *Confessio* manuscripts is, in itself, scarcely worth remarking. Many poems contain Latin tags or short sections of introductory verse, and glossed texts are of course common in the Middle Ages. What is unusual about the Latin glosses in Gower's manuscripts, however, is that they seem very likely to have been his own creation. This, as I shall argue, privileges the Latin work in a noteworthy way. G. C. Macaulay, who edited the full corpus of Gower's writings, was the first to suspect that emendations in several of the best copies of both the *Confessio* and the *Vox Clamantis* gave evidence of authorial correction.[2] John Fisher's subsequent review of the materials substantially corroborated Macaulay. Although the recent work of Peter Nicholson, as well as the thorough-going re-examination of all

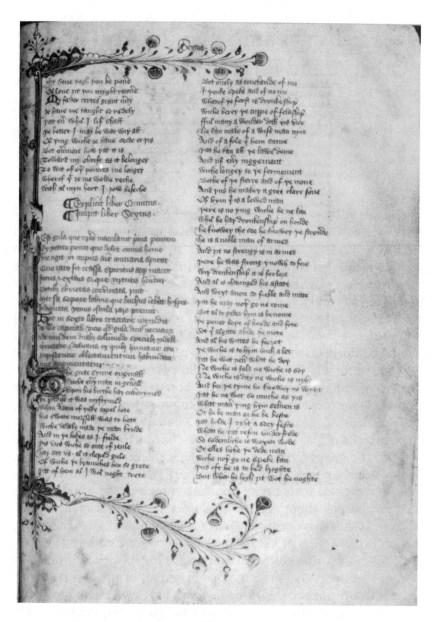

Figure 1

Beinecke Library, Yale University, MS. Osborn fa. 1, fol. 125^r. Photography appears by permission of the Beinecke Rare Book and Manuscript Library, Yale University.

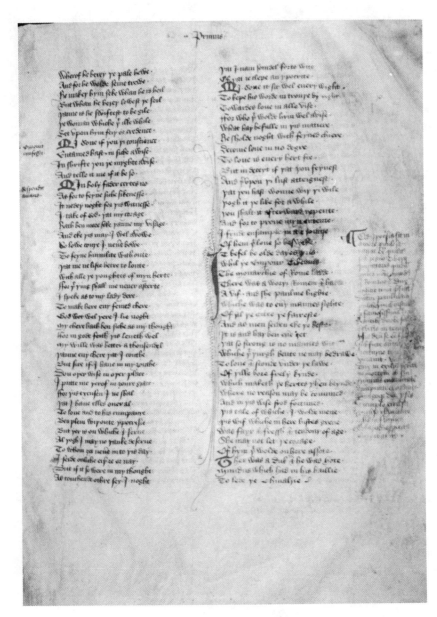

Figure 2
Beinecke Library, Yale University, MS. Osborn fa. 1, fol. 4^r. Photography appears by permission of the Beinecke Rare Book and Manuscript Library, Yale University.

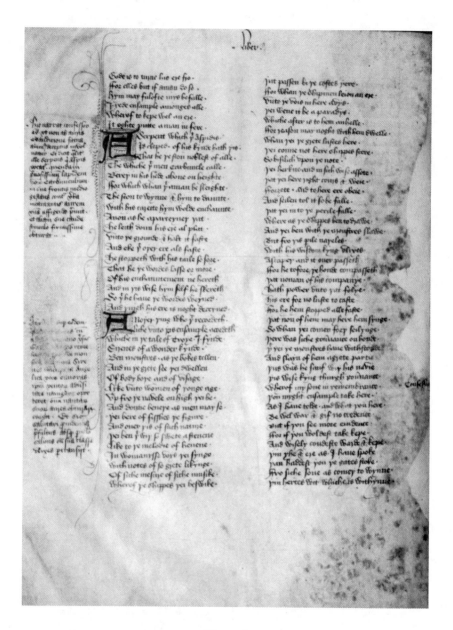

Figure 3
Beinecke Library, Yale University, MS. Osborn fa. 1, fol. 2ᵛ. Photography
appears by permission of the Beinecke Rare Book and Manuscript Library, Yale
University.

manuscripts, full and fragmentary, being carried out now by the team of Jeremy Griffiths, Kate Harris, and Derek Pearsall pointedly disagree with Macaulay and Fisher about how responsible Gower might have been for specific variations, they too appear content that Gower composed marginal glosses for his own poem.[3]

Such glossing of one's own text is indeed unusual, raising the question why might Gower have wished to create commentary, in Latin prose, for his major English work?[4] And, one might ask in conjunction, what prompted him to include the Latin hexameters as he did? Two very different lines of inquiry, leading to equally different but oddly related answers to both of these questions, suggest themselves.

One—the more purely aesthetic, perhaps—I have pursued in print already.[5] Gower, I believe, wished to make a point with his use of both Latin and English in the *Confessio*. In the Prologue and in the opening lines of Book I, he acknowledges his didactic intentions for the poem and evinces an awareness of how choices of subject matter, language, and style may affect his success. Reading devoted only to morally instructive things "dulleth ofte a mannes wit," Gower remarks, and therefore in this, perhaps his last poem, he will turn from the loftier topics he has chosen in the past to write instead of love. The "mateere" of the book will thus present "the middel weie," including:

> Somwhat of lust, somewhat of lore,
> That of the lasse or of the more
> Som man mai lyke of that I wryte . . . .
> (*CA* Pro. 19–20)

Language too is an issue of importance and requires decision. We receive an illuminating glimpse of the thoroughness of Gower's poetic planning when he continues, describing his choices:

> And for that fewe men endite
> In oure englissh, I thenke make
> A bok for Engelondes sake . . . .
> (*CA* Pro. 22–24)

Later on, in Book I, Gower once more calls attention to the problem of a proper style, with a further reference to his notion of the "middel weie":

> Forthi the Stile of my writinges
> Fro this day forth I thenke change

And speke of thing is noght so strange,
Which every kinde hath upon honde. . . .
(*CA*, 8-11)

Of course, by "stile" here Gower can be understood to mean several things. Primarily he was calling attention to that plainness of speech for which he has been often praised.[6]

What is less frequently noticed, however, is Gower's decision to write in "oure englissh," located among the lines above. The development of thought there seems to indicate Gower's sense of his native language as appropriately a "median tongue," neither as lofty as Latin nor as courtly as French—the mode rather of frank parlance and consequently well suited for a poem ostensibly a secular confession. Similarly, from the reticulation of ideas in these lines, we might conclude as well that English in Gower's mind was also a somewhat novel vehicle for major poetry.

In the 1380s, when Gower was composing the *Confessio Amantis*, Chaucer had probably finished *Troilus and Criseyde*, but may not have begun the *Canterbury Tales*, and Gower himself had written two lengthy poems and a sequence of ballades, but nothing, as far as we know, in English.[7] The decade of the *Confessio*'s writing is, then, best thought of as the infancy—albeit glorious—of Middle English poetry. Such an English poem might well be counted on to bring with it a desirable newness requiring and focussing attention.

If these inferences are correct, they have several things to tell us about Gower's poetics. First and simplest, they suggest that Gower included the Latin verses and commentary in his "low" English poem to give it credentials, to provide the learned polish that, judging from the style of both the *Mirour de l'Omme* and the *Vox Clamantis*, Gower so clearly admired. If, as the passages from the *Confessio* imply, Gower deliberately chose to write it in English, so did he choose to embellish his text with Latin verse and prose, which claim for their author a sophistication greater than the major language of the composition; on this level, the bilinguality of the *Confessio Amantis* is there to bulwark the reputation of a learned and sensitive man.

The second observation evoked by Gower's languages in the *Confessio*, however, brings us closer to our present topic. Primary among the "special effects" produced by the presence of the Latin verse and marginalia—and indeed by the appended French ballade sequences as well, in a particular manner[8]—is the multiplication of authoritative point of view, or what we might call authoritative "voice." By this I do not mean the points of view or voices of characters, either in the many narratives or in the larger *personae* of the frame story, Genius and Amans/John Gower. What indeed prevents the crowd of speakers in the total *Confessio* from raising an uninterpretable cacophony is precisely this absence of the authoritative voice from any of the fictional multitude. Not even the confessor figure Genius, the priest of Venus, has the credibility requisite to anchor the poem's direction. Genius is too carefully compromised for this, first because, despite the elaborate cosmetics, the confession we are overhearing is no true one, but a lover's. While Gower's audience accepted some overlap of the behavior proper to a good lover and to a good man, we ought to harbor no confusion about the stakes at the *fictive* level in Gower's poem: the salvation Amans seeks, like the absolution Genius may at last provide, is wholly limited to a secular attachment.[9] Amans confesses in order to purify himself sufficiently that a prayer to Venus to further his suit will stand a chance of success and bring his lady to his arms. Repentance and moral regeneration, while they occur, ultimately transforming Amans to aged John Gower praying "for the pes," are not the original goal of the Lover's confession.

In this limitation of viewpoint—and hence of the ultimate credibility of the directing voice—Genius shares certain important characteristics with the Pilgrim Dante of the *Inferno*, for there, hampered by his as yet unenlightened point of view, the Pilgrim must be reprimanded on several occasions by the guiding Virgil who, in this milieu at least, can be trusted as one who has achieved the requisite degree of detachment from earthly prejudices and misplaced sympathies. Like the Pilgrim, Genius is not a voice we can trust: the canto depicting Paolo and Francesca and the special character of Genius's catechism unfold to present the same messages.[10]

Nor is Genius helped in this regard by Gower's portrayal of his personality. Again the comparison with the *Divine Comedy* is a helpful contrast. Genius should be, after all, a guide figure, as is Dante's Virgil; but, rather than offering us the impression of knowledgeability and control, Genius seems at times argumentative, unprepared, even uncertain in the face of some of Amans' questions. Virgil, on the other hand, is aware of his failings of understanding and knows the reasons for them.[11] We are comfortable with Virgil because Virgil understands his place in a larger scheme of things; we trust him to guide us as far as he can. Yet Genius's uncertainties reduce the priest's authority in our eyes, render him but one voice among a number of characters' voices in the many minor narratives of the *Confessio*, who sometimes tell the truth and sometimes only the truth as they each know it, with no help for us to sort out the differences. In the end, we are left with a Genius who must be interpreted, neither interpreter nor key.

If, then, there is no directive voice emergent among the *personae* of the *Confessio*, where *do* we find it in the poem? Given Gower's clear didactic purposes, outlined in the Prologue and Book I and reiterated in the epilogue passages following Book VIII, it seems most unlikely that he would have risked leaving the body of the poem to indiscriminate interpretation. The answer, I believe, is to be found in a closer look at the Latin verses and marginalia, for what they have to tell us about Gower's reading of the text itself as sign. For if we are to comprehend what Gower thought possible for the *Confessio* as a poetic and didactic artifact, we must recognize the full dimensions of his plan. These included an attitude toward the entire page which, while it has more recent analogues, is arguably unique in medieval English literature. There *are* authoritative voices in the *Confessio Amantis*, but Gower's direction of them becomes apparent only if we step back from the fiction of the poem to consider the text in terms of the process by which it must be read.

So doing, we see that there are actually three "voices" requiring reading in the *Confessio*. The first is the fiction—the frame story of Amans and Genius, along with the many exempla told by Genius. To "read" this voice, we must interpret the fictional events one by one, finding and employing moments of irony, points of special information derived from allusions to sources, passages weighted to generate sympathy, laughter, repulsion, and scorn. Because we are concerned at this level with an overall reading, derived from the fitting-in of every element available, including all events and characters, we are able to find a "voice" for the work which requires no spokesman from within—no guide, in short. This is Chaucer's method in the *Canterbury Tales* and to some degree in the *Troilus*. Specific attention paid to its application in the *Confessio* has already yielded useful, specific results in the form of most standard interpretations of the poem.[12] This "voice" need not concern us here.

The second "voice" with both artistry and authority is heard through the Latin verses. Their function in the *Confessio* is to divide sections of narrative into wieldy size, to announce shifts in mood and speaker. Again the similarity to the *Canterbury Tales* is worth notice, if only to note the differences. In Chaucer's poem, the so-called headlinks and endlinks carry many of the same responsibilites as Gower's Latin verses do in the *Confessio*. The contrasts, however, are significant. Gower was a strong, if idiosyncratic, Latinist and the meaning of the "links" he wrote is frequently as problematic as his treatment of the hexameter line is skillfully musical. Aesthetically, the intent of the Latin verses is clear from their complexity: they are there to be read by a clerical audience whose Latin was sufficient to parse and appreciate their elegant, knotty beauty.[13]

In this, Gower's Latin "links" differ from Chaucer's Middle English ones, which are not ornamental but integral to the narrative flow of his poem, miniature dramas, joining together the otherwise unrelated tales. The voices we find in them are those of specific pilgrims, bantering, bickering, developing a context out of which the ensuing tale will grow. By contrast, Gower provides no dramatic or fictive involvement of the "voice" of his Latin verses. He does not, so to speak, *embody* it into the *Confessio*. No character, no fictive or even omniscient narrator, speaks these Latin lines; they appear as devices only, looking ahead for us to the unfolding of the larger narrative in English, providing a glimpse of what will be said and done. The result is a kind of unusual displacement of the Latin poetry, describable perhaps as a "present non-presence": what Blanchot has distinguished in *L'entretien infini* as the "narrative" voice which, unlike what he calls the "narratorial" voice of a character recounting any given story, is "neutral," and "utters [*dit*] the work from the placeless place where the work is silent."[14]

Such a "neutral" voice creates a special fiction about itself— about whether it should be "heard" as "present" or not. On one hand, in order to enjoy the narrative drama by entering into it with suspended disbelief (an effect Gower obviously strove to bring about for his readers through careful attention to establish the verisimilitude of his frame-story) we must forget that the Latin verses are there. On the other hand (and contrarily), as we read the Latin verses, we learn from them about the narrative. Thus, more contrarily still, they insist upon reminding us of the textuality of the experience, of its *un*reality, of its craftedness, even as we join in it, not as acknowledged participants simply in the fiction, but as *readers*, self-conscious of our distance from the text and its "voices." The effect is increased participation in an increasingly complex association of self and multiplicitous "other."

This "voice," then, of the Latin verses fulfills several loose purposes: aesthetically, in line with the argument advanced in the first half of this paper, it balances the "plain style" English of the larger poem, demonstrating to sophisticated audiences that their author John Gower can sing as well at the top as at the bottom of the scale. Moreover, it speaks up strongly for the recognition of the reading experience as the primary engagement between self and "other"—in this case, not a guide figure or a particularly imposing fictive character to whom we owe emotional allegiance (Dante's Virgil and Beatrice garner this, as does his Pilgrim; Chaucer's Troilus has taken on another shade of it by that poem's close); instead it is a *text* we are asked to consider and address, even be addressed *by*. And, finally, the "voice" of the Latin verses permits entry into the fictional world of frame and exempla an authoritative, directing presence which is also authorial. By reminding us continually that the fiction is text, neither self-productive nor uncrafted, the Latin verses bring us back to the source of such crafting. Partly in this way, the *Confessio* earns for itself its palinode: predictably vigorous Amans, we find, has been hoary John Gower all along. Thus the dream-tale told by a made-up character is transformed into that "prayer for the pes" commanded the character Amans/Gower by Venus, a prayer which is also the text in our hands, the work of the human being John Gower, connected consequently with his otherwise-perimetrical life as a lawyer and land speculator, as Geoffrey Chaucer's friend, and yet unconnected too, "narrative" in Blanchot's sense, speaking from beyond place and biographical isolation in time. Fiction is thereby grafted onto/transmuted into "fact" in a most unusual way, simultaneously being and pressed to bypass itself, to set up independently and remove itself from the poet (both as man and as mechanic act) altogether. Thus Amans/Gower, in writing an amorous poem as a prayer for peace, succeeds in stepping out of all roles by the *Confessio*'s end, transforming himself from narratorial lover to narratorial poet to "real" old man to— finally—"narrative" text unrelated to *persona* or personality.

This certainly is not Chaucer's method in *Troilus and Criseyde*, where the *persona* Troilus looks back to deny the world even as the narrator/poet/"voice" asserts itself and its powers over its creation most fully, to conclude with the "litel bok" sent off to do the poet's will, bringing him fame and salvation. Nor is it the method of the *Canterbury Tales*. There the "narratorial" voice is fictively enformed and located in "Geoffrey" the Pilgrim and in the individual Canterbury travellers. What results is humor, irony, and a necessary blurring, even loss, of any single lesson or point for the work as a whole. Nonetheless, a comparison of Chaucer's authorial presence in the *Canterbury Tales* with Gower's Latin verses is instructive. *Strategically* the attempt of both poets is analogous: for, through their respective means each poet has contrived to include a "voice" of his "own." This similarity of *strategy* is obscured by the differences in purpose. Gower's Latin hexameters attempt to enforce a single meaning on their context, while Chaucer's fictive narrators insist upon the opposite, offering instead a rich multiplicity of voices that denies unified effect, almost to the broadest extension of reading. Yet each poet succeeds at his task: we are required to read the text itself as "other," as autonomous presence, actual and active—as sign, in short—rather than as transparent conduit or medium beyond, or through, which the fictive world potentially unfolds. Chaucer's reminders of this, in the *Canterbury Tales*, are instructions slipped into the head- and endlinks, such as the Pilgrim/narrator's warning to the "gentils" before the "Miller's Tale" to "Turne over the leef and chese another" if we mind a little bawdy talk.[15] These links thus remind us that, first, Chaucer the poet has (had) power over his text and that we too, as readers with the volume now on our knees, have similar decisive control. Gower's Latin verses, which also serve his text as links, enforce similar demands by denying us the possibility of forgetting how fully and uniquely, in fact, we are engaged in an act of reading. In so doing, they provide us with a second "voice" in the *Confessio Amantis*.

There is also a third such "voice" active in the poem, the result of Gower's inclusion of Latin. Just as do the hexameter verses, so do the Latin prose marginalia bring us into touch with the text as significant "other." Their primary purpose, as I have elaborated elsewhere, is to "gloss" this poem of a first-person narrator by referring to the events from a third-person point of view, as for example in the following, taken from the margin in Book III, beside lines 2362 ff.: *Hic declarat per exemplum contra istos Principes seu alios quoscumque illicite guerre motores.*[16] The prose Latin "glosses" tell us what will happen, but more often what it means, and they further make reference to source texts from which a figure or a line is borrowed.[17]

Assuming these Latin marginalia to be Gower's own product, the nature of his intentions and their effects become especially interesting from the theoretical point of view. One may argue that the marginal "glosses" represent Gower's solution to the problem of didactic precision which confronts all moralists who trust important lessons to unavoidably misreadable fictions: Gower seeks to limit polysemy and avoid misunderstanding by directing the act of comprehension through an expansion of the poetic text to include the margins of his page.[18] Here meaning may be presented in a "distilled" state, exclusive of the demands of Blanchot's "narratorial" voices. The similarity of Gower's marginalia to the Glossa Ordinaria, and to a lesser degree the *Fasciculus Morum*, suggests Gower's model for the practice at the structural, though of course not at the theoretical, level.[19]

Yet if this explains some portion of what Gower may have hoped to accomplish with the Latin prose commentary in the margins, it does little to express the unusual quality of the decision. Composing marginal glosses for one's own poem, leaving the impression that they are the work of an unnamed "other" reader, is not common in the Middle Ages or any period. Indeed, we must go as far forward as Coleridge and "The Rime of the Ancient Mariner" to find a suitable parallel. The practice may well be a device of Gower's own invention, and as such it should be of interest in helping us categorize the boundaries of what was possible for a late medieval writer thinking about texts.

One certainty is that, for a man of his time, Gower was unusually concerned with the production and correction of his manuscripts. Although it now seems unlikely that the priory at St. Mary Overeys in Southwark, where Gower lived while writing the *Confessio*, had a scriptorium (as Fisher and others once surmised) in which his poems were copied under his oversight,[20] nevertheless, from the uniformity of many manuscripts, the consistent orthography showing the same mixture of Kentish and East Midland features, from certain additions and deletions of a type best explained as authorial, it seems Gower took a direct hand in bringing his work to the public.[21] In so doing he stands apart from Chaucer and other contemporaries, whose conceptualization of the book as an idea was quite different.[22]

This evidence is important for present purposes, because it renders more credible a suggestive line of inquiry. From Gower's other practices, it is apparent that he put much thought into the *look* of the page. Consistent orthography, such as we find in the many manuscripts of the three recensions of the *Confessio*, does not often appear where such concern is lacking. But to conceive of the page as a totality, an *environment*—that is, as a space to be inhabited poetically and spoken *from*—involves a shift of semiotic awareness we seldom grant medieval authors other than Dante. The question is one Jacques Derrida has recently attempted to define in terms of the "edge" ("le bord") of the text, in his doubled essay, "Living On: *Border Lines*" (p. 77). Significantly, Derrida here conjoins two texts, one printed in the margins of the page, one commenting freely (we would be correct to say "marginally," in two senses) upon the other. His purpose is "to create an effect of *superimposing*, of superimprinting one text on the other" (p. 83), to demonstrate graphically that "the text overruns all the limits assigned to it so far . . . everything that was to be set up in opposition to writing (speech, life, the world, the real, history, and what not, every field of reference . . .)," so that in the end we may "work out the theoretical and practical system of these margins, these borders, once more, from the ground up" (p. 84). He is, he says, "seeking merely [!] to establish the necessity of this whole problematic of judicial framing and of the jurisdiction of frames" (p. 88). His experiment brings him to conclude that in so encumbered[23] a case as a work with a "doubled" text, the narratives ("récits") become "synonymous, homonymous, anonymous," and the narrator innominate because "there is no guarantee that he does not have two [names]. . . " (p. 163).

This concern of Derrida's for the dissolution of jurisdictions—over margins, pages, books, and even authors' names themselves—is, I contend, John Gower's also, in his handling of the Latin marginalia in the manuscripts of the *Confessio Amantis*: that is, with what manner of vision did Gower perceive the possibilities of the page *qua sign* that allowed him to see it capable of such spatial signification? In the end, that is what he has produced, or come closest to producing, by stretching the limits of the meaningful in graphic ways. The noteworthy elements here are Gower's apparent recognitions that the page itself can embody the message, can become clearly a sign—in Derrida's phrase, "synonymous, homonymous, anonymous"; and that the text is, *must be*, an element actively making meaning, regardless of specific literary approach. We can see this clearly if we refer to the plates. Pages such as these, with their multiple cognitive foci, unfold toward the reader unwaveringly; indeed, they insist upon layered interpretation, one might say "conversational," or even choric, interpretation, given the several "voices" present in the marginalia, the poetic narrative in Middle English, and the Latin verses. (In many manuscripts of the *Confessio* these Latin sections are highlighted further by being written in red ink.) The act of reading the text thus becomes also an act of variable recreation of it, since the "voices" will be encountered in different orders by different readers—or by the same reader on different readings. Thus, in Gower's hands the blank sheet of vellum, which eventually becomes the manuscript page with the addition of writing, has also a "being," autonomous of the lines of text but relatable as a subsidiary, or "con-text," if pressed correctly to reveal the supporting mechanics of "voices." The result is an unusually rich field on which issues commonly considered *either* paleographic *or* theoretical may be seen to link, the one playing into, and informing analysis of, the other necessarily, through an inextricable association of the visual format and the comprehensible, or argumentative, poetic text. To "read" this text, the *Confessio Amantis*, is to recognize the page as sign, apparently with the full intent of the author, to draw meaning from its layout—its tactile surface, the very page one turns, to view another, "read," and turn again in a motion simultaneously distancing and enclosing. Such elements of poetic mechanics have long been advanced to favor the idea that Gower (for all his failures in not being Chaucer) was in possession of a breadth of vision which permitted him to look beyond the comparative security of tradition and to draw his own conclusions. If I am correct, and John Gower *was* responsive to the unique multiplication of the "voices" in his last poem and that he exploited and directed them, enforcing meaning through the physicality of the manuscript page itself, then something extraordinary has happened in the sophistication of how men envisioned, and perceived, manuscripts. In Gower's hands at least, they could join an enfolding realm of the meaningful; they could, in short, become signs.

NOTES

1. The arrangement of Latin verse headnotes and prose marginalia is reproduced in the primary modern edition of the *Confessio Amantis*: see G. C. Macaulay, ed., *The Complete Works of John Gower* (Oxford: Clarendon Press, 1901), II–III; rpt. as *The English Works of John Gower*, EETS, e.s., 81–82 (London: Oxford University Press, 1969). All references to the works of John Gower are to this edition.

2. See for example Macaulay's comments on the emendations in the manuscripts of the *Vox Clamantis*; *Complete Works*, IV, lix–lx; on the *Confessio* as evident in MS. Fairfax 3, see II, clvii–cix.

3. See John H. Fisher, *John Gower: Moral Philosopher and Friend of Chaucer* (New York: New York University Press, 1964), p. 117; Peter Nicholson, "Gower's Revisions in the *Confessio Amantis*," *Chaucer Review*, 19 (1984), 123–43; the work of Griffiths, Harris, and Pearsall is forthcoming from Garland Publishing, Inc.

4. I am grateful to Professor Sandra L. Hindman of the Department of Art History, Northwestern University, for calling my attention to the *Epistre Othéa* (MS. Paris fr. 848, produced ca. 1400), in which Christine de Pizan appears also to be glossing her own poem. Whether she was influenced by Gower is not known. For a detailed discussion of this manuscript, see Professor Hindman's forthcoming study, *Christine de Pizan's Epistre Othéa: Painting and Politics at the Court of Charles VI* (Toronto: Pontifical Institute, 1986).

5. R. F. Yeager, "òure englisshe' and Everyone's Latin: The *Fasciculus Morum* and Gower's *Confessio Amantis*," *South Atlantic Review*, 46 (1981), 40–53.

6. The "middel weie" as Gower applies it in the *Confessio* has been studied extensively. The most complete recent study is by Goetz Schmitz, "*The Middel Weie*": *Stil- und Aufbauformen in John Gowers Confessio Amantis* (Bonn: Gründman, 1974).

7. Fisher, *John Gower*, p. x, provides a helpful comparative chronology of the works of Gower and Chaucer.

8. The better manuscripts of the *Confessio* have appended to them the so-called "Traitié pour essampler les amants marietz," a collection of eighteen ballades with amorous themes composed in Anglo-Norman sometime after 1385. From the Latin prose headnote, it is clear that Gower intended to have them read as the last portion of his poem.

9. For example, see *CA* I, 148–97.

10. The Pilgrim Dante grows in his awareness of sin, and how it should be treated; compare his sympathetic weeping and swoon at the fate of Paolo and Francesca (*Inferno* V, 139–42) with Virgil's praise for his spurning of Filippo Argenti (VIII, 33–45).

11. See, for example, *Purgatorio* XXVII, 127–29.

12. I have in mind here interpretations such as Fisher's, *John Gower*, Russell A. Peck, *Kingship and Common Profit in Gower's Confessio Amantis* (Carbondale and Edwardsville: Southern Illinois University Press, 1978), and Paul Miller, "John Gower, Satiric Poet" in *Gower's Confessio Amantis: Responses and Reassessments*, ed. A. J. Minnis (Woodbridge, Suffolk: Boydell and Brewer, 1983).

13. That Gower considered this clerical audience when composing Latin poetry is apparent from his dedication of the *Vox Clamantis* to Thomas Arundell, Archbishop of Canterbury; see Macaulay, *Works*, IV, 1–2.

14. Quoted by Jacques Derrida in "Living On: *Border Lines*" (trans. James Hulbert), in *Deconstruction and Criticism* (New York: Continuum, 1979), p. 104.

15. See *Canterbury Tales* I, 3167–86.

16. "Here, using an example, he denounces those princes, or anyone else, who brings about war unlawfully."

17. See, for example, the marginal note beside Bk. I, 2705: "Salomon. Amictus eius annunciat de eo."

18. I discuss this point more fully in "our englisshe," pp. 46–47.

19. See "oure englisshe," pp. 43–47.

20. See Fisher, *John Gower*, pp. 60, 93.

21. Nicholson's research into the textual variations of the manuscripts has shown convincingly that many of what Macaulay thought were authorial revisions are in fact the work of bookshop scribes rendering the usual inconsistencies found in texts produced by multiple hands ("Gower's Revisions," p. 139). Nonetheless, the four manuscripts of the *Vox Clamantis* and MSS. Stafford and Fairfax of the *Confessio* seem to Nicholson as well to "support the belief that Gower supervised copying and production" (p. 136). On the bookshop production of *Confessio* manuscripts, see also A. I. Doyle and M. B. Parkes, "The Production of Copies of the *Canterbury Tales* and the *Confessio Amantis* in the Early Fifteenth Century," in *Medieval Scribes, Manuscripts and Libraries: Essays*

Presented to N. R. Ker, ed. M. B. Parkes and Andrew G. Watson (London: Scolar Press, 1978), pp. 163–210.

22. An intriguing reexamination of Chaucer's sense of the book as *idea* has been offered by Jesse M. Gellrich, *The Idea of the Book in the Middle Ages: Language Theory, Mythology, and Fiction* (Ithaca, N.Y.: Cornell University Press, 1985).

23. Derrida's actual term for this encumbering is "invagination"; "Living On," pp. 97–101.

The Latin Marginalia of the *Regiment of Princes* as an Aid to Stemmatic Analysis

MARCIA SMITH MARZEC

Thomas Hoccleve's *Regiment of Princes*, a verse treatise in the genre of advice to the king, was written in 1411/12 and addressed to Henry, Prince of Wales. It is based largely on Aegidius Romanus' *De Regimine Principum*, with the *Liber de Ludo Scacchorum* of Jacobus de Cessolis and the *Secreta Secretorum* as supplemental sources. However, it is probably Hoccleve's own additions—the autobiographical dialogue which constitutes the prologue, together with the contemporary illustrations and examples, and Hoccleve's own simple, honest style—which appealed most to fifteenth-century audiences, causing the *Regiment* to achieve a wide circulation, as is indicated by the number of manuscripts extant. The work survives in more manuscripts than any other Middle Englih verse with the exception of the *Prick of Conscience*, the *Canterbury Tales*, *Piers Plowman*, and the *Confessio Amantis*.[1]

As the forty-three extant manuscripts of the *Regiment*[2] are all fifteenth-century copies and nearly all represent a southeast midlands scribal dialect, the transmission of the text seems to have been chronologically and geographically limited. There were also no printings to indicate interest in the work prior to the 1860 Roxburghe Club edition by Thomas Wright.

Although the textual history of the work is neatly confined, the number of extant manuscripts creates an ambitious task for editors of the work, specifically in the charting of the affiliation of the manuscripts. No doubt the work was very popular in its time, as is evidenced by the number of manuscripts extant. And if forty-three manuscripts survive, we might assume that as many—possibly even twice that number—have been lost. There are, then, any number of unknown factors which complicate the stemma. Moreover, since many manuscripts seem to have been copied under identical circumstances, probably in scriptoria where several exemplars would have been available, there is reason to expect some conflation of manuscripts. Therefore, the method of separative and conjunctive errors as a procedure for stemmatic analysis has its limitations.

The diagram in Appendix A suggests the likely affiliation of the extant *Regiment* manuscripts based on a trial collation of the readings of 829 lines of the English text.[3] The manuscript relationships delineated represent the best hypothesis in light of the evidence, that is, necessitating the least amount of coincidental variance. But there are, to be sure, many pieces of contradictory evidence from the English texts for several problem groupings.

Having gathered what evidence of affiliation the English texts of the manuscripts offered, I turned to the Latin marginalia corresponding to the 829 lines of English text in those manuscripts which are glossed.[4] I had hoped to discover evidence which would support my conclusions as indicated in the postulated stemma, especially concerning those groupings for which evidence from the English is scant or contradictory. And, indeed, there was evidence to support many of the groupings—unfortunately, however, usually with groups already so clear as to need little support. The variants listed in Appendix C do confirm certain conclusions. Manuscripts varying together most frequently are $DiRy^2$, $GgHn^1Na$, $BoLaSeYa$ (and more frequently, $BoLaYa$), $GaKkSl^2SoTc$, $ArHa^2$, and $DuRy^3$. Further, these variants contribute to the evidence which supports the few cases in which I have posited one extant manuscript as exemplar of another, viz., the cases of $GgNa$, $DiRy^2$, and $KkSl^2$. In all three of these cases, the Latin glosses of the copies appear to be in the hand of the scribe. These are, no doubt, cases in which the production of the copy was an individual and independent effort, accomplished in each case by only one scribe using one exemplar throughout, including glosses.

This is not, however, the case with many of the early manuscripts, especially those more ornate manuscripts which Hoccleve himself had had produced for various patrons. There must have been at least five such patronic copies: the copy presumably presented to Prince Henry in 1412 (no longer extant); those copies presented to Edward, Duke of York, and John, Duke of Bedford, as is indicated by surviving dedicatory verses; the British Library MS. Arundel 38, bearing the arms of the FitzAlans, Earls of Arundel; and the British Library MS. Harley 4866, almost exactly like MS. Arundel 38 in bibliographical format. Moreover, there were other members of the royal circle who were patrons of other Hoccleve works and who would have been likely recipients of the *Regiment*, viz., Humphrey, Duke of Gloucester, Joan Beaufort, Countess of Westmoreland, Robert Chichele, and Joan FitzAlan, Countess of Hereford, possibly the recipient of the MS. Arundel 38.[5]

Stemmatic evidence in the English text indicates that not all patronic copies were made from Hoccleve's fair copy. The very fact that on a number of significant readings the manuscripts consistently vary in two groups, including a whole variant stanza in *Regiment* section 15, tells us that all extant manuscripts derive from one of two original copies. In Branch I, neither A nor Ha[4] can be that original manuscript, for both exhibit enough unique and incorrigible variants as to indicate a terminal position in the stemma. Separative errors among Branch-II manuscripts suggest at least two intermediate stages between the fair copy and the earliest extant manuscripts of the three distinct groups. The *alpha, beta,* and *gamma,* as well as the two original copies made from Hoccleve's fair copy, were all made quite early, probably during Hoccleve's lifetime as patronic copies. The fact that the *gamma* manuscripts Du and Ry[3] do not vary with other groups against the majority of manuscripts indicates a distinct and quite early stage in the transmission of the *Regiment* texts. Further, Du f. 89 lacks ll. 4978–5012, probably owing to the loss of one leaf in the exemplar, the leaf where the Chaucer portrait appears in the manuscripts which are illuminated—an illumination which seems from the very beginning to have been prized more highly than the Hoccleve text itself and, therefore, excised from some copies. Moreover, the fact that only Du and Ry[3] append to the Envoy the three dedicatory stanzas to John, Duke of Bedford, suggests that the *gamma* manuscript may itself have been that patronic copy, with Ry[3] copied before the excision and Du after. Overall, stemmatic evidence indicates that the early presentation copies of the text—all made during Hoccleve's lifetime, probably under his supervision, and perhaps even by his fellow clerks in the Office of the Privy Seal— entail at least three generations of copying, even though they were made virtually concurrently.

It is at this point in the stemma that the extra-textual evidence of rubrication is at once most helpful and most complicating. First, the complications: a scribe might use one exemplar for the English (if he did indeed use a single exemplar throughout) and the rubricator might use a different exemplar for the glosses. In the early, ornate copies, the script of the English text is different from that of the marginalia, whereas in the cheap privately-made manuscripts, the script in those manuscripts which are glossed is usually identical with that of the English text.[6] As the work became popular, there was evidently a demand for such copies, and these were turned out by anyone capable of the task, not necessarily the practiced and versatile scribes like those who executed the ornate copies for royal patrons. Yet not only are the scripts different in the ornate copies, but the hands may be as well. If numerous copies were intended initially for various of Hoccleve's patrons and if these copies were produced concurrently in a London scriptorium, it is reasonable to assume that a division of labor may have existed,[7] that the scribe and the rubricator of a given manuscript were not necessarily identical, and that the scribe rubricating a given text probably paid little regard to the English. This division of labor might then explain the very obvious contradictions between the English and Latin which can be found in some manuscripts, for example, the corruption introduced into l. 4500 by the scribe of MS. I who attributes a paraphrase to Isaiah, glossed correctly as Jeremiah 6—an interesting contradiction between the English and Latin maintained throughout Branch I in all manuscripts which are glossed and coinciding with the stemmatic division into two branches which the English evidence argues. Or the contradiction in the second *alpha* group: the Latin glosses read, "Qui odit auariciam longi fient dies eius," whereas the English texts from the inferred MS. #14 down read, "His dayes schulle encresse and multiplie / That auarice hathe . . . " (ll. 4533–34).

This complication in rubrication—another person or another exemplar—is seen in the two Branch-I manuscripts Di and Ry^2, which agree consistently in the glosses with the Branch-II *beta* group but not in any readings in the English:

Ide*m* cum deceat fontem habere os largum

Idem cum] Cum ergo tanto $DiRy^2$; $DoHn^2NeRy^1Sl^1$
largum] *add* quanto ex eo plures participare debet tanto decet Regem
largiorem esse &c $DiRy^2$; $DoHa^1Hn^2NeRy^1Sl^1$

No*ta quod* laudandus est ille quem pietas mouet releuamen prestar*e* indigenti

Nota . . . indigenti] *om.* DiGgRy^2; DoHa^{1}Hn^{2}NeRoRy^{1}Sl^1

Egidius in sec*und*a*m* pa*r*te j li p*ol*i*ticorum* a*ristoteles* ad Regem maxi*me* sp*ec*tat vt sit Rex s*ecundum* ve*r*itate*m*

 aristoteles] *adds* cum expositione surley ad Regem Do, *adds* cum expositione Burley ad nigem Ha^1, *adds* cum expositione burld ad regem Hn^2, *adds* cum expositione Durley ad regem Ne, *add* cum expositione burlei ad regem Ry^{1}Ry^{2}Sl^1

Sc*ri*ptum est, Qui amplectitur pace[m] in mentis hospicio

 hospicio] *add* mansionem preparat christo ArDoHa^{1}Ha^{2}NeRy^{1}Sl^1; Ry^2 (Hn^2 wants the pertinent leaves; Ro wants the gloss.)

Manuscripts collateral with Ry^2 are the unglossed Co and the Ha^5 manuscript, which consists of only the little glossed prologue to the poem. Therefore, there is no way to ascertain whether Ry^2 itself or its exemplar, the inferred MS. #4, was the manuscript into which *beta* glosses were introduced. Either way, the *beta* readings were probably introduced into the Branch-I manuscript rather than vice versa: even though Ry^2 is itself an early, ornate, possibly even a presentation copy, to suggest that the *beta* glosses were copied from the Branch-I manuscript is to maintain that the glosses are not originally recorded by Hoccleve.

Similarly, among the *beta* manuscripts, Ro, while clearly using a *beta* text for the English, is more likely glossed with an *alpha* text, as the following cases appear to argue:

Auaricia est ydolor*um* se*r*vitus

 Auaricia] Apostolus auaricia DoHa^{1}Hn^{2}NeRy^{1}Sl^1

Auaricia e*st* morb*us* incurabilis vt idem dicit

 Auaricia . . . dicit] *om.* in all *beta* and *gamma* manuscripts except Ro

Stanza 725 glossed: Est enim pax mala que est vere paci contraria & hoc est quando corda sunt in mala concordancia. talem pacem habuit Pilatus cum Herode &c ArHa^2; DoHa^{1}NeRy^{1}Sl^1; DiRy^2 (Hn^2 wants pertinent leaves.)

Item sc*ri*ptum est, Tantor*um* ergo te scias invadere bona qua*n*tor*um* de posses- sione tua poteris subuenire & no[n] vis

Item . . . vis] *om.* AsFi²Se; Ga; Ha³; Ro

Stanza 680 glossed: iiij^{or} virtutes Cardinales Prudencia temperancia fortitude & Iusticia BoLaSeYa; Ro

Stanza 744 glossed: Psalm*us*, Ecce qu*a*m bonum & qu*a*m iocundu*m* habitare fra*tr*es in vnu*m* AsBoFi²LaYa; Ro *om.* & . . . bonum

Et in te*rr*a pax hominib*us*

hominibus] *add* bone voluntatis AsBoFi²LaSeYa; Ha³; Ro

Et de tali pace loquitur psalmista Qui loqunt*ur* pacem cu*m* p*r*oxi*m*o suo mala autem &c

autem] *add* in cordibus eorum AsBoFi²SeYa; Ha³; Ro

No peculiarly *beta* glosses are ever found in Ro. The occurrence of Ha³Ro agreement may be due to contamination (in the glosses only) of Ha³ by the Ro text. There are two glosses found only in Ro and Ha³. The fact that the Latin of the Ha³ glosses is corrupt suggests that Ha³ is the copy.[8] The scribe of Ha³ seems to have been quite eclectic, and the English text itself is so hopelessly conflated that it defies classification other than as very basically a Branch-I manuscript.

On the helpful side, the system of stemmatic analysis by the study of separative errors is weakest the higher the point in the stemma, for there are fewer and fewer variants to delineate groups. However, variance in the glosses may at least supply more evidence for initial branches and groupings. For example, evidence from rubrics tends to confirm the placement of ArHa². The two are textually very close, but unique readings in each argue that neither is a copy of the other. The few times that the two manuscripts do vary with a group, it would seem to be with the *beta* group, although such evidence from the English text is scant:

4550 addition of gloss "scillicet necessitatis tempore" into the line ArHa²; DoHn²NeRoSl¹. The gloss is also found in DiRy², but marginally.

4711 or] *om.* Ar(CcGa)Ha²(Ha³Hh)Hn²(Kk)Ry¹(SjSl²SoTc), and DoHa¹NeRoSl¹

4829 hem] him Ar(DiGg)Ha²(Ha⁴Hh)Hn²(NaRy²)

5094 sensualitees] sensualite ArDo(Ga)Ha^{1}Ha^2(Ha^{3}Kk)NeRoSl^1(Sl^{2}So)

5422 men] man ArDo(Du)Ha^{1}Ha^2(Na)Ne(Ra^1)RoRy^1(Ry^3)Sl^1

Although the *beta* readings are a constant in this list, the presence of so many other manuscripts which share the readings and the insignificance of the variants themselves make a poor case for the *beta* affiliation. Marginalia in ArHa^2, however, prove more substantive:

Pr*o*bat philosophus iiij^{to} eth*icorum* iij^a r*ati*one q*uod* auaricia peior *est* pr*o*digalitate

prodigalitate] *add* et quod melius est infirmari morbo curabili qu*am* incurabili &c ArHa^2, *adds* quod in melius est infirmari morbo curabili quam incurabili Di, *add* primo enim melius est infirmari morbo curabili DoHa^{1}NeSl^1, *add* primo enim melius est infirmari morbo curabili quam incurabili Hn^{2}Ry^{1}Ry^2

Mulier fuit formata in paradiso. . . .

fuit formata] facta fuit ArHa^2; DoHa^{1}Ry^{1}Sl^1 (Hn^2 wants pertinent leaves.)

Pac*em* relinq*uo* vobis

Pacem] *add* meam ArHa^2; DoHa^{1}Ry^{1}Sl^1 (Hn^2 wants pertinent leaves; Ne wants the gloss.)

Stanza 663 glossed in ArHa^2; DiRy^2; DoHa^{1}Hn^{2}NeRy^{1}Sl^1: Tercio id*e*m di*cit* quod Rex positus est in Regno propter salutem Regni & vt prosit hijs qui in Regno sunt Auarus autem nulli prodest &c

quod] quia DoHa^{1}Hn^{2}NeRy^{1}Sl^1; DiRy^2
idem dicit] *om.* DoHa^{1}Hn^{2}NeRy^{1}Sl^1; DiRy^2

Sc*ri*ptum est Qui amplectitur pace[m] in mentis hospicio

hospicio] *add* mansionem preparat christo ArHa^2; Ry^2; DoHa^{1}NeRy^{1}Sl^1 (Hn^2 wants pertinent leaves; Ro wants the gloss.)

Stanza 725 glossed: Est pax mala q*uam* est vere paci contraria ta*l*lem pacem hab*u*it Pilat*us* cum Herode &c ArHa^2; DiRy^2; DoHa^{1}NeRy^{1}Sl^1

Of course, to use the glosses here as stemmatic evidence is risky, for there is no guarantee that the English and Latin exemplars of the inferred MS. #18 were indeed identical. But we know from the

English that Ar and Ha² are definitely Branch-II manuscripts, and whereas they share no really significant readings with the *alpha*, *beta*, or *gamma* manuscripts, they do at least share *beta* readings in the glosses.

Further, in that *beta* group, while the glosses do not supply sufficient evidence to solve the problem of the exact relationship of the manuscripts DoHa¹NeRoRy¹Sl¹, they at least show readings supporting the relationship hypothesized in the Appendix A stemma. While there are many readings to support the existent stemma, there are also some contradictory readings:

4488 ne mone] no mor (Cc)Do(Hh)NeRoSl¹

4511 soul] fowle (Hn¹)Hn²Ne

4547   þyn²] *om.* DoHa¹NeRoSl¹

4558 tytle] tale DoHa¹Hn²NeRoSl¹

4618 receyue] restreyne DoRoRy¹Sl¹, restheyue Ha¹

4685 or] of ArDoHa¹Hn²NeRo

4690 hyr] *om.* DoHa¹NeRy¹Sl¹

4696 a²] *om.* DoHa¹NeRo

4711 or¹] and DoHa¹NeRoSl¹

4773 lest] loste DoHa¹Hn²NeRoSl¹

4776 more] no more Hn²RoRy¹Sl¹

4786 Of] Of þe DoNeRoSl¹

4855 fycche þ] suthith DoHa¹, settith (DuGaKk)RoSl¹(Sl²SoTc), set Ry¹

5107 brow] boowe DoSl¹, bowe Ry¹

5288 werre] werre is RoSl¹

5422 handwerk] handly werke DoHa¹NeSl¹

What I have posited in the stemma concerning the *beta* group admittedly involves some coincidental variance and independent emendation, especially on the part of Ry^1. Yet my hypothesis involves the fewest number of such coincidences, and the glossing tends to support it. Aside from Ro, the *beta* manuscripts generally agree in glosses, and there is some evidence to mark the inferred manuscripts in the stemma:

MS. #21:
Scriptum *est* Auaricia est amor inmoderatus. . . .

amor] *om.* DoHa^{1}Ne

MS. #20:
Job 4° Quis resistet deo et pacem habuit. . . .

resistet] est qui resistet DoHa^{1}Ne, est qui resistat Ry^1, est qui resistit Sl^1

MS. #19:
Auaricia est ydolor*um* servitus

Auaricia] Apostolus auaricia DoHa^{1}Hn^{2}NeRy^{1}Sl^1

Esuriencium panis est quem tu detines nudor*um* vestimentu*m* est quod tu recludis

est^2] *om.* DoHa^{1}Hn^{2}NeRy^{1}Sl^1; Du

Dicit idem philosophus q*uod* *pro*digalitas e*st* morbus curabilis ab egestate v*el* etate

quod] et DoHa^{1}Hn^{2}NeSl^1
egestate . . . etate] etate . . . egestate
DoHa^{1}Hn^{2}NeRy^{1}Sl^1

Glosses also contribute evidence concerning the problem of the *alpha* manuscripts AsBoLaSeYa. The English texts of BoLaSeYa are very close; evidence also suggests a close affiliation of AsFi^{1}Fi^2. Yet there are readings in which AsSe vary against BoLaYa. A study of the Se codex reveals many of the readings in which Se agrees with BoLaYa to be contaminations (the erasures and corrections are quite clear in the manuscript). The glosses seem to support the original AsSe affiliation and suggest that the readings peculiar to BoLaSeYa were introduced by the scribe of the inferred MS. #11 rather than #9, arguing for a revision of that section of the stemma (see below):

Item sc*ri*ptum est Neq*ue* eni*m* minus est c*ri*minis h*a*benti tollere qu*a*m cum possis & habundans sis indigentib*us* necessar*ia* denegare &c

habundans] habundas AsLaSeYa

Stanza 647 wanting gloss in AsFi[2]Se; GaHa[3]Ro (Fi[1] wants pertinent leaves.)

Item Ne dicas amico tuo vade & reu*ertere* & cras dabo *tibi* cum statim possis dare

reuertere] reuerte AsSeYa

Stanza 687 glossed: Nota bene Tullius and Senek AsSe

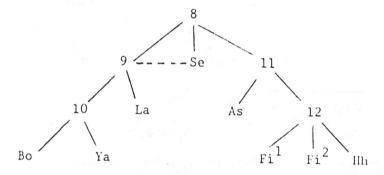

Further, glossing may explain the fact that although Bo and Ya agree a number of times against the English readings of all other manuscripts, Bo has certain readings in the English text which agree with readings prior to those variants introduced by the scribe of MS. #11. Although Bo was copied from Ya's exemplar, it would seem from the glosses to have been glossed from an earlier manuscript, as is indicated by the following:

Caueas ne int*ra* loc*u*los tuos includas salutem inopum & tanqu*am* in timulo ne sepilias vitam pauperum

intra] inter LaSeYa; Ry[1]
inopum] inipium Bo, imperium LaYa

Dicit idem philosophus q*uod* prodigalitas e*st* morb*us* curabil*is* ab egestate vel etate

quod] primo LaSeYa

De tali pace loqui*tur* psalmista ӡelam sup*er* iniquos pacem peccatorum videns &c

iniquos] inintos La, ininucos Se, inincos Ya

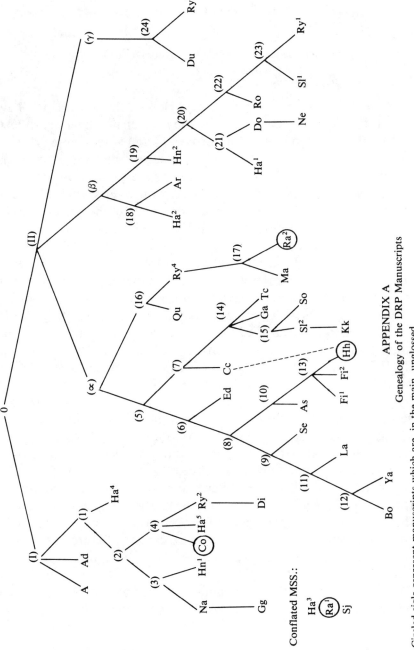

APPENDIX A

Genealogy of the DRP Manuscripts

Circled sigla represent manuscripts which are, in the main, unglossed.

Non veni inquit pacem mittere *sed* gladium &c

Non veni] Non venit Bo, Nemo LaYa
inquit] *add* venit LaYa

Psalm*us* Ecce q*ua*m bonu*m*. . . . (Gloss in AsBoFi^{1}Fi^{2}LaRoSeYa)

Psalmus] Psal*mista* Bo, *om.* LaYa

If Bo had an earlier exemplar for the glosses, the scribe could have used this text to elucidate cruces in the exemplar of his English text.

The glosses, then, can surely prove an *aid* to stemmatic analysis, although alone their authority is less secure because of the very problem of their authenticity: that is, was the glossing in Hoccleve's fair copy? There are a number of possibilities. First of all, none of the glosses may be authoritative if, for example, the original copies were made in a scriptorium and the glossing performed by, say, a foreman. (Even so, they may be authoritative if the glossing was performed under Hoccleve's supervision.) It is most likely, however, that Hoccleve glossed the work himself, either in full glosses or in brief citation for scribal direction. Hoccleve worked closely with his sources, using them in "block" fashion, often translating almost verbatim, and the identified glosses are true to his Latin texts, i.e., not a paraphrase composed by Hoccleve. Probably Hoccleve glossed the English passages straight out of the Latin source as he prepared his text.

With more familiar sources, however, particularly biblical sources, there is a greater chance of a gloss's originating with the scribe or rubricator, for he might recognize the English passage and record the Latin from memory. And even where such glosses originated in the fair copy, there is the issue of how much of the gloss was initially recorded by Hoccleve, as many glosses cite enough of the source passage for the reader's recognition, appending "&c" to the citation. Thus, problems of marginal space might cause the rubricator to omit words or phrases directly before the "&c"; similarly, if he had the space and the Latin was familiar to him, he might have extended the gloss. For example, in the gloss of stanza 744, the addition of "bone voluntatis" to the gloss "Et in terra pax hominibus" would be easy enough; similarly, the addition of "meam," giving "Pacem meam relinquo vobis," even though it is biblically inaccurate. Hoccleve's fair copy may have contained only the title and chapter citation for the rubricator to copy as gloss, further complicating the problem of authenticity.

Where space, time, or fatigue limits the rubricator, he may even omit the entire gloss. Because it is easier to omit a gloss than part of the text, omissions in the glosses are even weaker evidence of affiliation than are omissions in the text proper, nor do single-group occurrences of a gloss guarantee that the gloss is not authentic. For example, a long gloss from Aegidius is found only in the *beta* manuscripts; that MSS. I, *alpha*, and *gamma* all omit it independently is not extraordinary, for the Aegidius glosses here are so long that they fill the entire margin in most manuscripts, and this is the third such gloss in a row. In other words, it is not coincidental that two or three seminal manuscripts delete a gloss independently. It is only when the gloss enters the stemma further down that we might suspect its authenticity.

With the risk of being accused of using a circular argument, I would suggest that authenticity of the glosses can largely be supported by reference to the very stemma to which they contribute evidence. If, for example, the gloss can be found in early manuscripts of the two branches, or in at least two of the Greek-siglum manuscript groups, or even consistently in one major group, we might presume its authenticity and attribute it to Hoccleve's fair copy. Yet because there are also so many variables involved with the transmission of the glosses, the evidence they provide must be regarded as only supplemental. That is why, for example, I would be unwilling to infer the existence of a manuscript solely on the basis of evidence from the marginalia. Yet the glosses certainly do augment the evidence for manuscript affiliation found in the English texts. Even more important, they augment our understanding of the actual physical circumstances of production, giving us knowledge of which manuscripts were in the hands of which scribes or rubricators. Thus, the glosses can help explain coincidence of identical variants in the English texts in otherwise unrelated manuscripts or scribal emendation of presumably incorrigible variants. Herein lies their value.

APPENDIX B
List of Manuscript Sigla

A	British Library MS. Arundel 38
Ar	British Library MS. Arundel 59
Ad	British Library MS. Additional 18632
As	Bodleian Library MS. Ashmole 40
Bo	Bodleian Library MS. Bodley 221
Cc	Corpus Christi College, Cambridge, MS. 496
Co	Coventry Record Office MS.
Di	Bodleian Library MS. Digby 185
Do	Bodleian Library MS. Douce 158
Du	Bodleian Library MS. Dugdale 45
Ed	University of Edinburgh MS. 202
Fi^1	Fitzwilliam Museum, Cambridge, MS. McClean 182
Fi^2	Fitzwilliam Museum, Cambridge, MS. McClean 185
Ga	Princeton University MS. Garrett 137
Gg	Cambridge University Library MS. Gg.vi.17
Ha^1	British Library MS. Harley 116
Ha^2	British Library MS. Harley 372
Ha^3	British Library MS. Harley 4826
Ha^4	British Library MS. Harley 4866
Ha^5	British Library MS. Harley 7333
Hh	Cambridge University Library MS. Hh. iv. II
Hn^1	Huntington Library MS. El. 26. A. 13
Hn^2	Huntington Library MS. HM 135
Kk	Cambridge University Library MS. Kk.i.3. pt. 10–12
La	Bodleian Library MS. Laud Misc. 735
Ma	Magdalene College, Cambridge, MS. Pepys 2101
Na	National Library of Scotland Adv. MS. 19.I.II., pt. 3
Ne	Newberry Library MS. 6
Qu	The Queens' College, Cambridge, MS. 12
Ra^1	Bodleian Library MS. Rawlinson Poet. 10
Ra^2	Bodleian Library MS. Rawlinson Poet. 168
Ro	Rosenbach Foundation MS.
Ry^1	British Library MS. Royal 17 C. xiv.
Ry^2	British Library MS. Royal 17 D. vi.
Ry^3	British Library MS. Royal 17 D. xviii.
Ry^4	British Library MS. Royal 17 D. xix.
Se	Bodleian Library MS. Arch. Selden supra 53
Sj	St. John's College, Cambridge, MS. 223
Sl^1	British Library MS. Sloane 1212
Sl^2	British Library MS. Sloane 1825
So	Society of Antiquaries of London MS. 134
Tc	Trinity College, Cambridge, MS. R.3.22 (602)
Ya	Yale University MS. 493

NOTES

1. M. C. Seymour, "The Manuscripts of Hoccleve's *Regiment of Princes*," *Edinburgh Bibliographical Society Transactions*, 4.7 (1974):255.

2. For a list of the manuscript sigla, see Appendix B.

3. The designations of inferred manuscripts are tentative, the Branch I and II, *alpha*, *beta*, and *gamma* manuscripts so designated only for simplicity of reference in this paper. The transcriptions and lemma readings in this paper are from our copy-text, the MS. Arundel 38. Where our copy-text lacks the gloss, the transcription manuscript is otherwise designated, and lemma readings are those of the first siglum listed.

4. All *Regiment* manuscripts are glossed except for CoHhRa^{1}Ra^2.

5. Seymour, pp. 255–56.

6. It was not unusual for professional scribes in England to be versed in several scripts, in this period, viz., Textura (prescissa, quadrata, semiquadrata, or rotunda) among the book hands, and Anglicana, Anglicana Formata, Bastard Anglicana, Secretary book hand, and early Bastard Secretary deriving from the more cursive court hands. The scribes frequently used a mixture of script features, sometimes by design, sometimes by inadvertently slipping into a current or cursive style after beginning a piece in a more formal script. Scribes also used different scripts for different functions within a single manuscript. "Many fifteenth-century scribes were able to write well in more than one script," M. B. Parkes writes, "and manuscripts in which the scribe has used one script for the text and another for headings and commentaries are common" (*English Cursive Book Hands* [Oxford, 1969], p. xxiv). For examples of scribes who regularly used more than one script see H. C. Schultz, "Thomas Hoccleve, Scribe," *Speculum*, 12 (1937):71–81; R. A. B. Mynors, "A Fifteenth-Century Scribe: T. Werken," *Transactions of the Cambridge Bibliographical Society*, 1.2 (1950):97–104; A. I. Doyle, "The Work of a late Fifteenth-Century English Scribe, William Ebesham," *Bulletin of the John Rylands Library*, 39 (1957):298–325; P. J. Lucas, "John Capgrave, O.S.A. (1393–1464), Scribe and 'Publisher'," *Transactions of the Cambridge Bibliographical Society*, 5.1 (1969):1–35; M. B. Parkes, *English Cursive Book Hands*, pl. 19–23 with notes.

7. As early as the thirteenth century, a division of labor in book production was employed in the universities, with a system of renting separate quires of a work for reproduction. See Robert Steele, "The Pecia," *The Library*, 4 ser., 11.2 (1930): 230–34; J. A. Destrez, *La Pecia dans les manuscrits universitaires du xiiie et du xive siècle* (Paris, 1935); G. Pollard, "The *Pecia* System in the Medieval Universities," pp. 145–61 in *Medieval Scribes, Manuscripts & Libraries: Essays Presented to N. R. Ker*, ed. M. P. Parkes and Andrew G.

Watson (London, 1978). This pecia system may have had a counterpart in fourteenth- and fifteenth-century commercial production in the parceling out of sections for reproduction by scribes. See A. I. Doyle and M. B. Parkes, "The Production of Copies of the *Canterbury Tales* and the *Confessio Amantis* in the Early Fifteenth Century," pp. 163–210 in *Medieval Scribes, Manuscripts & Libraries.* We know that by the fifteenth century the art of book production entailed a rather complex subdivision of labor, often including different workmen for the script, the rubrics, the penwork initials, the painted and gilded initials, the borders, and the miniatures. See p. 89 of J. J. G. Alexander's article, "Scribes as Artists: The Arabesque Initial in Twelfth-Century English Manuscripts," pp. 87–116 in *Medieval Scribes, Manuscripts & Libraries*; A. W. Pollard, *Early Illustrated Books*, 2nd ed. (London, 1917), p. 2. The fact that often the marginalia appear cramped indicates that they were copied in batches after the text, and the fact that text and marginalia sometimes have different exemplars argues that a division of labor by function may have existed in established commercial scriptoria, as well as the process of book production entailing the parceling out of individual sections of the work, which Doyle and Parkes argue.

8.   Stanza 751 Nota de Auaricia et quemodo generat bellam Ro
         quemodo generat] quius querat Ha³
         Stanza 752 Contra adultores *et* de malis eorum moribus &c Ro
         eorum] dorum Ha³

Revising Shakespeare

GARY TAYLOR

I know of only two great creative artists who, according to orthodox interpretation, never revised their work. One is, of course, Shakespeare; the other is, of course, God.[1] This is part of a more general confusion between Shakespeare and God, prevalent in certain sects of the priesthood of literary criticism.

Nevertheless, textual critics have had to concede that the Shakespeare canon does contain clear evidence of certain *kinds* of revision. One kind is found in the good quartos of *Love's Labour's Lost* (Q1), *Romeo and Juliet* (Q2), and *Hamlet* (Q2). The quartos in question were apparently printed from Shakespeare's own manuscript draft. In the first two examples (Illustrations 1 and 2), the passage quoted on the left is, in the printed text, immediately followed by the passage on the right. The duplication of words and ideas between the right hand passage and the left hand passage has convinced most critics that Shakespeare first wrote the left hand passage, then for some reason decided it was unsatisfactory, and so redrafted it, immediately afterwards, in the form which it takes in the right hand passage. In *Hamlet*, there are apparently two false starts of this kind.

> For women feare too much, euen as they loue,
> And womens feare and loue hold quantitie,
> Eyther none, in neither ought, or in extremitie,
> Now what my Lord is proofe hath made you know,
> And as my loue is ciz'd, my feare is so,
>
> (H2)

The first line quoted has no rhyme-mate; moreover, its sense seems to be duplicated by the second line. In the third line, 'Eyther none' is extrametrical, and its sense seems to be duplicated by 'in neither ought'. The folio text omits both the unrhymed duplicated line and the extrametrical duplicated phrase.

285

1. *Romeo and Juliet*, Second Quarto (1599), D4ᵛ

(First Version)

The grey-eyde morne fmiles on the frowning night,
Checkring the Eafterne Clouds with ftreaks of light,
And darkneffe fleckted like a drunkard reeles;
From forth daies pathway, made by *Tytans* wheeles.

(Second Verison)

(night.
Fri. The grey-eyed morne fmiles on the frowning
Checking the Eafterne clowdes with ftreaks of light:
And fleckeld darkneffe like a drunkard reeles,
From forth daies path, and *Titans* burning wheeles:

2. *Love's Labour's Lost*, Quarto (1600), F2ᵛ-F3

(First Version)

And where that you haue vowd to ftudie (Lordes)
In that each of you haue forfworne his Booke.
Can you ftill dreame and poare and thereon looke.
For when would you my Lord, or you, or you,
Haue found the ground of Studies excellence,
Without the beautie of a womans face?
From womens eyes this doctrine I deriue,
They are the Ground, the Bookes, the Achadems,
From whence doth fpring the true *Promethean* fire.
Why vniuerfall plodding poyfons vp
The nimble fpirites in the arteries,
As motion and long during action tyres
The finnowy vigour of the trauayler.
Now for not looking on a womans face,
You haue in that forfworne the vfe of eyes:
And ftudie too, the caufer of your vow.
For where is any Authour in the worlde,
Teaches fuch beautie as a womas eye:
Learning is but an adiunct to our felfe,
And where we are, our Learning likewife is.
Then when our felues we fee in Ladies eyes,
With our felues,
Do we not likewife fee our learning there?

(Second Version)

O we haue made a Vow to ftudie, Lordes,
And in that Vow we haue forfworne our Bookes:
For when would you(my Leedge)or you, or you?
In leaden contemplation haue found out
Such fierie Numbers as the prompting eyes,
Of beautis tutors haue inritcht you with:
Other flow Artes intirely keepe the braine:
And therefore finding barraine practizers,
Scarce fhew a harueft of their heauie toyle.
But Loue firft learned in a Ladies eyes,
Liues not alone emured in the braine:
But with the motion of all elamentes,
Courfes as fwift as thought in euery power,
And giues to euery power a doub.e power,
Aboue their tunctions and their offices.
It addes a precious feeing to the eye:
A Louers eyes will gaze an Eagle blinde.
A Louers eare will heare the loweft round:/
When the fufpitious head of theft is ftopt,
Loues feeling is more foft and fenfible,
Then are the tender hornes of Cuckled Snayles.
Loues tougue proues daintie, *Bachus* groffe in tafte,
For Valoure, is not Loue a *Hercules?*
Still clyming trees in the *Hefperides*.
Subtit as *Sphinx*, as fweete and muficall,
As bright *Appolos* Lute, ftrung with his haire,
And when Loue fpeakes, the voyce of all the Goddes,
Make heauen drowfie with the harmonie,
Neuer durft Poet touch a pen to write,
Vntill his Incke were tempred with Loues fighes:
O then his lines would rauifh fauage eares,
And plant in Tyrants milde humilitie.
From womens eyes this doctrine I deriue.
They fparcle ftill the right promethean fier,
They are the Bookes, the Artes, the Achademes,
That fhew, containe, and nourifh all the worlde.
Els none at all in ought proues excellent.

Illustrations 1 and 2

In all three cases—and many other examples could be given, from elsewhere in these three plays, and from other plays like *Troilus and Cressida, Titus Andronicus*, and *Henry V*—we apparently see Shakespeare revising his work in the very act of composing it. The hypothesis of revision is, in such cases, based entirely upon a critical judgement that Shakespeare could never have intended *both* versions of these lines and ideas to be spoken, one after the other, upon stage. That critical judgement has been almost universally accepted, and these passages are regularly cited as evidence of Shakespeare revising himself.

In *Romeo, Love's Labour's Lost*, and *Hamlet* Shakespeare seemingly changed his mind in the very act of making it up. Consequently, 'revision' may seem a slightly misleading term. The rewriting is part of the original process of writing itself. One can cite these passages without consciously abandoning the image of Shakespeare as an unselfconscious artist. But another widely accepted example of revision is rather more disconcerting.

The first edition of *A Midsummer Night's Dream* (1600) was also apparently printed from Shakespeare's own foul papers. As a whole, this edition contains very little mislineation; most of the examples can be convincingly explained bibliographically, as the result of difficulty with fitting long lines into the compositor's measure, or difficulty with squeezing too much material (or expanding too little material) into quarto pages cast off in advance, for setting by formes.[2] But at the beginning of Act Five occurs a sudden infestation of mislineation, stretching over three quarto pages, for which no such bibliographical explanation is available. (I have boxed the affected lines in the facsimile; see Illustration 3.)

The.   More straunge then true, I neuer may beleeue
These antique fables, nor these Fairy toyes,
Louers, and mad men haue such seething braines,
Such shaping phantasies, that apprehend more,
Then coole reason euer comprehends. The lunatick,
The louer, and the Poet are of imagination all compact,
One sees more diuels, then vast hell can holde:
That is the mad man. The louer, all as frantick,
Sees *Helens* beauty in a brow of *Ægypt*.
The Poets eye, in a fine frenzy, rolling, doth glance
From heauen to earth, from earth to heauen. And as
Imagination bodies forth the formes of things

G2ᵛ

Vnknowne: the Poets penne turnes them to shapes,
And giues to ayery nothing, a locall habitation,
And a name. Such trickes hath strong imagination,
That if it would but apprehend some ioy,
It comprehends some bringer of that ioy.
Or in the night, imagining some feare,
How easie is a bush suppos'd a Beare?
    Hyp. But, all the story of the night told ouer,
And all their minds transfigur'd so together,
More witnesseth than fancies images,
And growes to something of great constancy:
But howsoeuer, strange and admirable.
        Enter Louers; Lysander, Demetrius, Hermia *and*
                            Helena.
    The. Here come the louers, full of ioy and mirth.
Ioy, gentle friends, ioy and fresh daies
Of loue accompany your hearts.
    Lys. More then to vs, waite in your royall walkes, your
boorde, your bedde.   (haue,
    The. Come now: what maskes, what daunces shall wee
To weare away this long age of three hours, betweene
Or after supper, & bed-time? Where is our vsuall manager
Of mirth? What Reuels are in hand? Is there no play,
To ease the anguish of a torturing hower? Call *Philostrate.*
    Philostrate. Here mighty *Theseus.*
    The. Say, what abridgement haue you for this euening?
What maske, what musicke? How shall we beguile
The lazy tyme, if not with some delight?
    Philost. There is a briefe, how many sports are ripe.
Make choyce, of which your Highnesse will see first.
    The. The battell with the *Centaures* to be sung,
By an *Athenian* Eunuche, to the Harpe?
Weele none of that, That haue I tolde my loue,
In glory of my kinsman *Hercules*,
The ryot of the tipsie *Bachanals*,

Tearing the *Thracian* singer, in their rage?
That is an olde deuise: and it was plaid,
When I from *Thebes* came last a conquerer.
The thrise three Muses, mourning for the death
Of learning, late deceast, in beggery?
That is some *Satire* keene and criticall,
Not sorting with a nuptiall ceremony.
A tedious briefe Scene of young *Pyramus*
And his loue *Thisbe*; very tragicall mirth?

3. *A Midsummer Night's Dream*

Folio
Variants

Folio
Variants

The. More ſtraunge then true, I neuer may beleeue
Theſe antique fables,nor theſe Fairy toyes,
Louers,and mad men haue ſuch ſeething braines,
Such ſhaping phantaſies,that apprehend more,
Then coole reaſon euer comprehends.The lunatick,
The louer, and the Poet are of imagination all compact,
One ſees more diuels, then vaſt hell can holde:
That is the mad man. The louer,all as frantick,
Sees *Helens* beauty in a brow of *Ægipt*.
The Poets eye,in a fine frenzy,rolling,doth glance
From heauen to earth,from earth to heauen. And as
Imagination bodies forth the formes of things
Vnknowne: the Poets penne turnes them to ſhapes,
And giues to ayery nothing, a locall habitation,
And a name Such trickes hath ſtrong imagination,
That if it would but apprehend ſome ioy,
It comprehends ſome bringer of that ioy.
Or in the night,imagining ſome feare,
How eaſie is a buſh ſuppoſd a Beare?
Hip. But,all the ſtory of the night told ouer,
And all their minds transfigur'd ſo together,
More witneſſeth than fancies images,
And growes to ſomething of great conſtancy:
But howſoeuer, ſtrange and admirable.
Enter Louers; Lyſander ,Demetrius,Hermia *and*
Helena.
The. Here come the louers, full of ioy and mirth.
Ioy,gentle friends, ioy and freſh daies
Of loue accompany your hearts,
*Lyſ.*More then to vs, waite in your royall walkes, your
boorde, your bedde. (haue,
The Come now:what maskes, what daunces ſhall wee
To weare away this long age of three hours,betweene
Or after ſupper, & bed-time? Where is our vſuall manager
Of mirth?What Reuels are in hand?Is there no play,
To eaſe the anguiſh of a tortaring howre? Call *Philoſtrate.*

Ege.   *Philoſtrate.* Here mighty *Theſeus.*
The. Say,what abridgement haue you for this euening?
What maske,what muſicke? How ſhall we beguile
The lazy tyme,if not with ſome delight?
Ege.   *Philoſt,* There is a briefe,how many ſports are ripe,
Make choyce,of which your Highneſſe will ſee firſt,
Liſ.   The, The battell with the *Centaures* to be ſung,
By an *Athenian* Eunuche, to the Harpe?
The.   Weele none of that,That haue I tolde my loue,
In glory of my kinſman *Hercules,*
Liſ.   The ryot of the tipſie *Bacchanals,*

The.   Tearing the *Thracian* ſinger, in their rage?
That is an olde deuiſe : and it was plaid,
When I from *Thebes* came laſt a conquerer.
Liſ.   The thriſe three Muſes, mourning for the death
Of learning,late deceaſt,in beggery?
The.   That is ſome *Satire* keene and criticall,
Not ſorting with a nuptiall ceremony.
Liſ.   A tedious briefe Scene of young *Pyramus*
And his loue *Thiſby*; very tragicall mirth?
The.   Merry,and tragicall? Tedious,and briefe? That is hot Iſe,
And wōdrous ſtrange ſnow. How ſhall we find the cōcord
Of this diſcord?

' Call *Egeus.*

Illustration 3

> Merry, and tragicall? Tedious, and briefe? That is hot Ise,
> And wōdrous strange snow. How shall we find the cōcord
> Of this discord?

As Dover Wilson observed in 1924, all of the mislined material could be omitted, without damage to its context, and some of the mislined material seems related to other mislined material.[3] All editors since Wilson have accepted that the mislined passages are mislined because they were written in the margin of Shakespeare's manuscript, and that they were written in those margins because they were written after the main body of the passage; they are afterthoughts. This example of revision differs from those already quoted because the very nature of the evidence for revision—extensive marginal additions—suggests strongly that Shakespeare did not write the offending material until after he had written at least fifty lines of the scene, and that he then went back over that part of the scene, making a number of belated alterations. How *much* later, we do not know; but it must have been at least a little later. Shakespeare thus apparently engaged in two kinds of revision: revision in the very act of composition, and revision at some time *after* initial composition— but still within the 'first draft' or 'foul papers' stage of composition.

Additional verse lines written in the margins of a manuscript confuse a printer because in such circumstances line-breaks may not have been indicated at all, or may have been obscured by the cramping of the material. A printer might also be misled by a marginal addition if he took it, not as an addition to the dialogue (which therefore did *not* belong where it physically occurred in the manuscript) but as a normal stage direction (which therefore *did* belong where it physically occurred in the manuscript). Thus, in the good quarto of *Romeo and Juliet* (Q2):

> Forbid this bandying in *Verona* streetes,
> Hold *Tybalt*, good *Mercutio*.
>
> *Away* Tybalt.
>
> *Mer*. I am hurt.
>
> (F3ᵛ)

Within the conventions of this quarto, '*Away* Tybalt.' is unmistakably intended as a stage direction. But it sounds much more like a speech: Shakespeare never elsewhere uses 'Away' as the verb in an exit direction, but does use it often in imperative speeches. W. W. Greg therefore conjectured, and subsequent editors have agreed, that '*A way* Tybalt' was a speech, written in the margin of the manuscript, which the printer misinterpreted as a stage direction.[4] This speech, noticeably, does not fit the metrical pattern of the verse into which it is inserted: without the two words, 'Hold *Tybalt*, good *Mercutio*. I am hurt' forms a typical Shakespearian pentameter, divided between two speakers; the added imperative 'speech' disrupts that pattern. The two words which Q2 treats as a stage direction were thus probably written in the margin of the manuscript, and probably written after the verse into which they intrude. Again, we cannot be sure when the addition took place.

In *A Midsummer Night's Dream* we infer that certain lines were written in the margin of a manuscript because they have been mislined in the printed text; in *Romeo and Juliet* we infer that a short speech was written in the margin because it was misinterpreted as a marginal stage direction. But in *Hamlet* certain lines are actually printed in the margin of the first authoritative edition. Illustrations 4 and 5 reproduce excerpts from H2 and H2^v, in which you can see these marginal lines; the first of these, you will notice, occurs just after a passage I have already referred to. There are no parallels for the way in which these two short speeches are printed in the 1605 quarto, or in any other Shakespeare quarto; there is no plausible bibliographical explanation for either anomaly. In the first example Hamlet's speech interrupts the Player Queen; yet there is no speech prefix to indicate that she resumes her speech after the interruption. And, of course, both passages make sense without the marginal speeches. Again, as in *Romeo* and *Dream*, it appears that Shakespeare marginally added to his own dialogue at some indeterminable point after initial composition.

But the examples from *Hamlet* and *A Midsummer Night's Dream* also have another feature in common. In both cases the apparent revision evident *within* the Quarto text coexists with related textual variation *between* the Quarto edition and a later text, printed in the 1623 First Folio. In *Hamlet*, the Folio text of this scene contains yet another brief speech by Hamlet, not printed in the Quarto at all.

> *Oph.* The King rises.
> *Quee.* How fares my Lord?
> *Pol.* Giue ore the play.

4. *Hamlet*, Second Quarto, H2

→ For women feare too much, euen as they loue,
   And womens feare and loue hold quantitie,
→ Eyther none, in neither ought, or in extremitie,
   Now what my Lord is proofe hath made you know,
   And as my loue is ciz'd, my feare is fo,
   Where loue is great, the litleſt doubts are feare,
   Where little feares grow great, great loue growes there.
   King. Faith I muſt leaue thee loue, and ſhortly to,
   My operant powers their functions leaue to do,
   And thou ſhalt liue in this faire world behind,
   Honord, belou'd, and haply one as kind,
   For husband ſhalt thou.
      Quee. O confound the reſt,
   Such loue muſt needes be treaſon in my breſt,
   In ſecond husband let me be accurſt,
   None wed the ſecond, but who kild the firſt.   *Ham.* That's
   The inſtances that ſecond marriage moue   wormwood
   Are baſe reſpects of thrift, but none of loue,
   A ſecond time I kill my husband dead,
   When ſecond husband kiſſes me in bed.
      King. I doe belieue you thinke what now you ſpeake,

5. *Hamlet*, Second Quarto, H2`

      Quee. Nor earth to me giue foode, nor heauen light,
   Sport and repoſe lock from me day and night,
   To deſperation turne my truſt and hope,
   And Anchors cheere in priſon be my ſcope,
   Each oppoſite that blancks the face of ioy,
   Meete what I would haue well, and it deſtroy,
   Both heere and hence purſue me laſting ſtrife,   *Ham.* If ſhe ſhould
   If once I be a widdow, euer I be a wife.   breake it now.
      King. Tis deeply ſworne, ſweet leaue me heere a while,
   My ſpirits grow dull, and faine I would beguile
   The tedious day with ſleepe.

Illustrations 4 and 5.

      King. Giue me some light, away.
      Pol.   Lights, lights, lights.
            (Second Quarto, H3)

      Ophe. The King rises.
→   *Ham*. What, frighted with false fire.
      Qu.   How fares my Lord?
      Pol.   Giue o're the Play.
      King. Giue me some Light. Away.
      All.   Lights, Lights, Lights.
            (First Folio, oo6ᵛ)

Likewise, in *Dream*, the first part of Act Five—where all the significant mislineation occurs—contains more variation between the Quarto and Folio than any other part of the play. (Folio variants are bracketed in the margin.)

      Enter Louers; Lysander, Demetrius, Hermia *and*
                  Helena.
      The. Here come the louers, full of ioy and mirth.
      Ioy, gentle friends, ioy and fresh daies
      Of loue accompany your hearts.
      Lys. More then to vs, waite in your royall walkes, your
    boorde, your bedde.   (haue,
      The. Come now: what maskes, what daunces shall wee
      To weare away this long age of three hours, betweene
      Or after supper, & bed-time? Where is our vsuall manager
      Of mirth? What Reuels are in hand? Is there no play,

[Call *Egeus*.] To ease the anguish of a torturing hower? Call *Philostrate*.

[*Ege*.] *Philostrate*. Here mighty *Theseus*.
      The. Say, what abridgement haue you for this euening?
      What maske, what musicke? How shall we beguile
      The lazy tyme, if not with some delight?

[*Ege*.] *Philost*. There is a briefe, how many sports are ripe.
      Make choyce, of which your Highnesse will see first.

[*Lis*.] *The*. The battell with the *Centaures* to be sung,
      By an *Athenian* Eunuche, to the Harpe?

[*The*.] Weele none of that, That haue I tolde my loue,
      In glory of my kinsman *Hercules*,

[*Lis*.] The ryot of the tipsie *Bachanals*,

      G3
      ——
      G3ᵛ

      Tearing the *Thracian* singer, in their rage?

[*The.*] That is an olde deuise: and it was plaid,
          When I from *Thebes* came last a conquerer.

[*Lis.*] The thrise three Muses, mourning for the death
          Of learning, late deceast, in beggery?

[*The.*] That is some *Satire* keene and criticall,
          Not sorting with a nuptiall ceremony.

[*Lis.*] A tedious briefe Scene of young *Pyramus*
          And his loue *Thisbe*; very tragicall mirth?

[*The.*] Merry, and tragicall? Tedious, and briefe? That is hot Ise,
          And wōdrous strange snow. How shall we find the cōcord
          Of this discord?

In the Folio the speeches of Philostrate are allocated instead to Egeus, thus bringing the thwarted father into the harmonies of the play's resolution: and Lysander—the son-in-law Egeus didn't want, but got—reads the list of proposed entertainments to Theseus.[5] This proximity of revision within texts and variation between texts may of course be coincidental; but then again, it may not.[6]

All modern editors accept that the anomalies in the first edition of *A Midsummer Night's Dream* result from authorial revision; all modern editors deny that the variation between Quarto and Folio results from the same process. Editors have been perfectly willing to accept that Shakespeare changed his mind in his foul papers; but they have steadfastly refused to believe that any of the variants between different editions result from authorial revision, revision which took place after completion of the first rough draft. In other words, when editors have only one extant text, they are happy to discern in it two layers of composition; but when editors have two substantive texts, they insist that both reflect only one layer of authorial composition. This editorial principle might be expressed by the mathematical formula: one sometimes equals two, but two always equals one.

Logically, there are only two possibilities.

1. Shakespeare never revised his work, after completing his initial manuscript draft.

2. Shakespeare did, at least occasionally, revise his work, even after completing his initial manuscript draft.

These hypotheses are of course mutually incompatible. Neither hypothesis can, as yet, be proven; yet editors must, in order to edit

Shakespeare at all, try to determine which hypothesis is, upon the available evidence, more *likely* to be right.

Most defenders of either hypothesis have offered 'literary,' rather than historical or bibliographical, 'proof.' Such proofs are intrinsically unstable. Advocates of the first hypothesis will allege that the differences between two early editions all result from corruption, rather than revision; they contend that the play only makes sense, or makes better sense, if we combine and conflate material from both early documents. Advocates of the second hypothesis, by contrast, allege that many variants result from revision, not corruption; they contend that the play only makes sense, or makes better sense, if we do *not* conflate material from two different documents, but recognize instead that each document has its own artistic coherence, that each body has its own soul. Both positions are equally and irredeemably subjective.

Of course, advocates of the first hypothesis have more to prove: they must attribute *every* variant to corruption; whereas advocates of the revisionist hypothesis only need to show that *some* variants result from revision. Moreover, advocates of the first hypothesis use an irrevocably subjective method to justify wholesale editorial emendation and reorganization; advocates of the revisionist hypothesis, more modestly, use an irrevocably subjective method in defense of the historical witnesses. But although advocates of revision may be more modest (intellectually, if not personally), their modesty does not make their 'literary' proof any more definitive than the 'literary' proof it seeks to supplant. 'Nothing neither way.'

Typically, advocates of traditional conflation argue that the conflated text is more 'complex' than either early document. But if you combine two atoms of hydrogen with one atom of oxygen you will, inevitably, produce a molecule more 'complex' than its constituent elements. That enhanced complexity does not prove that either oxygen or hydrogen is merely a 'corrupt' form of water. On the other hand, Shakespeare himself specializes in complex, open-ended, unstable artistic molecules; unlike *The Divine Comedy*, *Hamlet* has a form which permits interpolation and omission; and the kinds of complication (or even contradiction) produced by conflation are arguably difficult to distinguish from the kinds of complication (or even contradiction) already present in the acknowledged canon. I think the two *can* be rationally distinguished; but that is, after all, a personal judgement, no more infallible than the Pope's.

Shakespeare did revise, or he did not. How could you prove that one of these hypotheses is true, and the other false? You might hope to find reliable early testimony to Shakespeare's habits of composition. An autograph letter, for instance. 'Dear Anne, I'll be home next week, as soon as I finish completely revising that old play of mine, *King Lear*. Your loving Willy. London. 1 April 1610.'

In the absence of such authorial testimony we might look for depositions from Shakespeare's friends and colleagues. Two such statements in fact exist, both recorded in the preliminaries to the First Folio. As is well known, Heminges and Condell in their Preface allege that Shakespeare:

> as he was a happie imitator of Nature, was a most gentle expresser of it. His mind and hand went together: and what he thought, he vttered with that easinesse, that wee haue scarse receiued from him a blot in his papers.

Ben Jonson, in his *Discoveries*, repeats this claim:

> *I remember*, the Players have often mentioned it as an honour to *Shakespeare*, that in his writing, (whatsoever he penn'd) hee never blotted out line. My answer hath beene, would he had blotted a thousand. . . .[hee] had an excellent *Phantsie*; brave notions, and gentle expressions: wherein hee flow'd with that facility, that sometime it was necessary he should be stop'd:

How do we interpret this claim? It may be literally true: Shakespeare may not have blotted any—or many (depending on whether we believe 'scarse' or 'never')—of his lines, even when he intended to cancel them. If you look back at my first three examples, from *Romeo*, *Hamlet*, and *Love's Labour's Lost*, you will immediately realize that Shakespeare could not have blotted out the cancelled first version of those passages: if he had done so, the printer would have been unable to read them, and would in any case have realized that they were obviously meant to be cancelled. Shakespeare, when he wanted to omit something in his foul papers, may have simply used a marginal deletion mark, or may have used no mark at all, simply assuming that he could take care of such matters when he came to make his own fair copy of the play. Therefore, in some cases at least, the players' boast must have been literally true. But I think they intended the claim to have more than a literal significance; they intended by it to express the spontaneity and fecundity of Shakespeare's creative prowess, to distinguish him from imaginatively constipated writers like John Webster or Ben Jonson. But such a writer, whose mind overflows with images and ideas, filled with such imaginative impatience that he can hardly spill his mind out onto the paper fast enough—such a writer is not likely to be able to transform himself, when it comes to making a copy of his work, into a reliable human xerox machine. That very superabundance of talent makes it almost inevitable that he will continue impatiently rearranging, superfluously tinkering, overachieving, every time he copies his work. The claim that he never blotted a line thus tells us little about Shakespeare's attitude towards revision. If anything it suggests that he probably revised his work, one way or another, every time he copied it.

The other testimony in the First Folio—Ben Jonson's great encomium—is more explicit.

> Yet must I not giue Nature all: Thy Art,
>> My gentle *Shakespeare*, must enioy a part.
> For though the *Poets* matter, Nature be,
>> His Art doth giue the fashion. And, that he,
> Who casts to write a liuing line, must sweat,
>> (such as thine are) and strike the second heat
> Vpon the *Muses* anuile: turne the same,
>> (And himselfe with it) that he thinkes to frame;
> Or for the lawrell, he may gaine a scorne,
>> For a good *Poet's* made, as well as borne.
> And such wert thou.

Jonson, who had known Shakespeare since at least 1598, here explicitly claims that Shakespeare, either occasionally or habitually, 'struck a second heat' upon the muses' anvil.[7]

These two statements are the only external evidence we possess about Shakespeare's habits of composition. At worst, they contradict each other; at best, they both testify, implicitly or explicitly, that Shakespeare revised his work. But external evidence of this kind cannot finally decide the issue. Witnesses may, after all, have reasons to lie about a dead friend. Even if I did find that autograph letter, apologists for conflation could allege that Shakespeare himself was lying. Artists, after all, do, often enough, lie about their work. For all we know, 'revising *King Lear*' might have been Shakespeare's alibi, to cover an adulterous weekend.

We can only confidently deduce an author's habits of composition from the extant texts of his work. Either hypothesis—that

Shakespeare did, or did not revise—could be supported by the discovery of certain kinds of document. If we discovered two autograph manuscripts of one Shakespeare play, and if those two manuscripts contained no verbal variants, except perhaps for the odd slip of the pen, then we could reasonably conclude that—at least in that single case—Shakespeare did not revise his work when he copied it. The first hypothesis would not have been proven, for the first hypothesis claims to cover *every* case; but it would not have been disproven. Alternatively, if we discovered two autograph manuscripts, and those manuscripts did differ from one another in hundreds of readings, then we would have to conclude that Shakespeare did occasionally revise his work when he copied it: the second hypothesis would be proven. Unfortunately, autograph manuscripts of Shakespeare's plays do not survive in any noticeable abundance, so this kind of proof is unlikely to materialize.

The next best thing to two autograph manuscripts would be two independent editions of a single play, demonstrably printed from different manuscripts. This situation exists in the case of only three plays—and in fact the independence of the two editions involved has, in each case, only recently been established, on the basis of computer-assisted analyses of spelling and punctuation.[8] The three plays are *Henry the Fourth Part Two*, *Hamlet*, and *Othello*. For each of these plays there is a 'good' quarto and an independent Folio text printed from a manuscript. In each case, these editions differ from one another in hundreds of readings, including the presence or absence of extended passages of dialogue. Moreover, this control group of three can be doubled. For three other plays—*Richard II*, *Troilus and Cressida*, and *King Lear*—we possess two substantive editions. One is an early quarto, printed from manuscript. The Folio text has, in each case, been printed from a marked-up exemplar of a quarto; but the Folio corrects so many demonstrable Quarto errors in the dialogue that we can conclude, with absolute confidence, that an effort was made to collate the dialogue of the extant quarto with the dialogue of a manuscript now lost.[9] In all three cases, again, the two editions differ from each other extensively: the more thorough the correction of Quarto errors, the greater the number of verbal variants of other kinds between the two relevant texts. In each case, again, the variants include the presence or absence of extended passages of dialogue. We therefore possess six plays which come as close as possible to the ideal standard of proof, six plays for which the readings of independent manuscripts have been preserved in printed editions; all six contain massive verbal variation.

Further examples are provided by Shakespeare's sonnets, which we know circulated in manuscript at least ten years before they first appeared in print. A number of seventeenth-century transcripts of individual sonnets survive. For most sonnets only one manuscript exists, and it is difficult to determine the status and origin of the manuscript text. But two sonnets—number 2 and number 106— survive in more than one manuscript. In each case, again, the manuscript version differs significantly from the printed text. This can be seen from the parallel texts of Sonnet 2 (Illustration 6). A description and analysis of these two texts has recently been published in *The Bulletin of the John Rylands Library*.[10] Two other sonnets—138 and 144—also survive in two independent texts, one the Quarto of 1609, the other an octavo edition of *The Passionate Pilgrim*, printed ten years earlier; again, the two editions offer significantly different texts of the sonnets.

It might still be objected—indeed, it regularly is assumed—that these facts do not amount to proof that Shakespeare revised his work; for the variation between the two texts of these ten works might be the result of corruption in transmission. But this explanation is much more defensible if you are editing one work, than if you are editing the Complete Works. For these ten works have very different histories of transmission. The six relevant plays in the Folio, for instance, were set into type by at least five different compositors; three were set directly from manuscript, three from marked-up quartos; the manuscripts which lay behind these texts clearly have different kinds of provenance. Most, if not all, of the relevant quartos were apparently set from Shakespeare's own foul papers, but they were printed by four different printers, over the course of almost a quarter of a century, by (on current knowledge) nine different compositors. The only figure common to the transmission of all these texts is William Shakespeare. Therefore, if we wish to attribute the massive variation in all ten works to error and sophistication by agents of transmission, we must assume that such cavalier incompetence and irresponsibility affected virtually every agent entrusted with the transmission of Shakespeare's writings into print. Alternatively, we could conclude that everyone involved was reasonably competent, and that a single source of variation accounts for the divergences in all these texts: Shakespeare himself.

[THE MANUSCRIPT VERSION]

Spes Altera

When forty winters shall beseige thy brow
And trench deepe furrowes in y^t lovely feild
Thy youths faire liurey so accounted now
Shall bee like rotten weeds of no worth held
Then beeing askt where all thy bewty lyes
Where all ye lustre of thy youthfull dayes
To say within these hollow suncken eyes
Were an all-eaten truth, & worthlesse prayse
O how much better were thy bewtyes vse
If thou couldst say this pretty child of mine
Saues my account & makes my old excuse
Making his bewty by succession thine
This werr to bee new borne when thou art old
And see thy bloud warme when thou feelst it cold.

W.S.

[THE PRINTED VERSION]

2

When fortie Winters shall beseige thy brow,
And digge deep trenches in thy beauties field,
Thy youthes proud liuery so gaz'd on now,
Wil be a totter'd weed of smal worth held: 4
Then being askt, where all thy beautie lies,
Where all the treasure of thy lusty daies;
To say within thine owne deepe sunken eyes,
Were an all-eating shame, and thriftlesse praise.   8
How much more praise deseru'd thy beauties vse,
If thou couldst answere this faire child of mine
Shall sum my count, and make my old excuse
Proouing his beautie by succession thine.   12
This were to be new made when thou art ould,
And see thy blood warme when thou feel'st it could.

SHAKE-SPEARE

COLLATIONS OF THE MANUSCRIPT VERSION

The reading to the left of the bracket occurs in all eleven manuscripts, except those specified to the right of the bracket. Spelling and punctuation from the Westminster Abbey copy (W).

Spes Altera] Spes Altera A song F3; To one y^t would dye a Mayd B4, B5, F2, W,Y; A Lover to his Mistres N; The Benefitt of Mariage. R   1 forty] threescore B1; 40 B4 (?)   winters] yeares R   2 trench] drench R   feild] cheeke B2, B3   3 youths] youth B5, F3   faire liurey] fairer feild R   accounted] esteemed N   4 like] like like B5   weeds] cloaths F2.   5 beeing askt] if wee aske B3, B2; askt R   lyes] lye] W (cropped)   6 Where] Where's B1, B2, B3, F3, N, R   7 these] those Y; not in B4   8 eaten] beaten F2   prayse] pleasure B5   9 O] not in B5   much] far Y; not in B5   bewtyes] bewtious Y   10 pretty] little B2, B3   11 Saues] Saud Y   my] mine N   makes my old] makes me old B4; makes no old F2; yeilds mee an N; makes the old R; make no old Y   13 new borne] made younge B2, B3   14.1 W.S.] N (opposite title), B2 (table of contents)

Illustration 6

This still does not amount to a proof, of course. What we can prove is that most of the Folio compositors, and some of the Quarto compositors, and at least one of the scribes, were, in their other work, reasonably responsible and reliable, and that elsewhere they cannot be blamed for this quantity or kind of textual variant. We can prove that the censors did not elsewhere object to certain kinds of material.[11] *Normal* kinds of error and interference and sophistication will not account for the variants in these plays and sonnets, or for the fact that such variants occur in all ten.

We can also show that other playwrights and sonneteers of this period did revise their work in comparable ways. Such variation has been demonstrated in the sonnets of Spenser, Drayton, Daniel, and Constable, and in the plays of Jonson, Chapman, Beaumont and Fletcher, Dekker, Heywood, and Middleton. It perhaps does not surprise us to find such finicky self-preening in the work of consciously literary writers like Jonson and Chapman, or consciously gentlemanly writers like Beaumont and Fletcher; but Dekker and Heywood and Middleton were what Jonson called 'base fellows,' and what we would call 'hacks.' Professional playwrights like Shakespeare rather than 'men of letters' like Jonson and Chapman, they turned out a huge volume of work and showed little concern for their literary reputations *sub specie aeternitatis.* And E. A. J. Honigmann has shown that writers like Keats and Burns, who shared with Shakespeare an extraordinary imaginative fluency, a lack of higher education, and a certain carelessness of academic nicety, also revised their work in similar ways.[12] Even so, of course, such parallels do not *prove* that Shakespeare revised his work, because Shakespeare might be 'exceptional.'

In one sense, Shakespeare demonstrably was exceptional. He was the only playwright of his era who was also an actor and a sharer in its most successfull theatrical company, and who held that position for perhaps as long as twenty years. He was, as many witnesses conspire to inform us, the most popular and successful dramatist of that period. He is the only playwright whose works were collected and published posthumously by his theatrical company. He also named three actors in his will—the only playwright of this period, to my knowledge, who did so. We can confidently conclude that Shakespeare was exceptional, as a writer, in the strength and longevity and warmth of his relationship with a company of actors; exceptional, too, in the security of his position as a writer, both financially and institutionally; exceptional in his contact with and influence upon those people who were regularly responsible for transmitting his intentions from page to stage. If the transmission of Shakespeare's plays differed in any essential from the transmission of the plays of any of his contemporaries, it should have been in the relative scarcity of theatrical interference not sanctioned by the author himself.

Professor Fredson Bowers has rightly insisted that the basis of all textual editing and bibliographical investigation must be what he calls 'the postulate of normality.' 'No one should base a theory on abnormality instead of normality . . . unless there is overwhelming evidence in favour of the aberration.'[13] The hypothesis that Shakespeare never revised his work, after completing his first foul draft, is based upon five assumptions: (1) that those who transmitted the texts of his work were abnormally unreliable; (2) that Shakespeare was abnormal in the context of English Renaissance sonneteers and playwrights, and abnormal in the context of poets from all other periods, in his reluctance to revise his work; (3) that Shakespeare was abnormal in combining a willingness to revise in foul papers, with an unwillingness to revise thereafter; (4) that Shakespeare was normal only in the one respect in which we can demonstrate that he was instead unique: his relationship as playwright with the actors who performed his plays; (5) that the only ten control cases which we possess—the ten works which survive in two independent textual traditions—that these ten controls have, by a remarkable coincidence, and despite the variety of agents involved in their transmission, all suffered massive corruption, sophistication, and interference. The denial that Shakespeare revised his work can only be sustained if we accept all five assumptions, and accept them as an explanation for the variants in every text. Because once we admit the presence of revision as an operative source of variation in any one of these works, then we have inserted the thin end of that infamous wedge, and revision can no longer be ruled out as a possible explanation for variation in all the others. It seems to me that this set of interlocking assumptions no longer deserves our intellectual allegiance. It is like the pre-Copernican model of the universe: sustained only by the proliferation of improbable subsidiary complications.

Those few critics who have tried to defend the entrenched conflationist orthodoxy against the new revisionist onslaught have, to a man, done so by claiming that the case for revision is based on 'mere critical interpretation'—and bad interpretation, to boot. The pot proverbially calls the kettle black. But the evidence for revision is not solely, or even primarily, hermeneutical; it does not depend upon the single implausible Folio variant which hostile reviewers choose to quote. The hypothesis that Shakespeare, like every other author, revised his work, depends fundamentally upon the sheer weight of historical and bibliographical evidence for variation in the canon as a whole—variation which cannot be convincingly explained in any other way. That is why, although all previous editions have been based on the unexamined belief that Shakespeare did *not* revise his work, all future editions should be, and I believe will be, based on the recognition that he habitually did.[14]

NOTES

1. For evidence, if any were needed, that such attitudes about Shakespearian revision persist, even in the most elevated editorial circles, see for instance Harold Jenkins' new Arden edition of *Hamlet* (London: Methuen, 1982), *passim*. All extant editions of Shakespeare's works are, of course, based on similar assumptions.

2. See Robert K. Turner, Jr., 'Printing Methods and Textual Problems in *A Midsummer Night's Dream* Q1,' *Studies in Bibliography*, 15 (1962), 33–55.

3. *A Midsummer Night's Dream*, The New Shakespeare (Cambridge: University Press, 1924), pp. 80–86.

4. W. W. Greg, *The Shakespeare First Folio: Its Bibliographical and Textual History* (Oxford: Clarendon Press, 1955), p. 235, and George Walton Williams, 'A New Line of Dialogue in *Romeo and Juliet*,' *Shakespeare Quarterly*, 11 (1960), 84–87.

5. For a more extended discussion of the significance of these Folio variants, see Barbara Hodgdon, 'Gaining a Father: The Role of Egeus in the Quarto and Folio,' *Review of English Studies* (forthcoming).

6. An even more impressive example of foul paper revision linked to Folio variation is provided by *2 Henry IV*: see the extended discussion in John Jowett and Gary Taylor, 'The Three Texts of *2 Henry IV*,' *Studies in Bibliography*, 40 (1987), 31–50.

7. E. A. J. Honigmann first drew attention to the importance of this passage in his seminal book, *The Stability of Shakespeare's Text* (London: Arnold, 1965), pp. 30–31.

8. See Gary Taylor, 'The Folio Copy for *Hamlet*, *King Lear*, and *Othello*,' *Shakespeare Quarterly*, 34 (1983), 44–61, and 'Folio Compositors and Folio Copy: *King Lear* and Its Context,' *PBSA*, 79 (1985), 17–74. The evidence on copy for *2 Henry IV* will be published in a forthcoming article. If I were to be proven wrong about one or all of these three plays, they would simply fall into the second category (plays set from heavily-annotated printed copy); likewise, if current opinion were proven wrong about *Richard II*, *Troilus*, or *Lear*, they would simply rise from the second into the first category (manuscript copy). The argument of this paragraph therefore does not depend upon debatable hypotheses about the exact nature of printer's copy for the Folio.

9. For *Richard II*—the only one of these plays where manuscript consultation has sometimes been questioned—see John Jowett and Gary Taylor, 'Sprinklings of Authority: The Folio Text of *Richard II*,' *Studies in Bibliography*, 38 (1985), 151–200.

10. Gary Taylor, 'Some Manuscripts of Shakespeare's Sonnets,' *Bulletin of the John Rylands Library*, 68 (1985), 210–246.

11. For examples of such negative studies see the essays on censorship and compositors by Gary Taylor and Paul Werstine in *The Division of the Kingdoms: Shakespeare's Two Versions of 'King Lear,'* ed. Gary Taylor and Michael Warren (Oxford: Clarendon Press, 1983).

12. *Instability*, pp. 47–77.

13. *Bibliography and Textual Criticism* (Oxford: Clarendon Press, 1964), pp. 64–65.

14. Such editions need not and should not assume that every variant between two substantive editions results from authorial revision: allowances must always be made for normal kinds and quantities of compositorial (and in some cases scribal) error. Nor need acceptance of authorial revision entail adherence to the view that the so-called 'bad' quartos represent early plays of Shakespeare, later extensively revised by their author. The character of revision between the acknowledged good texts of Shakespeare differs fundamentally from the kind of variation found between the 'bad' quartos and their 'good' counterparts, and memorial reconstruction still seems to me easily the most plausible explanation for the peculiar nature of the 'bad' texts.

The Author as Scribe or Reviser? Middleton's Intentions in *A Game at Chess*

T. H. HOWARD-HILL

The eight surviving witnesses to the text of Thomas Middleton's celebrated play, *A Game at Chess*, reveal the playwright adapting an early, shorter, and structurally inferior version of the play to a fuller, perhaps final, version after he had presented his manuscript to the King's Company for performance. The material added to the short version—which survives in a single transcript—was probably written as a result of criticisms and demands made by the Company during rehearsals.[1] The two versions of the play offer ample testimony of the author's intentions, and one might think that when an editor has determined the character and priority of the witnesses, he may attempt a definitive edition of *A Game at Chess* that will, according to generally received principles, realise the author's final intention from amongst the welter of transmissional corruptions which obscure it. However, for a play it is necessary to recall that performance on the stage normally best represents a playwright's final intentions, whether or not his original conception of the work and the script which he delivered to the actors was modified by the exigencies of theatrical production. But in any particular instance, what happened to the text once it reached the theatre and how and to what extent the dramatist's intentions were realised in performance is problematic: contemporary accounts of performances of *A Game*, for instance, mention striking stage actions which have little or no warrant in the texts which have survived.[2]

On the other hand, a dramatist like Jonson, who was concerned to elevate the status of his plays to that of literary works, would revise plays to a form more appropriate for readers in the 1616 folio edition

305

of his *Works* or substitute his own writing for the contribution of an
earlier collaborator as in *Sejanus*. As G. Thomas Tanselle notes, an
editor in such cases can readily distinguish between versions which
represent distinct final intentions and edit the different texts according to his judgment of what these intentions were.[3] In the case of *A
Game*, the compositional genetics of which I have discussed elsewhere,[4] Middleton originally intended to write a religious allegory,
employing the device of chess-play to dramatize the age-old contention between good and evil. The political and satirical elements of the
play, which were responsible for its notoriety and the suppression of
its performances after the Spanish ambassador had complained to
the King, were either largely added to the text at the request of the
players or magnified by impersonation and stage-business during
performance so that the dramatist's basic conception of his work—
but not, perhaps, his final intention—was distorted and overshadowed. It is then possible to make a distinction between Middleton's
final intention for drama, the work *A Game at Chess*, and his final
intention for the theatre, realised on the stage in 1624 in the longest
run of consecutive performances of the same play known at that
time. Jonson's distinction between a *work* added to the enduring
body of literature and a *play* written for a transitory realisation in
performance needs to be borne in mind.[5]

The considerations become pointed for the leading case of
Middleton, a playwright who, having relinquished his play to the
stage, subsequently embarked on a premeditated course of preparing
texts of the play for sale, for presentation to patrons in hope of
reward, and for surreptitious publication. Six manuscripts, each with
significantly different textual characteristics, and two textually distinct quarto editions survive as witnesses to Middleton's intentions
for *A Game at Chess*.[6] The manuscript which preserves the earliest
version of the play is the Archdall-Folger. The title-page bears the
date 13 August, 1624 and the manuscript was therefore completed
three days before the Privy Council stopped performance of the
play. Middleton's dedication to the Malone manuscript in the
Bodleian Library—probably the last extant transcript to have been
prepared—claims that the play was not available from "Stationer's
Stall" and, because the manuscript was a new-year's gift, the
quartos, dated 1625? by Greg and STC, were apparently published
no earlier than mid-January of that year. The printer's copies for the
two quartos are textually related in a manner which it is not

necessary to specify here but which implies that, although Q3 is later than Q1, the manuscript from which it was printed was prepared about the same time. Analysis of the relationships amongst the witnesses reveals that, besides three non-extant manuscripts which must have existed by August 1624, at least seven more copies of the text must have been made subsequently in order to produce the six terminal copies which survive. Consequently, if publication of Q1 occurred quite shortly after the presentation of the Malone manuscript in January, at least thirteen copies of the play were made in the six months or so between performance and publication.

Middleton's handwriting is seen in three of the six surviving manuscripts, one of which (the Trinity College, Cambridge ms.) is entirely in his hand, and he wrote out the copy for Q1. Therefore, Middleton was closely involved in the multiplication of texts of his play after performances were stopped. Since the main object was to capitalise on the enormous sensation the play had made by its exceptionally bold presentation of contemporary political personages on the stage—for which Middleton may not have been himself mainly responsible—Middleton's participation in the transcriptional process with at least five other amanuenses was likely that of a scribe. Nevertheless, whenever an author shares in the transmission of the text, especially when he may have had second thoughts after presentation of his play on the stage, one should always consider closely the possibility of revision. In the easiest case for an editor to deal with, revision may be concentrated in a single manuscript which later transcripts will reproduce with differing degrees of accuracy according to the capabilities of the scribes and the distance of their copy from the revised text. Unfortunately, in *A Game at Chess* those variations which may be suspected to reflect authorial revision, that is, Middleton's progress towards the accomplishment of his final intention for the work, are not concentrated but rather dispersed through various witnesses and are therefore to be distinguished from scribal corruptions or sophistications only with considerable difficulty and rarely with certainty.

The editor's attempt to determine the author's final intentions for *A Game at Chess* is complicated by certain specific features of the witnesses which need be mentioned only briefly. (1) Although the witnesses were all prepared for readers, the scribes adopted rather different means to fit the text for the purpose; one manuscript (Malone) is a reading text radically different from the others. (2) The transcripts were written by at least six scribes who ranged in competence from the experienced professional, Ralph Crane, to the barely competent; Middleton himself may be included in the second category. (3) Moreover, since the author was involved in transcription, the exclusive variants of the two manuscripts where his presence is prominent (Trinity; Bridgewater-Huntington) may represent revisions but are in any event and most cases hard to distinguish from the unintentional variation or even intentional normalization which inevitably accompanies transcription, even when the scribe is the author. (4) Further, all eight witnesses are terminal, standing at the ends of lines of transmission of different lengths and complexity which demonstrate degrees of conflation and contamination.[7] (5) And, if all this were not enough, the surviving manuscripts contain intermittent textual alterations by *another* three hands which are not those of the six scribes.

I shall not attempt to consider all eight witnesses here but rather shall concentrate on those which evidently testify to Middleton's intentions for his work and his attitude to the text. Three of the witnesses are crucial for an editor, two because they are wholly (Trinity) or partially (Bridgewater-Huntington) in Middleton's hand, and the other (Q1) because it was printed from copy prepared by him. Another manuscript, the Archdall-Folger manuscript in the hand of Ralph Crane, is important because it reveals the earlier version of the work transcribed before the additions which enlarged the part of the Black Knight and introduced the Fat Bishop were incorporated in the other texts of the play. The Archdall manuscript is some 323 lines shorter than the "final" text. Even this transcript gives disturbing evidence of Middleton's attitude towards texts of his play. Middleton handled the transcript—there is a correction in his hand on f. 32—and must have known that it lacked a significant part of the action that was being presented on the stage when the transcript was finished on August 13th, yet he was prepared to let it go for sale, defective as it was.

When he transcribed the play himself, Middleton was no more scrupulous. The Trinity College manuscript in his hand lacks the last scene of Act IV, an omission which could not have occurred because a leaf is missing from the Trinity ms. as it has come down to us, because the following scene (V.i.) starts on the *verso* of leaf X2. The scene existed in the early version of the play and appears in all other witnesses. Because the omitted IV.v contains the Fat Bishop's attempt on the White Queen and his subsequent capture, it is essential to the action of the play: its omission is a serious oversight (to be charitable) by an author transcribing his own work. It reveals that the Trinity manuscript was not intended to be the source of any other manuscript; it was a transcript for sale or presentation. The omission apart, other indications of haste and carelessness seriously diminish the value of what is usually accounted the most authoritative witness. The Trinity manuscript shows some 81 substantive variants not attested to by other witnesses. Although many of them represent readings subsequently revised in other manuscripts, others are undoubtedly errors in the work of an author hurrying to copy his work for presentation or sale.[8]

An even more perturbing demonstration of Middleton's indifference to the completeness, and therefore the correctness of his text, appears in the Bridgewater-Huntington manuscript in which Middleton transcribed two quite extensive portions of the play. The manuscript was transcribed by two inexperienced scribes who had been assigned unequal shares of the play. Scribe A wrote from the start of the play and finished his stint in the middle of line II.ii.13. Scribe B started with the initial stage-direction of III.i and completed V.i; the transcript was continued and finished by Middleton himself. When the author put the two scribal stints together, he found that about 286 lines of II.ii were lacking.[9] Besides long speeches characterizing the Fat Bishop and initiating the Black Knight's plot against him, the scene contains the White Queen's Pawn's accusation before the assembled Houses of the Black Bishop's Pawn's attempted rape and a significant reversal of the White House's fortunes when the Black Knight successfully discredits the accuser. There is no possibility that II.ii could be detached from the play without structural damage; a reader would not make sense of the play without it. At this point in the process of transcription the gatherings of quarto halfsheets in which the scribes wrote were not sewn together; in any event, almost three pages of the gathering remained in which Middleton could complete the scene, and he could, of course, have continued on additional sheets. His method of filling the lacuna in order to complete the transcript of his play is startling, to say the least. He completed the verse (II.ii.13) left by scribe A and went on with the passage to the exit of the Fat Bishop's Pawn, another six verses (ll. 14–19). Then, omitting 27 verses of the Fat Bishop's soliloquy, he provided for the Black Knight's entrance with another twelve verses (ll. 48–60) into which he interpolated by interlineation a single verse (l. 78) from a passage subsequently omitted. Middleton now had the blank conjugate leaf of the gathering remaining to be filled and some 237 lines of II.ii yet to transcribe. At his usual frequency of 24 lines to a page Middleton would have required ten pages for the rest of the scene, that is, the existing leaf and two additional gatherings. He resolved his difficulty with Draconian effectiveness. He tore out the blank leaf, and altered the stage-direction with which Scribe B's portion of the manuscript began so that "Enter Fat Bishop" became "*The* Fat Bishop"; in short, the entrance which started III.i. became a speech-prefix for a character who (apparently) had not left the stage. While the gap between the two scribal portions was thus expediently filled, the resultant transcript lacks II.ii.61–293 through the deliberate choice of the author.

The manuscript which provided the truncated text of II.ii was the manuscript from which the authoritative Q1 was printed. Consequently, the Bridgewater-Huntington manuscript is the latest of the transcripts in the more or less direct line from Middleton's earliest papers. Middleton mutilated B-H. intentionally; B-H. is the last version of the text with which the author was patently involved. Is an editor therefore to believe that the B-H. manuscript, with its rump II.ii, incorporates Middleton's final intentions for the text of *A Game at Chess*? I think not, but pass to a more challenging problem of B-H., Middleton's performance as a scribe of V.ii, iii, and Epilogue, together with the part of II.ii just discussed.

As I have mentioned, the scribes of B-H. were inexperienced, writing unpracticed hands, and were not (so far as can be determined) otherwise employed for transcripts of *A Game*. In Scribe A's 763 lines there are 45 clear errors of transcription, most of which he corrected immediately, and another 51 substantive and manifest errors which could not possibly be construed as authorial revision in the scribe's copy. Scribe B wrote 1059 lines of B-H.; they show 125 scribal slips, false starts, miswritings and the like, and another 19 indubitable errors. Comparison of the scribes' performance with Middleton's in the 422 lines of B-H. in his hand shows that they were both about twice as careless as the author, who himself was hardly a model of accuracy or rectitude. (These calculations take no account of the errors transmitted through their copy which the scribes copied faithfully). It is remotely possible but not, I think, ultimately believable, that Middleton was conscious of the scribes' inadequate performance and charged someone else (whose presence cannot be detected elsewhere in the *Game* texts) to correct the manuscript. Nevertheless, there are some 409 markings in pencil by a contemporary hand which extend from the beginning of B-H. through Middleton's botched II.ii and all but the last four pages of Scribe B's stint. The pencil corrections range from the trivial to the substantial, but although they are intelligent and sometimes restore the text, none of them implies that B-H. was collated against copy. The pencil corrector in fact is a red-herring in B-H.[10] The significant fact is that although Middleton transcribed two portions of the manuscript and made a textual alteration to accommodate the adjustment of II.ii, there is no other indication by alterations in his distinctive handwriting that he so much as glanced over the work of the inexpert scribes in the B-H. manuscript. This observation creates a problem for an editor of *A Game*. One authorial transcript of *Game*, the Trinity manuscript, is careless and imperfect; the other, B-H., is error-ridden and deliberately defective at just that point where the author was most closely involved. What then should an editor make of the readings which are peculiar to B-H., which in theory reflect his later, even final, intentions for the text?

As human behaviour is notoriously inconsistent, it is possible to believe that Middleton was indifferent to the condition of his text throughout B-H. until he reached V.ii where, when he was actively engaged with his work as a scribe, the authorial instinct to refine or embellish his creation became paramount. If that is not true, we should at least like it to be true, because although editorial theory may incorporate the possibility of inconsistency, editorial practice is confounded by it. Therefore, if Middleton's attention to accuracy of the text is indifferent in Trinity and negligible in B-H., evidence that he cared to achieve a final correct text must be sought elsewhere, as a preliminary to judging the status of the authorial variants in B-H.

The first significant observation is that only one of the six *Game* manuscripts contains corrections by the author himself. In his Trinity manuscript, although he made some corrections *currente calamo*, usually by overwriting, Middleton did not go over the transcript, correcting it with reference to his copy. In the early Archdall-Folger manuscript, however, some corrections were made in the first part of the text (to l. 71 in II.i) to bring the transcript into conformity with the expansion and revision of the play which had been made in another nonextant manuscript, although, as mentioned earlier, Middleton did not care to incorporate in A-F. the substantial passages of the revision which distinguishes the other witnesses from A-F. Middleton's single correction in the six manuscripts of *Game* consists of the addition of a line (Trinity 712) at the end of (Trinity) 711, written in carelessly without indication of the speaker, in the vicinity of a correction made in another hand. Two other "correctors," who are also not otherwise to be observed in the *Game* manuscripts, made seven or eight substantial corrections. Five of them, in the hand which Susan Zimmerman Nascimento identifies as "Corrector 2," appear to respond to the concerns of the censor, the Master of the Revels; the others by "Corrector 3" are stylistic, literary deletions, additions and substitutions.[11] A couple of revisions were overlooked: two verses after Trinity 180 are found in no other witness and were thus deleted at an early stage in the ancestors of the surviving texts, and at l. 660 "Hugonites" appears as "Lutherans" in the other manuscripts, an alteration consistent with those that were made in A-F. Two other minor Crane singularities (at ll. 474 and 552) were overlooked, if indeed the transcript was read against copy, but these four instances apart, the early portion of A-F. contains no exclusive readings.[12]

The second point about Middleton's concern for the text is that only B-H. besides A-F. shows any attempt to ensure the correctness of the text.[13] However, the operations of the "pencil corrector" in the Bridgewater manuscript, although intelligent and serving to correct the grosser errors of the two scribes, give no evidence that he compared the transcript with copy, and besides, the last quarter of the text received no attention at all. Notwithstanding that most of his alterations are correct and helpful, they have no authority at all, and the very origin of the "pencil corrector," like the correctors of A-F., is mysterious and disturbing. Analysis of the relationships of the manuscripts indicate that emendation is likely to have occurred in the nonextant manuscript which is the common (but not immediate) source of the Rosenbach and Bridgewater-Huntington manuscripts and Q1, but the absence of clear indications that the playwright was concerned for the correctness of his text, and the presence of various "correctors" who worked to an extent independently of the playwright or authoritative copy, together do not lead to confidence that those emendations—even if they can be distinguished from scribal errors—correctly reflect the author's intentions.

Further conclusions about the character of Middleton's attitude to his text may be drawn from the Malone transcript in the Bodleian library, which is in the hand of Ralph Crane. This manuscript is unique amongst the surviving dramatic manuscripts of the period (to my knowledge) in that it is a condensation of the full version of the play which, while preserving all the characters and significant action, shortens the text by some 787 lines. Occasional variants, including two new part verses, were provided for the sake of smooth transitions between parts of speeches. One would normally conclude that the abbreviation of the play was the work of the author even though he was otherwise not directly connected with the manuscripts of this (the Crane) line. On the other hand, the contraction, which is skillfully achieved, was not beyond Crane's own capabilities; he was an author as well as an accomplished scribe of literary texts. But overall, although he had earlier revised the form of stage-directions in the copy for a number of printed texts,[14] the revision of the play in the Malone transcript is unexampled in his work. Therefore, it is somewhat more likely that Middleton marked up the copy from which Crane's Lansdowne manuscript had been transcribed for the scribe to copy for the Malone transcript. (That being true—and alternative explanations do not come readily to mind—Middleton must have intended to make several transcripts of the shortened version of the play; had he needed only one transcript he could have simply used the source of the Malone without undertaking the revision). When the transcript was finished it came into Middleton's hands: he inserted a dedication leaf in his own handwriting and arranged for the manuscript to be bound for presentation.[15] However, although Malone transmits the common errors of its line and adds exclusive variants of its own, and despite the special character of its text, there is no mark in the transcript to indicate that Middleton paid any attention to the text at all, either to ensure the correctness of the transmitted text or to approve fidelity to his "final" intentions in the revision.

The general conclusion to which one is led by consideration of Middleton's involvement in the Archdall-Folger manuscript, in his own early transcript, the Trinity, in the latest transcript, the Bridgewater-Huntington which contains 422 lines in his hand, and in the special revision of the play in the Malone, is that he was indifferent to both the correctness and the completeness of any of the texts of his play. The conclusion is reinforced when one notes that Crane's Lansdowne transcript (like Malone) lacks III.iii, and the

Rosenbach-Folger manuscript, for which Middleton wrote the title-page, also shows no sign of his attention to the numerous scribal errors which disfigure the text. In short, all the surviving manuscripts of *A Game at Chess* are grossly defective, with the acquiescence of the author.

Nevertheless, it is still possible that Middleton was more meticulous when he prepared the play for publication. The first quarto (STC 17882) was set by two compositors in the employ of an unidentified printer in 1625. The text shows 646 readings which are found in no other witness, amongst them variants in which it is reasonable to suspect the hand of the author; the most conspicuous example of these is the addition of a marginal stage-direction, *"A great shout and flourish"* at V.iii.161 (Harper's lineation) when the Black King is taken (sig. K3^v; Trinity 2378).[16] Variants which may be laid to the charge of the compositors—misprints, omissions, variations of number in nouns, misreadings, and other errors which have a more or less apparent paleographical origin—amount to 498, about one in every five lines of text. There are another 47 variants which may be classified as "indifferent," variations, for instance, between prepositions, relative pronouns, contractions and the like which may have been made by a compositor as readily as by an author transcribing a manuscript. Some 101 variants remain, most frequent in II.i,ii, III.i,ii and IV.ii but occurring overall about once in every twenty-five lines. Close analysis might show that some of them could be assigned to the compositors; not all transpositions, for instance, are so large or so significant as to be beyond a compositor's powers to effect. Nevertheless, there is a substantial residue which any editor would hesitate to relegate to compositorial inefficiency or highhandedness. It is impossible here to examine the possible authorial variants individually, but one instance can be given. At l. 2417 in all other witnesses the White Knight refers to the captured Black side as having been put into the "pitt." When Middleton had enlarged the play he strengthened the chess metaphor at the expense of the pit/hell analogy by incorporating references to the "bag" in which the pieces were fated to be confined as they were taken. The Q1 variation of "bag" or "pitt" develops the author's intention and is a reading which an editor, despite its absence from the two manuscripts written in the dramatist's hand, should prefer in an edition.

Notwithstanding suchlike morsels which an editor may glean from the variants which apparently indicate Middleton's attention to his work in Q1, an editor of *A Game* cannot simply plump for—compositorial errors aside—Q1 as the "best text." First, the large number of compositorial errors (which includes the omission of seven lines of text) proves that Middleton's concern for his play stopped at the printing-house door; the author did not proofread the sheets or supervise correction of the text. Second, Q1 includes no significant amount of revision through either the deletion or addition of passages; the possible authorial variants are sporadic and local and, for the most part, not much more significant than the kinds of variation which *any* author makes when transcribing his own work. And third, there is no evidence that Middleton attempted to correct the errors of the manuscript from which he transcribed the copy for Q1.[17]

Nevertheless, there is still the Bridgewater-Huntington manuscript to consider, particularly in that part of II.ii, and V.ii–iii, which the dramatist wrote out himself. However, analysis of the significant variants exclusive to B-H. (setting aside obvious slips of the pen) does not encourage one to believe that Middleton's final intentions may be found there. Of the 24 significant exclusive variants in this manuscript, two were made as part of the truncation of II.ii discussed earlier, and another eight are errors; there are only five readings which effect distinct but quite modest improvements, and the remaining nine variants are indifferent: they are of a kind characteristic of scribes and compositors; an editor would feel compelled to accept them if he decided to take the Middletonian portions of B-H. as his copy-text.[18]

That any of the variants in B-H. reflect Middleton's "final intentions" is doubtful. Although he effected some improvements in B-H. and in the copy for Q1, he did not consider them important enough to be transferred from one manuscript to the other. (Had he done so, they would not be exclusive variants, of course). Earlier I suggested that a playwright might continue to work towards a Platonic "final" form of a play after performance, but now it is clear that *A Game at Chess* was finalised for Middleton by the time he became deeply engaged in the transcription of texts. The "improvements" in the later witnesses are minor, local tinkerings; they are "final" only inasmuch as the texts stand at the ends of their respective lines of transmission and are "intentional" only to the limited extent they are improvements.[19] Against the testimony of a few "improvements" stands the clear evidence of Middleton's indifference to the integrity of the texts in which his play is found: they are neither complete nor correct, and for the most part responsibility is Middleton's alone. Although the editorial implications of Middleton's complicity in the debasement of his text are disheartening, in that it makes the establishment of a final text a complicated and uncertain endeavor, an editor may receive some comfort from the reflection that, *whatever* may be the character of his representation of Middleton's "final intentions," the author himself would have accepted it.

NOTES

1. Although there are some more purely literary revisions which involve diction, metre, and the like, most of the additions to the early version add the Fat Bishop's part for the actor William Rowley, who specialized in fat clowns, and improve details of staging. I have discussed the additions in "Stage-directions in Middleton's *Game at Chess*," an unpublished paper circulated to the Seminar on Stage-directions, Shakespeare Association of America annual meeting, Cambridge, Mass., April, 1984.

2. Don Carlos Coloma's report to Olivares mentioned that the White Knight "heartily beat and kicked the 'Count of Gondomar' into Hell" (E. M. Wilson and Olga Turner, "The Spanish protest against 'A Game at Chess,'" *MLR*, 44 [1949], 480), action supported by John Woolley in a letter to William Trumbull (Berkshire C. R. O. Trumbull alphabetical correspondence 48/134).

3. "The Editorial Problem of Final Authorial Intention," *Studies in Bibliography*, XXIX (1976), 192–93. In such a case as *The Duchess of Malfi* (1623) which Webster himself prepared for publication, an earlier theatrical version not surviving, the editor has no great need to consider a theatrical intention; the dramatist's final intention was to present a text for reading.

4. "The Origins of Middleton's *A Game at Chess*," *Research Opportunities in Renaissance Drama*, XXVIII (1985), 3-14.

5. *A Game at Chess* started as a work in dramatic form and was adapted for the theatre by the author and then the players. Although the players may have arrived at a satisfactory play, theatrical adaptation may have compromised the integrity of the work as the dramatist conceived it ideally. Therefore, after performances ceased, the playwright might have continued to work towards realisation of his final intention which, since the stage is no longer a factor, relates to the *work* rather than the play.

6. The quartos are Q1 (STC 17882) and Q3 (STC 17884); Q2 (STC 17883) is partly a reissue, partly a reprint of Q1 and has no independent value for determination

of the text. No account is taken here of Q3, or of Ralph Crane's Lansdowne transcript, made from an earlier transcript by him, which apparently Middleton did not see.

7. By "contamination" I mean the confusion in the genetic relationships of witnesses which results when a manuscript is copied from two or more other manuscripts of different origins and textual characters. "Conflation" is the importation into a manuscript of readings from another branch of a stemma, generally by interlinear or marginal corrections but sometimes by intermittent consultation.

8. Susan Zimmerman Nascimento ("Thomas Middleton's *A Game at Chesse*; a textual study," Ph.D. diss., University of Maryland, 1975) summarizes the status of Trinity manuscript thus: " . . . the Tr. MS. shows Middleton as a careless and probably hurried scribe. The change in the format of the act-scene divisions; the irregular marking of entrances and exits; the loose and frequently imprecise punctuation and lineation; the mistakes in speech-prefixes; the frequent messiness; and especially Middleton's willingness to omit IV.v and to let the errors in act V go uncorrected, argue that he did not give his full attention to this transcription" (p. 22).

9. The manuscript is described in "The Bridgewater-Huntington MS of Middleton's *Game at Chess*," *Manuscripta*, XXVIII (1984), 145–56.

10. The "pencil corrector" is discussed generally in the above article, pp. 153–55.

11. Corrections which may reflect censorship occur on p. 2 (Tr. l. 40), p. 5 (107), p. 6 (134), p. 13 (271), and p. 32 (710); the literary corrections are on p. 7 (144), p. 15 (330), p. (454), a phrase "crossed out in another ink" (Nascimento, p. 286), and p. 31 (690).

12. Speech-prefixes and stage-directions (which were revised for the later transcripts) are excluded from this statement. Setting aside speech-prefixes and stage-directions, A-F. has 74 exclusive readings from II.ii (906) onwards.

13. The "Corrector 2" distinguished by Nascimento (p. 27) is Scribe B.

14. Crane's influence on the stage-directions of the Folio *The Two Gentlemen of Verona, The Merry Wives of Windsor*, and *The Winter's Tale*, and the 1623 Q1 of Webster's *The Duchess of Malfi* is considered in my *Ralph Crane and Some Shakespeare First Folio Comedies* (Charlottesville: Published for the Bibliographical Society of the University of Virginia by the University Press, 1972).

15. Nascimento plausibly suggests that "Middleton supervised the final assembly of the manuscript" (p. 46).

16. There are no other indications that Q1 may have been printed from prompt-copy.

17. Those errors are represented by the agreement of B-H., Rs., and Q3 against the agreement of Tr., A-F. and Q1.

18. The indifferent variants are *found/save* (810) *has Wrought/do's work* (818), *count it strange/thinke it most absurd* (2075), *wch is the/this is the* (2098), *slid/light* (2154), *Was not seene/Was not knowne* (2161), *art/wert* (2190), *3 hundred/2 hundred* (2205), *a'th/of the* (2215). In the analysis of variants "indifferent" means that the variants show no clear sign of their probable origin (compositor, scribe, author); they offer no sure evidence of anything. However, "indifferent" does not imply that the variants have equal aesthetic value or the same meaning but merely that the benefit of accepting one variant and rejecting another in an established text cannot be shown. Usually an editor will accept into his text the indifferent readings of his copy-text for, even in the case of an author as slipshod as Middleton, there is no reason to reject them in favour of other equally suspect variants, and he will at least maximize the (unascertainable) probability of correct choices if he prints copy-text readings.

19. Since we believe that no author harms his work intentionally, errors are attributed to other agents whenever possible; similarly, consistent or widespread improvements are usually attributed to the author, because in usual circumstances no other agent assumes the function of improving the text in substantives. Errors—regardless of their source—are usually regarded as unintended, whereas improvements are intentional.

What is a Restoration Poem?
Editing a Discourse, Not an Author.

GERALD M. MACLEAN

"The proposition that the writer or artist is a creator belongs to a humanist ideology. In this ideology man is released from his function in an order external to himself, restored to his so-called powers. Circumscribed only by the resources of his own nature, he becomes the maker of his own laws."

Pierre Macherey[1]

Trained in the Cambridge school of "practical criticism" to regard a literary text to be not so much a closed formal unit but more an expression of life as it is being lived in a particular place, at a particular time, according to a particular structure of feeling governed, in the final instance, by the general mode of production (GMP),[2] I stand in an obviously difficult relation to the theory and practice of editorial criticism, a relation that marks the following discussion with what may seem like a naive or fatuous polemicism. Let me begin, then, by theorizing the terms of that polemic thus: the history of the institutions which govern the discourses and practices of both literary history and textual editing, is a history, among other things, of an ideological blindness—in the limited sense of a false consciousness—that has been noted by Jerome McGann in his *Critique of Modern Textual Criticism*, but which we here might specify further as the product of an *ahistorical aestheticism* and a *scientific positivism*. By "ahistorical aestheticism" I mean something similar to McGann's concerns over the problem of the *auteur*— an approach to the question of textual author–ity by way of a Romantic and ultimately bourgeois idolization of the integral author. By "positivism" here I wish to signal related but more fundamental problems concerning the status of texts and of history as *écriture*. Empiricist historians treat "history" as an assembly of people, events and facts that are knowable otherwise than in those very acts of conception, analysis and writing; in doing so they reify the textual object and deny the conditions of the historical subject. My concerns in this paper are political rather than moral, sociological rather than psychological. Beneath this polemicism, then, let me inscribe a traditional argument: the concerns of the literary historian and the textual editor are dialectically related rather than antithetically opposed, consequently either's theoretical advance will promote the health of both. In particular, redefinition of the tasks, questions and instruments of the literary historian bear directly upon the modes, manners and methodologies of the textual editor. Here I think of some important recent arguments within Marxist-feminism. To McGann's preferred line-up of Riffaterre, Said, Derrida, and De Man ("Shall These bones Live?" 21), let us here add the supplementary ghosts of Goldmann and Foucault, and the living names of Spivak, Coward, and Heath.

This paper examines some problems of establishing the *oeuvre* of Katherine Philips, since this will nicely illustrate what I have to say about discourses and authors. First, though, let me outline my general editorial project in order to approach the question of how new perspectives in literary history can help us avoid some of the fallacies still prevalent among literary historians when they try to talk about texts in ways that bear directly on the concerns of editorial theory and practice. In line with McGann's general contention in his *Critique* that we need a more "socialized" theory and practice of textual editing—one that both admits (of necessity) the editorial subject and the counter-problematics of subjectivity within the field of scientific knowledge—I offer the following notes on my editorial procedures working with the poems on the Restoration.

When editing a discourse, such as the poems on the Restoration, we find poetry and history come together in ways different from what we find when editing an author. The history of the author's life, to put it crudely, provides a center for focussing empirical data, those otherwise establishable facts, in ways that a discourse by its very constitution cannot. The status of the text alters when we see it not only in relationship with the authorial life and *oeuvre*, but also as more significantly related to a socio-cultural discourse of which it is a representative member; part of the body politic, as it were.

Twenty years ago when the enormously important Yale edition of *Poems on Affairs of State* started to appear, George de Forrest Lord addressed these problems and questions directly, forcefully, and accurately. In the section of the introduction entitled "The *State Poems* and HISTORY" Lord offers the following rationale for relating history and poetry the way he does:

> Political satire is related to historical events in two ways. It is a record of events, a "history," however distorted by partial views and private motives. It also exerts influence, however slight, upon the events themselves. The political verse of the Restoration played a considerable part in the determination of large issues in England: the question of a Protestant or a Catholic succession, for one, and the relative power of royal prerogative and Parliament for another. Viewed either as "history" or as an instrument of party warfare, Restoration political satire is marked by a circumstantial and highly personal approach to events. As history and as propaganda, it purports to tell the real story, to set the record straight, and its prime method is to present the reader with a plausible body of purported fact. For us who are studying these events three hundred years after they happened, two questions arise: How accurately do the *State Poems* reflect events? To what extent did they influence events? (1: xlii—xliii)

Keywords here are: "records of events," "partial views," "the events themselves," "purported fact," "accurately . . . reflect," and "influence." Lord's declared editorial practice, which accompanies this rationale, involves a tripartite classification of texts that, to a suspicious mind, could look rather like an upper-class of manuscripts that are rare or uniquely authoritative, a middle-class of manuscript collections, and a lower-order of printed texts. This preferential ordering precisely arranges extant texts according to their social status as defined by the condition of their production. Which is to say that a suspicious mind might believe it is not merely the rare or unique status of the manuscript that makes it more authoritative than the printed book, but rather the status of its relationship to the labor that produced it. Good-breeding and blood-lines count for a great deal here. The unique manuscript has closer direct ties to its progenitor than the text from an often promiscuous manuscript collection which is usually of a later generation anyway, having been reproduced at the hands of scribes. But the interference of the scribe is still preferable to that of the printing-shop compositor since, by this stage, the text has been thoroughly corrupted by a phase of mechanical reproduction that removes it even further from its origins in the author's genius, fancy or intention.

Lord's principles are indubitably correct and proper for these
subversive texts given the conditions of their production and dissemination.[3] The entropic rationale needs no defense, though I shall
return to the question of textual corruption. But, provisionally at
least, the editorial procedures and principles which I have formulated in accordance with my project differ from Lord's in several
respects for reasons both theoretical and material. For "How
accurately do the *State Poems* reflect events?" I shall substitute
"How do poems on the Restoration constitute a discourse?" and
suggest the following editorial procedures.

The governing principle from which I shall work is to chose as
copy-text that state of the text closest to the events it describes. As
initially conceived, this edition was only to involve the printed books
that appeared during the first year of Charles's reign which set about
the public legitimation of returning monarchy. For these printed
texts there are two obvious and immediate consequences of this
general principle: (a) to prefer in all cases the 1660 printed text where
other printed copies exist from later dates, and (b) to prefer a 1660
printed text to any manuscript. Choosing the 1660 printed text in
preference to a later version that might represent better the author's
final intentions is most relevant for certain celebrated works—such
as Dryden's *Astraea Redux*—both in respect of the text and of the
context in which it is reproduced. But could the case ever be made for
preferring the first state of inner form C which, as the California
edition makes clear, underwent some important stop-press corrections? Swedenberg's headnote to the California edition of Dryden's
panegyric discusses the poem in the context of a dozen printed
panegyrics (notably those in the Clark Library thirty years ago), thus
confirming the aesthetic status of *Astraea Redux* by viewing it as the
summation of the best that was written on the occasion before
moving to analyse it as anticipating the best in this author's *oeuvre*.
Yet my copy-text will still be the Herringman edition of 1660
(May/June) collated against the 1688 reprint and will doubtless
differ little, if at all, from the California text. Similarly with Richard
Flecknoe's "The Portrait of His Majesty," which was reprinted in
1673, and Thomas Fuller's *Panegyric*, which was substantially
re-written for republication at the end of the entry for
Worcestershire in the 1662 edition of the *Worthies* (182–4), the first
printed state will supply copy-text.

Difficulty, however, arises in the case of a poem like John Crouch's *A Mixt Poem* since two printings, one by Thomas Bettertun (Figure 1) and one by Daniel White (Figure 2), both declare "1660" on their title pages. George Thomason bought neither, so precise dating can only be provisionally established by other means. The more common Bettertun version[4] provides a longer text with fewer errors and could therefore provide copy-text on grounds of its greater general accuracy. Moreover, Crouch seems to have enjoyed a closer relationship with Bettertun than he did with White; Bettertun appears in Wing's *Short-Title Catalogue* for only one other production as a printer, *The Muse's Joy for the Recovery of Henretta* [sic] *Maria*, also by Crouch. White, on the other hand, published several other works under his name as a printer, but nothing else by Crouch, so the Bettertun text would seem to be closer to its author and so to its conditions of production.[5] White's text may also be earlier since it includes an errata list of seven misprints corrected—or at least not found—in Bettertun, and White's version shows general signs of having been printed in a hurry. All such evidence, however, is finally inconclusive since it can always point both ways; it may and must enter, but not necessarily determine, our decision regarding copy-text.

So, in the case of Crouch's *Mixt Poem*, I shall choose White's version since it seems to have a better claim to be closer to the events it describes. While I suspect it to be an earlier version than Bettertun's, such evidence as there is does at least indicate that it was printed in a hurry. The White title page is less carefully set. "Mixt Poem" stands out in bold type making the work seem to be primarily concerned with questions of genre in contrast to "Charls the Second" which is properly the visual center of Bettertun's title page. White's line divisions do not follow the sense as well as Bettertun's do: "Majes-ty" is divided against itself at lines 5/6, and the "&c" is obviously there to balance the line despite the trivializing effect. White's ordering of the three sub-topics is also interesting. Again, Bettertun balances his fonts, lines and subject more precisely by keeping "YORK" and "GLOCESTER" together while effecting a decorous descent from King, through Princes down to "State-martyrs" and the "Renowned Generall" before switching to the enemy "the *Rump* and its Appurtenances." Now White's order—

A

Mixt Poem,

Partly Hiftoricall, partly Panegyricall,

UPON THE

Happy Return of His Sacred MAJESTY

Charls the Second,

AND HIS

Illuftrious Brothers, the DUKES of

YORK and *GLOCESTER.*

With Honourable Refle&ions upon fome State-martyrs, and the Renowned Generall.

Not forgetting the *Rump* and its Appurtenances.

By J. C. Gent.

L O N D O N,
Printed for *Thomas Bettertun* at his fhop in
Weftminfter-hall. 1660.

Figure 1. John Crouch, *A Mixt Poem*, the Thomas Bettertun printing, 1660.
By permission of the Syndics of Cambridge University Library.

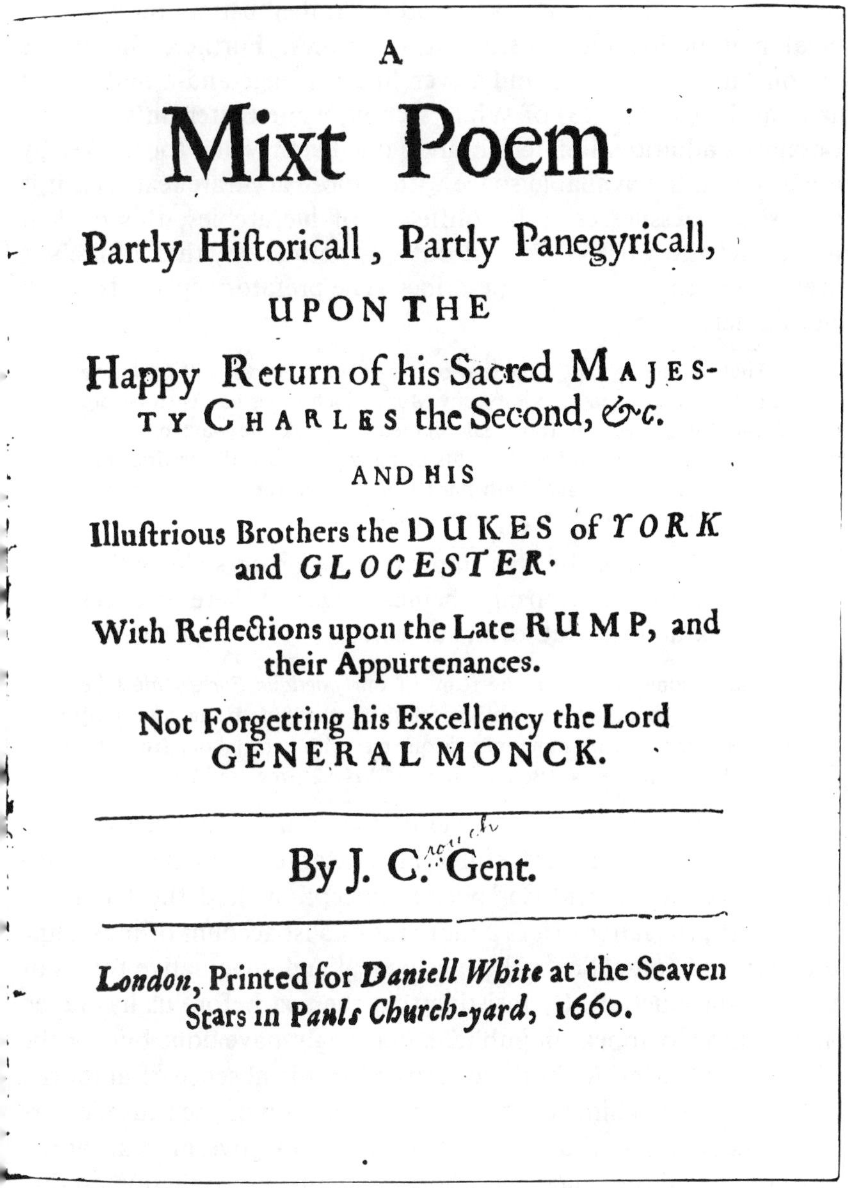

A

Mixt Poem

Partly Hiftoricall, Partly Panegyricall,

UPON THE

Happy Return of his Sacred M A J E S-
T Y C H A R L E S the Second, &c.

AND HIS

Illuftrious Brothers the D U K E S of *Y O R K*
and *G L O C E S T E R·*

With Reflections upon the Late R U M P, and
their Appurtenances.

Not Forgetting his Excellency the Lord
GENERAL MONCK.

By J. C. Gent.

London, Printed for *Daniell White* at the Seaven
Stars in *Pauls Church-yard,* 1660.

Figure 2. John Crouch, *A Mixt Poem,* the Daniell White printing, 1660. Cour-
tesy of The Newberry Library, Chicago.

King, Princes, Rump, Monk—captures rather better, though, the
social and political confusion of the times. Further, the White
version has more errors and fewer lines; a page-and-a-half is left
blank at the end (12–13) of White's book, while Bettertun's version,
containing additional material, gives one better value for money by
filling out all the available space with a more accurate text. But it is
in these carelessnesses, this confusion of hierarchies, this evident
rush to get the work done and out on the market, that White's is
surely closer to the events it describes. The prefatory epistle is worth
quoting here:

> That I come behind in the rear of our *Poetick Forces*, will I hope be
> imputed partly to my modesty; my Muse which never had been before
> in the Sun-shine, was too weak sighted to break the way: partly to
> unkind contingencies, her thoughts being conceived with the first; but
> by some misprisions met with hard labour from the midwifry of the
> press. [White, Sigs. A–A^v, reverse italics]

Bettertun's version of this improves the prose style but significantly alters the relationship being suggested here between the
printed book and the authorial subject:

> That I come behind in the reare of our *poetique Forces*, must be
> imputed to some unkind contingencies; my thoughts being conceived
> with the first, but by some misprisions met with hard labour from the
> midwifry of the Press. [Bettertun, Sigs. A2–A2^v, reverse italics]

The muscular Elizabethan style of the former has been refined,
gallicized into a more graceful syntax. Rather than the awkward
conceit involving the Muse, poetic conception, and the labors of
giving birth, the latter offers a more rationalist account of masculine
authority and control over the mechanical and imaginative forces of
textual re-production. By insisting that the text before us has taken
a longer time to appear in public than it might have done but for the
difficulties of printing, both versions mark the absence of authorial
control. Yet the White version, with its inclusion of the Muse, offers
a more fully nuanced account of the relations governing authorial
subjectivity and the social conditions of textual reproduction, and in
this sense comes closer to the events it describes not despite but
rather because of the greater number of errors, stylistic inelegancies
and careless packaging. In reprinting White's version, I will correct
the obvious errors—including those listed in the errata—but otherwise retain the accidentals and irregular orthography of the copy-text

as far as possible, while recording a full collation with Bettertun in the textual apparatus.

These procedures will, I trust, recreate the *historicity* of the text as closely as possible by replicating the order of its public production in the context of the king's return. I have in mind here Lucien Goldmann's genetic structuralism with its argument from homology.[6] After a generative process of confusion, pressure and delay, a work is produced—a king suddenly returned to his throne, a poem finally hurried through the press. Subsequent events and negotiations both alter and improve that initial work—king and commons debate, ratify and dispute the new juridico-political settlement throughout the weeks following Charles's arrival on English soil; author and printer refine, clarify and correct the celebratory text. The argument from authorial intention might prefer Bettertun's for better representing the author's intentions in their nearest to final form for 1660; it might even choose the 1663 reprint from *Census Poeticus* as representing the author's final intentions period. But a socialized theory of textual editing will prefer the White version for being closer not to its author's originary intention—though this is obviously relevant here—but to its public occasion, the king's return.

A second immediate consequence of this principle of choosing copy-text in relation to its discursive rather than authorial production is that I will prefer any 1660 printed version over any manuscript version. Authorial intention is here less important than public intervention, including the entropic "corruption" of the printing house, since corruption/production is viewed as a function of the socialization of the discourse at the level of its general mode of production (GMP). Elias Ashmole's *Sol In Ascendente* provides the best example I have so far found of the predicament in which a heavily edited draft in the author's hand and a single printed state both claim authority. I will probably take Nathaniel Brooks's printed version as copy-text and include a description of the manuscript in the textual apparatus. To do so will reverse exactly Lord's procedure with the *State Poems* which, for the early years at least, were not produced as part of an official print culture aimed at legitimating the *status quo*, but rather circulated in manuscript as primarily subversive interventions. The Restoration poems, on the other hand, were instrumental in bringing into being an official print culture geared to legitimating a return to dynastic power. While satirical *Poems on Affairs of State* typically entered the public domain in the form of manuscripts, poems on the Restoration which appeared in 1660 were typically printed and so subject to different forms of entropic interference.

But it also follows, then, that the most important challenge to a socialized theory of textual editing appropriate for the special case of English poems on the Restoration, will be those poems which exist only in manuscript form. Here again, just as the aristocracy in 1660 constituted less a homogeneous socio-political class, than a heterogeneity of interest, allegiances and juridico-political powers, so the manuscript poems on the Restoration will, I suspect, offer greater and more significant variety than similarity: meanwhile, a theory based on heterogeneity will take precedence over one based on homogeneity.[7] When I first projected this edition, I had not intended to include manuscript verses since they did not fully enter into the public domain as instruments shaping public opinion in quite the same way printed books did and do. The problem of dating too is specially irksome here where the chronological status of a manuscript is inconclusive or simply missing from our records. A manuscript poem composed after the event it describes clearly does not have the same status as one composed at the time. A poem describing the Restoration composed after the Glorious Revolution of 1688, say, cannot be said to influence opinion regarding the Restoration settlement and the return of Charles II. But the pressure of the materials, the fact, if you like, that these manuscript poems started showing up asking to be accounted for, puts a strain on the initial theoretical principles. A subtler theory of "history" than that which depends upon mysteriously but objectively knowable facts—"the events themselves"—is needed. Indeed, this silencing of the textual witness that makes such "events" seem knowable becomes specially suspicious as increasing numbers of poems existing only in manuscript form continue to surface. It becomes increasingly necessary to pose two difficult questions: (a) what *was* the Restoration? and (b) how does the public/private dichotomy operate here?

There is a clear difference, as I said, between the Restoration as the conditions under which a particular dynastic chief was allowed to resume power, and the Restoration as the conditions under which support for that or any other dynastic claim was continued. Poems on the Restoration were not uncommonly used during the eighteenth century as part of the propaganda campaigns involving later kings, queens, and dynasties. There is a slide here to the conditions of production governing the *State Poems*, especially the Jacobite use of the Restoration during the early eighteenth century.

On the public/private dichotomy, let us return to the principal rationale of the edition in the first place. Poems on the Restoration constitute a public discourse constructed from an armory of traditional poetic devices, tropes, modes, figures, topoi, etc., all neatly assembled to make the king's return not only thinkable, but acceptable. To understand their ideological effectiveness we need to view the public/private divide not by emphasizing one term and silencing the other, but by articulating them both together as the mode of this discourse's operation. In the almost total absence of contemporary responses to the reading of poems on the Restoration at the time of Charles's return—such as we might find amongst the diaries and letters of later generations to whom it was not unusual, say, to comment in detail upon the experience of a text[7]—one of the few ways we have of measuring, judging and evaluating the "consumption" of these poems on the Restoration is to notice that people continued to write them long after the events of 1660. May 29th did not become quite the same sort of conventional poetic topic that the events of November 5th had done, rather we find three broad categories of post-Restoration poems on that event:

i. First we find poems written or published after 1660 celebrating Charles's return; for instance none of Katherine Philip's panegyrics appeared in print until the 1664 pirated edition of the *Poems*, though we may presume they were written and circulated at earlier times. The anonymous *The Glory of the English Nation, or an Essay on the Birth-Day of "King Charles" the Second* did not appear until 1681 when it looked nostalgically back to earlier times of national unity under the Stuarts.

ii. Next we can mention attacks on Charles that remind us of his return for satiric purposes; *An Historical Poem* of around 1680 once included in the Marvell *oeuvre* is relevant here.[8]

iii. Then there is a large and heterogeneous group of later poems, variously associating kings other than Charles with "restored" monarchy as a political principle of varying applicability. The "Ode On His Majesties Return" printed by Steele at the end of the 1727 second edition of his *Poetical Miscellany* is a blatant piece of Whig propaganda on the coronation of George II. Ballads aimed at mobilizing moderate Tory sympathies had led the way here: *An Excellent Old Ballad, made at the Restauration of K. Charles II* of

1711 was reprinted the next year. *A New Song on St. George's Day . . . to the Glorious Memory of Queen Anne. With the Restauration of K. Charles the 2nd* presumably appeared in or around 1713/4. Several such ballads appeared during the twenties displaying the colours of the Jacobite cause. Among the Roxburghe ballads in the British Library, at least two ballads of this period bear the title *King Charles the Second's Restoration*, while *A Knave at Bottom, The Dealers Sure of a Trump* declares itself more covertly to be about the Restoration, since it constantly alludes to political events of the 1720's.

With notable exceptions, most of these poems will not be included in the edition but will, rather, be registered in a check-list since their concern is with the Restoration as a past principle rather than as a present moment. But for those poems on the Restoration that exist only in undatable manuscript form, problems persist since these texts clearly possess a greater claim to inclusion. Indeed, to omit them would be to misconceive the very project being undertaken and endanger its claim to record a discourse rather than pay tribute to the individual genius of the best poetry. For in these unpublished manuscripts, whether they were ever intended for publication or not, we do not find—as with *State Poems* from later in the century—a key to the dominant mode of production, but rather we find the best record we have of a relatively "private" response to the "public" dialogues of the Restoration, and that will open up the question of "subjectivity" in both senses.

Now the public/private divide as the terms of subjectivity has been a cornerstone of feminist thought and practice since the slogan "The personal is political" provided the consciousness-raising movement with a socialized theory and practice for destabilizing the bourgeois myth of a unified, gender-specific self. Having been subjected to the silences required by a patriarchal culture, we have been told, women have been taught to regard pain, suffering, frustration, and misery as self-generated problems to be endured or displaced by exercises of self-control, self-discipline, and self-analysis rather than by collective social analysis that will liberate them, at least, from the mystifications of their own subjectivity. It is not coincidental, then, that I have chosen for an example a manuscript poem that has been attributed to Katherine Philips, the so-called "Matchless Orinda," one of the earliest token females of the masculine literary establishment in England. Her reputation has long rested on the high-minded neoplatonism of her verses to other women which, though written in that wicked age, are not smutty like Mrs. Behn's plays. From the standard and still cited biography of 1931 by Philip Souers—entitled *The Matchless Orinda*—emerges a refined creature who might very well have achieved life in the ideal space of platonic abstraction, and whose intensity of feeling reminds one of Dorothy Wordsworth rather than, say, her closer contemporary, the Duchess of Newcastle. One important omission from Souers's account is the evidence of the dedicatory poems to Philips's *Poems* which repeatedly invite the reader to prefer these poems to those of none other than Sappho. Cowley's complimentary verses, "Upon Mrs. *Philips* her Poems," may sound mildly tongue in cheek, but it is surely without sarcasm or irony or smutty intent that he reminds us of her reputation:

> They talk of *Sappho*, but, alas! the shame
> Ill Manners soil the lustre of her fame.
> *Orinda's* inward Vertue is so bright,
> That, like a Lantern's fair enclosed light,
> It through the Paper shines where she doth write.
>   (Sig. C) [reverse italics]

The modern biographer, however, lives in a post-Victorian age when sapphic discourse has, apparently, become unutterable.[9] We shall notice again this desire of author-centered scholarship to exclude, to deny, at the confrontation with sexuality, but will turn now to the poem attributed to Philips.

"Upon His Majesties most happy restauration to his Royall Throne in Brittaine" is a twenty-two line manuscript poem in the Bodleian written on a loose sheet where it is followed by twenty lines "Upon the Hollow Tree into w[hi]ch his M[ajes]tie escaped after the unfortunate Battle at Worcester." Under six horizontal slashes, the two sets of verses are signed "Cecinit Domina Phillips agro Pembrokia" in the same hand that copied the verses. These texts have not excited much scholarly commentary, but what little notice they have received is curiously marked by minor errors associated with this theoretical problem regarding the defensive idolization of the author.

In 1951 Paul Elmen concluded that a new edition of the works of Katherine Philips is "one of the pressing needs in seventeenth-century scholarship," (57) having examined some manuscript poems in the National Library of Wales. Elmen ignores the Bodleian manuscript under consideration here, which is fair enough, though it would only support his general argument regarding the Orinda *oeuvre*. In her *First-Line Index*, however, Margaret Crum tentatively attributes these two manuscript poems to Philips at entries "A 1937" and "H 38," keyed to the initial letter of the opening line. In 1977, Catherine Mambretti once again raised the question of Philip's *oeuvre* partly by way of addressing Crum's *Index*. It is doubtless significant, though of what I am less certain, that these two reports of the manuscript have generated no fewer than six types of directly misleading information in addition to misquotation.

First, Crum inconsistently reports the two sets of verses. Under A 1937 we read:

> [Philips, Katherine (?)], 'Upon his Majesties most happy restaura-
> tion . . . ', 1660, subscribed 'Cecinit Domina Phillips agro
> Pembrokiae'.
> Pr. bk. Firth b. 20, fol. 136.

while H 38 reads:

> Philips, Katherine, 'Upon the Hollow Tree into which his Mtie.
> escaped.'
> Not amongst her printed poems.
> Pr. bk. Firth b. 20, fol. 140.

One might have expected similar information, orthography and format to signalize the identical status of the attribution to an author. The former entry, moreover, mistranscribes the scribal attribution—"Pembrokiae" instead of "Pembrokia"—and mis-records the Bodleian shelf-mark as "Firth b. 20, fol 136." On these entries we would be misled further to imagine:

> i. that A 1937 is attributed to Philips by an unreliable
> scribal witness
> ii. that H 38 is more certainly by her than A 1937
> iii. that the two poems appear on different sheets
> iv. that A 1937 is among her printed poems

On the evidence of the manuscript, however, there is no reason to distinguish the authority of the attribution in this way since both poems appear on the same side of a single sheet that has been attached to Firth b. 20 at folio 140—probably by Harold Brooks in the 1930's.

Mambretti adds two further kinds of errors in her report. Twice she identifies A 1937 as "1 937," indicating a poor memory of the opening line—"Awake Britannia." And in referring to the text of the manuscript, Mambretti miscounts as well as misquoting: line 13 of A 1937 is called "1. 14," line 3 of H 38 is misquoted "with bloody beake" for "with the bloody beake," and "Pembrokia" is, perhaps following Crum, rendered "Pembrokiae" (451). Since Mambretti quotes fewer than thirty words of the manuscript—which she is, we should notice here, eager to dismiss from Orinda's *oeuvre*—this seems like a very high degree of textual corruption for so few lines of unedited verse. But I offer these observations not to sound smug over the inaccuracies of others, but rather to bring together the theoretical terms "corruption" and "subjectivity" in this editorial context. What links the desire to exclude this text with both its history of entropic corruption and its ascription to this female poet? A literary historian expresses a covert design when she introduces her argument.

> Any such additions to Orinda's canon [as those suggested by Crum's *Index*] should be accepted only if the manuscripts in which they appear descend from sources close to the poet or Cotterell, whose testimony regarding the Philips canon is well informed. (443)

The argument sounds uncontroversial enough, but what happens to it if we play with it in a Derridean fashion by putting "any such," "should," and "only" under erasure?[10] Instead of this exclusionary formula we achieve instead one that seeks to include. Why should a literary historian or critic wish to define Orinda's canon by an exclusionary practice in this way?

Let us continue to misread the argument. After two sentences on Cotterell's authority, she begins a new paragraph: "New poems attributed to Katherine Philips must also conform to the subdued and dignified style of her published poems" (444). We do not need deconstruction to be suspicious of "must also conform," or "subdued and dignified style." The phrases resonate too strongly with the imaginatively frigid tones of a humorless analytical positivism, a certain petit-bourgeois will to offer elegant discriminations in *no uncertain terms*. Notice the rising charge of the slide from "should be accepted" to "must also conform" in a disturbingly dogmatic aestheticism that may or may not fit the facts of the case. But as a theoretical principle it will persuade only those who believe in the unitary nature of the authorial self as being incapable of radical alterity, and that surely is a dangerous principle in the context of theories of an authorial canon based on questions of style. Let us think, rather, "additions to a poet's canon may be accepted if the manuscripts in which they appear descend from sources close to the poet," and "new poems attributed to a poet may also conform to the style of her published poems, but then again they may not." For the desire thus to exclude, to silence, to close off what seeks to remain open, and the urge to create the self which is at one with itself, these are among the most dangerous ideological instruments of patriarchal phallogocentrism.[11]

Again, let me insist that I am seeking not to criticize a Mambretti, but the typical false consciousness in that commitment to the unified authorial self who produces a text, viewed as a reified object the history of which is necessarily "corruption." One *may* possibly be right to argue that the Bodleian manuscript poem was neither composed nor conceived by Philips. But in failing even to ask why the anonymous scribe should have *wanted* to write that it was sung by "Domina Phillips" from Pembroke, we may also fail to ask why a scholar should *want* to argue that it was not. The stylistic reasons we are offered for dismissing the text are no more conclusive than the ascription. For is it not the case that the argument from style in verifying attributions—a highly topical problem with current debates over manuscripts attributed to Dryden and Shakespeare[12]—can only ever be of strictly limited reliability? While such debates at their best produce new information regarding authors and exciting reassessments of styles, to argue that an attributed text is not by a known author precisely because of stylistic difference from an otherwise established chart of that author's style is to efface the historical conditions of subjectivity in the cause of the united self.

Philips was, it is known, one of the very few women to have written poems on Charles's return; indeed she wrote several that appear in the "authorized" printed *Poems* of 1667. If, then, the scribe of the Bodleian manuscript was wrong to write that these were by Philips, we have some context in which to set that error, but no obvious leads to whether it was deliberate misrepresentation or unknowing complicity. Philips was hardly a controversial figure with a reputation for having publicly celebrated Cromwell—the predicament of Dryden, Cowley, and Waller—though she was involved with Waller and public dispute towards the end of her life. But even so, given her acute concern over the private control of her poetry, a concern that led to the celebrated anxiety over the pirated edition of her *Poems* in 1664, it is hardly unimaginable that, if she had composed these verses, she might also have sought to suppress them herself. Here is a diplomatic transcription:

> ### Upon his Majesties most happy restauration,
> ### to his Royall Throne in Brittaine.
>
> 1 Awake Britannia, rouse thy selfe, and say
> Good Morrow to thy sonns, bid them good day;
> This Sun's returned to thaw thee with his light,
> And by his Radiant Beames has banisht night.
> 5 God cleansd thy face from Blood, from Sweat, and Teares,
> Which has defac'd thy Beuties twenty yeares.
> Thou art now a Bride, a Royall Queene noe more,
> A wretched widdow growling on the flore.
> The base ambitious Giant Race are feld,
> 10 That would thee, and thy Jupiter have Queld;
> He lightning has, Thunder, and forked Darts,
> If they revive againe, to wound their harts:
> Then god adornd thy selfe as heretofore,
> When his great Syre the sacred Septer bore;
> 15 Anoint, perfume, and dresse thy selfe in Pride,
> And hasten to him, as a love sick Bride;
> Present thy selfe unto his roiall hand,
> Thou in thy Jupiter shalt all command:
> 'Twas he alone could save thee, set thee free,
> 20 ffrom Bloody Rape, and Tyrannous Anarchy.
> Then I. O. sing and Paeans to his praise
> And round thy Temples, winde the verdant Bayes.

By 1662, once Charles had married Catherine of Braganza, the central conceit of "Upon his Majesties most happy restauration," the marriage of nation and king, simply became inappropriate. The apostrophe to Britannia to rouse herself in preparation for receiving her husband's body would fit very neatly with Philips's address to the bridegroom in her *"Arion on a Dolphin, To his Majesty at his passage into England"* (*Poems*, 3-5) and is partly anticipated in her verses "On the numerous Access of the *English* to wait upon the King in *Flanders*" which tells how *"England* (though grown old with woes) will see / Her long deny'd and Sovereign Remedy" (2). And it is in keeping with Philips's general policy and poetic theory that she would have preferred the opportunity to address a woman personally rather than the nation by personification. A real queen, a real human relationship, these are topics better suited to her humanistic neoplatonism than the personified nation:

> Hail Royal Beauty, Virgin bright and great,
> Who do our hopes secure, our joys compleat.
> We cannot reckon what to you we owe,
> Who makes Him happy who makes us be so. (6)

By contrast, the Bodleian verses seem dangerously risqué in their approach to sexuality. "Virgin" appears here technically, made to sound abstract being "bright and great." The female body in the manuscript, however, is more directly addressed and imagined, and there is a constant strain of sexual innuendo running from line eleven to the end. Yet if Philips did compose the manuscript verses between the time of Charles's return and marriage, she would subsequently have had plenty of reason to reject them herself as unsuitable for more than stylistic reasons.

At this juncture in this discussion of editorial subjectivity and textual production/corruption, I should like to reintroduce myself as representative of readers trained to disregard questions of author and then, as a reflex, impatiently demand "So what happens if we *read* the poem?"[12] Nor need this necessitate the unthinking reification of the "text itself" provided we bear in mind the traces of our own suspension of disbelief in authors rather than willfully engaging in the mysteriously a-historical self-discipline of critical close-reading.

The most striking feature of the verses as they appear in my transcription is that they do not really make much sense in a number of places. We clearly cannot trust that comma at the end of line 7—which is where it appears in the manuscript—since the syntax demands differently. Let us move it back:

> Thou art now a Bride, a Royall Queene, noe more
> A wretched widdow growling on the flore.

The bestial image may still be unpleasant and startling, and the rhythm of the lines becomes twisted, but at least this makes sense. But there are more than rhythmic problems with lines 12 and 13 however we may change the punctuation:

> Then god adornd thy selfe as heretofore
> When his great Syre the sacred Septer bore.

"Then god adorned thy selfe"? At best this is clumsy; at worst part of a general confusion that starts back in line 2 when the poem first switches subjects, from the personified female figure of Britannia to the "Sun" who has "thaw"-ed her and then again in line 5 to the "god" who "cleansd" her face for her. The direct address to Britannia returns in outlining the change in her marital status and continues in the next lines which reassure her that her enemies have been vanquished for all time. "Jupiter" may initially seem to present a further complication, since we cannot be utterly certain of his identity with the "God" of line 5, but that disturbance of the temporal scheme of the poem which occurs at "then" reintroduces the term "god" and thereby reminds us that the absolutist ideology being voiced here depends upon this sort of systematic mystification of temporal and political relationships. From the first line, the poem has been moving forward into the immediate future, glancing backwards in lines 5 and 6, but offering a reassurance for the future in the lines immediately preceding that "Then":

> He lightning has, Thunder, and forked Darts,
> If they revive againe, to wound their harts:
> Then god adornd thy selfe as heretofore,
> When his great Syre the sacred Septer bore.

This break from the expected time scheme works nicely to reinforce the peculiar transition of the addressee from widow to royal bride, and anchors the poem firmly in its immediate historical circumstances—the "political fiction" as Larry Carver has called it—of the Stuart Restoration.[14] For assembled here are several distinctive features of poems written on the occasion of Charles's return: the need to assure the nation of immediate short-term benefits from the king's return, an assurance that rests on no stronger foundations than some clearly exaggerated personal virtues of the king (here, typically, the celebration of his power to maintain peace by suppressing those who might rebel); a compulsive habit of mind which, when confronted with the future following Charles's return, responds by turning back to the moment of his father's execution; and the reintroduction of those patriarchal principles which make the elision here of "Sun," "God," with "Jupiter" and the "god" whose "great Syre" was killed not so much a confusion of terms but a necessary structure of belief. Royal power, being divine, passes immediately from father to son without interruption; the king is dead, long live the king.

But this sort of historical contextualization also serves to highlight the deficiencies of the poem as an affective formal composition. The slide of Sun/God/Jupiter/Charles remains awkward and contrived, constantly straining the syntax and taxing the reader's acquiescence rather than enforcing it by the pleasures of agile stimulation such as fully achieved conceits offer. It was just this sort of congestion in the historical allusion that Dryden receives due praise for having re-solved—following Denham and Waller—by dropping the impacted conceit in favour of a more lucid and precise exposition. *Astraea Redux* is itself marked by not dissimilar difficulties when situating Charles's return and his father's execution at the basis of immediate negotiations between crown and nation (e.g. lines 250—277), but nothing there is as arbitrary as this catalogue of kingly attributes or as clumsy as "Then god adornd thy selfe."

One editorial impulse that interferes with reading the Bodleian verses is that which seeks to improve them in the way one sometimes edits a student's verses. Here, that obviously unreliable comma in line 7, the general history of errors in reporting this text, and the post-structuralist challenge that all texts are finally indeterminate, add weight to this impulse. Moreover, a little will achieve a lot. Simply by reading, in two identical constructions, four "d"s as mistranscriptions for final "e"s, we solve nearly all of the difficulties of the first half of the poem. If for "God cleansd" and "god adornd" we substitute "Goe cleanse" and "goe adorne," the clustering of synonyms for returning monarchy is simplified and the imperative address to Britannia is regularized, making consistently better sense especially at line 13:

> Then goe adorne thy selfe as heretofore,
> When his great Syre the sacred Septer bore.

The phrase makes sense now. The reflexive pronoun works correctly. "Then" becomes part of the argumentative structure—"in conse-quence of which you should"—rather than that excessively startling dislocation of the time pattern: "heretofore," with its trisyllabic disturbance of the rhythm and rhyme, sufficiently marks the break in the historical scheme of things introduced with the memory of martyred monarchy. And the whole poem flows together rather better as a persistent address. "Then goe . . . Annoint, perfume, and dresse thy selfe in Pride / And hasten to him, as a love sick Bride.''

What makes this editorial emendation of ''e'' for ''d'' even more compelling is the symmetry of the constructions in which they would occur; just the sort of thing that an (inevitably?) imperfect transcription might produce. And, from the stance of feminist-deconstruction, this substitution is doubly effective for it erases the name of the patriarchal will to power in the very act of empowering the female subject by suggesting, at least, that she is capable of cleaning and adorning her own body. But we do not, surely, need to think of Pope's revisions to *The Rape of the Lock*, which suggest that some women do, indeed, need divine assistance with their *toilette*, to recognise the systematic trivialization of female power from which no editorial intervention can rescue a text intent upon legitimating the Restoration of 1660 in such gender-specific terms as this one offers. What such a suggestion as this substitution of ''e'' for ''d'' nevertheless illustrates is the degree to which authors are never entirely in control of their texts. In turn, this dislocation of the argument from authorial control discloses what might not—but should—have been apparent before: this poem's resolute anti-feminism. Whether we read ''God'' or ''Goe,'' the female subject is only ever constructed here as precisely *that*, a subject, at every stage entirely dependent for her identity upon a structuring order of masculine will, force and mobility.

The theoretical stakes here seem more considerable than principles of authorial integrity—based upon the circular collapsing of questions of authority into matters of style—can properly weigh. Since it is by articulating a personal engagement with a public discourse that any text comes into meaning, too earnest a regard for the reputation of authors may lead us to miss the more important questions of a poem's *stance*,[15] in this case the way the text gives voice to an expression of an ideological fix regarding the possibilities of female liberation. For that, after all, is what this poem purports to describe, the freeing of Britannia. What we find is a reformulation of a double-bind implicit in the most progressive and seemingly liberating tenets of Renaissance discourse on women: the fiction that marriage offers freedom. Here, Britannia is being invited to substitute the intolerable conditions of her widow-hood for the ''maximized obligations and minimal redress''[16] of the affective marriage to the one man who ''alone could set [her] free.''

With the king's return, the former struggles between crown and people which had brought civil war become domesticated in a happy marriage; continuing class conflict between crown and subject is resolved into the good-humoured self-subjection of the obedient wife. Whatever the textual minutiae, whoever their author, these lines express their historical moment precisely by celebrating female subordination as though it were general liberation. Where this text "deconstructs" itself, where it most loudly signalizes the stress of its production, is where the tortured syntax strains to situate and relate the structures of absolutist ideology, at the moments of textual indeterminacy where "god" hides an imperative to action. Which is to say no more, perhaps, than that editorial questions directed at authors may mislead us from the more engaging questions that can be asked if texts are more fully entered into the general conditions of their production.

I shall include the verses as they appear in the manuscript and are reproduced here, leave the comma "uncorrected" noting that I have done so, follow them with the verses "Upon the Hollow Tree" under a general headnote that reproduces the subscripted attribution to "Domina Phillips," include references to this debate, and index them under "Philips, Katherine (?)."

To conclude, then. Editing a discourse involves principles of multiplicity different from those employed in editing an author. Against the centrality of the creative author we may oppose the discursive heterogeneity of the mode of production. Computerization has made this ideal only barely imaginable; programs that would replicate a text in its full historical trajectory by means of alternating displays, though, may be needlessly expensive and finally unreadable. For an edition in the form of a printed book, the ideal of a fully socialized and historicized editorial theory and practice may raise more problems than it would solve. If textual corruption is, indeed, a law and not an ideology, then it follows that no attempt to reproduce exactly all the orthographic minutiae of a seventeenth-century poetic text could ever be achieved—even supposing that it were desirable. In the case of poems on the Restoration, though, the ideal may nevertheless be worth pursuing since if the printed collections of *State Poems* with which Lord and others worked were published late within a discourse characterized by the subversive and unnofficial character of the manuscript mode of production, then the printed book was the dominant mode in 1660—right down to the interference of rushed settings from numerous fonts at a time of irregular control over orthographic convention. Multifont setting of camera-ready copy is as much a fact of the modern scholarly editorial scene as the need to read against the grain of "corrupt" texts was back in 1660.

Original research for this paper was subsidized by grants from the Ahmanson Foundation, the Social Sciences and Humanities Research Council of Canada, and Wayne State University. I wish to acknowledge my gratitude to Lucy Brashear, Jackson Cope, Elaine Hobby, Donna Landry, Ian McKillop, Rachel Weil and the staffs of: the William Andrews Clark Memorial Library, UCLA; the Newberry Library, Chicago; the Bodleian Library, Oxford; and the University Library, Cambridge.

NOTES

1. *A Theory of Literary Production* (66). Once we have deplored and displaced the reification here, in this "translation," of the generic male creator, we may recuperate the French theorist's parodic intent—"We have defined literary discourse as parody, as a contestation of language rather than a representation of reality" (61)—for what it signalizes.

2. This tradition of "Cambridge English" can be traced from Matthew Arnold's *Culture and Anarchy* (1869; rpt. 1875), directly to F. R. Leavis's response, a century later, to the social and educational movements of the sixties in his *English Literature in Our Time and the University* (1969). Francis Mulhern's *The Moment of Scrutiny* (1979) provides a useful historical analysis of the Leavis phenomenon and its relation to the persistence of certain values and attitudes outside the academic study of English. With *Culture and Society* (1958), Raymond Williams had paved the way for materialist cultural studies, but not until his *Marxism and Literature* (1975) did he provide a clear and thorough theoretical explanation of what had been his own critical practice as a socialist working in academic criticism. Central to Williams's contribution has been the willingness to read outside the native tradition—not just the literary figures such as Ibsen and Brecht, but theorists like Lukács, Goldmann and, perhaps most importantly, Volosinov. Though he moved to Oxford, Williams's student Terry Eagleton (1976 and 1983) has developed links between the European intellectual traditions and the study of English. While Williams endeavoured to demystify the ideological assumptions from which he works by bringing non-canonical writers into the scope of "English"—notably the work on the European dramatists and the inter-generic work in *The Country and the City* (1973)—Eagleton's theoretical studies frequently display a wittily dismissive character (he used to speak of *Literary Theory* as a "bluffer's guide") that enables him to continue writing on already canonized authors. His own monographs on Shakespeare (1967), the modernists Conrad, Waugh, Orwell, Greene, Eliot, Auden and Lawrence (1970), the Brontës (1975), Richardson

(1982) and a study of Shakespeare for the Blackwell's "re-reading" series of which he is general editor, may seem curiously reformist since they effectively recuperate a tradition of major English writers. Yet the peculiarly "Cambridge" approach to literary studies persists in Eagleton's continuing attempt to chart the socio-political position and importance of literary study in an age when criticism "has become incorporated into the culture industry," *The Function of Criticism* (107).

3. But editors working on subsequent volumes of the *Poems on Affairs of State* project found it necessary to revise these principles when faced with the intractable evidence of the material evidence. See Galbraith Crump's statement of policy for volume 4 (1968, xli—xliii) which later editors developed.

4. In Donald Wing's *Short-Title Catalogue*, Bettertun's printing is listed for London, Cambridge, Harvard, the Newberry, Folger and Yale collections. White's is listed as a Bodleian *unicum*. The Newberry copy is, in fact, by White.

5. See entries for Bettertun and White in Morrison's *Index*.

6. See "Structure: Human Reality and Methodological Concept," and *The Hidden God* (3-21).

7. See my "So what *does* Thomas Gray's *Progress of Poesy* have to do with Progress?," for an example of how we can reconstruct the historical conditions of the "consumption" of literary texts in mid-eighteenth-century England.

8. It is worth noting here the aesthetic debate over this poem. Donno (1972) approves Margoliouth's (1927) opinion that "it seems to me a great mistake to continue to print among Marvell's poems inferior stuff which has long been considered spurious," Margoliouth (1:236) cited Donno (218). Oddly, while Margoliouth—and Legouis (1971) following him—include *An Historicall Poem*, Donno doesn't even mention it in her check-list of "Other attributions" (217-8) which draws specifically on poems included in the important Bodleian manuscript, Eng. poet. d. 49 which contains the basis for most editions of Marvell's poetry. As Legouis points out, Lord used non-inclusion in this manuscript collection as the rationale for excluding this poem from his edition of Marvell (1:426); but in Donno's account, it merely disappears behind the approval of Margoliouth's opinion. Legouis takes a more favorable view of the poem's relation to Marvell, as does Mengel when editing it for *Poems on Affairs of State*, Vol. 2, cited by Legouis (1:426).

9. Philips's possible lesbianism has received some attention, but not a lot; see Faderman, *Surpassing the Love of Men* (69-71). On this general silence about lesbianism as a theoretical topic of importance to feminists and literary historians generally, see the "Lesbian Issue" of *Signs* (Summer 1984). In a footnote to a subsequent *Signs* article—"Sapphistries" (44)—Susan Gubar notices Philips's sapphics and draws attention to her poem "To my Most

Excellent Lucasia: On Our Friendship," which, with Sandra Gilbert, she has edited for the recent *Norton Anthology of Literature by Women* as the only example of Philips's poetry. The headnote to the Norton mentions that "her most loving poems are addressed to female friends" (81), but nothing is mentioned of Philips's debts to Sappho as either woman or poet. In *The Weaker Vessel* (1984), Antonia Fraser follows Souers to insist on the integrity of the neoplatonic position. "It would," she writes, "be wrong to read anything covertly sensual into these relationships, however overtly passionate. That would have been quite outside the Platonic tradition. As Orinda herself wrote on the nature of friendship, such 'flames' were free from 'grossness or mortality' " (338, cf. 337).

10. See Gayatri Chakravorty Spivak, "Translator's Preface," to Jacques Derrida *Of Grammatology* (xiv—xvii).

11. These marginalizing practices are among the most remarkable achievements of culture under the capitalist mode of production. They have been exposed by the articulation of Marxism and feminism made possible by Spivak's deconstructive practice. It is not, perhaps entirely coincidental that Eagleton concludes his discussion of *The Function of Criticism* (120-4) by endorsing the work of John Brenkman, one of Spivak's students. Thus mediated by a male writer, Spivak's argument that marginalization-centralization is "a structure . . . that assures the stability of cultural explanation in general" ("Explanation and Culture" 214) enables Eagleton to turn, via Brenkman's division of "mass" culture, to herald the women's movement as an instance of a "counterpublic sphere" in which the cultural/political stakes make criticism legitimate once more. For from the culture of the "other,"—of the masses, of women—a politically serious criticism might be developed.

12. On Dryden, see John Barnard and Paul Hammond, "Dryden and a poem for Lewis Maidwell," which offers a transcription of a poem signed "J. Drydon" with the case for including it in the master's canon; and Alan Roper's reply which sensibly legitimates an aesthetic judgment to exclude the verses by carefully weighing historical detail. The celebrated attribution to Shakespeare of some verses in the Bodleian has received due attention in the periodical press. Most recently see Gary Taylor's edition of the verses with the case for including them, and Robin Robbins's counter argument in the *TLS*.

13. After presenting a version of this paper at the STS conference in 1985, I returned to the Bodleian and was horrified to discover that my own long-hand transcription of the manuscript was corrupt in no fewer than eight places. The institutionalized training of reading without regard for authors derives, largely, from I. A. Richards's *Practical Criticism* (1929), which codifies the results of undergraduate essays on "anonymous" poems. Richards's conclusion is worth recalling: "The protocols show . . . how entirely a matter of authority the rank of famous poets, as it is accepted and recognized by public opinion, must be. Without the control of this rather mysterious, traditional authority, poets

of the most established reputations would very quickly and surprisingly change their places in general approval. . . . There cannot be much doubt that when we know we are reading Milton or Shelley, a great deal of our approval and admiration is being accorded not to the poetry, but to an idol" (315-6).

14. See Carver (1977) and MacLean (1985) for discussions of these features of poems on the Restoration.

15. See Williams's development of the term "stance" throughout *Marxism and Literature* (e.g. 149, 176), to designate the always already-ideological positioning of literary texts or, in his precise terms: "a mode of basic (social) organisation which determines a particular kind of presentation" (183).

16. Lisa Jardine, *Still Harping on Daughters* (1983), 44. Jardine elaborates this double-bind to criticize feminists who are over-eager to celebrate representations in Renaissance texts of the bourgeois marriage as the site of female emancipation.

References

Arnold, Matthew. *Culture and Anarchy.* 1869, rev 1875. Ed. John C. Wilson. 1932. Cambridge: Cambridge University Press, 1969.

Ashmole, Elias. *Sol in Ascendente.* 1660.

Barnard, John and Paul Hammond. "Dryden and a poem for Lewis Maidwell." *Times Literary Supplement* 4234 (May 25, 1984): 586.

Carver, Larry. "The Restoration Poets and Their Father King." *Huntington Library Quarterly* 40 (1977): 332-51.

Coward, Rosalind. *Patriarchal Principles: Sexuality and Social Relations.* London: Routledge and Kegan Paul, 1983.

Crouch, John. *A Mixt Poem.* 1660 (variant printings).

———. *Census Poeticus: The poet's tribute paid in eight loyal poems.* 1663.

———. *The Muse's Joy for the Recovery of that weeping Vine, Henretta Maria, the Queen-Mother, and her royal brothers.* 1660.

Crum, Margaret. *First-Line Index of English Poetry 1500-1800 in Manuscripts of the Bodleian Library Oxford.* 2 vols. Oxford: Clarendon Press, 1969.

Derrida, Jacques. *Of Grammatology.* Trans. Gayatri Chakravorty Spivak. Baltimore: Johns Hopkins University Press, 1976.

Dryden, John. *Astraea Redux.* 1660.

———. *The Works of John Dryden.* Ed. H. T. Swedenberg et al. 22 vols to date. Berkeley and Los Angeles: University of California Press, 1956-.

Eagleton, Terry. *Criticism and Ideology.* 1976. London: Verso, 1978.

———. *Exiles and Emigres: Studies in Modern Literature.* New York: Schocken, 1970.

———. *Literary Theory: An Introduction.* Oxford: Blackwell, 1983.

———. *Myths of Power: A Marxist Study of the Brontës.* London: Macmillan, 1975.

———. *Shakespeare and Society: Critical Studies in Shakespearean Drama.* New

York: Schocken, 1967.

——. *The Function of Criticism: From "The Spectator" to Post-Structuralism.* London: Verso, 1984.

——. *The Rape of Clarissa: Writing, Sexuality and Class Struggle in Samuel Richardson.* Minneapolis: University of Minnesota Press, 1982.

Elmen, Paul. "Some Manuscript Poems by the Matchless Orinda," *PQ* 30 (1959): 53-57.

An Excellent Old Ballad, Made at the Restauration of K. Charles II. 1711. Rpt. 1712.

Faderman, Lillian. *Surpassing the Love of Men.* New York: William Morrow, 1981.

Flecknoe, Richard. "The Portrait of His Majesty," in *Heroic Portraits.* 1660. Rpt. as "The Pourtrait of His Majesty, Made a little before His Happy Restauration," in *A Collection of the choicest Epigrams and Characters of Richard Flecknoe.* 1673.

Fortescue, George. *Catalogue of the Pamphlets, Books, Newspapers . . . collected by George Thomason.* 2 vols. London: British Museum, 1908.

Foucault, Michel. *The Order of Things: An Archaeology of the Human Sciences.* 1970. Trans. Alan Sheridan. New York: Random House, 1973.

Fraser, Antonia. *The Weaker Vessel.* 1984. New York: Vintage, 1985.

Fuller, Thomas. *A Panegyric To His Majesty, On His Happy Return.* 1660. Rpt. in *The History of the Worthies of England.* 1662.

Gilbert, Sandra, and Susan Gubar, eds. *The Norton Anthology of Literature by Women: The Tradition in English.* New York: Norton, 1985.

The Glory of the English Nation, Or, an Essay on the Birth-day of 'King Charles' the Second. 1681.

Goldmann, Lucien. "Structure: Human Reality and Methodological Concept," in *The Structuralist Controversy: The Language of Criticism and the Sciences of Man.* Ed. R. Macksey and E. Donato. Baltimore: Johns Hopkins University Press, 1970. 98-110.

——. *The Hidden God: A Study of Tragic Vision in the Penseés of Pascal and the Tragedies of Racine.* Trans. Philip Thody. London: Routledge and Kegan Paul, 1964.

Gubar, Susan. "Sapphistries." *Signs* 10 (1984): 43-62.

Jardine, Lisa. *Still Harping on Daughters: Women and Drama in the Age of Shakespeare.* Brighton: Harvester, 1983.

Heath, Stephan. *The Sexual Fix.* London: Macmillan, 1982.

King Charles the Second's Restoration. Two separate ballads of this title at Roxburghe III. 758 and III. 760. [1720].

A Knave at Bottom. The Dealers Sure of a Trump. [1720/30].

Leavis, F. R. *English Literature in our Time and the University.* London: Chatto, 1969.

Lord, George de F., et al. eds. *Poems on Affairs of State: Augustan Satirical Verse, 1660-1714.* 7 vols. New Haven: Yale University Press, 1963-71.

Macherey, Pierre. *A Theory of Literary Production.* 1966. Trans. Geoffrey Wall. 1978. London: Routledge and Kegan Paul, 1980.

MacLean, Gerald M. "So What *does* Thomas Gray's *Progress of Poesy* have to do with Progress?.'' *Postscript: Publication of the Philological Association of the Carolinas* 2 (1985): 67-74.

———. "The King on Trial: Judicial Poetics and the Restoration Settlement." *Michigan Academician* 17 (1985): 375-88.

Mambretti, Catherine. " 'Fugitive Papers': A New Orinda Poem and Problems in her Canon." *PBSA* 71 (1977): 443-52.

Marvell, Andrew. *The Complete Poems.* Ed. Elizabeth Story Donno. 1972. Harmondsworth: Penguin, 1976.

———. *The Poems and Letters of Andrew Marvell.* Ed. H. M. Margoliouth. 1927. 3rd ed. revised Pierre Legouis and E. E. Duncan-Jones. 2 vols. Oxford: Clarendon Press, 1971.

McGann, Jerome. "Shall These Bones Live?," *TEXT 1: Transactions of the Society for Textual Scholarship.* New York: AMS Press, 1984. 21-40.

———. *A Critique of Modern Textual Criticism.* Chicago: University of Chicago Press, 1983.

Morrison, Paul G. *Index of Printers, Publishers and Booksellers in Donald Wing's STC.* Charlottesville: Bibliographical Society of America, 1955.

Mulhern, Francis. *The Moment of Scrutiny.* London: Verso, 1979.

A New Song on St. George's Day. And to the Glorious Memory of Queen Anne. With the Restauration of K Charles the 2nd. [1714].

"Ode on His Majesty's Return." In *Poetical Miscellanies. Consisting of Original Poems and Translations.* Ed. Richard Steele. 2nd ed. 1727.

Philips, Katherine. *Poems.* 1664.

———. *Poems.* 1667.

Richards, I. A. *Practical Criticism: A Study of Literary Judgement.* 1929. New York: Harcourt, Brace, 1930.

Robbins, Robin. " . . . and the counter-arguments." *Times Literary Supplement* 4316 (Dec. 20, 1985): 1449-50.

Roper, Alan. Reply to Barnard and Hammond. *Times Literary Supplement* 4238 (June 22, 1984): 696.

Signs: A Journal of Women in Culture and Society 9 (1984).

Souers, Philip W. *The Matchless Orinda.* Cambridge: Harvard University Press, 1931.

Spivak, Gayatri Chakravorty. "Explanation and Culture: Marginalia." *Humanities in Society* 2 (1979): 241-46.

———. "Feminism and Critical Theory." *Women's Studies International Quarterly* 1 (1978): 241-46.

Taylor, Gary. "A New Shakespeare Poem? The evidence . . . . " *Times Literary Supplement* 4316 (Dec. 20, 1985): 1447-8.

Thomason. See "Fortescue."

Williams, Raymond. *Culture and Society: 1780-1950.* 1958. Harmondsworth: Penguin, 1963.

———. *Marxism and Literature.* Oxford: Oxford University Press, 1975.

———. *The Country and the City.* New York: Oxford University Press, 1973.

Wing, Donald, et al., eds. *Short-Title Catalogue of Books Printed in England, Scotland, Ireland, Wales, and British America and of English Books Printed in Other Countries, 1641-1700.* 2nd ed. 2 vols. to date. New York: MLA, 1972-.

Eighteenth-Century Thorns, Twentieth-Century Secretaries, & Other Prickly Matters

ROBERT H. ELIAS

We work in an age of textual consciousness. We tend to agree that we want authenticity. Whether it is a poem, a novel, or an essay, we wish, in publishing it, to be faithful to its author's intention and achievement: to reproduce what he said just as he said it—and yet, when we extend our activity to the reproduction of correspondence, we inevitably have difficulties rendering the author's intention, with achieving a consensus concerning authenticity. Because of our sensitivity to the nature of history and the details of biography, because of a division in our loyalties, because of conflicting interests, we—if we are not to remain paralyzed—must conclude with compromises that forever leave us partly dissatisfied.

Since I have managed to edit or co-edit two sets of letters (fairly extensive sets—approximately three hundred letters each time), I have obviously succeeded in avoiding paralysis and therefore, you can infer, stand before you dissatisfied.[1]

Why?

One of my correspondents was a twentieth-century writer (Theodore Dreiser, but it could have been John Dos Passos or Sherwood Anderson or some other contemporary who did not spell or punctuate conventionally while at the same time occasionally employing typists who did); the other was an eighteenth-century Revolutionary figure (Thomas Digges, author of an early, probably the first, American novel but better known as a correspondent of Franklin's, Adams's, Jefferson's, Madison's, among others whose letters are at present being edited according to what we term the expanded method). The problems I encountered are familiar enough.

They begin quite obviously with the very act of reproducing in public form a document written as a private communication (and I am talking of personal letters, not open letters or manifestoes in the guise of letters), in which the private codes, symbols, mannerisms now become the subjects of editorial responsibility. Squiggles have to be accounted for. Because of the limitations of type and the requirement of what we call "readability," an individual's quirky ampersand frequently has to be like all ampersands, and all ampersands very often are spelled "a-n-d." Abbreviations that are obscure to strangers may, when rare, be footnoted and when frequent be extended within brackets or simply expanded without notice beyond the volume's introductory textual note. We editors tamper; we stand between, helping—and hindering.

When we edit the work of our contemporaries, of course, we are not likely to do violence to the text in the way we do violence to older texts. With twentieth-century writers, for example, we encounter habits of punctuation that are usually likely to be more self-conscious, more deliberate, more reflective of what we can in our time recognize as meaning than what we encounter in the eighteenth century. The eighteenth-century writer of letters strikes us as idiosyncratic; sporadic or vague in paragraphing; uncertain about whether to use commas, colons, or periods; given to the use of dashes that resemble "equals" marks; careless about capitalizing the beginnings of sentences that follow marks of ambiguous character or that simply start a new line following one that terminates at a margin without punctuation of any sort—I could add to this list. In the letters of our twentieth-century writer we find no need to wonder whether some diacritical mark has to be explained to the twentieth-century reader, or translated, modernized, or "normalized," as the euphemism has it: the question does not arise.

What enters the present century as a special problem for editors, though, is not the use of unfamiliar signs and symbols but the employment of the secretary and her (usually *her*) typewriter. There were secretaries (usually male) in the eighteenth century; they made "fair copies"; they often corrected spelling and modified capitalization and punctuation. But the extent of their copying that has to be taken into account by present-day editors is negligible compared with what has to be taken into account when one edits the letters of a writer such as Dreiser. If we believe that we should reproduce documents in a form approximating their original, what do we do when we have a writer who employed secretaries to copy rough drafts or take dictation and then produce the final, corrected copy to be signed (along with a carbon), or who was himself less a misspeller than a terrible typist? He employed a secretary to produce corrected copy, but he himself was incapable of such production. The secretary is in these instances the writer's first editor. Shall we accept that version or go behind it to the manuscript draft? Let us suppose we cannot find the original drafts but must work from secretaries' carbons. And let us say there are mistakes *there*, misspellings or whatever. Whose are those errors? Do we reproduce *them* faithfully? Or do we assume we can determine that our writer's misspellings occur in only his handwritten letters and that letters typed by secretaries contain no such errors? Do we think it anything but a distraction to produce a volume or more of texts so glaringly inconsistent? Is it really enlightening? Is it fair to the writer? Is it helpful to the reader? What is the purpose or value of this kind of textual fidelity?

Documents from the earlier periods emphasize the critical nature of that last question. In editing older documents we have options that require us to take peculiar effects into account. Editors ordinarily eliminate from serious consideration reproduction through facsimiles. They are useful if we are examining some of the poems of Emily Dickinson, say, but the editor's hand is finally needed there, too. Basically, facsimiles merely make the reader the editor. There is certainly a temptation to adopt what is closest to the facsimile: the so-called literal method, whereby (except in very illiterate manuscripts) we adhere strictly to the original spelling, capitalization, punctuation; preserve tildes and thorns; raise superior letters and print them in smaller type; hope our typesetter has all the necessary diacritical marks; and maybe even preserve the use of the long-tailed and bob-tailed letters. But if we do that, what have we accomplished? What effect have we produced? We provide a glimpse of the past but not as the past saw itself, of the writer but not as he was within his society. It is like the difference between the sound of a harpsichord in the ears of someone who has never heard the modern piano and the sound of the harpsichord in the ears of someone who has.

Perhaps, though, we do not care about how the *past* viewed itself. We care only about our own view—only about what our perspective indicates is peculiar to the past. We will be selective in what we preserve. The long-tailed *s*'s and bob-tailed *j*'s we will translate into their modern equivalents. We will expand certain presently abandoned abbreviations, especially those signaled by tildes and apostrophes and by the various kinds of ampersands and thorns. What we will retain are idiosyncratic punctuation, spelling, and capitalization, inconsistent paragraphing, and all kinds of errors that leave no ambiguity. Explaining all this in a textual note, we will provide a healthful environment that keeps out the dreadful *sic*.

When we have managed this with as much consistency as diligence and aspirin can create, we may feel that we have opened the way for today's reader to participate fully in yesterday's communications. This is the method the editors of the papers of Thomas Jefferson and his contemporaries have used, and with minor modifications it is the method Eugene Finch and I used with Thomas Digges.[2] It makes the texts more accessible to the twentieth-century reader than the literal method does: it relieves the reader of most editorial responsibilities.

But if one of the purposes of publishing letters is to contribute to an understanding of their author's personality, then may not even the expansion of the ampersand be risky? Form is itself content. Surely there are times when—particularly when writing longhand— we ourselves prefer ampersands to "a-n-d," and not just to save time. Poets there are who certainly so prefer. I cannot say what the difference in meaning is, but I know there are times when *I* would not want to substitute the expanded spelling for the simple sign in *my* handwritten letters, although I do not use it when I type. Moreover, even if it is not used to save time, it may be used to affect pace—as contractions are. Like rhythm in poetry, pace in prose contributes to total meaning. So, in modifying signs and symbols and expanding abbreviations we may often offer readers an accessibility that at the same time limits—even distorts—what we are providing access to. Yet I have already suggested that if we tamper less, preserving as much of the antiquated as we can and thereby enlisting our readers as collaborating editors, we do not do any better: we do not really immerse them in the past; we simply create the barriers of self-consciousness. The thorn provides a sense of its time only beyond its time; the flavor of the eighteenth century does not have a distinct taste in the eighteenth century. So whether we tamper or whether we do not, we either misrepresent the author or impede the reader.

Confronted with this impasse should we not then throw up our hands—tell ourselves that all editing of letters must in part be like translating a foreign language and that we should forsake all vestiges of literalism for equivalences? But the issue there is once again primarily that of fidelity to texts.[3] We need to broaden the issue. How about loyalty to authors? When I edited Dreiser's letters I undertook to "normalize" the texts. Partly I was guided by my consulting editors, who had been my mentors;[4] partly, and I think more compellingly, by my feeling that to call repeated attention to the contrast between the spelling in Dreiser's handwritten letters and the spelling in the letters typed by his secretaries would be not only distracting but also unfair to him. I felt a personal commitment to him. He had been generous in helping me when I was working on my biography of him. Knowing from what he had written Louise Campbell, among others, how he had regarded his own uncertain editorial skills, I even developed a fantasy about what he would say about my preparing his letters for print were he then still alive; it was to this effect: "if you're actually going to *publish* these letters, then fix them up—I'm such a bad editor—and you can take care of all those errors: spelling, punctuation, and so on." So I covered it all with a textual note that listed the most frequent of his misspellings and recommended (my tone was, I fear, not a little condescending) that readers who found that sort of thing edifying should consult the original manuscripts and collect all instances.

Why *not* edit in Dreiser's behalf (or any author's)? Misspellings—simply to consider them as an example—are visible primarily to readers who spell correctly and are strangers. Intimates, whether they themselves spell correctly or not, look right through the misspelling of their friend to the author and his message. Unlike ampersands, misspellings provide no pace; but like ampersands they are part of the person one knows. Since the intimacy is impossible for outsiders, the misspellings are more likely to distract and mislead; and when one is editing for a readership of outsiders, one wants to avoid misleading. To serve the author, then, one should correct the spelling but perhaps let the ampersands alone.[5]

As to the thorns?

I suspect that most of us still hanker for a recovery of pastness, for a rendering of otherness. We accept the self-contradictions and futility inherent in our forays into earlier times and other personalities and find pleasure in a sense of our evolution beyond them. But I hope we do not take too much pleasure from it, for in it there is some falsification or betrayal of what we are undertaking to preserve. And I hope I have made clear that I see no escape from compromises that some will judge wholly arbitrary. Change nothing, change everything, change some things—there is no end to editorial options and the rationale each of us will subjectively formulate to defend what we did.

And yet, with loyalty to authors in mind, I wonder whether there is not still another kind of compromise we should consider, one that arises out of the difference between what we do when we edit a *collection* of letters and what we do when in the course of an article we quote a letter or two. Collections are in a sense total works; they can be viewed as their authors' final books; their editors are their Maxwell Perkinses (or at least their knowledgeable literary executors). Our concern should be to make these final works as available to readers (and these are not just scholarly readers, as we now know) as were the novels and poems these authors published during their lifetime. We should help them send their composite "letter to the world." We would not "clean up," expurgate, modify, or otherwise tamper with substance in the texts as some editors did in the last century and early years of this one. We would confine ourselves to form and format. This view of editorial responsibility places more emphasis on mind than on mannerism, more on substance than on shorthand, more on idea than on idiosyncrasy. The price we pay is admittedly a loss of some of the sense of the epistolary form, a loss, though, already partially suffered anyway when letters are removed from the context of an entire life and assembled in a volume in which each letter cannot escape becoming part of the larger unit. The gain is in an effect of wholeness and immediacy. We enable authors to escape their own times to become our contemporaries. To indulge our hankering for the vicarious plunge into yesterday, we can in our articles, where we simply quote a few documents, preserve all the peculiarities we wish. The choice is ultimately between preserving the sense of an individual in the act of writing a letter on the one hand and his communicating as immediately and cogently as possible what that letter not only said but still says on the other.

To shift the perspective once more and for the last time, in order to bring our quandaries into sharper focus, let us ask ourselves how we would want our own letters edited—if, say, they could be taken back into the past or rocketed into the future. Would we want them published just as we wrote them, which means that our norms might look like oddities to our fancied readers and thus impair understanding, or would we want to be normalized, for communication's sake, by editors who must seem odd to us?

NOTES

1. This paper was originally presented at the Third International Interdisciplinary Conference of the Society for Textual Scholarship, 25 April 1985, in the CUNY Graduate Center, New York, as part of a panel discussion on "Editing Letters: Quandaries and Queries."

2. We considered it important, as our textual note makes clear, that the presentation of Digges's letters should be compatible with the presentation, already in progress, of the letters of those of his notable contemporaries with whom he was most frequently in correspondence (Franklin, Adams, and Jefferson). For details see Digges lxxix–lxxxiv.

3. The various ways editors of literary correspondence have recently dealt with this issue are described by Robert Stephen Becker in a survey he made a few years ago of forty-seven editions published after 1900. In conjunction with his examination, Becker corresponded with thirty-two scholarly editors whose ideas helped him "formulate better ground rules for the transcription of literary letters."

4. Sculley Bradley and Robert E. Spiller had invited me to undertake the project, promising advice and support. When I raised questions about Dreiser's spelling and other matters related to the distractions of presenting inconsistent texts, they unhesitatingly recommended that I "normalize" the text (Dreiser).

5. In instances of extraordinary eccentricity editors will choose to devise special methods. No typesetter could do justice to the visual effect of a letter from John Cowper Powys, for example; in the course of writing a letter of whatever length Powys often would reach the last page of the paper at hand and then, in his bold and almost impenetrable script, filling slanted margins and crossing or writing between lines already there, work his way back to the first page to conclude. A photograph of a typical letter would be imperative, whatever editorial approach was adopted. Whenever his friend Dreiser received such a letter from him, Dreiser was likely to glance at it to sense Powys's presence and then ask his secretary to type out a copy in a more conventional form so that he could find out what it said. Letters to Dreiser are in the Dreiser collection in the Charles Patterson Van Pelt Library of the University of Pennsylvania; one to me is in the John M. Olin Library of Cornell University.

Eighteenth-Century Continental Books: Some Problems of Bibliographical Description

J.-A. E. MCEACHERN

In preparing my bibliographies of Jean-Jacques Rousseau's *Emile* and *La Nouvelle Héloïse*, I have examined approximately 170 editions printed between 1760 and 1800 in France, Holland, Switzerland, Germany, Denmark, Italy, England, Scotland, Ireland, and the United States. In this relatively small sample, I have observed a variety of printing practices which would merit further study. As R. A. Sayce pointed out in his lengthy article, "Compositorial Practices and the Localization of Printed Books,"[1] more detailed study of the practices peculiar to and/or characteristic of a certain place at a certain time would not only constitute a substantial contribution to our general knowledge of the history of printing, but might also enable us, eventually, to identify the origins of books with false imprints and/or dates. This problem is particularly relevant to my own research, for the majority of the editions I have described bear a false imprint and, as I have been able to prove in some cases, a false date.

It is unfortunate that so little has been done to enlarge upon or refine Sayce's work. As he himself pointed out, "the sample chosen [2800 books] is too small to enable really firm conclusions to be drawn" (p. 2). In order to make valid generalisations about the printing practices of any region in any period, we would need information on a vast corpus of books: this is particularly true of the second half of the eighteenth century, when, as Sayce pointed out, continental practices tended towards ever-greater uniformity. Any undertaking to gather such information would be an enormous enterprise, probably too great for any individual, although it might be attempted by a team. However, such a project would involve much time and much expensive travel, with no certainty that it could ultimately provide sufficient evidence for the making of valid generalisations. The obvious alternative was proposed by Sayce himself in the conclusion to his study: "It might also be suggested . . . that standard methods of bibliographical description should be modified to include more detailed and precise information . . . which may be of considerable importance" (p. 45).

Clearly, if every bibliographer dealing with continental books included the sort of information suggested by Sayce, sufficient material might eventually be amassed to provide a solid point of departure for further study by an individual or a team. However, the methods traditionally used to describe English books provide no guidelines for the description of features which are peculiar to the continent. At present, this is the crux of the problem. I propose, therefore, to review some of those features for which traditional bibliographical methods have proven inadequate, and to ask that bibliographers dealing with continental books reach a consensus on how these features might best be described without departing too radically from established practices. This will lead also to some suggestions about areas open to immediate research, as well as to some proposals for future research.

Finally, we might note in passing the particular difficulty of discussing these problems in the French language, or indeed any of the Romance languages, since no consensus has yet been reached on the terminology of analytical bibliography and of modern textual editing.[2]

1. Title-page

1.1 Ornaments

The bibliographer attempting to describe books produced on the continent in the eighteenth century labours under a number of disadvantages unknown to his colleagues dealing with English books, not the least of which is the paucity of adequate works of reference. Reference works of printers' ornaments, for instance, can greatly simplify the bibliographer's task, since he need not, in fact, describe an ornament which is found in a reference work: "When a title-page border has been listed by McKerrow and Ferguson, or by some other authority . . . the proper reference takes the place of a description" (Bowers, p. 144)[3]; "Ornaments are very difficult to identify, . . . when identifiable, a citation of the reference book or article is appropriate" (Bowers, p. 145). Not only do such reference works ease the bibliographer's task, they also help identify the printers of books bearing false imprints, or, at least, narrow down the dating of books with false dates.

At present, the value of ornaments as evidence is not as great as it would be if we had adequate reference books. This is certainly an area for immediate research, and the work is, in fact, being done. Giles Barber is currently making a collection of European printers' ornaments, although it may be some time before the collection is published. Until the day comes when we may describe ornaments merely by referring to the Barber number, it might be useful to consider an alternative to verbal descriptions or expensive photographic reproductions: each published bibliography might have attached an envelope of microfiches providing inexpensive reproductions of all ornaments described in the text.

1.2 Printers and booksellers

As with ornaments, students of English books are amply provided with reference works enabling them to identify printers, booksellers and bookbinders.[4] For students of French books, no such wealth of material is available in published form: Augustin-Marie Lottin, *Catalogue chronologique des libraires-imprimeurs de Paris* (Paris, 1789) and Paul Delalain, *L'imprimerie et la librairie à Paris de 1789 à 1813* (Paris, 1900) are inadequate to the purpose and ought to be superseded. This, again, is an area susceptible to immediate research, although it is likely to be a long-term project and would probably be best approached by a team of researchers.

1.3 Long ∫

Finally, I have noticed in some recent bibliographies that long ∫ is no longer always distinguished in the transcription of the title-page. Although this problem is by no means confined to continental books, I note it in passing because the tendency strikes me as unfortunate. The presence or absence of long ∫ may provide contributory evidence concerning the dating of an edition, or, if the date is known, concerning the edition's origin. This may be of special significance when dealing with the transitional period in the last half

of the eighteenth century, since the change to the modern lowered
form was certainly made at different times in different places.

2. Formula

Traditionally, the collation ignores any differences of type-face
found in the signatures. In many editions of *Emile*, for example, the
index is printed in smaller type than the text. As a result, the
signatures in the index are in small capitals, a fact which goes
unrecognized in the collation—and rightly so, since it is clearly of no
bibliographical significance.

On the other hand, the use of italics in preliminary gatherings
signed with the lower case alphabet may prove to be of some use in
identifying the origin of a book. At present, however, there is no way
that italics may be indicated in the collation, since italics, if used at
all, are normally used in this context to indicate an inferred
signature. I wonder whether it would be permissible to treat lower
case alphabets used for prelims in the same way that one treats
symbols, and reproduce them exactly as they stand, roman or italic,
while enclosing inferred signatures in square brackets.[5]

3. Contents

In listing the contents of an eighteenth-century book, should one
use pagination or signing for reference? I have asked this question of
various colleagues and received conflicting advice. Bowers permits
the use of pagination, but points out, nonetheless, that this method
has some serious drawbacks: "The only argument for page reference is its ease . . . Its accuracy is not complete . . . However, the
main objection is that it is not a structural system . . . When the sole
reference is to pages, the relation of the contents to the makeup of
the book is completely obscured . . . These difficulties are serious
ones, but the advantages of quickness of reference in eighteenth-
century books and later are usually felt to outweigh the objections to
pagination reference" (Bowers, pp. 315–316).

A further disadvantage of using pagination is that the method
cannot be followed consistently: unpaginated preliminary matter or
an unpaginated index, for instance, can be referred to only by
signature. One edition of *Emile* has unpaginated section-titles, which
the printer's pagination does not allow for, so that the (simplified)
statement of pagination for one volume reads:1–298 [2] 299–546. If
pagination is used for reference, how should one refer to the two

unnumbered pages? Is it not disturbing, when reading a list of page references, to read suddenly "T6ʳ"?

My solution to this problem has been to provide both signatures and page numbers: for example, "H4ᵛ (p. 96), blank." Where no page number can be inferred, only the signature is given. While this solution may be considered pedantic and clumsy, it has the merit of retaining the advantages of both systems. Further discussion of the question might lead to the development of a more concise and elegant method.

4. Signatures

4.1 Text

4.1.1 Position in the line

The position of the signature in the direction-line, whether in the centre or to the right of centre, is not normally noted in a bibliographical description. Sayce observed that "Books with catchwords on every page naturally tend to have the signature at or near the centre; others tend to have it on the right" (p. 26). This would appear to be of no bibliographical significance. However, in the latter half of the eighteenth century, when page-catchwords were gradually being abandoned in favour of quire-catchwords, editions are found which have quire-catchwords, and the signature in the centre. The obvious conclusion is that a book presenting this combination of features was produced by a printer who had only recently abandoned the use of page-catchwords. Sayce found only three examples of this kind, but expressed the hope that the matter would be studied further: "If this practice were corroborated by a more thorough investigation it might furnish valuable evidence for identification at a time when . . . more obvious traditional distinctions are becoming blurred" (p. 26). I have found more examples from the second half of the eighteenth century of books having quire-catchwords and signatures in the centre, and the presence of this feature in one edition bearing the imprint "Paris, 1799" provides contributory evidence of the fact that the imprint is false.

In my descriptions, the position of the signature in the line is noted in the statement of signing, and I would suggest that other bibliographers describing continental books do likewise.

4.1.2 Position on the page

The signature may be found at the bottom of the page or between the text and the footnote. The latter practice appears, in my experience, to be confined to editions which have page-catchwords and extra catchwords for the footnotes. In such cases, the signature is placed on the same line as the catchword for the text, except for $1, which is always placed at the bottom of the page, regardless of the presence of notes. I have found no editions with quire-catchwords and the signature between text and note, but such may exist. In any case, the position of the signature on the page may prove to provide evidence for identification, and should therefore be noted.

4.1.3 Number of leaves signed

Sayce demonstrated conclusively that the number of leaves signed is "one of the most useful indications of origin" (p. 26). Traditional methods of description allow the bibliographer to state the number of leaves signed in a concise, effective way: for a duodecimo, we need only write "$6 signed" (or $5 or $7, as the case may be). However, a problem arises when we are faced with a duodecimo in eights and fours, a common continental format. My solution has been to write "$4 signed in gatherings of 8, $2 signed in gatherings of 4", a statement which avoids ambiguity, but seems clumsy and unnecessarily lengthy. However, in future I intend to provide a shorter, simpler statement, such as "$4, $2 signed," leaving the size of the gatherings to be understood, or perhaps simply "half signed".

4.1.4 Signature numeration

Sayce observed that "from about 1630 to about 1780 roman figures strongly suggest French, especially Parisian, or perhaps French Swiss origin. Conversely, arabic figures will constitute a strong argument against Parisian (although not necessarily against French) origin. During the same period a mixture of the two may suggest Geneva or the French provinces and borderlands" (p. 24). I would add that a mixture of the two may also suggest a printer who is just in the process of abandoning roman figures for arabic, and who occasionally falls back into his old habits: I have seen more than one obvious case of this kind.[6] It is important, therefore, to note the method of signature numeration in a continental book, since this may help to identify its origin. In describing editions which have signatures numbered with roman numerals, I have noted the fact in the statement of the signing, for example: "$6 signed to the right, numbered with roman numerals." This seems unnecessarily verbose; a more concise statement which reproduced what actually appears in the book would not only be more elegant, but would also be more easily grasped by the reader, for example: "$vj signed to the right."

In my volume on *Emile*, a typical description of the signature reads as follows:

> *Signatures*. Half the leaves of each gathering are signed to the right, numbered with roman numerals, $4 in gatherings of eight, $2 in gatherings of four ($2 with arabic figures: CE).

The same information could be given more concisely, yet more clearly:

> *Signatures*. $iv, $ij signed to the right ($2: CE)

4.2 Preliminaries

The paragraph describing the signing of a continental book should include a separate statement for the signing of the preliminaries. Even leaving aside the use of symbols, considerable variety is found in the use of the lower case alphabet. Sayce oversimplified the problem by failing to distinguish roman and italic forms: "The roman and italic forms are here treated together. The almost universal practice was to italicize the signature if the text above it was in italics, and obviously this has no special significance. Where this is not the case and an italic signature accompanies a text in roman, the result may be of some interest" (p. 10). In my experience, there were a number of printers who consistently used italics, or a combination of roman and italic forms, for the preliminary signatures, regardless of the type-face used in the preliminary text. Since this will almost certainly prove, eventually, to be of some significance in identifying origin, the use of italics should be noted.

Like the text, the preliminary signatures may be numbered with roman or arabic figures, and again this should be noted, particularly as there are numerous editions in which the signatures in the main series are numbered with arabic figures, while the preliminary signatures are numbered with roman figures. Further study may show this feature to be characteristic of a particular region or printer.

Thus, where lower case alphabet is used to sign the preliminaries, there are eight possible forms to be distinguished: *aij*, aij, *a*ij, a*ij*, *a2*, a2, *a*2, a*2*. According to established conventions, italics are used in a bibliographical description to indicate an inferred signature. Accordingly, the statement "a2 is signed '*aij*'" would be a contradiction in terms incomprehensible to the traditional bibliographer, who would be forced to assume, because of the italics, that a2 is, in fact, *unsigned*. However, the alternative, a verbal description of the eight possible variations, is not only clumsy, but may even be misleading because of the possible confusion between "roman" *face* and "roman" *figure*:

> *aij* italic face letter with italic face roman numeral
> aij roman face letter with roman face roman numeral
> *a*ij italic face letter with roman face roman numeral
> a*ij* roman face letter with italic face roman numeral

Thus, the description of the preliminary signatures in an edition with a–c^{12}, where half the leaves of each gathering are signed, might read as follows:

> *Prelims.* $6 signed, with lower case roman letter and italic roman numeral.

Because this is exceedingly difficult to visualize, and in order to avoid any possibility of ambiguity, I normally add an example in quotation marks, "a*ij*".

This description would be just as comprehensible if the verbal description were omitted, but the example retained:

> *Prelims.* $vj signed, italic numeration, e. g. '*aij*'

In any case, it is clear that the preliminary signatures of a continental book should be described *exactly* as they appear: italics and roman numerals should not be passed over in silence, even though we may be as yet unsure of their precise significance. What is required is a method of describing these differences which can be easily integrated into the established conventions.

5. Catchwords

5.1

Sayce distinguishes four types of catchword: page-catchwords, catchwords on every page except those bearing signatures, leaf-catchwords and quire-catchwords. In the eighteenth century, we are concerned mainly with page-catchwords and quire-catchwords, and their usefulness as evidence of origin. I have observed yet another type of catchword, for which I have no name, in one duodecimo edition of *Emile*, dated "Amsterdam, 1773", although the imprint may be false. This edition has catchwords on 4^v and 12^v, clearly to ensure the proper placement of the four centre-leaves of the gathering. Since this type of catchword appears to be rare, further investigation may enable us to identify its origin.

5.2

Another feature, which is somewhat more common, is the use of quire-catchwords for the text, but page-catchwords for the footnotes; that is, wherever a note is carried on to the following page, it is given a catchword, regardless of its position in the gathering. This may be characteristic of printers who have recently abandoned the use of page-catchwords, although I have discovered no evidence to that effect.

5.3 Position of catchword

Like the signature, the catchword may be found at the bottom of the page or between the text and the footnote. The latter feature is normally found in editions which have an additional catchword for the note, although this is not invariably the case: there are editions which have no catchword for the notes, but in which the catchword is placed between text and note nevertheless. It may prove useful, therefore, to note whether the edition has catchwords for the notes, and the position of the catchword on the page.

5.4 Length of catchword

I have observed that page-catchwords tend to be short, often giving only the first one or two syllables of the word, followed by a hyphen, whereas quire-catchwords tend to give the entire word, irrespective of length. However, quire-catchwords are occasionally found which give only the first syllable of a word. A large number of such examples in one edition might serve as an indication that the printer has only recently abandoned page-catchwords for quire-catchwords and might help to identify him.

We have noted already that, when a printer abandoned page-catchwords for quire-catchwords, he tended for some time to continue printing the signature in the centre of the line, and that the signature drifted only gradually towards the right. It seems possible that the printing of the catchwords followed a similar pattern: that is, when he first abandoned page-catchwords, he continued for some time to print only the first syllables of the quire-catchwords, and only gradually fell into the habit of printing the entire word. This is only a hypothesis, of course, and must be tested. I would suggest that lists of anomalous and incorrect quire-catchwords should include abbreviated catchwords.[7]

6. Running-title

In the examples that I have seen, typographical errors and variations in the running-title appear to have less significance than they apparently have in English books. Variants are certainly repeated, but no pattern is discernible in their repetition. One of the running-titles in the first edition of *Emile*, for example, is easily recognizable: it has one letter from the wrong fount of type, one letter with a broken accent, and another letter with a broken serif. This running-title is found once in nearly every gathering of the first volume, but its appearances follow no pattern: my attempts at skeleton analysis, therefore, were doomed to failure, since, apparently, this printer used no skeleton. This holds true for all the continental editions I have seen, so that it is not possible to use the concise method proposed by Bowers and state that variant A, for example, appears on 2^r. One can only note each variant and list all its positions, one by one.

7. Paper

I have observed numerous watermarks which are listed in neither Churchill nor Heawood.[8] This is, presumably, just as great a problem for the bibliographer describing English books as it is for the continental bibliographer, although the few English editions that I have examined show considerably less variety than the continental ones. (I realize that this may not be generally true, however.) Since it is exceedingly difficult, if not impossible, to give a satisfactory verbal description of a watermark, and since it is clearly not feasible to reproduce facsimiles of all watermarks in an author-bibliography, a complete collection of eighteenth-century watermarks would certainly be welcome.

8. Copies examined.

At present, each bibliography that appears has a list, which may run to several pages, of abbreviations used for libraries. This seems rather extravagant. Would it not be possible to produce, in the form of a pamphlet, a single list of abbreviations, following the method used for American libraries? The national union catalogue for Switzerland, for example, has produced a list of abbreviations for Swiss libraries, similar to the American system: GeP (Geneva, Bibliothèque publique et Universitaire), LzZ (Luzern, Zentralbibliothek), NeV (Neuchâtel, Bibliothèque publique de la Ville). Similar abbreviations might be invented for all the libraries listed in the *World of Learning*: e.g., CDN-ToU (Canada, Toronto, University of Toronto Library), D-BU (Germany, Berlin, Universitätsbibliothek), F-PBN (France, Paris, Bibliothèque nationale), GB-OxB (Great Britain, Oxford, Bodleian), etc.

Conclusion

Any number of the apparently minor differences which are obscured or ignored by established Anglo-American bibliographical conventions may ultimately prove to be meaningful for the student of continental books. The constant, consistent accumulation of these small details may enable future researchers to study the problem of the localisation of books on a much larger scale than Sayce or any individual could accomplish. The fact that we are as yet unsure of the significance of certain features makes it all the more important that they be noted. In the first edition of his *Principles* (1949), Bowers advised that press figures be listed, although their significance was unknown: "Although not very much is precisely known about press numbers as yet, they will prove to have an interesting bibliographical significance" (p. 317). The same holds true for the details discussed above: until they are proven conclusively to be of no importance whatsoever, they should be included in every bibliographical description. It remains only to agree upon a methodology, that is to say, how these features may best be described within the context of established bibliographical conventions.

NOTES

1. R. A. Sayce, "Compositorial Practices and the Localization of Printed Books, 1530–1800," *The Library*, 5th. Ser., XXI (March 1966), 1–45.

2. This question was discussed at the Fifth International Congress on the Enlightenment in 1979. See Jean Varloot, "Terminologie et édition critique," *SV*, 193 (1980), 1759-62. "On reconnaît . . . la nécessité urgente, dans un premier temps, d'un lexique technique minimal" (p. 1762).

3. Fredson Bowers, *Principles of Bibliographical Description* (1949; rpt. New York, 1962).

4. Ronald B. McKerrow, et al., *A Dictionary of Printers and Booksellers in England, Scotland and Ireland, and of Foreign Printers of English Books, 1557-1640* (London, 1910), Paul G. Morrison, *Index of Printers, Publishers and Booksellers in A. W. Pollard and G. R. Redgrave, A Short-Title Catalogue* (Charlottesville, Va., 1950), and *Index of Printers, Publishers, and Booksellers in Donald Wing's Short-Title Catalogue of Books, 1641-1700,* (Charlottesville, Va., 1955), Henry R. Plomer, *A Dictionary of the Booksellers and Printers Who Were at Work in England, Scotland and Ireland from 1641 to 1667* (London, 1907), and *A Dictionary of the Printers and Booksellers Who Were at Work in England, Scotland and Ireland from 1668 to 1725,* ed. Arundell Esdaile (London, 1922), Henry R. Plomer, G. H. Bushnell, and R. R. McC. Dix, *A Dictionary of the Printers and Booksellers Who Were at Work in England, Scotland and Ireland from 1726 to 1775* (London, 1932), Ian Maxted, *The London Book Trades, 1775-1800: a Preliminary Checklist of Members* (London, 1977), and William B. Todd, *A Directory of Printers and Others in Allied Trades, London and Vicinity, 1800-1840* (London, 1972).

5. In my own descriptions, square brackets indicate inferred signatures and I have used no italics at all. Where prelims are signed italic, this fact is noted in my statement of the signing, but is ignored in the collation.

6. For example, a single pirate was responsible for ten editions of *Emile*, dating from 1763 to 1792. His early editions are numbered roman; the later editions are numbered arabic; the middle editions have a mixture of the two.

7. An example of this is the printer of the ten pirated editions of *Emile* mentioned in note 6. His early editions have the catchword "coquet-" for "coquetterie," while the later editions give the entire word.

8. W. A. Churchill, *Watermarks in Paper in Holland, England, France, etc. in the XVII and XVIII Centuries,* (1935; rpt. Amsterdam, 1967), and E. Heawood, *Watermarks mainly in the 17th and 18th Centuries* (Hilversum, 1950; rpt. Amsterdam, 1970).

Recording from Coleridge's Voice

CARL WOODRING

Hazlitt was the first to complain that Coleridge talked when he should have been writing. Among the hundreds who listened to Coleridge's conversation with awe or irritation, scores attempted to write down what they thought they had heard him say. A few tried to record what they heard him say in public lectures.

Coleridge did his sharpest thinking in direct response to the thought of others. Frequently he left his responses for friends and posterity in the margins of a book he was reading or in a notebook with the stimulant (here I mean a book) before him. In public lectures he drew like most lecturers from his reading, creatively if he had thought about the subject previously, often with a directness now regarded as plagiarism if he were getting up a lecture to meet an announced schedule. Although this procedure resulted in some of the finest and most influential literary criticism ever uttered in English, service as public conveyancer is not Coleridge at his most subtly philosophical. The intellectual subtlety apparent in his notebooks and marginalia is seldom equally evident in his performances for an audience or a publication.

As we are seldom told by reporters what remarks by others drove Coleridge to private lectures or monologues in dining or drawing rooms, we can assume, and sometimes can demonstrate, that he was keenest when rehearsing what he oft had thought but never before quite so well expressed. Of the many contemporaries who boasted of listening to Coleridge, or of being present and not listening, about one-third declare him either unintelligible or gaseous, a living embodiment of his friend Beddoes' Pneumatic Institution for treatment with "factitious airs." At least one-third of those reporting prove that the third that called him unintelligible reveal more about themselves than about Coleridge's performance. Carlyle sneered at Coleridge's adenoidal snuffling, and others complained of his

Devonshire accent, but those who understood him best were not from Devon.[1]

The subject before us is not the quality of his thought but the ascertainable degree of accuracy in what we take to be his lectures and conversation. For these two sources of knowledge about his thought and expression, we are largely dependent upon the notorious unreliability of witnesses. The listener mishears a key word or misunderstands its meaning and obliterates the precision or the ambiguity of the original with a presumed synonym, which in turn emerges in an altered and simplified context. Even an editor of a written text has strong temptations to dissolve apparent ambiguities; paraphrase from the spoken word normally eliminates intended ambiguity of phrase except when the reporter deadens the ambiguity by explaining it. An attempt to preserve a spoken emphasis, even when the reported words are accurate, may be lost upon a later reader. The hearer may unconsciously translate the speaker into thoughts nearer to—or, in reaction, further from—the hearer's own position. The hearer who disagrees with what she hears has a tendency to make the speaker's point more emphatic than the disinterested reporter would make it. As the hearer who reports also has an audience, there may be further translation into the idiom, or toward the expectancy, of the audience as conceived by the reporter. Of many of Coleridge's lectures we know nothing, and of others next to nothing. Of his lectures in Bristol in 1795 on politics and religion, some have been published in the collected works from his manuscript notes and others from self-censored versions that he printed; still others are lost or available only in manuscript fragments. For most of the later, more significant lectures, we have no versions published by Coleridge and no complete versions in his hand. It follows,then, that those who take seriously the Coleridge who spoke must take seriously those reports that survive. How near do they bring us to Coleridge's own words?

Our sources for his later lectures are principally of four kinds: (1) For a few we have substantial notes made by Coleridge in preparation for the public occasion. (2) For some we have fragmentary notes either intended for particular lectures or usable for lectures and coinciding, more or less, with what he is thought to have said or what it is thought appropriate for him to have said. (3) For some we have newspaper reports, on occasion a brief summary in one paper more or less confirming a longer report in another. (4) For some of the lectures in two of the series we have transcriptions from shorthand reports commissioned by friends of Coleridge.

When some of these materials first appeared in the *Literary Remains*, edited by Henry Nelson Coleridge, this nephew combined available jottings for the lectures with discovered notes on a subject known to be pertinent because it was announced in the surviving prospectus of the series concerned.[2] He did not in any of his editing take dating or sequence seriously. He sometimes expanded the extant jottings into paragraphs appropriate to his own sense of what Coleridge would have said. One of several flaws in this eclectic procedure is that Coleridge gave several series on or including Shakespeare, and the nephew was trying to piece out only one series of 1818. Conflation inevitably resulted.

After attempts by two intervening editors, Thomas M. Raysor provided three volumes of Coleridge's literary criticism with an aim of including all pertinent evidence concerning the literary lectures.[3] Raysor was generally alert to the problems of chronology and to the distinctions among notes, marginalia, and transcriptions from reports from hearers, but he often accepted the nephew's amplifications, partly in the realization that an editor working a century later could come no closer to Coleridge's intentions and partly in the pious hope that H. N. Coleridge might have had at least partial warrant for which there is now no documentary evidence. In most instances, we believe we know what H.N.C.'s primary sources were; from those sources, we know that he felt free not only to consolidate, but also to improve.[4]

Kathleen Coburn's 1949 edition of the philosophical lectures of 1818–19 demonstrates some of the steps that can be taken with extant materials.[5] The basic manuscript for these lectures is a transcription made from the record of an inadequately informed shorthand reporter employed by Coleridge's friend John Hookham Frere. The chief sources for correcting this fallible copy-text are notes made in advance by Coleridge for each lecture, some in a notebook and some on miscellaneous scraps of paper. Names, words, phrases, and sentences can sometimes be corrected from other notes by Coleridge on subjects discussed in the lectures. Because he was not so myriad-minded as never to return to the same subject, corrections can also be proposed from similar assertions or allusions in his letters, marginalia, printed writings, and conversations recorded by persons more closely attuned than was the shorthand reporter. Any corrections from such sources, and any expansion from Coleridge's lecture notes, should of course be clearly identified not only in a diplomatic but also in a reading text of matter as uncertain as a lecture not read from a surviving manuscript. What is available in the extant materials is a "potential" rather than an "actual" text.

Of the lectures the best illustration is of the series of 1811–12 on Shakespeare and Milton. In 1883 Thomas Ashe gathered evidence from several sources. He reprinted from John Payne Collier seven of the announced seventeen lectures; from various newspapers briefer reports of three of the seven and of three others; and from Henry Crabb Robinson's diary brief comments on the lectures in general and on several in particular. Raysor reprinted virtually the same material.

When Collier first printed the *Seven Lectures on Shakespeare and Milton* "by the late S. T. Coleridge" in 1856, he was beginning to be charged publicly with forgery and falsification of records. In publishing his reports on Coleridge's lectures and conversation, he had as one of his purposes the defense of pretended discoveries that had been challenged by other scholars. In one or two brief passages he made Coleridge support his own fabrications, but most of Collier's many changes between manuscript and print would seem to be attributable merely to his irrepressible creative urges.

Collier said that most of his original shorthand notes had been destroyed and his transcriptions long mislaid. The materials he used for his edition of 1856—his transcriptions of the seven lectures and his diary recording remarks by Coleridge in conversation—survive in the Folger Shakespeare Library, which also holds photostats made in 1937 of two of Collier's shorthand notebooks that presumably survive somewhere yet. R. A. Foakes issued an interim report on these materials in 1971.[6] A fully annotated text, edited by Professor Foakes, will appear soon in the Collected Works of Coleridge published by the Princeton University Press. We can know what changes Collier made from his own transcriptions, and we can know that his transcriptions amplify and alter in other ways his shorthand notes. We know from the briefer reports by others that Coleridge is more responsible than Collier for most of what we quote as from Coleridge's series of 1811–12. What we do not know, and seem likely never to know, is the degree of congruence between Coleridge's words in 1811–12 and the words now available. Only a portion can be confirmed from records of what Coleridge said on other occasions. Not only demonstrably more reliable early in life than later, Collier by his abilities rather than by his character is the most nearly reliable reporter we have on what Coleridge said in public on Shakespeare at any one time.

My own responsibility in the Collected Works is for the *Table Talk*. The nephew's collection as it is generally known from his second edition of 1836 includes entries from Coleridge's notebooks and marginalia as well as from conversation originally recorded by Henry Nelson Coleridge and his brother John Taylor Coleridge. My copy-text for H.N.C.'s record—the most important single source for Coleridge's conversation—is taken from three work-books which include a diary that quickly became a dated record of remarks by Coleridge. The bulk of the record appears in the middle work-book, now in the library of Victoria University (in the University of Toronto) among papers of S. T. Coleridge. The beginning and end of the record are in the Harry Ransom Center of the University of Texas, Austin, among the papers of H.N.C. and other members of the family. After the earliest segment, of 1822-27, H.N.C. was both nephew and son-in-law. His notes increased from mere topic-headings at first to summaries of an argument and on to paraphrases of the core discussion on any topic. In print he sometimes fleshes out an early entry from a later return to the same subject. When he prints words, sentences, or paragraphs not in the manuscript diary and we find no other manuscript authority, he may be reporting conversation heard at another time, he may be drawing upon a manuscript source now unknown, he may be giving in his own words what he believes to be Coleridge's thought, or of course he may—however unconsciously—be giving his own thought in his own words. He makes no claim at any time in the *Table Talk* to report Coleridge's exact words.

Coleridge himself, arguing in *Confesssions of an Inquiring Spirit* that the Holy Bible, though certainly not dictated by God, was divinely inspired, imagines for analogy works by William Roper on Sir Thomas More and by William Rawley on Bacon containing "a series of *dicta* and judgments attributed to these illustrious Chancellors," with "many and important specimens of their table discourses."[7] First we must ask if there are any grounds "to doubt either the moral, intellectual, or circumstantial competence of the biographers." As Roper and Rawley pass this test, Coleridge pro-

poses two standards for checking new material against documents
and conversations reported previously by others:

> Suppose, moreover, that wherever the opportunity existed of collating
> their documents and quotations with the records and works still
> preserved, the former were found substantially correct and faithful, the
> few differences in no wise altering or disturbing the spirit and purpose
> of the paragraphs in which they were found, and that of what was not
> collatable, and to which no test *ab extra* could be applied, the far larger
> part bore witness in itself of the same spirit and origin; and that not
> only by its characteristic features, but by its surpassing excellence, it
> rendered the chances of its having had any other author than the
> giant-mind, to whom the biographer ascribes it, small indeed! (p. 28)

The tests he applies to the word of God can be applied to the
reported conversation of the "giant-mind" Coleridge. When we
distinguish credibility of content from credibility as rhythms of
speech, however, authenticity of content is called in question whenever we can produce a verbatim document from Coleridge himself.
Authenticity of content cannot assure authenticity of spontaneous
conversation on a declared date.

This second question comes to the fore in several diagrams that
appear in the midst of talk in H.N.C.'s printed versions. Is the reader
to imagine Coleridge drawing pyramids in the air with his finger, or
checking off one column with his left hand and a column of algebraic
equivalents with his right? Is one to imagine that Coleridge gave a
complicated explanation of these matters which the nephew simplified into a diagram for the reader? Collier's printed recollections
include a list of twenty-nine triads which Coleridge is said to have
"enumerated off-hand, and on-hand, for he noted them in succession upon his fingers"—with "some others, which I cannot remember."[8] We cannot believe that Collier remembered in detail what
Coleridge enumerated, not merely because this list is absent from
Collier's manuscript, but because we cannot believe that anybody at
any time reeled off such a list without being locked up at once as
insane. For H.N.C.'s diagrams, two happier explanations are available. We have similar diagrams in Coleridge's hand and in works
that he himself saw into print. We can imagine that he sketched such
diagrams on available paper or that he pointed to a diagram already
drawn. Most likely, for one or two of the diagrams or tables of
equivalents, H.N.C. borrowed appropriately from cognate
Coleridgean sources and called it conversation. A diagram on

"Blumenbach's scale of dignity," which appears in H.N.C.'s manuscript, is altered and transferred to a different date in the printed versions.[9]

H.N.C. offers the gist and not the exact wording. Memories were better trained then than now, however, and comments by Coleridge in print or in manuscript often confirm H.N.C.'s fidelity to disciplined vocabulary and verbal triumphs as well as to sense. For the student wishing to quote Coleridge, H.N.C. often gives a clearer and simpler version of a salient point than one can find in Coleridge's prose. It was not unusual for a hearer to follow Coleridge closely on a subject of special interest to the hearer. H.N.C. is one of only three or four who could (and did) give a convincingly faithful report of what Coleridge said on Thucydides, Rabelais, Kepler, the Council of Trent, atonement, hydrophobia, galvanism, and Wordsworth.

The dates of the printed versions are not those of the manuscript dairy, but the sequence is generally faithful. H.N.C. seems not to have made notes in Coleridge's presence, but it is probable that he sometimes made an intermediate record, perhaps on slips of paper now lost. Since the Coleridge family seldom threw away anything in the handwriting of any member of the family, the absence of any writing once extant points almost inevitably to a bad conscience rather than to carelessness—to an impression by some member of the family that no such record should reach posterity. In any event, revisions in the notebooks make the habit of an intermediate record by H.N.C. seem less likely than an occasional intermediate notation. There are two extant stages of parts of the whole between the work-books and the printed version of 1835, but they do not bear upon the reliability of the original record of spoken performance. Everything we know about Coleridge, as well as H.N.C.'s own statements, indicates that compression occurs everywhere in the record. Only persons with the intent of parodying Coleridge's manner attempted to suggest his transitions from one subdivision to another of a subject that in his mind was both extensive and seamless.[10]

Nothing has made the editing of H.N.C.'s manuscript more worth while than the censorship that intercepted many of Coleridge's remarks between manuscript and print. We learn of no illegitimate children or of months spent in a madhouse, and Coleridge's scatalogical raciness in letters and notebooks is absent from H.N.C.'s record of talk, perhaps censored out between ear and pen.

But the printed versions show Coleridge more reverent than the manuscript indicates toward the Bible, the Church, the clergy, and some of his less famous relatives and more famous friends.

Occasionally I have been able to determine from other sources, ranging from Coleridge's letters and notebooks to books that Coleridge read and encyclopedias that I have consulted, that H.N.C. heard a word incorrectly or not at all. The editor's nastiest chores arise when H.N.C. cannot read his own hand, when he finds the content too puzzling for confident transcription, or when he knew both originally and later that his notation was inadequate. In none of these cases is the editor simply confronted with an author's illegible manuscript: the performer S. T. Coleridge is always ready to speak through his nephew's manuscript to any editor who can overhear.

The nephew heard Coleridge refer to a lyric by Goethe that he particularly liked, but neither H.N.C. nor I have made anything of the scribbled abbreviations. The printed versions say, misleadingly, "Goethe's small lyrics are delightful." Under the published date of July 13, 1832, Coleridge is made to describe Herder as "seriously annoyed with himself" because he once failed to remember one name in a table of an electoral family. After years of reading journals and biographies of Herder (which puzzlingly omitted to mention that he *had* a memory), I was led by Coleridge's disciple John Sterling to the discovery that Coleridge must have said, not Herder, but—as incidental to the identification—"Herder's editor." Elsewhere in the record what may have been originally jewels have become pancakes. In oral transmission we may expect errors such as that in the New England ballad about the vessel "Amford Wright," which G. L. Kittredge deciphered as the *Amphritite*. Much more often, when the account is in prose, we may assume loss of detail: lyrics, not a particular lyric; Herder, not the editor of Herder.

Even the mishearing of a word can have unexpected consequences. As printed in the *Specimens of Table Talk* under the date of December 27, 1831, Coleridge is reported to have said, "the old definition of beauty in the Roman school of painting was, *il più nell'uno*—multitude in unity; and there is no doubt that such is the definition of beauty." We know from several sources that Coleridge preferred this definition of beauty to all others: no problem there. In H.N.C.'s manuscript this phrase is attributed to "Francesco Tessela." But he could not later find any account or other mention of this Francesco Tessela, nor could I. Sometimes Coleridge wrote the phrase as "uno nel più," the one in the many, so that the appearance of "il più nell'uno" three times in an identical form in the *Table Talk* itself indicates editorial care. In a manuscript note to a letter of July 1829 to William Sotheby, Coleridge wrote, *"PIÙ NEL UNO* is Francesco de Salez' brief and happy definition of the Beautiful. . . . "[11] Now, one logical explanation of this guise for St. Francis of Sales, pronounced by Coleridge as something near "Francesco Tessela," is that he owned a copy of an Italian translation of St. Francis's *Traité de l'amour de Dieu*. From the French or from its sense at the end of the first chapter of this work, that God reduces the multitude and distinctions of what is to a perfect unity, one would expect to find Coleridge's phrase in the Italian translation, but it has not been found there. From H.N.C.'s bad guess that his nonexistent "Tessela" belonged to "the Italian school of painting," the late Gian Orsini was led in desperation to propose that Coleridge might have heard the Italian phrase from some guide in a museum, presumably in Rome.[12] If in Rome, then Coleridge heard the phrase twenty years before he began to use it.

A sadist has been defined as one who is kind to masochists. By this definition, one who reports without a tape recorder the spoken words of another is kind to the future editor or biographer of that other.

NOTES

1. The reports in *Coleridge the Talker*, ed. Richard W. Armour and Raymond F. Howes (1940; 2nd ed., New York: Johnson Reprint Co., 1969), will be extended in the two volumes of *Table Talk* in *The Collected Works of Samuel Taylor Coleridge* in Bollingen Series LXXV of the Princeton University Press.

2. *The Literary Remains of Samuel Taylor Coleridge*, ed. Henry Nelson Coleridge (4 vols., London: Pickering, 1836–39).

3. *Notes and Lectures upon Shakespeare and Some of the Old Poets and Dramatists*, ed. Sara Coleridge (2 vols., London: Pickering, 1849); *Lectures and Notes on Shakspere and Other English Poets*, ed. T. Ashe (London: Bell, 1883); *Miscellanies Aesthetic and Literary*, ed. T. Ashe (London: Bell, 1885); Coleridge, *Shakespearean Criticism*, ed. T. M. Raysor (2 vols., Harvard University Press, 1930; 2nd, rev. ed. Everyman's Library, 1960); *Coleridge's Miscellaneous Criticism*, ed. T. M. Raysor (Harvard University Press, 1936).

4. Excessive faith in H. N. Coleridge's fidelity to sources, partly under the guise of attribution to Sara Coleridge, has been enunciated as a principle for a future

edition of *Biographia Literaria* by Norman Fruman, "Review Essay: Aids to Reflection on the New *Biographia*," *Studies in Romanticism* (Spring 1985), 24:141–73.

5. *The Philosophical Lectures of Samuel Taylor Coleridge*, ed. Kathleen Coburn (New York: Philosophical Library, 1949).

6. *Coleridge on Shakespeare: The text of the Lectures of 1811–12*, ed. R. A. Foakes (Charlottesville: University Press of Virginia, 1971).

7. "Edited from the Author's MS by Henry Nelson Coleridge Esq MA" (London: Pickering, 1840), pp. 27–28.

8. J. Payne Collier, "Preface," *Seven Lectures on Shakespeare and Milton by the late S. T. Coleridge* (London: Chapman and Hall, 1856), pp. xxix–xxxi.

9. *Specimens of the Table Talk of the Late Samuel Taylor Coleridge* (2 vols., London: Murray, 1835), I, 56.

10. One example, and the most famous, appears in Keats's journal-letter of 16 April 1819, *The Letters of John Keats*, ed. Hyder Edward Rollins (2 vols., Cambridge, Mass.: Harvard University Press, 1958), II, 88–89.

11. *The Collected Letters of Samuel Taylor Coleridge*, ed. Earl Leslie Griggs (6 vols., Oxford: Clarendon Press), VI, 799n.

12. *Coleridge and German Idealism* (Carbondale and Edwardsville: Southern Illinois University Press, 1969), p. 170.

Stevenson's Revisions of
Treasure Island:
"Writing Down the Whole Particulars"

DAVID D. MANN
and WILLIAM H. HARDESTY, III

The cornerstone of Robert Louis Stevenson's reputation, *Treasure Island* (serialized 1881-2, book version 1883), deserves more careful textual study than it has previously been given.[1] Because the book is often thought of as simply a children's story—one on almost everyone's list of favorite books—its textual history has largely been ignored.[2] Few people realize the importance of Stevenson's textual revisions to the success of the novel and to an understanding of his career.

The novel, Stevenson's first, was utterly unlike the novel he had long wanted to write. In 1876, he wrote to his confidante Mrs. Fanny Sitwell that he was writing a novel to be patterned on George Meredith's novels of manners, but the attempt was abandoned after several weeks.[3] Later, in May 1877, Stevenson wrote Mrs. Sitwell that he was beginning another novel, even giving her the plot of his anticipated tale.[4] But this too never got much farther than the planning stage. Putting this kind of novel aside for a while, Stevenson tried his hand at the horror tales, which he called "crawlers," and produced several short stories, but still no novel.

Between these early attempts at novel writing and his beginning of *Treasure Island*, Stevenson's personal life changed significantly.[5] He went to France, met Fanny Osbourne, an American married woman with two children, followed her to America, and, after her divorce, married her in California. The couple returned to Scotland for a reconciliation with Louis's displeased parents. In part because of their son's tuberculosis, the elder Stevensons not only accepted

Louis's new family but even spent a vacation period in the summer of 1881 with them at Braemar, Scotland. It was in this setting that *Treasure Island* began to take shape.

In order to entertain his stepson, Samuel Lloyd Osbourne, Louis began to tell a story about a map he had drawn: suddenly from the map Stevenson saw characters emerging, "fighting, and hunting treasure on these few square inches."[6] *Treasure Island* thus was born as a yarn including a boy narrator with whom Lloyd could identify. Writing to his friend W. E. Henley, Stevenson called the tale "The Sea Cook, or Treasure Island: A Story for Boys"—an indication of the author's early interest in Long John Silver. Since Stevenson worked without a plan, the narrative structure was necessarily episodic; early along he even confided to Henley that he had no notion of how he was going to end the tale.[7] Stevenson wrote in the morning and read after dinner to Lloyd; Fanny and Stevenson's parents joined the reading, as did occasional visitors, including Edmund Gosse.

Another visitor was Alexander Hay Japp, a correspondent who came to discuss an essay that Stevenson had written on Thoreau.[8] During his visit, Japp, hearing a portion of "The Sea Cook," asked the author if he could take the early chapters of the manuscript to James Henderson, a fellow Scot and editor of *Young Folks*. Agreeing to run the story in his weekly periodical for children, Henderson stipulated that the title be altered to *Treasure Island; or The Mutiny of the Hispaniola*, and that the tale be published under the pseudonym "Captain George North." Stevenson was now committed to finishing the novel.

What had been a lark turned into a chore when the family relocated from Scotland to Davos, Switzerland, because of Stevenson's poor health. He had been writing steadily, but now the narrative flow seemed to dry up: "Fifteen days I stuck to it, and turned out fifteen chapters, and then, in the early paragraphs of the sixteenth, ignominiously lost my hold. My mouth was empty; there was not one word more of *Treasure Island* in my bosom."[9] En route to Davos, Stevenson stopped to call on George Meredith at Weybridge. Despite the company and encouragement of the older novelist, he made little progress with his tale. He had reached a crucial point in the narrative where the story could no longer plausibly be continued from the boy narrator's point of view, and Stevenson was at a loss for a solution to this technical problem. He did, however, read proofs of the opening chapters and return them to Henderson.

Louis, Fanny, and Lloyd arrived in Davos as the first installments appeared in *Young Folks*, at a rate of about two chapters a week, beginning 1 October 1881. The move had broken Stevenson's concentration, yet he needed to press his work to completion. The problem was an all-too-familiar one, given his past writing history: a novel started in a great burst of energy, only to be abandoned when that initial surge gave out. Stevenson must have felt a desperate need to get on with the story, to recapture the lost momentum, despite his poor health and the added anxiety caused by the publication of the early chapters of his tale in *Young Folks*.

Hastily resettled, he resumed work on the novel. He solved the narrative problem by shifting the point of view from Jim to Dr. Livesey, who narrates three chapters (16 to 18 in the book text), after which Jim resumes the story and continues it to the conclusion. Stevenson describes the resumption of the novel thus: "down I sat one morning to the unfinished tale, and behold! it flowed from me like small talk; and in a second tide of delighted industry, and again at the rate of a chapter a day, I finished *Treasure Island*."[10] By the end of November 1881, Stevenson sent off the remaining chapters to Henderson. The eighteen-part serial wound to a conclusion in the *Young Folks* issue of 28 January 1882, without having stirred up much interest: Robert Leighton, of Henderson's staff, reported that Stevenson's serialized story did not raise the circulation "by a single copy."[11] So, quite casually, *Treasure Island* became the first book-length fiction by this writer who had wanted to write a novel for years but had instead produced only essays, short stories, and travel books.

That *Treasure Island* was crucial in Stevenson's writing career becomes apparent when we consider the pressures caused by the circumstances of its serial publication. As the date of relocation approached, the exhausted narrative flow was halted completely by worry over the details of the removal. Moreover, the presence of the author's parents—who not only disapproved of Stevenson's chosen profession as a writer, but also of his giving up his legal career—surely created tense moments. When Stevenson started his boys' yarn and the family became involved, tensions eased. Indeed, his father Thomas joined the spirit of the creative process by suggesting such items as the contents of Billy Bones's sea chest and Ben Gunn's love of cheese. In a way the tale helped Stevenson gain a psychological victory by reuniting the parents with their son and his new family. Still, Thomas was supporting not just Louis, but Fanny and Lloyd as well. Louis had enough pride to desire independence from his father's purse strings; he surely wished to support himself and his family by the craft of writing. On the other hand, he openly wondered how any craftsmanship could be involved in writing boys' books.[12] Nevertheless, having committed himself to the project, he would have to go through with it, for both money and pride. His father's stern Calvinism had taught him that much. Thus, hastily concluded under great stress, full of inconsistencies and infelicities, the manuscript was dispatched to Henderson.

With Henley looking after his literary interests in London, Stevenson could look after his own health at the sanitorium, aided by his physician, Dr. Ruedi, and the clear air. Yet even before the last chapters had been printed, Stevenson wrote to his father that he wanted to rework his novel: "You may be pleased to hear that I mean to re-write Treasure Id [sic] in the whole latter part, lightening and *siccating* throughout."[13]

It was not until 1883, however, that Henley, acting on Stevenson's behalf, sold the story to Cassell's, and Louis had the opportunity to turn his serialized yarn into a novel. After the contract for the novel was signed for the author by his lawyer Charles Baxter on 2 June 1883, Stevenson began to revise the manuscript. During that same summer, residing in Hyères in the south of France, he continued his revisions of *Treasure Island*, while writing *Black Arrow* (another serial running in *Young Folks*) and adding chapters to *Prince Otto*. Despite this activity, the revision of the serialization must have gone well, for he wrote to his father on 30 August 1883 that everything was submitted to Cassell's except the map, which he had to redraw because the original map was lost.

Whether Stevenson used the *Young Folks* text or his original manuscript for his revision, we cannot know because the manuscript and galleys have disappeared. Cassell's, in fact, does not know where they may be, or if they even exist, for the firm's archives were destroyed during the blitz of London.[14] A set of the serial parts with suggested changes is in the Beinecke Stevenson collection at Yale (item #1008), but the recommended alterations, mostly minor and probably the work of Stevenson's father, were largely ignored in the revision and subsequent book publication.[15]

When the book was prepared for the "Christmas market," only 500 of the approximately 2000 copies were bound. But the book version of *Treasure Island* succeeded beyond the publisher's, and perhaps the author's, expectations. Considering the lack of enthusiasm for the serialized version, *Treasure Island* was astoundingly successful as a book. Almost from the first appearance of the reviews in early December, 1883, the book was a classic. And the reviews were spectacularly good.[16] Cassell's, of course, bound the remaining copies and printed more to meet the demands of the English market. The American text, published by Roberts Brothers, Boston, in February, 1884, from stereotyped plates supplied by Cassell's, added four drawings. These drawings evidently encouraged Cassell's to publish an illustrated edition the following year with a decorated title page and twenty-one drawings, two from the American edition. Cassell's continued to pay royalties to Stevenson's estate until the copyright expired in 1944.[17] One hundred years after publication, the book is still in print and available from at least twenty-eight different publishers in the United States alone.

Since Stevenson had planned to revise his novel from as early as 1882, we believe that substantive additions and deletions must be those of the author himself. Although some accidentals can be identified as the house style of Cassell's, the "lightening and *siccating*" must have been done by Stevenson. A copy editor could, of course, have made minor suggestions, but it is unlikely that he would, without authority, tamper with the text. That Stevenson's instincts as a teller of oral narrative are correct is demonstrated by the fact that the published book has the same plot, cast of characters, and settings as the original yarn: most of that tale read aloud in Braemar survives in the first Cassell's edition of 1883—the most reliable text. But Stevenson's revisions of the serialized version show how the writer shifted the episodic, oral tale to a novel. These revisions are the subject of this essay. A close comparison of the two versions (serial and book text) demonstrates that he eliminated the unessential and flabby parts of the serial and touched up portions of the narrative with his additions. A study of these two versions, in fact, shows the extent of Stevenson's development in his craft.[18]

The deletions accelerate the events of the novel, eliminating unnecessary descriptions and purple passages and tightening up the action. After looking at the serialized version, a reader can easily notice the improved style: the writing is tighter, and extraneous details are cut, as in this passage (pp. 191–92; *Young Folks*, #575, deleted passages italicized):

> . . . I beheld huge slimy monsters—soft snails, as it were, of incredible bigness—two or three score of them together, making the rocks echo with their barkings. *Now they would wrestle, one with another, but whether in play or in earnest, I could in no way make out, now, as I say, they would drop from their rocks upon the water, for all the world like people bathing.*

Such editing has lightened the texture; moreover, it often accelerates the pace of the narration, since the reader is not forced to pause in the midst of the action for a descriptive or moralistic aside. This effect can also be seen in the following passage (p. 189; *Young Folks*, #575, deletions italicized):

> I glanced over my shoulder, and my heart jumped against my ribs. There, right behind me, was the glow of the camp fire. The current had turned at right angles, sweeping round along with it the tall schooner and the little dancing coracle; ever quickening, ever bubbling higher, even muttering louder, it went spinning through the narrows for the open sea.
>
> *I remembered the words of John Silver, that the channel "had been dug out with a spade." In a sudden lightening of the fog above me, I caught a glimpse of Skeleton Island, hard on my left hand. The coracle gave a bound like a stag's. A wave broke close by me with a glow of phosphorescence. The current had begun, grating on either shore, to give forth a low continuous growl.*
>
> Suddenly the schooner in front of me gave a violent yaw, turning, perhaps, through twenty degrees; and almost at the same moment one shout followed another from on board; I could hear feet pounding on the companion ladder; and I knew that the two drunkards had at last been interrupted in their quarrel and awakened to a sense of their disaster.

Stevenson's revision not only drops Jim's recollection of earlier events because it impedes the swiftness of the action, but also eliminates the didactic incorporation of facts found in the serial. All too frequently in Victorian fiction for children, writers were prone to be instructive in their tone and comments; Stevenson had followed the trend with unnecessary information about phosphorescence and geography. In the following passage he makes a similar cut, removing a few short paragraphs of indirect didacticism (p. 193; *Young Folks*, #575, deletions italicized):

... the coracle would bounce a little, dance as if on springs, and subside on the other side into the trough as lightly as a bird.

Speaking of birds, the gulls hung about me, fishing; seemed to have but little fear of my presence, and came with their white wings flashing past my head.

I lay, moving as little as might be, and made my breakfast of a biscuit. One only of my store was dry; the rest were soaked with salt sprays, and having no water with me, I had sense enough to leave these alone.

By the time I had done, up came the sun above the island, sparkled on the sea around me, and ran glinting down the craggy sides of the mountain. It warmed my heart through my jacket.

In sum, Stevenson deletes to make the events move swiftly, and to eliminate overwritten passages, didactic commentary, and excessively detailed description.

Since Victorian readers were used to windiness, such stylistic changes could not have been solely responsible for the runaway success of the novel. More significant are the changes Stevenson made in the characters he visualized emerging from the map, "fighting, and hunting treasure." The revisions that affect characterization fall into two groups: first, changes in the section narrated by Dr. Livesey, which make the doctor more humane and differentiate him more clearly from Squire Trelawney;[19] second, changes made in other major and minor characters, especially in the narrator and his adversary, to increase their complexity and to make their motivations more plausible.

The sort of revision that Stevenson performed to sharpen characterization can be clearly seen in a lesser figure, the marooned Ben Gunn, whom we observe in the serialized version as a shadowy Robinson Crusoe, clad in goatskins and concerned about his soul. Stevenson's father, in a letter written shortly after the conclusion of the serialization, pointed out both the shallowness of Ben's characterization and his resemblances to Crusoe. Thomas Stevenson further suggested inserting a passage "that should be a kind of religious *tract*."[20] The revisions only slightly modified Ben's attire, but did add eleven lines (p. 121, bracketed below) to explain Ben's going wrong. However, Stevenson's tone in the revised version lacks the piety his father might have desired:

"Jim, Jim," says he, quite pleased apparently. "Well now, Jim, I've lived that rough as you'd be ashamed to hear of. But it were Providence

that put me here. [Now, for instance, you wouldn't think I had had a
pious mother—to look at me?'' he asked.
"Why, no, not in particular,'' I answered.
"Ah, well,'' said he, "but I had—remarkable pious. And I was a
civil, pious boy, and could rattle off my catechism that fast, as you
couldn't tell one word from another. And here's what it come to Jim,
and it begun with chuck-farthen on the blessed gravestones. That's
what it begun with, but it went further'n that; and so my mother told
me and predicked the whole, she did, the pious woman.'']

During this chapter (15), Stevenson thus establishes an ironic parallel
between Jim and Ben, whom Jim describes as "like myself" (p.120).
Though both have affection for their mothers, they tend to ignore
their upbringing and to act on impulse. Both have reason enough to
regret rash actions, too: Jim's stowing away in the pirates' boat to
come ashore makes him a witness to murder, and his later running
away from the camp ultimately places him in the pirates' hands.
When Jim hears of Ben's yielding to an innocent impulse, Jim may
wonder if he has fallen into some moral trap that will cause him to
end up like the pirates.[21]

But beyond this, the book text gives an extra quality of native
sagacity to the apparently slow-witted, marooned sailor, a trait
which justifies Ben's finding and moving the treasure. More importantly, the empathy between Jim and Ben makes credible Ben's
throwing in his lot with the loyal party. Thus, Stevenson has
reinforced Ben's character with his additions, and these in turn affect
the plot. So while these additions poke gentle fun at the old
castaway, Ben Gunn becomes more sympathetic in Jim's and the
reader's eyes.

Stevenson's handling of hero and villain in the book text also
produces a depth not present in the serial. Not only does Stevenson
make the character of Jim Hawkins more believable, but he also
makes the character of Long John Silver more calculatingly subtle
through several additions. When Jim first meets the one-legged
innkeeper at Bristol, the Long John of the serial text is merely a bluff
seaman. By contrast, in the first edition, he becomes a consummate
actor who cleverly fools Jim after Black Dog's escape from the
Spyglass Inn by pretending not to know the pirate (pp. 65–66):

[Here I have this confounded son of a Dutchman sitting in my own
house, drinking of my own rum! Here you comes and tells me of it
plain; and here I let him give us all the slip before my blessed
dead-lights! Now, Hawkins, you do me justice with the cap'n. You're

a lad, you are, but you're smart as paint. I see that when you first came
in.]

Stevenson's addition to this monologue reduces Jim's suspicions
about Long John Silver, who blames himself for Black Dog's escape;
but note that, at the same time, he includes Jim in the general guilt—
"[he] give *us all* the slip" (our emphasis). He also flatters Jim so that
the boy will do him justice with Trelawney, here called "cap'n" to
increase the Squire's importance. Silver, thus, is shown to be a more
wily man of affairs. Stevenson's additions now better support Jim's
earlier remark that the old sea cook "was too deep, and too ready,
and too clever for me" (p. 65). And readers can more easily
understand why Jim "would have gone bail for the innocence of
Long John Silver" (p. 65).

Silver's increased geniality leads to a greater shock for the reader
during the first events on Treasure Island, when Jim witnesses
Silver's villainy. Stevenson revises the passage narrating Silver's
murder of the seaman Tom to show Long John as a more controlled
and ruthless pirate than we had imagined. *Young Folks* reads (#570,
deletions italicized):

> With a cry, John whipped the crutch out of his armpit, and, *bereft of
> his support, rolled face forward on the ground; but, at the same instant,*
> that uncouth missile, hurtling through the air, struck poor Tom, point
> foremost, and with stunning violence, right between the shoulders in the
> middle of the back.

Contrast this with the book text (pp. 114–15, additions bracketed):

> With a cry, John [seized the branch of a tree,] whipped the crutch out
> of his armpit, and [sent] that uncouth missile hurtling through the air.
> [It] struck poor Tom, point foremost, and with stunning violence, right
> between the shoulders in the middle of the back.

Silver's calculated actions and his coolness in the situation demonstrate his right to be leader of the pirates. No longer does he act in a
hot-headed fashion and then roll absurdly on the ground; rather, he
commits a carefully premeditated murder as if it were all in a day's
work. Stevenson has thus made Silver both more ruthless and more
self-controlled.

Besides this careful sharpening of Silver's villainous character,
Stevenson makes Jim Hawkins a more consistent protagonist, who
has a greater control of the situation than in the serialized version.
It is, in fact, this strengthening of Jim that might be said to overcome

the story's lack of success in *Young Folks*. Since the events of the novel are mainly his story, Stevenson gives him additional self-assurance and competence in order to increase his heroism and to improve the reader's identification with him. Several passages pointing out exhaustion or physical weakness are deleted, as is a paragraph criticizing the adults in the loyal party. On the other hand, Stevenson's additions promote greater empathy by giving the reader a glimpse of Jim's mental state—particularly his most secret hopes and fears.

Very early in the story, for example, Jim is paid by Billy Bones to be on the lookout for "the seafaring man with one leg." The book text (p. 4, additions bracketed below) goes into much more detail than the two sentences of the serialized version:

> How that personage haunted my dreams, I need scarcely tell you. On stormy nights, when the wind shook the four corners of the house, and the surf roared along the cove and up the cliffs, I would see him in a thousand forms, and with a thousand diabolical expressions. [Now the leg would be cut off at the knee, now at the hip; now he was a monstrous kind of creature who had never had but one leg, and that in the middle of his body. To see him leap and run and pursue me over hedge and ditch was the worst of nightmares. And altogether I paid pretty dear for my monthly fourpenny piece, in the shape of these abominable fancies.]

What Stevenson has done here is to give Jim's personality a depth not found in the serialization. In the original transaction between Jim and Billy Bones, Jim simply watches for the seafaring man with one leg and is rewarded with a fourpenny piece. But in the book text, Jim experiences such frightful dreams that he lives in continual fear. The addition emphasizes Jim's constant anxieties through the repeated use of the word "now" and the extended infinitive phrase.

With the rewritten passage, Stevenson better sets up the incident in chapter 8 when Jim actually meets the one-legged Silver at the Spyglass Inn. The genial tavernkeeper is utterly unlike the fearful, protean monster of Jim's nightmares. Jim (and the reader) are consequently lulled into trusting Silver, despite Jim's explicit fears (p. 62) that the innkeeper may turn out to be the specter of the dreams. The nightmares begin to come true when, in the apple barrel (chapter 11), Jim hears Long John's bloody threats, but he does not witness Silver's full depravity until, on the island, Long John fells a seaman with his crutch and stabs his defenseless body (chapter 14). Jim's "abominable fancies" have become a reality.

Stevenson's additions also emphasize Jim's romantic expectations about the treasure hunt. For instance, when Jim leaves home with Redruth to go to Bristol, he originally remarks: "I said good-bye to mother and the cove where I had lived since I was born, and the dear old 'Admiral Benbow.'" Stevenson then adds this sentence to Jim's remarks about his departure: "[One of my last thoughts was of the captain, who had so often strode along the beach with his cocked hat, his sabre-cut cheek, and his old brass telescope]" (p. 58). Here Jim looks nostalgically backward to Billy Bones, who changed his life with the treasure map. But the added sentence also looks forward to the emblems that Jim expects to find when he encounters other pirates: a cocked hat, physical mutilation, a telescope. And this remembrance precludes any sentimentality in Jim's first departure from his home and mother: "next moment we had turned the corner, and my home was out of sight."

Whereas such additions tend to give Jim greater psychological complexity, the deletions seem designed to reduce certain unpleasant traits in his original characterization: he becomes less priggish and less querulous. Gone are such passages as this complaint about the adults' handling of the defense of the stockade (p. 155; deletions from *Young Folks*, #573, italicized):

> . . . the three chiefs got together in a corner to discuss our prospects. *I do not mean to blame anyone, but it might have been better if they had taken us more fully into their confidence. The result of that council, and the various questions discussed, were of great importance to all; yet we never knew their decision till long after.*

Gone, too, are long-winded explanations, such as this one, where Jim is shown as indecisive and voicing ideas that sound much more like Dr. Livesey (p. 185; deletions from *Young Folks*, #575, italicized):

> One cut with my sea-gully, and the *Hispaniola* would go humming down the tide.
>
> *So far, all was well for my adventure. But there was another side to the question. If this strong tide were the very thing required to strand the ship, it was likewise the very thing to make my return impossible.*
>
> *Plainly, in this unmanageable boat, and with this rapid current, it was out of the question to go back. But then I could still go forward; the current was bound to throw me on the west shores of the anchorage;*

> *thence going round by the heads of the rivers, over the shoulder of the*
> *Spyglass, and past the place where I had met Ben Gunn, I could avoid*
> *the pirates' camp, and get safely back to the stockade. I had the map*
> *very clear in my head, and I saw it would be a mere pleasure walk of*
> *eight or ten, or, at the outside, twelve miles, to give me an appetite for*
> *dinner.*

Besides making additions and deletions, Stevenson completely recast some passages. In them, Jim's stance is made more self-confidently heroic, as on p. 193 (brackets; deletions from *Young Folks*, #575, italicized):

> I began [after a little] *immediately* to [grow very bold] *be filled with*
> *hope*, and *at once* sat up to try my skill at paddling.

When Jim returns to the stockade to find the pirates in possession, he is made less of a childish braggart than he was originally in the serial (deletions from *Young Folks*, #577, italicized):

> *And if you ask me how I did it, tortures wouldn't drive me, in the first*
> *place; and, in the second, much good it would do you, now the harm's*
> *done, and you ruined. And now you can kill me, if you please. The*
> *laugh's on my side. I've as good as hanged you, every man, and I'm not*
> *fifteen till my next birthday.*

In the book text, Jim bargains, rather than brags; he is more honorable and more obviously in control of both himself and the situation (p. 232):

> [The laugh's on my side; I've had the top of this business from the first;
> I no more fear you than a fly. Kill me, if you please, or spare me. But
> one thing I'll say, and no more; if you spare me, bygones are bygones,
> and when you fellows are in court for piracy, I'll save you all I can. It
> is for you to choose. Kill another and do yourselves no good, or spare
> me and keep a witness to save you from the gallows.]

In such additions to the book text, Stevenson has shifted from the oral style to a more subtle texture meant for careful reading.

What may be a quintessential example of the additions occurs during the period between Jim's acquisition of the map and his setting out for the island. Jim in the serial version merely lives on at Trelawney's house, "full of sea-dreams and the most charming anticipations of strange islands and adventures." The following passage is added in the book text (p. 54):

> [I brooded by the hour together over the map, all the details of which
> I well remembered. Sitting by the fire in the housekeeper's room, I

approached that island, in my fancy, from every possible direction; I explored every acre of its surface; I climbed a thousand times to that tall hill they call the Spyglass, and from the top enjoyed the most wonderful and changing prospects. Sometimes the isle was thick with savages, with whom we fought; sometimes full of dangerous animals that hunted us; but in all my fancies nothing occurred to me so strange and tragic as our actual adventures.]

Jim's daydreams show him as a highly imaginative boy, eager for adventure. The passage thus increases empathy between the reader and the protagonist, who jointly share enthusiasm for excitement and vicarious danger. More importantly, the addition affects the reader in two ways. First, it whets the reader's interest by promising new landscapes and new adversaries. Second, it sets up for more alert readers a series of ironies, by indicating directions the novel is not going to take. There will be no savages, but there will be the expected pirates—criminals capable of actions every whit as despicable as those of any savages. Neither will there be wild animals, unless one counts the often drunken and sometimes bestial buccaneers—who are, indeed, compared with (or referred to as) animals of various sorts.[22]

Jim romantically expects a clean, well-lighted adventure, without realizing that life is always less tidy and glamorous than daydreams. He clings to these expectations, despite having already met Pew, Billy Bones, and Black Dog—clearly denizens of the seamy underside of British life. He has also survived the pirates' night attack on the Admiral Benbow Inn. When Jim actually reaches Treasure Island, he (and the reader) should not be surprised at spending no time on Spyglass Hill but a good deal in the miasmic swamps. The real adventure is terrifying (witness Silver's murder of Tom, discussed above), as well as both dirty and dangerous.[23] During his time on Treasure Island, Jim lives with death and the threat of death: he almost drowns in his attempt to recapture the ship, he is wounded in his fight with Israel Hands, and he is twice saved from pirate executioners.

The revised text both recalls the fictional past and foreshadows later occurrences while the reader is tantalized by expectations and denials. In some later events, Jim's fancies come to naught; in others his most extravagant imaginings are more than fulfilled. Jim's yearning for adventure is stressed in Stevenson's revisions but so is his anxiety. His psychological make-up is thus validated. Such increased complexity is typical of Stevenson's manipulation of the conventions of the nineteenth-century boys' novel.[24] The stylistic excellence of Stevenson's novel and, more importantly, the sharpened characterization set this book apart from the genre into which it was born. Insofar as these are heightened by Stevenson's revisions, the process of turning yarn into book was also the turning of mere story into art. The *Young Folks* text has the tale, but the full impact depends on "the whole particulars," as Jim calls them in the first paragraph of the novel. The key, as Jim himself says, is writing them down.

NOTES

1. We wish to acknowledge the valuable help of Jay Berry, now of the University of Iowa, for his assistance in the collation of the texts.

2. Roger G. Swearingen, *The Prose Writings of Robert Louis Stevenson: A Guide* (Hamden, CT: Shoe String Press, 1980), pp. 63-70, is one literary historian who has examined the circumstances involved in the publication of the novel.

3. Stevenson's platonic relation with Mrs. Sitwell, later Lady Colvin, is described by David Daiches, *Robert Louis Stevenson and his World* (London: Thames and Hudson, 1973), pp. 27-28.

4. *Letters: Vol. I, 1859-1879*, ed. Sir Sidney Colvin, *Works*, Skerryvore Edition (London: William Heinemann, et al., 1926), 27: 303, 311-314.

5. We have used J. C. Furnas, *Voyage to Windward: The Life of Robert Louis Stevenson* (London: Faber & Faber, 1952), James Pope Hennessy, *Robert Louis Stevenson* (London: Methuen, 1974), and Jenni Calder, *Robert Louis Stevenson: A Life Study* (New York: Oxford University Press, 1980), to supply biographical information in this part of our discusssion.

6. "My First Book," in *Treasure Island*, *Works*, Skerryvore Edition (London: William Heinemann, et al., 1924) 2: xxx. References to the text of the novel are to the first edition (London: Cassell and Company Ltd., 1883); citations to chapter and page are included in the text of our essay. A Xerox copy of the *Young Folks* serialization (#565 to #582) was generously supplied to us by the Osborn Collection of the Toronto Public Library.

7. *Works, Letters: Vol. II, 1880-1887*, Skerryvore, 28: 58.

8. Alexander Hay Japp, *Robert Louis Stevenson* (London: T. Werner Laurie, 1905), p. 162.

9. Swearingen, p. 65.

10. Quoted in Swearingen, p. 66. He also cites Fanny Stevenson's recollection that the novel was only finished "intermittently," and that, if the serialization had not already begun, "I doubt if it would ever have been finished."

11. In Hammerton, *Stevensoniana*, pp. 54–56, cited by Furnas, p. 437. See also James Dow [proofreader at *Young Folks*], "Robert Louis Stevenson and the *Young Folks* Reader," in Masson, ed., *I Can Remember Robert Louis Stevenson* (1922), p. 209, cited by Swearingen, p. 66.

12. *Letters, II*, 57. Also in *Robert Louis Stevenson: the Critical Heritage*, ed. Paul Maixner (London: Routledge & Kegan Paul, 1981), pp. 124–25.

13. National Library of Scotland, Acc. 7165, quoted by Swearingen, p. 66. By "siccating," we assume that Stevenson meant a drying out of, perhaps, the over-lush prose descriptions. A number of these passages are deleted or reduced.

14. Letter from Cassell's to the authors, April 1976.

15. We wish to thank Professor David H. Jackson, Centenary College of Louisiana, for assisting us in our inquiries into this marked, pasted-up scrapbook. Our essay describing Stevenson's response to these proposed changes is in progress.

16. Examples may be found in Maixner, pp. 128–41.

17. Swearingen, pp. 63, 67.

18. Because of limited space in this article, we are unable to provide a complete listing of the more than two thousand changes made in the book text; this must await our critical edition of *Treasure Island*. Many of the deletions, however, come in the chapters (19 and following) when Jim resumes the narrative, written during, or shortly after, the move to Davos. Clearly, Stevenson's attempts at composition lacked the usual drive.

19. These revisions are discussed at length in P. W. Hardesty, W. H. Hardesty, and D. D. Mann, "Doctoring the Doctor," *Studies in Scottish Literature*, 21 (1986), 1–26.

20. Maixner, pp. 126–27. T. E. Stevenson's letter of 26 Feb. 1882. Emphasis in original.

21. Another parallel is simultaneously set up. Since Ben Gunn is a simple, good man led astray, he appears less a pirate by nature than because of bad companions. Later (chapters 28–32), we read about a young pirate, Dick, who

is led astray but who clings to his Bible. The actual phrases about Dick and his Bible are also added in the first edition. For example, when the pirates hear Ben Gunn wailing in the trees about Darby McGraw, Stevenson adds: "Dick had his Bible out, and was praying volubly. He had been well brought up, had Dick, before he came to sea and fell among bad companions" (p. 270). Stevenson is, thus, consistent in the various echoes he sets up in his additions to the novel. When we read about Dick, we may be expected to remember how, years ago, Ben Gunn fell among similar evil companions.

22. Such as "dogs" (p. 132), "owls" (p. 195), "bulls" (p. 213), "food for fish" (p. 218), "cats upon a mouse" (p. 244), "bird" (p. 247), and "bear" (p. 260).

23. Ironically, one of the first killed is Redruth, the retainer who protected Jim when he dreamed the daydreams at Trelawney's house.

24. W. H. Hardesty and D. D. Mann, "Stevenson's Method in *Treasure Island*: 'The Old Romance, Retold,' " *Essays in Literature*, 9 (1982), 180–193.

Technological Artifacts as Historical Documents

ROBERT ROSENBERG

In *The Historian's Craft*, Marc Bloch says, "It would be sheer fantasy to imagine that for each historical problem there is a unique type of document with a specific sort of use. . . . In an age when the machine is supreme, should a historian be allowed to ignore how machines are designed and modified?"[1] That brazen and singular pronouncement aside, it would not be hard to make the introduction to this discussion negative; that is, to point out how, time and again, a historical or literary editor has avoided including nonverbal material in a definition of documents. But that would be unfair, because until quite recently editors have dealt with political, literary, and scientific figures whose intellectual traces have been verbal documents such as letters, diaries, and manuscripts—documents composed of words or mathematical symbols. A fundamental premise of historical editing has been that the essence of the persons treated has lain in those writings. In the last few years, documentary editors have take the opportunity to tackle figures of a new kind— inventors and engineers. Presenting them in letterpress form has introduced some interesting problems, for the most significant aspects of their thought and work were not always presented in words. It is increasingly an article of faith among the historians and philosophers of technology that the core of technological thinking— design—involves nonverbal reasoning. As one historian has said, such reasoning is "involved in most intellectual activity . . . , but in technology it has to be central."[2] The manifestation of technological thinking is often a drawing or an artifact.

At the Edison Papers, we have had to meld the traditions of documentary editing with the often nonverbal legacy of Edison's career. Edison was, of course, more than an inventor. He was also an

393

entrepreneur, an innovator, a businessman, and early enough in life a folk hero, and the hundreds of thousands of verbal documents in the West Orange archive illuminate him in these roles. But his inventions were the heart of his work. They are the reason he has our attention in the first place. And Edison's artifacts contain information that is not otherwise available—not in published descriptions of the instruments and their uses, not in his notes, and not in drawings. Consequently, we have decided not only to include Edison's sketches and drawings as documents, but also to go one step further and treat the devices themselves as documents. That is, not only are we treating artifacts in the volumes, but we are using the traditional tools and forms of documentary editing to do it.

In developing a method for editing artifacts, we have found that a strong analogy can be drawn between verbal and artifactual documents, especially with respect to two fundamental characteristics, authorship and date. In the same way that a written text embodies verbal intellection, a physical artifact embodies a design. Just as the writer may use a pen or an amanuensis, the inventor may build a device or have it built. In either case, authorship belongs to the conceiver, not the recorder, of the ideas. We know that Edison almost always had machinists constructing his inventions. By analogy, he often gave his secretary the general sense of a reply to a letter, which the secretary then fleshed out. Just as he was the author of that letter, so was he the designer of his device, and it is irrelevant whether the machinist chose this or that screw size in embodying Edison's idea in three dimensions.

Dating an artifact is similarly analogous to dating a verbal document. The time of composition of the original document determines the date assigned. For an artifact, "time of composition" becomes the appearance of the first of a type, and all preliminary models, sketches, and writings are as notes for a manuscript. Depending on the method of manufacture, subsequently created artifacts of that type may be seen as transcriptions or as copies of an edition, with states, issues, cancels, and so on. Occasionally we have the original artifact, but far more often we have a transcription or copy.

Reducing editorial theory to practice is, of course, most of the work. We had to decide which artifacts to present, what form to use, how to treat them editorially, and what information to provide as annotation.

Document selection is always a challenge for historical editors faced with too much to publish. The basis for selection is the importance of the information contained in the document. This is as true for artifacts as for other documentary forms. For example, in the years around 1870 Edison devised scores of telegraphic devices. Many were minor variations on his basic designs for printing telegraphs or trivial adaptations of earlier devices, not immediately practical and created for protection against patent encroachment or at a patron's request. We bring this work of Edison's to the readers' attention, but artifacts embodying such patents will not be selected. Some artifacts, however, were significant for their technological novelty, their technological antecedents, their place in Edison's business dealings, or their commercial importance. Those will appear in the books.

The Edison National Historic Site in West Orange, New Jersey, the central repository for Edison's papers and artifacts, has relatively few artifacts from the first years of Edison's inventive and manufacturing career, when he dealt primarily in printing, automatic, and multiplex telegraphy. The site's principal artifactual resource for that period is officially designated as Catalogue #551. Assembled around the end of 1872, it comprises 50 photographs of early printing telegraph instruments. Some are Edison's; some are not. Fortunately, the reconstructed Menlo Park laboratory in Henry Ford's Greenfield Village in Dearborn, Michigan, contains nearly all of Edison's early patent models as well as a few production instruments. The Smithsonian also holds a few Edison artifacts from this period.

One can learn a remarkable amount by handling or working an artifact of any kind. When a Smithsonian team got the pioneering nineteenth-century locomotive "John Bull" on the track and running in 1980, they gained "insights into the history and design of the locomotive . . . [that] could only have come from the actual hands-on experience of running and operating the engine."[3] Similarly, when historian Robert Howard researched the interchangeability of parts in nineteenth-century American firearms, he did more than read accounts and discuss the question with manufacturers and collectors; he had the guns disassembled and the parts tested for interchangeability.[4] There is no substitute for manipulating the machines at first hand. Since, however, only the most dedicated or fortunate researchers will have such an opportunity, the Edison

Papers staff members have to supply as much of that information as possible.

Just as the published transcription of a verbal text ought to reflect the original as closely as possible, the transcription of an artifactual document ought to be a faithful reproduction. Accordingly, in the best of all possible worlds, our readers would have in hand full-size, authentic copies of instruments. Failing that, we have discussed several alternatives. Holograms would be wonderful, but are obviously on the wrong side of the technological and economic frontier. Images on videotape or videodisc could convey a great deal of information, but budgetary considerations as well as editorial constraints—particularly the difficulty of satisfactory integration with the other documents—preclude such treatment. The artifacts will be presented in the volumes as photographic reproductions. A great deal is lost in the transcription—motion, noise, smells—even more, perhaps, than in a four-square-inch black and white reproduction of a Monet painting—but for the present it is the only practical solution.

Traditionally, documentary editions present annotative information in headnotes, footnotes, and textnotes. Because it is impossible to footnote a photograph, we have divided our annotation between a headnote that introduces the artifactual document and a textnote that follows the photograph and discusses the particular artifact chosen. There is frequently a footnote appended to the date of the artifact. The main editorial departures introduced by this treatment are: first, each artifactual document has a headnote, which few verbal documents in such large collections do; and second, the textnote contains considerably more information than for an average verbal document.

I can best illustrate what all this means with two examples. The first is Edison's universal stock printer (Figures 1 and 2). Edison designed it in early 1871, roughly three and a half years after Edward Calahan invented the stock ticker, and its basic form became an industry standard for over two decades. The introductory headnote discusses the instrument generally, beginning with information about design and manufacture. From accounting records, we know that Edison made a wooden model and two prototypes before beginning production; we know when he began production; and we have a record of the dates on which the serially numbered machines were delivered. Although we have had to assign dates to some artifacts

Figure 1

Figure 2

with uncertainties of months, in this case the account books allow us to date the universal stock printer to within a few weeks. From other sources we have a good idea of where and how the instruments were used.

The next portion of the headnote is a discussion of the technical aspects of the machine. This is not a detailed description of the printer's mechanism or circuitry, which can be best obtained from the patent specifications available in our microfilm edition. Its purpose is only to give a schematic notion of the technical principles involved and to show which elements of the universal stock printer (including the overall form) were adapted from Edison's earlier work, which were from others' work, and which were new. The annotation's technical level is just deep enough to illuminate the kinds of problems encountered and solved in the machine's design. Additionally, we have in this case sketches that appear to show Edison working out solutions to a couple of the machine's design problems (Figures 3 and 4). These drawings will accompany the headnote as captioned illustrations.

The headnote also discusses what is perhaps the most interesting mechanical aspect of the universal stock printer—something of which we could not be sure without having the artifacts at hand. Its parts were interchangeable. Edison managed this not by stringent manufacturing standards, but by designing the machine to be sufficiently adjustable to accommodate the parts he made. The claim of interchangeability was made in a company instruction pamphlet and supported by shop records of "boxes of parts shipped," but such claims had been unjustifiably made before by other manufacturers. In this case it was confirmed by examining the artifacts at Dearborn. Edison's cotton instruments—the design supplanted by the universal stock printer—had numbers stamped on their individual parts; the universal's parts had no such numbers. (These numbers were used when parts were not made precisely enough to fit together on first assembly. They enabled workers to keep track of parts for reassembly after the machine was dismantled and the parts filed to make them fit.)[5] I have also spent several hours actually adjusting a machine to get it working, and I learned first-hand that a large manufacturing tolerance could be forgiven by the universal stock printer's design.

The end of the headnote mentions the many notes and drawings

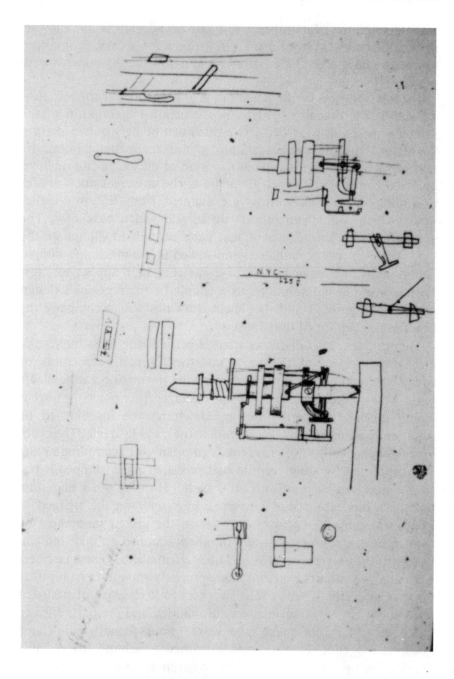

Figure 3

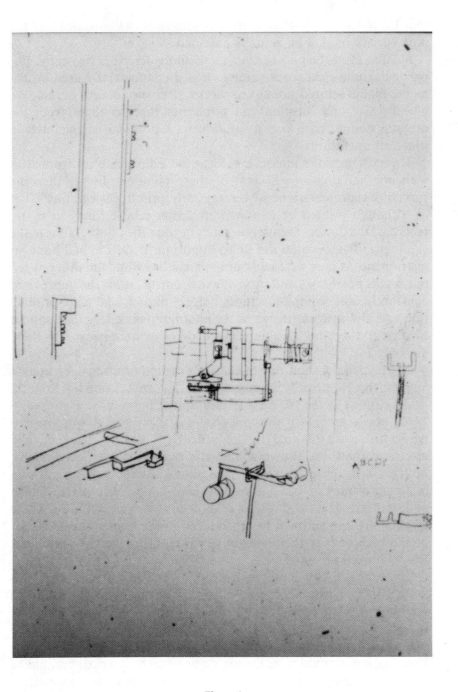

Figure 4

that Edison made describing modifications of the universal and the nine variations that he actually patented.

Finally, after the photographs, a textnote describes this copy, this particular universal stock printer. It is a commercially used instrument, manufactured about ten weeks after production began. We give its size and location and point out three changes from the original design, each one a solution to a problem encountered in practical operations.

The existence of Catalogue #551 at the Edison site confronted us with another decision. Several of these photographs are the only surviving representations of certain early printing telegraphs. That is, although printed or handwritten documentation may exist, no record of the devices themselves exists beyond the photographs in the catalogue. These would not be so important if Edison had built his instruments as they were laid out in patent drawings and other plans, but, as his notebooks and surviving instruments show, he improvised constantly, altering the machines before, during, and after production. As the instruments in these photographs reflect that sort of tinkering, they are invaluable records of contemporary working machines.

Figures 5 and 6 show one of Edison's earliest printing telegraphs—his fourth. He created it in collaboration with Franklin Pope, a leading figure in the New York telegraphic community. Designed in 1870, one year before the universal stock printer, it was used to report the price of gold to the offices of brokers, bankers, and merchants and was known as the gold printer. These photographs, both from the catalogue mentioned above, are the only images of a real gold printer we have, although there is a wooden patent model at Dearborn. Hence, these serve as a historic transcription of the original artifact and will be reproduced in the book. This is hardly unprecedented, for the analogous procedure for verbal documents has long been accepted.

For example, we have an Edison verbal document—what was known as a caveat, a sort of preliminary patent application filed to establish priority. It is not in Edison's hand, and we have no original. It was apparently copied from the original by one of Edison's manufacturing partners, a semiliterate fellow named Joseph Murray. Punctuation is random, as Edison's was when he hurried, but, unlike Edison's writing, the spelling is capricious and the sense often obscure (as when he writes, "B is a friction pulling rotated by foot or

Figure 5

Figure 6

other power, and carries the type wheel shaft A are used by friction"). The diagram to which the document's many letters and numbers refer is missing. The gold printer photographs are in many ways like that caveat copy. Just as there is information lost to us in the transcription of the caveat by Joseph Murray, so is there information irrevocably lost in the photographs. Shortcomings in clarity of focus, depth of field, and contrast—to say nothing of the views we do not have, like the underside of the base—all of these frustrate us terribly when we try to understand artifacts in historic photographs. In the gold printer, what happened to the switching device that, according to the patent drawing, ought to be in the middle of the base? The original design had only two binding posts for wires; the photographs show four. What were the circuits?

We can surmise, but we do not know. One point in favor of the historic photograph, however, is that if we can date it accurately we do not have to worry about whether the text is corrupt—that is, whether the device we are describing has been altered or restored between that date and the present, which is always a concern when dealing with artifacts. It is an interesting difference between verbal and artifactual material that what would usually be a corruption in a verbal text is often—even from the perspective of authorial intent—an improvement in an artifact, whether made by the author or another.

What do we have to say about the gold printer? The structure of the headnote that introduces these pictures is much like that for the universal stock printer. It begins with a statement of authorship—that is, that Edison and Pope designed it—of purpose—that they designed it in order to sell patent rights to a specific company—and of actual use. In this case, we have no manufacturing data of any sort. The technical portion of the headnote elucidates the working of the gold printer (which is especially clever) in the same fashion as the note on the universal stock printer did.

Because we have few notebooks or sketches for Edison's earliest years, we have had to use the date of the signing of the patent application as the date for the gold printer as well as for several other artifacts. This is unfortunately inaccurate, rather like dating a manuscript by the resultant book's publication date.

The textnote, appended to the photographs, again describes the specific machine pictured, labeling it a historic transcription, giving its size—in this case, since we have only photographs, an estimated size—and pointing out the questions that arise from differences between its appearance and the patented design.

Edison's artifacts, whether extant, as the universal stock printer, or transcribed photographically, as the gold printer, do more than just provide useful information. They give an almost tactile sense of Edison's achievements, and they provide an important complement to the discussion of those achievements. We have many sources of information, and most wind up in footnotes. To relegate the artifacts to footnotes or to use them as mere illustrations for verbal documents would subordinate the substance of technology to its description. Although treating artifacts as documents seems only natural in Edison's case, it raises new issues in documentary editing. We at the Edison Papers are not certain that we have found the best way to deal with this new documentary source—at least new to documentary editing—but we think that presenting the artifacts as annotated documents will bring the reader a fuller sense of Edison's work and world.

NOTES

1. M. Bloch, *The Historian's Craft* (New York: Vintage Books, 1953), pp. 67-68.

2. Eugene Ferguson, "The Mind's Eye: Nonverbal Thought in Technology," *Science*, 197 (1977):827-36. See also Edwin Layton, Jr., "Technology as Knowledge," *Technology and Culture*, 15 (1974):31-41; *idem*, "Science and Engineering Design," *Annals of the New York Academy of Sciences*, 424 (1984):173-81; Brooke Hindle, *Emulation and Invention* (New York: New York University Press, 1981), esp. pp. 93, 136-37.

3. Quoted in D. Stapleton's review of John H. White, *The John Bull: 150 Years a Locomotive* (Washington, D.C.: Smithsonian Institution Press, 1981), in *Technology and Culture*, 23 (1982):640.

4. Robert A. Howard, "Interchangeable Parts Reexamined: The Private Sector of the American Arms Industry on the Eve of the Civil War," *Technology and Culture*, 19 (1978):636, n. 4.

5. D. Hounshell, *From the American System to Mass Production* (Baltimore: The Johns Hopkins University Press, 1984), chapter 2 and appendix 2.

LEGENDS

Figures 1 and 2. Edison's 1871 universal stock printer.

Figures 3 and 4. In these sketches Edison is proposing designs for several components of his universal stock printer, notably the mechanism for shifting the typewheels back and forth so one or the other would print and a design for the "unison stop" that prevented individual tickers from getting out of step with others on the same circuit.

Figures 5 and 6. Edison and Pope's gold printer.

The Fading Coal vs.
The Gothic Cathedral
or
What To Do about an Author both
Forgetful and Deceased

EDWARD MENDELSON

All editors—I imagine all readers—carry around with them one of two archetypal models of the process by which works of literature get written. All the sophisticated, rigorously logical theories of editing and of authorship that have appeared over the past few decades are, I think, elaborate versions of one or the other of these primary models. An editor's preference for one rather than the other is, almost certainly, a matter more of temperament than of logic. This means that no one is going to be persuaded by argument to abandon one model for the other—although I think it probable that some editors do, on their own, outgrow one and embrace the other.

The first of these models, and in the past two centuries surely the more popular, received its most emphatic expositon in Shelley's "Defence of Poetry." Shelley wrote:

> The mind in creation is as a fading coal, which some invisible influence, like an inconstant wind, awakens to transitory brightness. . . . Could this influence be durable in its original purity and force, it is impossible to predict the greatness of the results; but when composition begins, inspiration is already on the decline, and the most glorious poetry that has ever been communicated to the world is probably a feeble shadow of the original conception of the Poet.

This means, in the version of Shelley's argument believed by many readers and editors, that the most significant, the most revealing, moment of literary composition is the earliest, that we understand most about a work when we make the closest possible approach to its original idea. Everything that comes afterward is more or less dross. I do not know of any editor who has sought to publish a version of a text so close to an author's original idea that it precedes the composition of the text, but any editor who strives to present an early or original version of a text is almost certainly a partisan of the fading-coal model of authorship. In practice, this is an editor who believes that later revisions are not only less important than early drafts, but that they ought not to be trusted—because the author who revises, though he bears the same name, is almost certain to have grown out of sympathy with the author who composed. This sort of editor can be counted on to champion an author's younger and more vigorous self against his older and presumably more cautious one, and prefers (as who would not?) a red and glowing coal to a grey and fading one.

Now, among the editors whose work is based on this model, the more thoughtful ones recognize that it can seldom be put into practice without elaborate and damaging compromises. For one thing, in almost every case, simple practicality requires that a "reading edition" be based on a version that has seen at least some authorial revision, and probably quite a bit of it. If the editor of a novel chooses to work from, say, the work's first appearance in book form, then that editor has chosen a version that was revised first in the course of preliminary drafts, then perhaps during preparation of a fair copy, then perhaps in preparing a partial or complete text for periodical publication, and then again in one or two sets of proofs— and all these revisions may have come to a halt, not because of anything inherent in the author's working methods, but because the publisher insisted that the book get printed in time for the Christmas rush. If an editor is preparing an edition of a long novel—or a volume of poems written over a period of, say, four years—then some of the text will have gone through as much as four years of revision, some perhaps as little as four months. Certain segments of the coal prove to be more glowing than others.

The second model, for which a convenient metaphor is the gothic cathedral, is less thrilling to think about, but it corresponds more closely to the way books probably get written. In this model, a work of art is not a pale shadow of a grand and inaccessible idea, but the substantial product of all the detailed and even contradictory decisions through which the work of art was made. The decisions that shape a poem or novel are comparable, despite the difference in scale, to the decisions that altered the form and detail of a great cathedral over the centuries in which it was constructed, yet left the completed building a reasonably (or retrospectively) harmonious whole. It is only to be expected that a writer's idea of a work should alter while the work is in progress—or even after he thinks he has finished it, only to find that it needs a different form and different details from those he first imagined. In the gothic-cathedral model, there is no clear way of distinguishing composition from revision, nor should there be: composition is an activity that may be interrupted for brief or extended intervals, but only death or distraction can bring it to an end.

So, like a gothic cathedral, any lengthy work of literature will exhibit thousands of details that its author could never have imagined when the work was first conceived, and, again like a gothic cathedral, the work will probably have a rather different form than the one the author imagined when making his initial plans. The work, whatever Shelley thought about the matter, is infinitely richer than the idea. And, to take up a related matter, just as the carvings of a medieval cathedral are the work of different stonemasons working within a common style, so the details of a work of literature are products of the various moods and intentions of the author, who is never precisely the same person every time he sits down at the writing-table.

Now, since those who favor one model are unlikely to be persuaded to abandon it for the other, I will not spend any more time trying to convince the partisans of the coal to switch sides to the cathedral. The rest of this essay can be better spent exploring some of the very real difficulties that the gothic-cathedral model, for all its merits, can still come up against.

One problem that never arises with cathedrals, but does arise with literature, is the problem of contradictory changes in different states of a work. A piece of stonework either gets carved or it does not, and, once carved, either gets altered or doesn't. It can't exist in two states simultaneously. But a poem or novel can exist in two states at the same time, and often does. I want to focus on a book by W. H. Auden published in 1941 in the United States as *The Double Man* and in the same year in England as *New Year Letter*. Auden revised the American and British texts in slightly different ways during a period of a few weeks, and in some instances there is no way of disentangling the later versions from the earlier, or even of deciding which is which. The problems of this book do not end there. Revising its poems in later years, Auden made changes for an American collection published in 1945 that he apparently forgot when preparing the text of a British collection in 1965. In most instances, fortunately enough, the changes do not contradict each other, and an editor can fairly safely conflate them. There is a dogma, now perhaps somewhat discredited, that forbids publishing eclectic texts; but this dogma ignores, I think, the way an author's mind actually works. No one keeps the full text of a book in his head simultaneously. Even while first composing their books, authors forget what they had written a few pages earlier—Trollope, for instance, could never get the names of his minor characters to stay the same from one end of a novel to the other, and once (in *Ayala's Angel*) made a letter that had been torn to bits in one chapter reappear, miraculously complete, in another. And when an impatient author like Auden goes back in 1965 to revise page 50, it is hardly likely he would notice he is using an edition that lacks the revisions he made twenty years before to page 60. An editor who refuses to correct an author's oversight in this matter is, to say the least, being fussy and discourteous. The gothic-cathedral model is an editor's best guide here. All revisions made to a work, at whatever moment, become part of that work. If authors can be inconsistent in composition, there is no reason to demand that they become consistent in revision.

But there are instances where an author's revisions do contradict each other, where they cannot be conflated, and here the gothic-cathedral model no longer serves an editor as an adequate guide. The chart on p. 416 presents in simplified form one of the problems resulting from Auden's different revisions of the poems in *The Double Man*. (Solid lines in the chart represent unquestionable lines of descent, dashed lines probable but not absolutely demonstrable ones.) In the earliest, and most of the later, states of the sonnet-sequence "The Quest" Auden headed the individual sonnets with either numbers or titles, but not both. And he seems to have chosen different headings alternately. By the end of the story, the evidence gets so tangled that neither alternative seems correct. Up to a point, texts deriving from the first American edition of *The Double Man* use titles for the sonnets, while texts deriving from the first British edition, *New Year Letter*, use numbers. Incidentally, this first British edition got the title *New Year Letter* not because Auden chose it, but because T. S. Eliot did. Auden had initially given the book to the Hogarth Press, who announced it for publication under Auden's own title *The Double Man*. But Eliot, who superintended Auden's work at Faber and Faber, pointed out that Auden was under a contractual obligation to Faber and made the Hogarth Press give up the book. Then, because Eliot did not want to publish a title that had already been announced by some other publisher, he changed it to *New Year Letter*. He tried to get Auden to change the American title also, but Auden either ignored him or got the message too late. The first American edition happened to precede the first British by a couple of months, but there is a possibility that Auden mailed the typescript of the British edition across the Atlantic before he delivered the typescript of the American edition to his publishers in New York.

Now, there is no way of knowing whether Auden, having added titles to the "Quest" sonnets for the American edition, deliberately or accidentally omitted them from the British. In a letter to Eliot in February 1941, almost three months after the titles had appeared in the *New Republic* version, Auden referred to the sonnets by number only. So he seems to have used both kinds of heading at about the same time. What *is* certain is that when he went back to the sequence two or three years later to revise it for a collected edition, he used the American text and in so doing retained the titles. Whether he retained them by choice or whether he unthinkingly used the text he happened to have in front of him because he was living in America, working on an edition commissioned by his American publisher, is impossible to say. It happened that this American *Collected Poetry* was not published in England. Instead, Faber published in 1950 a somewhat different volume titled *Collected Shorter Poems 1930–1944*. This, unlike the American collection, did not include the poems that had appeared in *The Double Man*. Again, the decision behind this was not Auden's but Eliot's. When Eliot first proposed the British collection, in 1948, Faber had a large stock of copies of *New Year Letter* in the warehouse. At a time of postwar austerity, Eliot did not want to include the contents of these copies in a new book that would immediately dry up the market for the old one. Auden accepted Eliot's decision.

And there matters stood until 1965, when Faber commissioned yet another collected edition, which appeared (in both England and

America) under the title *Collected Shorter Poems 1927–1957*. Auden was living in Europe at the time he worked on this book. His British publishers, having commissioned the book, helped him prepare it by pasting up pages of their earlier editions of his poems—including *New Year Letter*. So Auden, revising "The Quest" in 1965, worked from a 1940 text that used numbers instead of titles and apparently forgot that he had published a text in 1945 that had used titles instead of numbers.

The printer's copy for this 1965 revision of "The Quest" consists of the pages of the 1940 *New Year Letter* text, with revisions written out in Auden's hand. This *New Year Letter* text already had the numbers (no titles) printed on the page, and Auden simply let them stand—or *almost* simply, as one of the sonnets was so extensively revised that he retyped it and also retyped its number. So in this new 1965 version Auden used numbers instead of titles, and the one retyped sonnet provides evidence that he actively chose to use the numbers. This may be significant; but, within a few weeks of finishing the revisions for the Faber collection, Auden gave his Italian translator, Aurora Ciliberti, a fair copy of the new version of one of the sonnets, and in writing this out he did so *with the title*. He was still in Europe, and he was presumably still using the same editions he used when he made the revisions, but his act of writing restored the title that his somewhat less active editing had ignored. (The reason Auden sent this manuscript to his translator was that she was working on a bilingual edition of his poems. She happened to be using the 1945 American text as the basis of her work, but she altered her translation to include the revisions Auden made while she was working; and so her edition alone combined the titles that Auden had added late in 1940 and the textual revisions he made in 1965.)

It is quite possible that Auden wrote out the title only because he was writing out a single poem and would have omitted it had he been writing out the full sequence. But, taken together, the evidence of all these versions suggests, first, that Auden actively added the titles in 1940, and, second, that he sometimes continued to use the titles when he had occasion to write out one of the sonnets. He ignored the titles only when he was revising a printed text that already ignored them. This would indicate to an editor that the titles conceivably should now be restored. At least this is what the evidence suggested to me in 1971, when I asked Auden whether he wanted the titles put back into some future edition. He answered that the sequence should *not* have titles, and that was the end of that: he died two years later. I believe that in these last years he had grown accustomed to the text that used numbers instead of titles, and I like to imagine that, had I had the nerve to ask him to follow all the steps I have just gone through, I perhaps might have shown him that the titles belonged there instead. Perhaps not. As an editor, I *think* I have no choice but to accept Auden's emphatic final statement on the matter. I do not much like it—it seems to perserve an early version instead of a later one—but I do not know of anything in any of the gothic-cathedral theories that points a way out of the dilemma.

There are other problems with the gothic-cathedral model as well. An edition that presents an author's work in the form it achieved when the author was obliged by death to abandon it is all too often an edition that could satisfy no one but the author—and he is not around to take any satisfaction in it either. If it is an edition of James or Auden, it leaves out too much; if it is an edition of Wordsworth or Dickens, its language is too tame. These tend to be *our* judgements, of course, and not those of the people who actually wrote the works, but they are judgements we are properly determined to sustain.

One way to accommodate those judgements is to base an edition, not on *any* theory of authorship, but on a sense of literary history with all its arbitrariness—that is, to present the text that a work's first audience read, reviewed, and incorporated into their own awareness of literature and history. Carried to its logical extreme, this procedure would require an edited text to retain all the misprints and errors of the original while ignoring the corrections the author sent the publisher two hours after the presses began rolling. Like every other procedure for editing a work, this too requires compromises that are only barely tolerable. The truth of the matter is that *all* editions serve some legitimate purposes and neglect others. And the conclusion to be drawn is not, simply, that all editions are wrong, but that we can never have enough of them.

NOTE

This paper was delivered at the 1984 convention of the Modern Language Association of America. The text printed here retains the manner of an informal talk, and has not been rewritten for the printed page.

416 T E X T

[heading and first line of the opening sonnet in "The Quest"]

[holograph fair copy, before November 1940? (Berg Coll., NYPL)]:
I
Out of it steps the future of the poor,

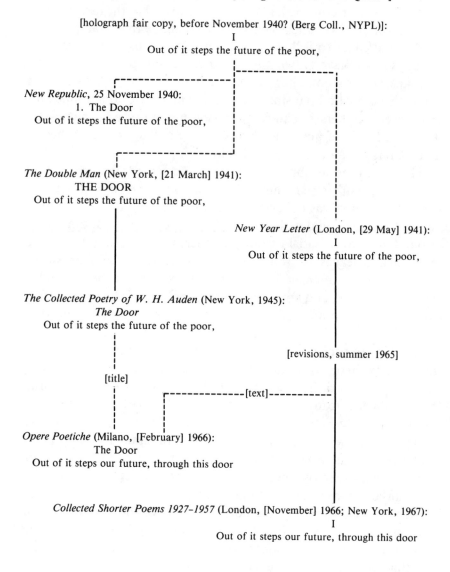

New Republic, 25 November 1940:
1. The Door
Out of it steps the future of the poor,

The Double Man (New York, [21 March] 1941):
THE DOOR
Out of it steps the future of the poor,

New Year Letter (London, [29 May] 1941):
I
Out of it steps the future of the poor,

The Collected Poetry of W. H. Auden (New York, 1945):
The Door
Out of it steps the future of the poor,

[revisions, summer 1965]

[title]

[text]

Opere Poetiche (Milano, [February] 1966):
The Door
Out of it steps our future, through this door

Collected Shorter Poems 1927-1957 (London, [November] 1966; New York, 1967):
I
Out of it steps our future, through this door

What Is the Text of a Film?

E. RUBINSTEIN

To begin with, let me enunciate three general considerations that will to a large degree govern my subsequent remarks.[1]

First, I do not mean to pursue the ontological or epistemological implications of my somewhat presumptuous title, except briefly to note that, with regard to film, the problem of the "whatness" of the text, which shades at once into the problem of the "whereness" of the text, is even more troublesome than similar problems attendant upon a literary text. One simple preliminary question should suffice to adumbrate the trouble: even leaving aside the whole area of cutting and editing, does the true text of a film come into existence when the camera first makes its recording of the world, when the film stock is developed, or only when the film is projected? Answers, even the most tentative, are outside the scope of this paper.

Second, the field of textual scholarship is not my own. At the same time, I have known enough discussion in more familiar academic fields to feel assured that in this one, as in any other, positions have been taken, battles waged, and enemies cultivated; if, by any of my statements, I seem to be endorsing a still-controversial point of view or vocabulary, and succeed thereby in earning myself a battalion of new enemies, I do so through inadvertence and through ignorance, not through partiality.

Third, since the topic of much that follows will be a Hollywood Western, I must point out that I lack the time and space even to raise the question of the academic validity of the field now generally known as "cinema studies," a field, I am well aware, not yet endorsed and adopted by some universities. So I end this prefatory statement on a plea for a truce with anyone reading these words who finds the serious study of film, and particularly of the American studio film, more eccentric or perverse than the study of any more distant or obscure "popular" art.

To the subject, then: What is, in the simplest, the least debatable sense of the word, the "text" of a film, and how is the accuracy of such a text to be assessed?

I

In a recent study of the classic American director Howard Hawks, Gerald Mast devotes ten pages to what he calls "A Note on the Text of *Red River*." I wish to go through a few of his observations, explicating, expanding, and at times questioning them. These observations, let me say, seem to me reasonable and interesting: my aim is not to challenge Mast but to demonstrate some ways in which his observations isolate issues that also concern textual scholars who might wonder about the role of their colleagues in the area of film. Mast opens with a few sentences that will almost certainly carry familiar resonances:

> Before making any critical or interpretive surmises about what an artist may intend in a text, it is obviously necessary to know precisely what the text is. The problem of determining the authoritative text precedes the problem of explicating any text's meaning. This determining of authoritative texts is a common enough one in literary study— particularly with those early texts which were not personally and carefully prepared by the author for the printer. . . . It may seem strange that film, a uniquely contemporary art, should produce as many textual problems as those older literary texts, but indeed there is probably not a single major film whose textual authenticity might not be questioned or at least examined. As this study has shown, several different evolving scripts precede the filming itself. Many changes in that script occur during shooting. After the film has been shot, many filmed scenes never become part of the finished film. Even after the film has been "finished" . . . the maker may desire to add or delete material.

But wait. The script, it seems, is not the "text"; it is, in fact, only a sort of —literally—*pre*text for the filmic text. But what if the script is by, say, William Faulkner or Scott Fitzgerald or—no need to go on: nearly all the major figures of American fiction and drama of their day wrote for Hollywood, Hemingway standing as the major exception. The job of the scholar interested in Faulkner—*not* in Hawks—would at very least be that of ascertaining (1) which if any sequences of the script Faulkner actually wrote (writing "credits" in Hollywood were often exercises in sheer whimsy), (2) how much of the verbal continuity (that is, the words we hear when we watch the finished movie) remain faithful to what Faulkner wrote, and (3) what happened to what Faulkner wrote but somehow got rewritten or discarded or altered or forgotten either before or during production. (Southern Illinois University Press is, in fact, now publishing a series devoted to the movie scripts of well-known writers.) Similarly, if one were interested in Aaron Copland or Erich Korngold, the question of text would be the question of the musical component of the film. (Here, by the way, the scholar's burden might be heavier still, for he or she may be obliged to collate Copland's concert suite of the music he wrote for *The Red Pony* with the score heard in the film *The Red Pony*: composers as a rule tried harder than writers to force some extra mileage out of their work for the movies.) And so on, down the line of credits to—well, let us halt at the costume designer. Yet when Mast uses the word "maker," he means—and expects us to know that he means—the director.

The cult of the director—like the very sanctity of the notion of "authorship"—may be dying out, but at heart most students of film are still, to some degree at least, its adherents. Its shibboleth, born in the pages of *Cahiers du Cinéma* in the 1950s and passed on to America in the 1960s, is, of course, *auteur*. I bring all this up not in order to establish my own version of the history of film criticism over the last generation but in order to suggest that the concept of *auteur*ship sheds considerable light on the theory and practice of textual scholarship in relation to the Hollywood film. For without the concept of the *auteur*, how can we properly speak of "authorial intention?" And without the concept of authorial intention how can we discuss the standards by which to establish a text? (There are answers to these rhetorical questions, I know, but too seldom are the questions even raised in film scholarship.) And so it is here that we may locate one point at which the received assumption of film criticism and the methodology of textual criticism seem to come together: in the concept of the author, of the shaping imagination, misguided or wise, self-advertising or self-effacing, to which we may refer all final questions of accuracy and responsibility. But is the whole *politique des auteurs* not rooted in this apparently Romantic, but just as apparently inviolable, identification of "author" and "authority"? In any case, *Red River*, if it is to be experienced as a work worthy of serious attention, is assumed to be a *Hawks* film, and we automatically suppose that any changes made in it are, to use Mast's all-revealing term, "extra-artistic."

If, in the arena of literary study, one of the perennial ogres goes by the name of "publisher," so in film study the still more dreadful villain goes under the name of "producer." And when, as in the case of *Red River*, the producer goes under the specific name of Howard Hughes, a whole mythological apparatus is set in motion. Now, I doubt neither the general mythology in circulation concerning Howard Hughes nor the particular spiteful gestures of which Mast accuses him in relation to Hawks and the making of *Red River*. Yet since in the vast majority of cases it was the producer or the studio who hired the director for purposes other than any that the director—the mere *metteur-en-scène*—had in mind, should it not be Hughes's intention that rightly claims our interest here, whatever our moral qualms about the man?

Popular legend notwithstanding, it is not to be supposed automatically that the producers were by definition inferior in taste and in judiciousness to even the most prominent and gifted of directors. It is instructive to read the vituperative memo that David O. Selznick fired at Alfred Hitchcock on the subject of the preliminary treatment that Hitchcock and his collaborators submitted for Hitchcock's first American film, *Rebecca*.[3] Without going into detail one can assert that, if Hitchcock had had his way, *Rebecca* would not be the film we have today. Moreover—here one can only speculate—would *Rebecca* have been the film that established Hitchcock's immense popularity and allowed him such rare artistic liberty in the American industry? Whether the unSelznickized *Rebecca* might be more fun to watch is doubtful, full as it would have been of vomit jokes and other perhaps half-conscious expressions of Hitchcock's distaste at being ordered to film a little Daphne du Maurier romance which he despised. Hitchcock, who in this instance had not much choice, essentially executed Selznick's wishes, not his own, and all of those matchless directorial effects he achieved may quite properly be understood as his contribution to the realization of *Selznick's* intention. (To be sure, he also cheated, and more than a little, when Selznick, preoccupied with *Gone with the Wind*, was not looking.)

The problem I raise here is one common to all the collaborative arts. If we try to imagine the original staging of *Le Sacre du printemps*, it is less Roerich's or Nijinsky's or Stravinsky's intention that we must try to reconstruct than Diaghelev's. And what was

Diaghelev himself if not a "producer," a man whose double genius lay in assembling talent and raising money?

All this, the hypothetical film critic will say, is devil's advocacy, especially the rather strained reference to Diaghelev. And the film critic would not be far off the mark. I have mounted my argument only to stress (1) the collaborative nature of film and (2) the severity of the limits placed on the director in the typical Hollywood enterprise—two points which, for all their obviousness, must constantly be invoked in any consideration of authorial intention. Moreover, given the enormous expense of commercial film production, a good deal of what we may know of the director's own feelings lies in the realm of the unrealized—the realm, that is, of hearsay. We rarely have two integral versions of any film, indeed of any sequence of any film, for if the producers or the studio or the New York office—the "bosses," as we like to say, casting a Mafia-like shadow over the whole operation—did not or could not nip the director's independent impulses in the bud, much more often than not they could distort those impulses beyond recognition in the final cutting and editing of the film.[4] Not for nothing has the phrase "cutting-room floor" come down to us as a metaphor for a world of forgotten efforts and lost images.

Red River, for reasons that Mast details in his discussion of the changes that Hughes attempted to effect, is an exception:

> [The] general problem can be illustrated by attempting to define an authoritative text of *Red River*, for two radically different versions of the film survive today. One of the existing negatives, which I will call the "Book Version," uses the consistent visual imagery of handwriting on paper, clearly the pages of the book "Early Tales of Texas," for its essential narrative transitions. The second existing negative, which I will call the "Voice Version," uses the voice-over narration of [one of the characters] to provide those same transitions. The Book Version is about seven and a half minutes longer than the Voice Version.

That Mast can write with such assurance—and such precision—is, if not quite a miracle, at least a dramatic exception; the particular circumstances (which Mast explains in detail) that allowed two versions of *Red River* to survive were seldom duplicated. But even if variant texts of a film like *Red River* did somehow appear, how might they be assembled and disseminated? The luxury available to the literary scholar, the luxury of at least being able to *opt* for an "eclectic" edition, is seldom available to the film scholar: consider the expense of collating two editions, intercutting shots or whole scenes from the one with shots and scenes from the other. And as for an "edition" based on the model of a literary variorum edition, what would such an edition of a film look like, and how many would sit through it? A film imposes its length upon the viewer in a way that, say, a novel does not upon its reader, and a film that includes all possible variants—all the scenes shot and discarded, even if by some chance they happen to have survived—would surely prove intolerable, even to the most dedicated student. Normally, then, at least with respect to any given single screening, the scholar *must* opt for editorial judgment as the standard by which to decide which version of the film will be projected. Printed critical editions of the continuity script, with verbal descriptions of, and, when possible, frame enlargements from, other received texts, will have to serve the viewer in lieu of the actual experience of seeing variants of the film. The fact is as unfortunate as it is, in most cases, inescapable, for in this sense, the fully annotated text of a film is not the text of a *film*.

II

But the problem of the authenticity of a filmic text is not limited to Hollywood sound films. Let me quote Mast one last time:

> There are enormous differences in the existing prints of even classic films like *The Birth of a Nation, Intolerance*, and *Potemkin*. To put the question into an historical perspective, when an audience one hundred years from now sees [a Hawks film] or any other film by any other director, what film will they see? This kind of question bodes well for the cinema scholars of the future.

What need of "historical perspective"? The question "bodes well," if that be the phrase, for a film released the day before yesterday as seen by a film scholar tomorrow afternoon. But even more to the point, if any works in film history testify to the operation of a single imagination, they are Griffith's *The Birth of a Nation* and *Intolerance* and Eisenstein's *Potemkin*: why have *these* texts not come down to us intact? Are we to blame the various censors or distributors or the sheer physical decay of the prints themselves (and of the negatives from which they were struck) for missing or awkwardly assembled sequences? Each film in history will, alas, generate its own pattern of problems for the textual scholar.

Even the two great Griffith epics and *Potemkin* embody a complex collaborative effort compared to the film I wish now to consider, a film which happens to have occupied a good deal of my own attention over the last years. I refer to the celebrated short documentary that Luis Buñuel shot in 1932 in the appalling land of Las Hurdes outside Salamanca.[5]

The film was made for about $2,000 donated by a friend of the director: there were no "bosses" to spoil the brew. The actual production crew, if it can even be called that, consisted of the cameraman, Eli Lotar, the writer, Pierre Unik, and Buñuel himself. (Two interested bystanders, a Professor Sanchez Ventura and the schoolteacher who gave Buñuel his rather laughable capital, apparently joined the expedition.) Since the film takes the form of a travelogue—a grimly parodistic travelogue—there were no professional actors to contend with. Buñuel oversaw Lotar's camera work and specifically collaborated with Unik on the verbal commentary. Indeed, according to Lotar, "during shooting Buñuel maintained an almost infantile tyranny over the group." The grotesquely incongruous musical score—excerpts from the Brahms Fourth Symphony—was selected by Buñuel, who also did the final editing (under the most primitive conditions imaginable). When banned by the Republican government of Spain because of the unflattering light it shed on the motherland, the film was withdrawn: no censor tampered with the text. Can there be a purer instance of a film for which absolute authorship might be claimed?

And what is the name of this film? It is sometimes referred to as *Tierra sin pan (Land without Bread)*, sometimes simply as *Las Hurdes*: which title did Buñuel prefer? The circulation print owned by the Museum of Modern Art in New York goes under still a third title, *Unpromised Land*. Now this third, somewhat "literary" title—encountered, as far as I know, only on this print and copies of it and obviously printed on stock different from that used in the rest of the film—might seem totally spurious, appended perhaps by an overly imaginative distributor somewhere along the line, except for the rather unsettling fact that the print in question was given to the Museum by Buñuel himself in 1940, when he was in the Museum's employ. (The records of the Museum's Film Study Center contain no comments or explanations on Buñuel's part.)

The title, one might argue, is of relatively small moment. But what about the all-important voice-over narration? I have encountered three versions of *Land without Bread* (to opt for the most commonly encountered title), one in French and two in English (the Museum print and the print owned by the City University of New York). Since the first official release was in France in 1937, following the ban in Spain, and since Unik and Buñuel wrote this version in French, we might suppose it to constitute the definitive verbal narration. Why then do neither of the English versions follow it exactly, and why are there discrepancies between the two English versions? (And why is the narrator not the same man in the two versions?) Some of these discrepancies are of considerable importance. The rhetorical point of the narration resides in the virtually emotionless voice in which it comments on the horrific images of life among the Hurdanos, so that a major shift in tone and meaning is effected when, for example, the word "quaint" is used in place of the word "barbarous" in regard to local festival customs. Many other such discrepancies are in evidence, but no clear or meaningful pattern is to be discerned. And to repeat, neither version is an exact translation of the French, though the CUNY print is considerably closer in places.   And anyway, how can one know whether the French print of today reproduces the French narration heard in 1937?

The images, too, reflect some palpable differences. To take but one example: André Bazin, in his magisterial essay on Buñuel's *Los olvidados*, alludes to a certain shot present in none of the three prints of *Land without Bread* I have seen.[6] In the essay I recently prepared on the film, I suggested that Bazin must have conflated two images in his memory in order to arrive at the shot he describes. The editor of the journal in which my piece was to appear wrote back to ask if I might wish to delete my phrase about Bazin's memory, since the print she uses does indeed contain the shot in question. Dutifully I returned to the CUNY print: the shot isn't there.

How do shots get lost? Shown over and over in various theatres and universities, prints are of course mutilated—by faulty projection equipment, even, I am ashamed to say, by projectionists who remove sections of a film that they wish to add to their personal collections. (Silent films in particular, by the way, were even in their first release often shortened, or bowdlerized, by individual theatre owners, who seldom bothered to restore the footage they literally excised before returning the print to the distributor.) And the negatives, as I said earlier, have all too frequently been either lost or destroyed. Where then does one turn?

In the case of *Land without Bread*, one would have to begin by seeking out still further prints of the film in various *cinémathèques* and universities and private collections throughout the world and attempting to trace the provenances of these prints. One would certainly have to visit the *cinémathèque* of Toulouse, where there exist four reels of film shot in Las Hurdes (donated by Buñuel's sister) which Buñuel chose not to include in the original, no part of which, to my knowledge, has ever been included in any distribution print, but which *might* . . . . But there is no need to go on: for all the special problems I have attempted to identify in these pages, the methods of the film scholar and those of scholars in other fields will, in the last analysis, seem less consequential than the familiar and unavoidable similarities of their everyday methods.

NOTES

1. These remarks, in substantially their present form, were delivered at the annual meeting of the Society for Textual Criticism in New York on April 22, 1983.

2. Gerald Mast, *Howard Hawks, Storyteller* (New York: Oxford University Press, 1982), pp. 337–346.

3. *Memo from David O. Selznick*, ed. Rudy Behlmer (New York: Avon Books, 1972), pp. 306–311.

4. Nor is it to be supposed that American studios were unique in their practices. See Joseph L. Anderson and Donald Richie, *The Japanese Film: Art and Industry*, Expanded Edition (Princeton: Princeton University Press, 1982)—or for that matter, see virtually any interview with Akira Kurosawa—for evidence that the Japanese film industry, to name only one, was hardly more respectful of the wishes of most directors.

5. Most of my information on the making of the film is from Francisco Aranda, *Luis Buñuel: a Critical Biography*, trans. and ed. David Robinson (New York: Da Capo Press, 1976), pp. 85–99. My essay on the film, to which I later allude and on which I draw in this discussion, is "Visit to a Familiar Planet: Buñuel Among the Hurdanos," *Cinema Journal*, 22, No. 4 (Summer, 1983), 3–17.

6. Bazin, "Los olvidados," trans. Sallie Iannotti, in *The World of Luis Buñuel: Essays in Criticism*, ed. Joan Mellen (New York: Oxford University Press, 1978), pp. 194–200.

The Society for
Textual Scholarship

The Society for Textual Scholarship, founded in 1979, is an organization devoted to the interdisciplinary discussion of textual theory and practice. The Society's members are scholars from many different fields, including English, American, French, Spanish, Italian, German, Slavic, and Oriental Languages and Literatures, Classics, Biblical Studies, History, Linguistics, Musicology, Folklore, Art History, Theater History, Legal History, Cinema Studies, Epigraphy, Palaeography, Codicology, Enumerative, Analytical, and Descriptive Bibliography, Textual Criticism, and Computer Science. The Society convenes at a biennial conference (usually three or four days, with seventy-five to one hundred speakers), where members and invited guests present papers in plenary or special sessions. Members may also organize discussion groups at the conferences. Each conference features a special address by the current president of the Society, the first four presidents being G. Thomas Tanselle, Paul Oskar Kristeller, Fredson Bowers, and Eugene A. Nida. The last three conferences held in New York City in 1981, 1983, and 1985 attracted scholars from several countries, including (in addition to the U.S.A. and Canada) England, Scotland, Ireland, France, Germany, Sweden, Saudi Arabia, and Australia. The fourth conference of STS was held in April 1987, again in New York City. The Society also meets periodically under the auspices of the various professional conventions (e.g., the Modern Language Association of America).

The Society publishes an annual hardback volume of contributions, *TEXT*, which contains articles selected from papers given at the biennial conferences, together with articles submitted independently.

The Editors welcome contributions for future volumes of *TEXT* from scholars concerned with any aspect of the enumeration, description, transcription, editing, or annotation of texts in any discipline. Submissions are read and evaluated by selected members of the STS Advisory Board. The Society also publishes periodic Bulletins, and a Newsletter, which contains correspondence, reviews, and bibliographies of interest to scholars in various disciplines.

The Society for Textual Scholarship welcomes applications for membership. All inquiries, or submissions to *TEXT*, should be sent to:

D. C. GREETHAM, *STS Executive Director*
Ph.D. Program in English
Graduate Center
The City University of New York
33 West 42nd Street
New York, N.Y. 10036

Contents of Previous Volumes